CUSTOMARY INTERNATIONAL LAW AND ITS INTERPRETATION BY INTERNATIONAL COURTS

It is notorious that international courts and tribunals have greatly contributed to the development of customary international law (CIL) by, for instance, articulating the constituent elements of custom and clarifying the conditions required for its modification. This volume demonstrates that they have also been actively engaged in the interpretation of CIL. In elucidating CIL interpretation before and by international courts and tribunals, the volume chooses three focal points: theory, method and normative interactions. Viewing CIL and its interpretation from these vantage points leads to a more complete picture of the role and function of CIL interpretation in international courts. The volume encourages readers to question orthodox theories on CIL and its interpretation, to look anew at what has long been labelled as mere identification of custom, and to take a systemic approach to CIL, which, even in the process of interpretation, remains unwaveringly connected to treaties and general principles of law.

This title is also available as Open Access on Cambridge Core.

MARINA FORTUNA is Assistant Professor at the University of Groningen and member of the TRICI-Law project team. Her research focuses primarily on the practice of international courts, which she examines from the perspective of various topics in general international law.

KOSTIA GOROBETS is Assistant Professor of International Law at the University of Groningen. He specialises in analytical jurisprudence and philosophy of international law, as well as in their interplay.

PANOS MERKOURIS is Professor of International Law at the University of Groningen. He is Principal Investigator of the TRICI-Law project (ERC Grant Agreement No. 759728). Professor Merkouris has written extensively on the law of treaties, sources and interpretation, most recently authoring *Interpretation of Customary International Law: Of Methods and Limits* (2024).

ANDREAS FOLLESDAL is Professor of Political Philosophy at the Faculty of Law, University of Oslo. He co-directed PluriCourts and was Principal Investigator of ERC Advanced Grant MultiRights 2011–16. He publishes in the field of political philosophy, mainly on international political and legal theory, globalisation/Europeanisation and human rights. He is Fellow at Wissenschaftskolleg zu Berlin 2023–24.

GEIR ULFSTEIN is Professor Emeritus of International Law at the University of Oslo, where he also co-directed PluriCourts. He is President of the Norwegian Branch of the International Law Association (ILA) and winner of the University of Oslo Research Award 2021 (with Andreas Follesdal). He has published in various areas of international law, including the law of the sea, international environmental law, international human rights, international institutional law and international courts.

PAULINE WESTERMAN is Professor of Philosophy of Law at the University of Groningen, a member of staff at the Academy for Legislation in The Hague and a member of the Royal Dutch Academy of Sciences. Her research focuses on the making of law, the formation of soft law and the emergence and development of international law.

THE RULES OF INTERPRETATION OF CUSTOMARY INTERNATIONAL LAW

Established in 2021, the *TRICI-Law Book Series* is a limited series that aims to publish monographs and edited volumes on topics that shed light on legal interpretation in international law, with a particular emphasis on the interpretation of customary international law. Titles appearing in the series examine the interpretation of customary international law from a theoretical and practical perspective, and compare the characteristics of legal interpretation in international law across courts, regimes and sources as they have evolved and continue to do so through time. The *TRICI-Law Book Series* is a joint initiative between Cambridge University Press, the European Research Council and the University of Groningen. The titles in this series are available as Open Access thanks to the generous funding from the European Research Council (ERC) under the European Union's Horizon 2020 Research and Innovation Programme (Grant Agreement No 759728) and the University of Groningen.

CUSTOMARY INTERNATIONAL LAW AND ITS INTERPRETATION BY INTERNATIONAL COURTS

Theories, Methods and Interactions

Edited by

MARINA FORTUNA
University of Groningen

KOSTIA GOROBETS
University of Groningen

PANOS MERKOURIS
University of Groningen

ANDREAS FOLLESDAL
University of Oslo

GEIR ULFSTEIN
University of Oslo

PAULINE WESTERMAN
University of Groningen

CAMBRIDGE
UNIVERSITY PRESS

CAMBRIDGE
UNIVERSITY PRESS

Shaftesbury Road, Cambridge CB2 8EA, United Kingdom

One Liberty Plaza, 20th Floor, New York, NY 10006, USA

477 Williamstown Road, Port Melbourne, VIC 3207, Australia

314–321, 3rd Floor, Plot 3, Splendor Forum, Jasola District Centre, New Delhi – 110025, India

103 Penang Road, #05–06/07, Visioncrest Commercial, Singapore 238467

Cambridge University Press is part of Cambridge University Press & Assessment, a department of the University of Cambridge.

We share the University's mission to contribute to society through the pursuit of education, learning and research at the highest international levels of excellence.

www.cambridge.org
Information on this title: www.cambridge.org/9781009541329

DOI: 10.1017/9781009541312

First published 2024

A catalogue record for this publication is available from the British Library.

Library of Congress Cataloging-in-Publication Data
Names: Merkouris, Panos, editor. | Føllesdal, Andreas, editor. | Ulfstein, Geir, 1951– editor. | Westerman, Pauline, editor. | Gorobets, Kostia, editor. | Fortuna, Marina, 1995– editor.
Title: Customary international law and its interpretation by international courts : theories, methods, and interactions / edited by Panos Merkouris, Rijksuniversiteit Groningen, The Netherlands; Andreas Follesdal, Universitetet i Oslo; Geir Ulfstein, Universitetet i Oslo; Pauline Westerman, Rijksuniversiteit Groningen, The Netherlands ; Kostia Gorobets, Rijksuniversiteit Groningen, The Netherlands; Marina Fortuna, Rijksuniversiteit Groningen, The Netherlands.
Description: Cambridge, United Kingdom ; New York, NY : Cambridge University Press, 2024. | Series: Tric the rules of interpretation of customary international law | Includes bibliographical references and index. | Contents: The illusion of gold-digging : interpretation of state practice / Pauline Westerman – Addressing the chronological paradox : constitutive rules and the constructive interpretation of CIL / Henrique Marcos – Interpreting the plural sources of CIL / Harlan Grant Cohen – Interpretation dynamics in CIL : an entropic approach / Eleni Micha – The application of logic and reason in CIL interpretation / William Worster – The interpretation of 'direction and control' in the investor state arbitration : the case of state-owned enterprises / Paula Baldini Miranda da Cruz – The Court of Justice of the EU and CIL interpretation : close encounters of a third kind? / Tamaś Molnař – Judicial effectiveness or judicial ambiguity : is CIL an instrument for judicial activism in excess? / Leoni Ayoub – Judicial dialogue between international courts in the interpretation of customary international human rights law / Silviana Cocan – 'General principles of law' and the interpretation of CIL / Craig Eggett – The role of treaties and general principles of law in the interpretation of customary rules / Marina Fortuna – Reconciling conflicting norms of CIL-towards a mode of practical concordance at the ICJ / Raphael Oidtmann – Indicators of coherence and interpretation of CIL / Charalampos Giannakopoulos.
Identifiers: LCCN 2024020480 | ISBN 9781009541329 (hardback) | ISBN 9781009541312 (ebook)
Subjects: LCSH: Customary law, International – Interpretation and construction. | International courts.
Classification: LCC KZ1277 .I58 2024 | DDC 340.5–dc23/eng/20240509
LC record available at https://lccn.loc.gov/2024020480

ISBN 978-1-009-54132-9 Hardback

CONTENTS

CONTRIBUTORS

LEONI AYOUB obtained her PhD in 2021 after successfully defending her thesis 'Judicial Activism and Restraint in the Creation of the International Judicial Function: How Have Activism and Restraint Shaped the International Courts?' She holds an LLB from the University of Kent in Canterbury, an LLM in public international law from the University of Kent in Brussels and a Specialisation Masters (LLM) in European law from the Free University of Brussels (2015). She was called to the English Bar (Lincoln's Inn) in 2013 and the Cypriot Bar in 2018, and since April 2020 has served as a consultant to the World Bank Group in Washington, DC.

PAULA BALDINI MIRANDA DA CRUZ is a lawyer specialising in international law and dispute settlement. Her research interests cover the development and implementation of international law, legal culture and institutions. She is a PhD candidate at the Grotius Centre for International Legal Studies and a qualified attorney admitted to the Brazilian and Portuguese Bars.

SILVIANA COCAN is a lecturer at the Université de Montréal Faculty of Law and a BCL/JD candidate at McGill University. She holds a double PhD in international law from Université Laval Faculty of Law and Université de Bordeaux Faculty of Law and Political Science. Her thesis, 'The Dialogue between International Jurisdictions and Quasi-Jurisdictions Protecting Human Rights: The Example of the Prohibition of Torture and Other Cruel, Inhuman or Degrading Treatment or Punishment', published by LGDJ in 2020, won the Louis Joinet thesis prize from the Francophone Institute for Justice and Democracy and the thesis prize of the Quebec Society of Comparative Law. Her research interests focus on public international law, international human rights law, comparative law and international refugee and migration law.

HARLAN GRANT COHEN is Professor of Law at Fordham University Law School, prior to which he held the positions of Gabriel M. Wilner/ UGA Foundation Professor in International Law and Faculty Co-director of the Dean Rusk International Law Center at the University of Georgia School of Law. His scholarship focuses on international legal theory, global governance, international trade and US foreign relations law, particularly with regard to sources, authority, communities of practice and the role of history in international and foreign relations law.

CRAIG EGGETT is Assistant Professor of International Law at Maastricht University. His PhD research focused on the nature and functions of general principles of law in the international legal system. His current research interests include the rights of future generations, the role of courts and tribunals in international law-making and normative interaction in international law. He is Convenor of the Maastricht International Law Discussion Group and a member of the Maastricht Centre for Human Rights.

ANDREAS FOLLESDAL is Professor of Political Philosophy at the Faculty of Law, University of Oslo. He was Co-director of the PluriCourts Centre for the Study of the Legitimate Roles of the Judiciary in the Global Order and Principal Investigator for European Research Council Advanced Grant MultiRights 2011–16 on the legitimacy of a multilevel human rights judiciary. He holds a PhD in philosophy from Harvard University. His published works in the field of political philosophy cover international political and legal theory, globalisation/Europeanisation, human rights and socially responsible investing. He is General Editor (with Geir Ulfstein) of two book series published by Cambridge University Press: Studies on Human Rights Conventions and Studies in International Courts and Tribunals.

MARINA FORTUNA is Assistant Professor at the University of Groningen and a member of the TRICI-Law project. Her research on the interpretation of customary international law in international courts and tribunals is funded by the European Research Council and focuses on the practice of international courts and quasi-judicial bodies, especially the ICJ, human rights courts and international criminal tribunals, examined from the perspective of various aspects of general international law. In 2023, she successfully defended her thesis

'Interpretation of Customary International Law in International Courts: A Mosaic of Methods'.

KOSTIA GOROBETS is Assistant Professor of International Law at the University of Groningen. He specialises in analytical jurisprudence, philosophy of international law and their interplay. In 2022, he successfully defended his thesis 'Contemplating an Uneven Landscape: The Authority of International Law'.

CHARALAMPOS GIANNAKOPOULOS is Senior Research Fellow at the Centre for International Law (CIL) and Adjunct Assistant Professor at the Faculty of Law, National University of Singapore. He holds a PhD in international law from the Graduate Institute of International and Development Studies in Geneva, an LLM in public international law from University College London and an LLB from the University of Athens. His principal areas of research are international investment law and arbitration, ASEAN investment law and policy, international adjudication, treaty interpretation and legal theory. His monograph *Manifestations of Coherence and Investor-State Arbitration* was published by Cambridge University Press in 2022.

HENRIQUE MARCOS is currently preparing a double doctorate at Maastricht University (Foundations and Methods of Law) and the University of São Paulo (International and Comparative Law). He is also a researcher at the University of São Paulo's Centre for Research in International Courts (Núcleo de Estudos em Tribunais Internacionais – NETI).

PANOS MERKOURIS is Professor of International Law at the University of Groningen. He is Principal Investigator for the TRICI-Law project (funded by European Research Council grant agreement no. 759728). He has written extensively on the law of treaties, sources and interpretation, and is the author of *Interpretation of Customary International Law: Of Methods and Limits* (Brill, 2023) and co-author, with Professor Malgosia Fitzmaurice, of *Treaties in Motion* (Cambridge University Press, 2020).

ELENI MICHA teaches at the University of Athens Law School and is a visiting lecturer at Frederick University in Cyprus and a practising human rights lawyer. She holds a doctorate in law from the University of Athens and a diploma from the ICRC. She specialises in public international law, with a particular interest in the international protection of human rights, international humanitarian law, international criminal law and geopolitics. Her most recent work deals with jurisdictional and evidentiary issues at the International Criminal Court and the execution of judgments of the European Court of Human Rights in the domestic legal order.

TAMÁS MOLNÁR is a legal research officer at the EU Agency for Fundamental Rights in Vienna. He is a visiting lecturer on international migration law in the Department of International Relations at Corvinus University of Budapest. He holds an LLM in EU law and a PhD and a "habilitation" (post-doctoral teaching and research quantification) in international law, and has published widely in the fields of international and EU migration law and the relationship between legal orders. His latest monograph, *The Interplay between the EU's Return Acquis and International Law*, was published by Edward Elgar in 2021. He is also the co-author, with Ramses A Wessel, of *Interactions between EU Law and International Law. Juxtaposed Perspectives* (Edward Elgar 2024).

RAPHAEL OIDTMANN currently serves as a parliamentary and legal advisor at the Hessian State Parliament as well as an adjunct lecturer in international law at the Mannheim Law School. He holds Master's degrees in political science (Johannes Gutenberg University Mainz), international and comparative law (University of Mannheim, University of Adelaide) and international relations (University of Cambridge) and is currently an external PhD candidate at Goethe University Frankfurt. His principal teaching and research interests pertain to (general) international law, international criminal law, the history of international law, human rights and the law of armed conflict, as well as international relations theory and history, geopolitics, international security studies and European Union integration.

GEIR ULFSTEIN is Professor Emeritus of International Law at the University of Oslo and was Co-director of the PluriCourts Centre for the Study of the Legitimate Roles of the Judiciary in the Global Order. His publications cover various areas of international law, including the law of the sea, international environmental law, international human rights, international institutional law and international courts. He is General

Editor (with Andreas Follesdal) of two book series published by Cambridge University Press: Studies on Human Rights Conventions and Studies in International Courts and Tribunals.

PAULINE WESTERMAN is Professor of Philosophy of Law at Groningen University Law, serves on staff of the Academy for Legislation in The Hague and is a member of the Royal Dutch Academy of Sciences. Her interests centre on the making of law, the formation of soft law arrangements and the emergence and development of international law. Her book *Outsourcing the Law: A Philosophical Perspective on Regulation* was published by Edward Elgar in 2018. She has also co-edited two volumes: *Conceptual (Re)Constructions of International Law*, with co-editors Kostia Gorobets and Andreas Hadjigeorgiou, published by Edward Elgar in 2022, and *Legal Validity and Soft Law*, with co-editors Jaap Hage, Stephan Kirste and Anne Ruth Mackor, published by Springer in 2018.

WILLIAM THOMAS WORSTER teaches public international law, the law of international organisations and international migration/refugee law at The Hague University of Applied Sciences and the University of Missouri–Kansas City. He earned a JD from Chicago–Kent College of Law and an LLM in Public International Law from Leiden University. He is also currently an external PhD candidate at the University of Amsterdam. His research interests correspond to his areas of teaching, with a particular focus on international legal actors, nationality law and sources of international law.

PREFACE

This edited volume is the result of the teamwork of the TRICI-Law project, the PluriCourts Centre, and the Department of Transboundary Legal Studies of the University of Groningen. The volume had its origins in the second TRICI-Law conference, *Interpretation of Customary International Law: Methods, Interpretative Choices and the Role of Coherence*, co-organised by those teams and held in The Hague in December 2021.

The TRICI-Law project, headed by Professor Panos Merkouris, is a five-year research project funded by the European Research Council (ERC) Horizon 2020 programme (Grant Agreement No. 759728). The project is dedicated to in-depth study of customary international law (CIL) interpretation and identification of the rules that guide this process. It is the first of its kind, introducing the lens of interpretation as a distinct aspect to be studied in the life cycle of a CIL rule.

The PluriCourts Centre for the Study of the Legitimate Roles of the Judiciary in the Global Order studies the legitimacy of international courts and tribunals (ICs) from legal, political science and philosophical perspectives. The Centre examines the normative, legal and empirical soundness of charges of illegitimacy in order to understand and assess how ICs do, could and should respond. It also explores the multidimensional legitimacy standards, which include multilevel separation of authority, independence and accountability, performance and comparative advantages.

The Department of Transboundary Legal Studies of the University of Groningen is a unique mix of legal and political philosophers, international lawyers, technology lawyers and other scholars who transcend the traditional boundaries of the legal domain. Since its formation in 2017, the Department has contributed especially to the collaborative work of the sections of legal philosophy and international law on the topics of customary international law, authority of international law and international legal normativity.

The conference had an ambitious aim. We invited international legal scholars, legal philosophers and practitioners to address some of the trickiest questions regarding the interpretation of customary international law. To what extent do internationally accepted principles of legal interpretation provide general guidance on how to interpret CIL, thereby guiding and restricting ICs' discretion? What are the methods of interpretation of CIL used by ICs? Are there commonalities and patterns in the ways that ICs belonging to different fields of international law interpret customary rules? How do interpretative choices in CIL interpretation vary across ICs? And finally, do ICs strive for coherence in their interpretation of CIL, or does coherence serve as a method or a guiding principle rather than a goal?

The call for papers for the conference attracted a lot of interest, and we were particularly delighted to see that many of the abstracts submitted offered insights into CIL and its interpretation that bridged international law and legal philosophy. This was testament to the fruitful collaboration between the disciplines, which also informed the composition of the organising committee and the overall philosophy of the conference. Therefore, in our selection of abstracts, we tried to strike a balance between, on the one hand, contributions that discussed broader conceptual issues of CIL and its interpretation and, on the other, contributions that engaged in a more narrowly focused and practice-oriented analysis. The conference, and ultimately the chapters of this edited volume, reflect this balance.

The edited volume comprises thirteen chapters, divided into three parts. Part I is dedicated to traditional conceptual issues of CIL and its interpretation. The contributions in this part scrutinise both orthodox and modern theories of CIL and their critiques; they look at the conceptual image of the interpretation of state practice; address the problem of the chronological paradox and its impact on the interpretation of CIL; explore the possibility of plural sources of CIL; and offer an entropic approach to CIL interpretative dynamics. Part II takes a closer look at some of the interpretative choices that ICs make when engaging with CIL. The contributions in this part discuss the use by ICs of logic and reason in their approach to CIL interpretation; look at examples of CIL interpretation more specifically in investment arbitration; and examine the role of judicial dialogue and judicial activism in the identification and interpretation of CIL. Part III shifts the focus to the place of CIL in the normative universe of international law, thus putting the spotlight on the interaction between CIL and other sources of international law. The chapters in this part scrutinise the interplay between CIL, treaties and general principles of law and issues of reconciliation of conflicting norms. This part also enquires into the different roles that coherence plays in ICs' interpretative practices.

We thank the contributors of this edited volume for their thorough and ambitious texts, which will doubtless advance the understanding of the interpretation of CIL. We also thank the other speakers and chairs at the 2021 conference, whose presentations and comments inspired many of the discussions developed in this volume. We are particularly grateful to His Excellency Judge Liu Daqun for his keynote speech on CIL interpretation by international criminal courts and tribunals.

This edited volume continues a set of publications dealing with a wide variety of issues connected to CIL interpretation. We are very grateful to Cambridge University Press for publishing this research collection as the TRICI-Law Book Series. We are also indebted to Ms Marianne Nield for her invaluable assistance and unending patience in the preparation of this volume and those that are still to come, and to Mr Tom Randall and the Cambridge University Press editing team for their unfailing support throughout the publication process. A special mention is owed to the ERC and the University of Groningen, without whose generous financial help this edited volume, as well as the TRICI-Law Book Series, would not have been possible.

This publication has been made open access thanks to generous funding from the European Research Council (ERC) under the European Union's Horizon 2020 Research and Innovation Programme (Grant Agreement No. 759728) and the University of Groningen.

ABBREVIATIONS

Acta Phys Pol A	*Acta Physica Polonica A*
ADPILC	*Annual Digest of Public International Law Cases*
AJES	*American Journal of Economics and Sociology*
AJIL	*American Journal of International Law*
All ER	*All England Law Reports*
Arb Int'l	*Arbitration International*
ARIEL	*Austrian Review of International and European Law*
ARSIWA	Articles on the Responsibility of States for Internationally Wrongful Acts
Asian JIL	*Asian Journal of International Law*
ASIL Proc	*Proceedings of the Annual Meeting of the American Society of International Law*
Aus YIL	*Australian Yearbook of International Law*
BCLR	*Boston College Law Review*
BFSP	*British and Foreign State Papers*
BJIL	*Brooklyn Journal of International Law*
BJPhS	*British Journal for the Philosophy of Science*
BSTJ	*Bell System Technical Journal*
BULR	*Boston University Law Review*
BVerfGE	*Entscheidungen des Bundesverfassungsgerichts*
BYBIL	*British Yearbook of International Law*
Can YIL	*Canadian Yearbook of International Law*
CDE	*Cahiers de droit européen*
Chinese JIL	*Chinese Journal of International Law*
CIL	customary international law
CJEU	Court of Justice of the European Union
CJICL	*Cambridge Journal of International and Comparative Law*
CJIL	*Chicago Journal of International Law*
CJLJ	*Canadian Journal of Law and Jurisprudence*
CLR	*California Law Review*
CoE	Council of Europe
CWR J Int Law	*Case Western Reserve Journal of International Law*

CYIL	*Canadian Yearbook of International Law*
CYELS	*Cambridge Yearbook of European Legal Studies*
Denv J Intl L & Pol'y	*Denver Journal of International Law and Policy*
DLJ	*Duke Law Journal*
DSU	Dispute Settlement Understanding
ECCC	Extraordinary Chambers in the Courts of Cambodia
ECHR	European Convention on Human Rights
ECLI	European Case Law Identifier
ECtHR	European Court of Human Rights
ECR	European Court Reports
EJIL	*European Journal of International Law*
Envtl L	*Environmental Law*
EP	*European Papers*
EQdF	*Enrahonar Quaderns de Filosofia*
ESIL	European Society of International Law
Eur L Rev	*European Law Review*
FCAFC	Federal Court of Australia Full Court
GJICL	*Georgia Journal of International and Comparative Law*
GJIL	*Georgetown Journal of International Law*
GLJ	*German Law Journal*
GlobCon	*Global Constitutionalism*
GYIL	*German Yearbook of International Law*
Har L Rev	*Harvard Law Review*
Heidelberg J Intl L	*Heidelberg Journal of International Law*
HHRJ	*Harvard Human Rights Journal*
HILJ	*Harvard International Law Journal*
HRC	Human Rights Committee
HRLJ	*Human Rights Law Journal*
HRLR	*Human Rights Law Review*
IACtHR	Inter-American Court of Human Rights
ICC	International Criminal Court
ICJ	International Court of Justice
ICJ Rep	*Reports of the International Court of Justice*
ICL	international criminal law
ICLQ	*International and Comparative Law Quarterly*
ICLR	*International Community Law Review*
ICRC	International Committee of the Red Cross
ICSID	International Centre for Settlement of Investment Disputes
ICSID Rev	*ICSID Review – Foreign Investment Law Journal*
ICTL	*Information and Communications Technology Law*

ICTY	International Criminal Tribunal for the Former Yugoslavia
IHL	*International Humanitarian Law*
IJCL	*International Journal of Constitutional Law*
IJGLS	*Indiana Journal of Global Legal Studies*
IJSL	*International Journal for the Semiotics of Law*
ILA	International Law Association
ILC	International Law Commission
ILDC	*Oxford Reports on International Law in Domestic Cases*
i-lex	*i-lex – Rivista di Scienze Giuridiche, Scienze Cognitive e Intelligenza Artificiale*
ILM	*International Legal Materials*
ILSA J Intl Comp L	*International Law Students' Association Journal of International Law and Comparative Studies*
IO	*International Organization*
ITLOS	International Tribunal for the Law of the Sea
ITLOS Rep	*Reports of the International Tribunal for the Law of the Sea*
IUSCT	Iran-United States Claims Tribunal
J Marshall L Rev	*John Marshall Law Review*
J Philos	*Journal of Philosophy*
J Soc Public Teachers of Law	*Journal of the Society of Public Teachers of Law*
JICJ	*Journal of International Criminal Justice*
JIDS	*Journal of International Dispute Settlement*
JLS	*Journal of Legal Studies*
Law Philos	*Law and Philosophy*
LJIL	*Leiden Journal of International Law*
LLALR	*Loyola of Los Angeles Law Review*
LPICT	*Law and Practice of International Courts and Tribunals*
Melb JIL	*Melbourne Journal of International Law*
Mich L Rev	*Michigan Law Review*
MJIL	*Michigan Journal of International Law*
Monash UL Rev	*Monash University Law Review*
MPEPIL	*Max Plank Encyclopedia of Public International Law*
NCJIL	*North Carolina Journal of International Law*
NILR	*Netherlands International Law Review*
NJIL	*Nordic Journal of International Law*
NLH	*New Literary History*
NYIL	*Netherlands Yearbook of International Law*

NYUJILP	*New York University Journal of International Law and Politics*
NYUL Rev	*New York University Law Review*
OJLS	*Oxford Journal of Legal Studies*
Open Thermodyn J	*The Open Thermodynamics Journal*
PCA	Permanent Court of Arbitration
PCIJ	Permanent Court of International Justice
PCIJ Rep	*Reports of the Permanent Court of International Justice*
Philos Public Aff	*Philosophy and Public Affairs*
Philos Q	*Philosophy Quarterly*
Philos Rev	*Philosophical Review*
Philos Sci	*Philosophy of Science*
Phys Rev	*The Physical Review*
PYIL	*Polish Yearbook of International Law*
RdC	*Recueil des cours* (Collected Courses of the Hague Academy of International Law)
RBEF	*Revista Brasileira de Ensino de Fisica*
RDI	*Rivista di diritto internazionale*
RDUNED	*Revista de Derecho de la Universidad Nacional de Educación a Distancia*
Res	Resolution
RGDIP	*Revue générale de droit international public*
RMP	*Reviews of Modern Physics*
SCSL	Special Court for Sierra-Leone
SDILJ	*San Diego International Law Journal*
STL	Special Tribunal for Lebanon
Tex L Rev	*Texas Law Review*
TILJ	*Texas International Law Journal*
UC Irvine J Intl Transl Comp L	*UC Irvine Journal of International, Transnational, and Comparative Law*
UCLJLJ	UCL Journal of Law and Jurisprudence
UCLR	*University of Chicago Law Review*
UJIEL	*Utrecht Journal of International and European Law*
UMSLR	*University of Manchester Student Law Review*
UN	United Nations
UNCITRAL	United Nations Commission on International Trade Law
UNCTAD	United Nations Conference on Trade and Development
UNGA	United Nations General Assembly

UNRIAA	*United Nations Reports of International Arbitral Awards*
UNSC	United Nations Security Council
UNSG	United Nations Secretary-General
UNTS	United Nations Treaty Series
UPJIL	*University of Pennsylvania Journal of International Law*
URLR	*University of Richmond Law Review*
VCLT	Vienna Convention on the Law of Treaties
VJIL	*Virginia Journal of International Law*
VJTL	*Vanderbilt Journal of Transnational Law*
VLR	*Virginia Law Review*
VUWLR	*Victoria University of Wellington Law Review*
WLR	*Weekly Law Reports*
WRLAE	*Wroclaw Review of Law, Administration and Economics*
WTO	World Trade Organization
Yale LJ	*Yale Law Journal*
YILC	*Yearbook of the International Law Commission*
ZaöRV	*Zeitschrift für ausländisches öffentliches Recht und Völkerrecht*

TABLE OF CASES

Permanent Court of International Justice (PCIJ)

Case Concerning Certain German Interests in Polish Upper Silesia (Merits) [1926] PCIJ Rep 5, Series A No 7

Mavrommatis Palestine Concessions (Greece *v.* Britain) (Objection to the Jurisdiction of the Court) [1924] PCIJ Series A No 2

Nationality Decrees Issued in Tunis and Morocco (Advisory Opinion) [1923] PCJ Series B No 4

S.S. 'Lotus' case (France *v.* Turkey) [1927] PCIJ Series A No 10

S.S. 'Wimbledon' (UK, France, Italy and Japan *v.* Germany) [1923] PCIJ Series A No 1

Status of Eastern Carelia (Advisory Opinion) [1923] PCIJ Rep 6

International Court of Justice (ICJ)

Accordance with International Law of the Unilateral Declaration of Independence in Respect of Kosovo (Advisory Opinion) [2010] ICJ Rep 403

Anglo-Norwegian Fisheries (United Kingdom *v.* Norway) (Judgment) [1951] ICJ Rep 116

Application of the Convention on the Prevention and Punishment of the Crime of Genocide (Bosnia and Herzegovina *v.* Serbia and Montenegro) (Judgment) [2007] ICJ Rep 43

- Joint Declaration of Judges Shi and Koroma

Application of the Convention on the Prevention and Punishment of the Crime of Genocide (Croatia *v.* Serbia) (Judgment) [2008] ICJ Rep 413

Arbitral Award of 31 July 1989 (Guinea-Bissau *v.* Senegal) [1991] ICJ Rep 53

Armed Activities on the Territory of the Congo (Democratic Republic of the Congo *v.* Uganda) (Judgment) [2005] ICJ Rep 168

- Separate Opinion of Judge Elaraby
- Separate Opinion of Judge Kooijmans

Armed Activities on the Territory of the Congo (Democratic Republic of the Congo *v.* Uganda) (Reparations, Judgment) [2022] ICJ Rep 1

Armed Activities on the Territory of the Congo (New Application: 2002) (Democratic Republic of the Congo *v.* Rwanda) (Jurisdiction and Admissibility) [2006] ICJ Rep 6

Arrest Warrant (Democratic Republic of the Congo *v.* Belgium) (Jurisdiction and Admissibility) [2002] ICJ Rep 3

- Separate Opinion of Judge Koroma
- Joint Separate Opinion of Judges Higgins, Kooijmans, and Buergenthal
- Dissenting Opinion of Judge van den Wyngaert

Avena and Other Mexican Nationals (Mexico *v.* United States of America) (Judgment) [2004] ICJ Rep 12

Barcelona Traction, Light and Power Company Limited (New Application: 1962) (Belgium *v.* Spain) [1970] ICJ Rep 3

Case Concerning the Temple of Preah Vihear (Cambodia *v.* Thailand) (Merits) [1962] ICJ Rep 39

- Separate Opinion of Vice-President Alfaro

Case of the Monetary Gold Removed from Rome in 1943 (Preliminary Question) [1954] ICJ Rep 19

Certain Iranian Assets (Islamic Republic of Iran v. United States of America) (Preliminary Objections) [2019] ICJ Rep 7

- Separate Opinion of Judge ad hoc Brower

Certain Phosphate Lands in Nauru (Nauru *v.* Australia) (Preliminary Objections) [1992] ICJ Rep 240

Certain Questions of Mutual Assistance in Criminal Matters (Djibouti *v.* France) (Judgment) [2008] ICJ Rep 177

Colombian-Peruvian Asylum Case (Judgment) [1950] ICJ Rep 266

Continental Shelf (Libya/Malta) (Judgment) [1985] ICJ Rep 13

Corfu Channel (United Kingdom *v.* Albania) (Judgment) [1949] ICJ Rep 4

- Separate Opinion of Judge Azevedo

Delimitation of the Maritime Boundary in the Gulf of Maine Area (Canada/USA) (Judgment) [1984] ICJ Rep 246

Diallo Case (Guinea *v.* DR Congo) (Judgment) [2007] ICJ Rep 582

Difference Related to Immunities from Legal Process of a Special Rapporteur of the Commission on Human Rights (Advisory Opinion) [1999] ICJ Rep 62

Dispute Regarding Navigational and Related Rights (Costa Rica *v.* Nicaragua) (Judgment) [2009] ICJ Rep 213

East Timor (Portugal *v.* Australia) (Judgment) [1995] ICJ Rep 90

- Dissenting Opinion of Judge Weeramantry
- Dissenting Opinion of Judge Skubiszewski

Fisheries (UK *v.* Norway) (Judgment, Dissenting Opinion of Judge Reed) [1951] ICJ Rep 116

Fisheries Jurisdiction Case (UK *v.* Iceland; Germany *v.* Iceland) (Merits) [1974] ICJ Rep 3

Frontier Dispute (Burkina Faso/Republic of Mali) (Judgment) [1986] ICJ Rep 554

Gabčíkovo-Nagymaros Project (Hungary *v.* Slovakia) (Merits) [1997] ICJ Rep 7

- Separate Opinion of Judge Bedjaoui

Immunities and Criminal Proceedings (Equatorial Guinea *v.* France) (Preliminary Objections) [2018] ICJ Rep 1

Interhandel (Switzerland *v.* United States of America) (Preliminary Objections) [1959] ICJ Rep 6
International Status of South West Africa (Advisory Opinion) [1950] ICJ Rep 128
Interpretation of the Agreement of 25 March 1951 between the WHO and Egypt (Advisory Opinion) [1980] ICJ Rep 73
- Separate Opinion of Judge Guillaume

Jadhav Case (India *v.* Pakistan) (Merits) [2019] ICJ Rep 418
- Declaration of Judge Robinson

Jurisdictional Immunities of the State (Germany/Italy; Greece intervening) [2012] ICJ Rep 99
- Dissenting Opinion of Judge Trindade

Kasikili/Sedudu Island (Botswana *v.* Namibia) (Judgment) [1999] ICJ Rep 1045
LaGrand Case (Germany *v.* United States of America) (Judgment) [2001] ICJ Rep 466
Legal Consequences for States of the Continued Presence of South Africa in Namibia (South West Africa) Notwithstanding Security Council Resolution 276 (1970) (Advisory Opinion) [1971] ICJ Rep 16
Legal Consequences of the Construction of a Wall in the Occupied Palestinian Territory (Advisory Opinion) [2004] ICJ Rep 136
Legality of the Threat or Use of Nuclear Weapons (Advisory Opinion) [1996] ICJ Rep 226
- Dissenting Opinion of Judge Schwebel
- Dissenting Opinion of Judge Higgins

Legality of Use of Force (Serbia and Montenegro *v.* Belgium) (Preliminary Objections) [2004] ICJ Rep 279
Maritime Delimitation and Territorial Question between Qatar and Bahrain (Qatar *v.* Bahrain) (Merits) [2001] ICJ Rep 40
Maritime Delimitation in the Area between Greenland and Jan Mayen (Denmark *v.* Norway) (Merits) [1993] ICJ Rep 38
Maritime Delimitation in the Indian Ocean (Somalia *v.* Kenya) (Preliminary Objections) [2017] ICJ Rep 3
Maritime Dispute (Peru *v.* Chile) (Judgment) [2014] ICJ Rep 3
Military and Paramilitary Activities in and against Nicaragua (Nicaragua *v.* United States of America) (Jurisdiction and Admissibility) [1984] ICJ Rep 392
Military and Paramilitary Activities in and against Nicaragua (Nicaragua *v.* United States of America) (Merits) [1986] ICJ Rep 14
North Sea Continental Shelf Cases (Germany/Netherlands; Germany/Denmark) (Judgment) [1969] ICJ Rep 3
- Separate Opinion of Judge Ammoun
- Dissenting Opinion of Judge Tanaka
- Dissenting Opinion of Judge Sørensen
- Dissenting Opinion of Judge Lachs

Nottebohm (Liechtenstein *v.* Guatemala) (Preliminary Objections) [1953] ICJ Rep 111.
Nottebohm (Liechtenstein *v.* Guatemala) (Judgment, Second Phase) [1955] ICJ Rep 4
Nuclear Tests (Australia *v.* France) (Judgment) [1974] ICJ Rep 253

Obligation to Negotiate Access to the Pacific Ocean (Bolivia *v.* Chile) (Merits) [2018] ICJ Rep 507

- Dissenting Opinion of Judge ad hoc Daudet

Oil Platforms (Islamic Republic of Iran *v.* United States of America) (Preliminary Objections) [1996] ICJ Rep 182

Oil Platforms (Islamic Republic of Iran *v.* United States of America) (Judgment) [2003] ICJ Rep 161

- Separate Opinion of Judge Higgins
- Separate Opinion of Judge Kooijmans

Pulp Mills on the River Uruguay (Argentina *v.* Uruguay) (Judgment) [2010] ICJ Rep 14

- Separate Opinion of Judge Trindade

Questions of the Delimitation of the Continental Shelf between Nicaragua and Colombia beyond 200 Nautical Miles from the Nicaraguan Coast (Nicaragua *v.* Colombia) (Preliminary Objections) [2016] ICJ Rep 100

- Declaration of Judge Robinson

Questions Relating to the Obligation to Prosecute or Extradite (Belgium *v.* Senegal) (Judgment) [2012] ICJ Rep 422

Questions Relating to the Seizure and Detention of Certain Documents and Data (Timor-Leste *v.* Australia) (Provisional Measures) [2014] ICJ Rep 147

Reparation for Injuries Suffered in the Service of the United Nations (Advisory Opinion) [1949] ICJ Rep 174

- Opinion of Judge Alvarez
- Dissenting Opinion of Judge Krylov

Reservations to the Convention on the Prevention and Punishment of the Crime of Genocide (Advisory Opinion) [1951] ICJ Rep 15

- Joint Dissenting Opinion of Judges Guerrero, McNair, Read and& Hsu Mo

South West Africa (Liberia *v.* South Africa) (Judgment) [1966] ICJ Rep 6

Territorial and Maritime Dispute (Nicaragua *v.* Colombia) (Judgment) [2012] ICJ Rep 624

Territorial and Maritime Dispute between Nicaragua and Honduras in the Caribbean Sea (Nicaragua *v.* Honduras) (Judgment) [2007] ICJ Rep 659

Territorial Dispute (Libyan Arab Jamahiriya *v.* Chad) (Judgment) [1994] ICJ Rep 6

United States Diplomatic and Consular Staff in Tehran (USA *v.* Iran) (Judgment) [1980] ICJ Rep 3

Voting Procedure on Questions Related to Reports and Petitions Concerning the Territory of South West Africa (Advisory Opinion) [1955] ICJ Rep 84

- Separate Opinion of Judge Klaestad
- Separate Opinion of Judge Lauterpacht.

Western Sahara (Advisory Opinion) [1975] ICJ Rep 12

Whaling in the Antarctic (Australia *v.* Japan; New Zealand intervening) (Judgment) [2014] ICJ Rep 226

- Separate Opinion of Judge Cançado Trindade

Memorials in ICJ Cases

Corfu Channel, Memorial of the UK (30 September 1947) <www.icj-cij.org/sites/default/files/case-related/1/1489.pdf>
Jurisdictional Immunities of the State (Germany *v.* Italy) Memorial of the Federal Republic of Germany (12 June 2009) <www.icj-cij.org/sites/default/files/case-related/143/16644.pdf>
Jurisdictional Immunities of the State (Germany *v.* Italy) Counter-Memorial of Italy (22 December 2009)
Jurisdictional Immunities of the State (Germany *v.* Italy) Rejoinder of Italy (10 January 2011) <www.icj-cij.org/sites/default/files/case-related/143/16652.pdf>
Maritime Delimitation and Territorial Questions between Qatar and Bahrain (Qatar *v.* Bahrain) Verbatim Record CR 2000/12
Obligations Concerning Negotiations Relating to Cessation of the Nuclear Arms Race and to Nuclear Disarmament (Marshall Islands *v.* Pakistan) Counter-memorial of Pakistan (Jurisdiction and Admissibility) (1 December 2015)
Oil Platforms (Islamic Republic of Iran *v.* United States of America) Reply and Defence to Counter-claim submitted by the Islamic Republic of Iran, vol I (10 March 1999) <www.icj-cij.org/sites/default/files/case-related/90/8630.pdf>

International Criminal Court (ICC)

Decision on the Prosecution's Application for a Warrant of Arrest against Omar Hassan Ahmad Al Bashir, ICC-02/05-01/09 (4 March 2009)
Situation in the State of Palestine, 'Prosecution Request Pursuant to Article 19(3) for a Ruling on the Court's Territorial Jurisdiction in Palestine' Decision (5 February 2021) ICC-01/18
The Prosecutor *v.* Dominic Ongwen, ICC-02/04-01/15 (4 February 2021)
The Prosecutor *v.* Omar Hassan Ahmad Al Bashir ICC-02/05-01/09 (6 June 2005)
The Prosecutor *v.* Omar Hassan Ahmad Al Bashir, ICC-02/05-01/09-1 (4 March 2009)
The Prosecutor *v.* Omar Hassan Ahmad Al Bashir, ICC-02/05-01/09-94 (12 July 2010)
The Prosecutor *v.* Omar Hassan Al Bashir, ICC-02/05-01/09, AC ICC-02/05-01/09 OA2 (6 May 2019)
The Prosecutor *v.* Omar Hassan Al Bashir, ICC-02/05-01/09-397-Anx1 (6 May 2019)
The Prosecutor *v.* Omar Hassan Ahmad Al Bashir (Judgment in the Jordan Referral re Al-Bashir Appeal) ICC-02/05-01/09-397-Corr (6 May 2019)
The Prosecutor *v.* Uhuru Muigai Kenyatta, ICC-01/09-02/11 (18 October 2013)

- Separate further opinion of Judge Eboe-Osuji

International Criminal Tribunal for the Former Yugoslavia (ICTY)

The Prosecutor *v.* Aleksovski (Judgment) ICTY-95-14-1-A (24 March 2000)

The Prosecutor *v.* Aleksovski (Appeals Chamber Judgment) ICTY-95-14/1-A (24 March 2000)
The Prosecutor *v.* Delalić and ors (Judgment) ICTY-96-21-T (16 November 1998)
The Prosecutor *v.* Delalić and ors (Judgment) ICTY-96-21-A (20 February 2001)
The Prosecutor *v.* Duško Tadić (Interlocutory Appeal) ICTY, IT-94-1-A (2 October 1995)
The Prosecutor *v.* Duško Tadić (Appeals Chamber Judgment) ICTY-94-1-A (15 July 1999)
The Prosecutor *v.* Furundžija (Judgment) ICTY-95-17/1 (10 December 1998)
The Prosecutor *v.* Hadžihasanović and ors (Interlocutory Appeal) ICTY-01-47-AR72 (16 July 2003)
- Dissenting Opinion of Judge Shahabudeen

The Prosecutor *v.* Kordic and Cerkez (Judgment) ICTY-95-14/2-T (26 February 2001)
The Prosecutor *v.* Kordic and Cerkez (Judgment) ICTY-95–14/2-A (17 December 2004)
The Prosecutor *v.* Krstic (Judgment) ICTY-98-33-T (2 August 2001)
The Prosecutor *v.* Kunarac and ors (Judgment) ICTY-96-23-T and ICTY-96-23/1 (22 February 2001)
The Prosecutor *v.* Kupreškić (Judgment) ICTY-95-16-T (14 January 2000)
The Prosecutor *v.* Prlić and ors (Judgment vol 1) ICTY-04-74- A (29 November 2017)
The Prosecutor *v.* Radovan Karadzic (Judgment) ICTY, IT-95-5/18-T (24 March 2016)

Special Court for Sierra Leone (SCSL)

Prosecutor *v.* Charles Ghankay Taylor (Judgment) SCSL-03-01-T (18 May 2012)
Prosecutor *v.* Morris Kallon and Brima Buzzy Kamara (Decision on Challenge to Jurisdiction) SCSL-2004-15-AR72(E) (13 March 2004)

Special Court for Lebanon (STL)

Prosecutor *v.* Ayyash and ors, STL-11-01/I (Interlocutory Decision on the Applicable Law, 16 February 2011)

Extraordinary Chambers in the Courts of Cambodia (ECCC)

Prosecutor *v.* Chea, Case 002 (Pre-Trial Chamber, Decision on Appeals by Nuon Chea and Ieng Thirith against the Closing Order, 15 February 2011)
Prosecutor *v.* Chea and Samphan, Case 002/02 (Judgment, 16 November 2018)

Arbitration

Blockade of Portendic (Great Britain *v.* France) [1843] 42 BFSP 1377

Différend concernant l'accord Tardieu-Jaspar (Belgium/France) Award of 1 March 1937, UNRIAA, vol III, 1713
Georges Pinson Case (France/United Mexican States) Award of 13 April 1928, UNRIAA, vol V, 422
Lance Paul Larsen *v.* The Hawaiian Kingdom (Final Award) (2001) PCA
The South China Sea Arbitration (The Republic of Philippines *v.* The People's Republic of China) (Final Award) (2016) PCA
Trail Smelter Arbitration (United States *v.* Canada) [1941] 3 RIAA 1905, 1965

International Centre for Settlement of Investment Disputes (ICSID)

Alex Genin, Eastern Credit Limited, Inc. and A.S. Baltoil *v.* Estonia (Award) ICSID Case No ARB/99/2 (25 June 2001)
Asian Agricultural Products Ltd. (AAPL) *v.* Republic of Sri Lanka (Award) ICSID Case No ARB/87/3 (27 June 1990)
Azurix Corp *v.* Argentina (I) (Decision on Jurisdiction) ICSID Case No ARB/01/12 (8 December 2003)
Bayindir Insaat Turizm Ticaret Ve Sanayi AS *v.* Pakistan (Award) ICSID Case No ARB/03/29 (27 August 2009)
Cable Television of Nevis, Ltd and Cable Television of Nevis Holdings, Ltd *v.* St Kitts and Nevis (Award) ICSID Case No ARB/95/2 (13 January 1997)
CMS Gas Transmission Company *v.* Argentina (Decision on Jurisdiction) ICSID Case No ARB/01/8 (17 July 2003)
Compañía de Aguas del Aconquija SA and Vivendi Universal SA (formerly Compañía de Aguas del Aconquija, S.A. and Compagnie Générale des Eaux) *v.* Argentina (I) (Decision on Annulment) ICSID Case No ARB/97/3 (3 July 2002)
Consortium RFCC *v.* Morocco (Decision on Jurisdiction) ICSID Case No ARB/00/6 (16 July 2001)
Corn Products International, Inc *v.* United Mexican States (Award) ICSID Case No ARB (AF)/04/1(18 August 2009)
- Separate Opinion of Andreas F Lowenfeld

Deutsche Bank AG *v.* Sri Lanka (Award) ICSID Case No ARB/09/2 (31 October 2012)
Emilio Agustín Maffezini *v.* Spain (Decision of the Tribunal on Objections to Jurisdiction) ICSID Case No ARB/97/7 (25 January 2000)
Enron Creditors Recovery Corporation (formerly Enron Corporation) and Ponderosa Assets, LP *v.* Argentina (Decision on Jurisdiction) ICSID Case No ARB/01/3 (14 January 2004)
Gustav F W Hamester GmbH & Co KG *v.* Ghana (Award) ICSID Case No ARB/07/24 (18 June 2010)
Helnan Inqsazternational Hotels A/S *v.* Egypt (Decision on Objection to Jurisdiction) ICSID Case No ARB/05/19 (17 October 2006)
Hussein Nuaman Soufraki *v.* The United Arab Emirates (Award) ICSID Case No ARB/02/7 (7 July 2004)

European Court of Human Rights (ECtHR)

Mamatkulov and Askarov *v.* Turkey, App no 46827/99 and 46951/99 (4 February 2005)
McElhinney *v.* Ireland, App no 31253/96 (21 November 2001)
Oleynikov *v.* Russia, App no 36703/04 (14 March 2013)
Radunović and ors *v.* Montenegro, App no 45197/13, 53000/13 and 73404/13 (25 October 2016)
Rinau *v.* Lithuania, App no 10926/09 (14 January 2020)
Sabel El Leil *v.* France, App no 34869/05 (29 June 2011)
Soering *v.* United Kingdom, App no 14038/88 (7 July 1989)

Inter-American Court of Human Rights (IACtHR)

Mayagna (Sumo) Awas Tingni Community *v.* Nicaragua (Merits, Reparations and Costs) Inter-American Court of Human Rights Series C No 79 (2001)

Iran–United States Claims Tribunal (IUSCT)

Eastman Kodak Company *v.* the Government of Iran (Award No 329-227/12384-3) IUSCT Case No 227 (11 November 1987)
Flexi-Van Leasing, Inc *v.* Iran (Award No 259-36-1) IUSCT Case No 36 (13 October 1986)
Foremost Tehran, Inc, Foremost Shir, Inc, and ors *v.* Iran, the Ministry of Economic Affairs and Finance, and ors (Award No 220-37/231-1) IUSCT Case Nos 37 and 231 (11 April 1986)
International Technical Products Corporation and ITP Export Corporation, Its Wholly Owned Subsidiary *v.* Iran and Its Agencies, the Islamic Republic Iranian Air Force and the Ministry of National Defense, Acting for the Civil Aviation Organization (Award No 196-302-3) IUSCT Case No 302 (28 October 1985)
Otis Elevator Company *v.* Iran and Bank Mellat (formerly Foreign Trade Bank of Iran) (Award No 304-284-2) IUSCT Case No 284 (29 April 1987)
PepsiCo, Inc *v.* Iran, Foundation for the Oppressed, Zamzam Bottling Company, and ors (Award No 260-18-1) IUSCT Case No 18 (13 October 1986)
Schering Corporation *v.* Iran (Award No 122-38-3) IUSCT Case No 38 (16 April 1984)
SEDCO Inc *v.* National Iranian Oil Company and Iran (Award No 419-128/129-2) IUSCT Case Nos 128 and 129 (30 March 1989)

- Opinion of Judge Khalilian

Court of Justice of the European Union (CJEU)

A and ors *v.* Minister van Buitenlandse Zaken (C-158/14) [2016] ECLI:EU:C:2016:734
A Racke GmbH & Co *v.* Hauptzollamt Mainz (C-162/96) [1998] ECR I-3655
Aboubacar Diakité *v.* Commissaire général aux réfugiés et aux apatrides (C-285/12) [2013] ECLI:EU:C:2013:500
Ahlström Osakeyhtiö and ors *v.* Commission (89/85, 104/85, 114/85, 116/85, 117/85 and 125/85 to 129/85) (Woodpulp) [1993] ECLI:EU:C:1993:120

Air Transport Association of America (ATAA) & ors *v.* Secretary of State for Energy and Climate Change (C-366/10) [2011] EU:C:2011:864

Amministrazione delle finanze dello Stato *v.* Denkavit italiana Srl (61/79) [1980] ECR 1205

Anklagemyndigheden *v.* Peter Michael Poulsen and Diva Navigation Corp (C-286/90) [1992] ECR I–6019

Council of the European Union *v.* Front populaire pour la libération de la saguia-el-hamra et du rio de oro (Front Polisario) (C-104/16 P)[2016] ECLI:EU:C:2016:973

Danisco Sugar AB *v.* Allmänna ombudet (C-27/96) [1997] ECR I-6653

Firma Brita GmbH *v.* Hauptzollamt Hamburg-Hafen (C-386/08) [2010] ECLI:EU:C:2010:91

Front populaire pour la libération de la Saguia el-Hamra et du Rio de oro (Front Polisario) *v.* Council of the European Union (T-279/19) [2021] ECLI:EU:T:2021:639

Front populaire pour la libération de la Saguia el-Hamra et du Rio de oro (Front Polisario) *v.* Council of the European Union (T-344/19 and T-356/19) [2021] ECLI:EU:T:2021:640

Hauer *v.* Land Rheinland Pfalz (44/79) [1979] ECR 3727

Hellenic Republic *v.* Commission of the European Communities (C-203/07 P) [2008] ECR I-8161

Helm Düngemittel GmbH *v.* Hauptzollamt Krefeld (C-613/12) [2014] ECLI:EU:C:2014:52

Hungary *v.* Slovakia (C-364/10) [2012] ECLI:EU:C:2012:630

J Nold, Kohlen- und Baustoffgroßhandlung *v.* Commission of the European Communities (4/73) [1974] ECR 491

Janko Rottman *v.* Freistaat Bayern (C-135/08) [2010] ECLI:EU:C:2010:104

- Opinion of AG Maduro, ECLI:EC:C:2009:588

Kadi and Al Barakaat International Foundation *v.* Council of the European Union and Commission of the European Communities (C-402/05 P and C-415/05 P) [2008] ECR I–6351

LG *v.* Rina SpA, Ente Registro Italiano Navale (C-641/18) Opinion of AG Szpunar [2020] ECLI:EU:C:2020:3

LTTE *v.* Council (T-208/11) [2014] ECLI:EU:T:2014:885

Omega Spielhallen- und Automatenaufstellungs-GmbH *v.* Oberbürgermeisterin der Bundesstadt Bonn (C-36/02) [2004] ECR I–9609

Opel Austria GmbH *v.* Council of the European Union (T-115/94) [1997] ECR II-39

Opinion 2/15 (Free Trade Agreement between the European Union and the Republic of Singapore) [2016] ECLI:EU:C:2016:992

Ahmed Mahamdia *v.* People's Democratic Republic of Algeria (154/11) Opinion of AG Mengozzi [2012] ECLI:EU:C:2012:309

Raad van bestuur van de Sociale verzekeringsbank *v.* LF Evans (C-179/13) [2014] ECLI:EU:C 2014:2015

Western Sahara Campaign UK *v.* Commissioners for Her Majesty's Revenue and Customs and Secretary of State for Environment, Food and Rural Affairs (C-266/16) [2018] ECLI:EU:C:2018:118

- Opinion of AG Wathelet, ECLI:EU:C:2018:1

Yvonne van Duyn *v.* Home Office (42/74) [1974] ECR 1337

Other Courts and Judicial Bodies

AA Megalidis *v.* Turkey [1932] 4 Annual Digest of Public International Law Cases 395
GATT, Dispute Settlement Panel Report on United States Restrictions on Imports of Tuna (1994) 33 ILM 839
Lake Lanoux (France *v.* Spain) (1957) 12 RIAA 281
M/V 'Norstar' (Panama *v.* Italy) (Preliminary Objections, Order of 15 Mar 2016) ITLOS Reports 2016
Responsibilities and Obligations of States Sponsoring Persons and Entities with Respect to Activities in the Area (Advisory Opinion) ITLOS Reports 2011
Responsibilities and Obligations of States with Respect to the Activities in the Area (Request for Advisory Opinion Submitted to the Seabed Dispute Chambers) Advisory Opinion, ITLOS Reports 2011
WTO, Turkey – Restriction on Imports of Textiles and Clothing Products, Report of the Panel (31 May 1999) WT/DS34/R

Decisions of National Courts

Australia, Federal Court, Ure *v.* The Commonwealth of Australia [2016] FCAFC 8
Canada, Supreme Court, Nevsun Resources Ltd *v.* Araya, 2020 SCC 5
Canada, Supreme Court, R *v.* Hape, 2007 CSC 26
England and Wales, Court of Appeal, R *v.* Bottrill, ex parte Kuechenmeister [1947] 1 KB 41
England and Wales, House of Lords, Maclaine Watson *v.* Department of Trade [1989] 3 All ER 523
England and Wales, House of Lords, R *v.* Bow St Metropolitan Stipendiary Magistrate, ex parte Pinochet Ugarte (Pinochet III) [(1999] 2 WLR 827
France, Conseil Constitutionnel, Decision no 94–352 (18 January 1995)
Germany, Bundesverfassungsgericht, Order of First Senate (17 December 1975) 1 BvR 63/68
Germany, Bundesverfassungsgericht, Order of First Senate (3 November 1987) 1 BvR 1257/84
Germany, Bundesverfassungsgericht, Order of First Senate (7 March 1990) 1 BvR 1215/87
Singapore, Court of Appeal, Van *v.* Public Prosecutor (20 October 2004) SGCA 47
Switzerland, Federal Criminal Court, A *v.* Office of the Attorney General of Switzerland, BB.2011.140 (25 July 2012)
Switzerland, Federal Supreme Court (12 October 2012) BGE 139 I 16
United States, Supreme Court, Jacobellis *v.* Ohio (378 U.S. 184)

TABLE OF TREATIES AND INTERNATIONAL DOCUMENTS

Treaties

1945 Charter of the United Nations (adopted 26 June 1945, entered into force 24 October 1945) 892 UNTS 119

1945 Statute of the International Court of Justice (adopted 26 June 1945, entered into force 24 October 1945) 33 UNTS 993

1947 Understanding on the Rules and Procedures Governing the Settlement of Disputes, Annex 2 to the 1994 Agreement Establishing the World Trade Organization (1947) 1869 UNTS 401

1948 Convention on the Prevention and Punishment of the Crime of Genocide (opened for signature 9 December 1948, entered into force 12 January 1951) 78 UNTS 277

1950 European Convention for the Protection of Human Rights and Fundamental Freedoms (adopted 4 November 1950, entered into force 3 September 1953) 23 UNTS 2889

1955 Treaty of Amity Economic Relations and Consular Rights between the United States and Iran (adopted 15 August 1955, entered into force 16 June 1957) 284 UNTS 93

1957 Treaty on the Functioning of the European Union [2016] OJ C202/47

1965 Convention on the Settlement of Investment Disputes between States and Nationals of Other States (adopted 18 March 1965, entered into force 14 October 1966) 575 UNTS 159

1969 Vienna Convention on the Law of Treaties (adopted 23 May 1969, entered into force 27 January 1980) 1155 UNTS 331

1972 European Convention on State Immunity (signed 16 May 1972, entered into force 11 June 1976, 4 October 1979 in UK) 1495 UNTS 182

1976 International Covenant on Civil and Political Rights (adopted 16 December 1966, entered into force 23 March 1976) 999 UNTS 171

1983 Agreement between the Government of the United Kingdom of Great Britain and Northern Ireland and the Government of the Republic of Panama for the Promotion and Protection of Investments (signed 7 October 1983, entered into force 7 November 1985) 2107 UNTS 300

1983 Annex to Treaty between the United States of America and the Republic of Senegal Concerning the Reciprocal Encouragement and Protection of Investment (signed 6 December 1983, entered into force 25 October 1990)

1984 Convention against Torture and Other Cruel, Inhuman or Degrading Treatment or Punishment (adopted 10 December 1984, entered into force 26 June 1987) 1465 UNTS 85

1982 United Nations Convention on the Law of the Sea (adopted 10 December 1982, entered into force 16 November 1994) 1833 UNTS 3

1992 Agreement on the European Economic Area (adopted 2 May 1992, entered into force 1 January 1994) 1801 UNTS 3

1998 Rome Statute of the International Criminal Court (adopted 17 July 1998, entered into force 1 July 2002) 2187 UNTS 3

2004 United Nations Convention on Jurisdictional Immunities of States and Their Property (adopted 2 December 2004, not yet in force) UN Doc A/59/508

2008 Treaty between the Government of the United States of America and the Government of the Republic of Rwanda Concerning the Encouragement and Reciprocal Protection of Investment (adopted 19 February 2008, entered into force 1 December 2012)

2018 Agreement for the Reciprocal Promotion and Protection of Investments between the Argentine Republic and the United Arab Emirates (signed 16 April 2018, not in force)

2021 China-EU Comprehensive Agreement on Investment (adopted 22 January 2021)

International Documents

UN Documents

International Law Commission (ILC)

ILC, 'Draft Articles on Responsibility of States for Internationally Wrongful Acts with Commentaries' (23 April–1 June and 2 July–10 August 2001) UN Doc A/56/10

ILC, 'Draft Articles on the Responsibility of International Organizations' (2011) UN Doc A/66/10

ILC, 'Draft Conclusions on Identification of Customary International Law, with Commentaries' (30 April–1 June and 2 July–10 August 2018) UN Doc A/73/10

ILC, 'Fifth Report on Peremptory Norms of General International Law (*jus cogens*)' (2022) UN Doc A/CN.4/747

ILC, 'Fifth Report on the Law of Treaties' (1966) UN Doc A/CN.4/183 and Add.1–4

ILC, 'First Report on General Principles of Law' (29 April–7 June and 8 July–9 August 2019) UN Doc A/CN.4/732

ILC, 'Fragmentation of International Law: Difficulties Arising from the Diversification and Expansion of International Law, Report of the Study Group of the International Law Commission' (13 April 2006) UN Doc A/CN.4/L.682

ILC, 'Guiding Principles Applicable to Unilateral Declarations of States Capable of Creating Legal Obligations' (1 May–9 June and 3 July–11 August 2006) UN Doc A/61/10

ILC, 'Immunity of State Officials from Foreign Jurisdiction: Texts and Titles of the Draft Articles Adopted by the Drafting Committee on First Reading' (31 May 2022) UN Doc A/CN.4/L.969

ILC, 'Second Report on General Principles of Law' (27 April–5 June and 6 July–7 August 2020) UN Doc A/CN.4/741

ILC, 'Third Report on General Principles of Law' (18 April–3 June and 4 July–5 August 2022) UN Doc A/CN.4/753

ILC, 'Third Report on Identification of Customary International Law by Michael Wood, Special Rapporteur' (4 May–5 June and 6 July–7 August 2015) UN Doc A/CN.4/682

ILC, 'Ways and Means for Making the Evidence of Customary International Law More Readily Available' (1950) YILC II

United Nations General Assembly (UNGA)

UNGA, 'Affirmation of the Principles of International Law Recognized by the Charter of the Nuremberg Tribunal' (11 December 1946) UN Doc A/RES/95

UNGA, 'Report of the International Law Commission on the Works of Its Fifty-Ninth Session' (8 January 2008) UN Doc A/RES/62/66

UNGA, 'Request for an Advisory Opinion of the International Court of Justice on the Consequences of Legal Obligations of States under Different Sources of International Law with Respect to Immunities to Heads of State and Government and Other Senior Officials' (18 July 2018) UN Doc A/73/144

UNGA Res 1803, 'Permanent Sovereignty over Natural Resources' (14 December 1962) UN Doc A/RES/1803/(XVII)

UNGA Res 2099(XX), 'Technical Assistance to Promote the Teaching, Study, Dissemination and Wider Appreciation of International Law' (20 December 1965) UN Doc A/RES/2099(XX)

UNGA Res 217A(III), 'Universal Declaration of Human Rights' (10 December 1948) UN Doc A/RES/3/217 A

UNGA Res 2625, 'Declaration on Principles of International Law Concerning Friendly Relations and Co-operation among States in Accordance with the Charter of the United Nations' (24 October 1970) UN Doc A/RES/2625(XXV)

UNGA Res 3201, 'Declaration on the Establishment of a New International Economic Order' (1 May 1974) UN Doc A/Res/3201(S.VI)

UNGA Res 3281, 'Charter of Economic Rights and Duties of States' (12 December 1974) UN Doc A/Res/3281/(XXIX)

UNGA Res 48/46, 'Activities of Foreign Economic and Other Interests Which Impede the Implementation of the Declaration on the Granting of Independence to Colonial Countries and Peoples in Territories under Colonial Domination' (10 December 1992) UN Doc A/RES/48/46

UNGA Res 49/40, 'Activities of Foreign Economic and Other Interests Which Impede the Implementation of the Declaration on the Granting of Independence to Colonial Countries and Peoples in Territories under Colonial Domination' (9 December 1994) A/RES/49/40

UNGA Res 50/33, 'Activities of Foreign Economic and Other Interests Which Impede the Implementation of the Declaration on the Granting of Independence to Colonial Countries and Peoples in Territories under Colonial Domination' (6 December 1995) UN Doc A/RES/50/33

UNGA Res 56/83 'Annex, Responsibility of States for Internationally Wrongful Acts' (12 December 2001) UN Doc A/RES/56/83

United Nations Security Council (UNSC)

UNSC 8233rd meeting (14 April 2018) UN Doc S/PV.8233 (Provisional) <https://documents-dds-ny.un.org/doc/UNDOC/PRO/N18/108/91/PDF/N1810891.pdf?OpenElement> accessed 30 April 2022

UNSC, 'Letter Dated 29 January 2002 from the Under-Secretary-General for Legal Affairs, the Legal Counsel, Addressed to the President of the Security Council' (12 February 2002) UN Doc S/2002/161

UNSC Res 827 (25 May 1993) UN Doc S/RES/827, as amended by UNSC Res 1877 (7 July 2009) UN Doc S/RES/1877

UNSC Res 955 (8 November 1994) UN Doc S/RES/955

UNSC Res 1593 (31 March 2005), UN Doc S/S/RES/1593

United Nations Secretary-General (UNSG)

UN Secretary-General, Question of the Death Penalty: Report of the Secretary-General (2 July 2012) UN Doc A/HRC/21/29

Other UN Documents

Declaration of the UN Conference on the Human Environment (Stockholm, 16 June 1972) in UN Doc A/CONF. 48/14 and Corr. 1

HRC, General Comment 24, 'Issues Relating to Reservations Made upon Ratification or Accession to the Covenant or the Optional Protocols Thereto, or in Relation to Declarations under Art. 41 of the Covenant' (1994) CCPR/ C/ 21/ Rev.1/ Add.6

UNCITRAL, 'Report of Working Group III (Investor–State Dispute Settlement Reform) on the Work of its 36th Session (Vienna, 29 October–2 November 2018)' UN Doc A/CN.9/964 (6 November 2018)

UNCTAD, 'Fair and Equitable Treatment', UNCTAD Series in International Investment Agreements II, UN Doc UNCTAD/DIAE/IA/2011/5 (2012)

International Law Association (ILA)

ILA Committee on Complementarity in International Criminal Law, Final Report (Lisbon Conference 2022) <www.ila-hq.org/en/committees/complementarity-in-international-criminal-law> accessed 29 March 2024

ILA Committee on Formation of Customary (General) International Law, Final Report: 'Statement of Principles Applicable to the Formation of General Customary International Law' (London Conference, 2000) <www.ila-hq.org/en_GB/committees/formation-of-customary-general-international-law> accessed 29 March 2024

ILA Study Group, on the Content and Evolution of the Rules of Interpretation <www.ila-hq.org/en_GB/study-groups/content-and-evolution-of-the-rules-of-interpretation> accessed 29 March 2024

Mendelson M, 'Formation of International Law and the Observational Standpoint' in ILA Committee on Formation of Customary (General) International Law, 'Report of 63rd Conference: Annex to the 1st Interim Report of the Committee' (Warsaw 1988)

Merkouris P and Peat D, 'Final Report on the Interpretative Practice of the PCIJ/ICJ' (International Law Association, 79th Biennial Conference, Kyoto, 2020)

Other International Documents

Advisory Committee of Jurists, 'Procès-Verbaux of the Proceedings of the Committee' (Permanent Court of International Justice 1920)

African Union Commission, Office of the Legal Counsel and Directorate for Legal Affairs, 'Legal Opinion on the Legality in the Context of International Law, Including the Relevant United Nations Resolutions and OAU/AU Decisions, of Actions Allegedly Taken by the Moroccan Authorities or Any Other State, Group of States, Foreign Companies or Any Other Entity in the Exploration and/or Exploitation of Renewable and Non-Renewable Natural Resources or Any Other Economic Activity in Western Sahara' (14 October 2015)

CoE, Committee of Ministers Res (68)17, 'Model Plan for the Classification of Documents Concerning State Practice in the Field of Public International Law' (28 June 1968)

European Union Guidelines on Promoting Compliance with International Humanitarian Law (IHL) [2005] OJ C327/04

ICC, 'Towards a More Just World Every Day', Annual Report of the Office of the Prosecutor (1 December 2022) <www.icc-cpi.int/sites/default/files/2022-12/2022-12-05-annual-report-of-the-office-of-the-prosecutor.pdf> accessed 29 March 2024

ICJ, 'Address by HE Judge Gilbert Guillaume, President of the International Court of Justice, to the United Nations General Assembly, 26 October 2000' <www.icj-cij.org/public/files/press-releases/9/2999.pdf> accessed 29 March 2024

ICSID, *History of the ICSID Convention: Documents Concerning the Origin and the Formulation of the Convention on the Settlement of Investment Disputes between States and Nationals of Other States* (1968) vol II-1

Institut de Droit International (Bath Session, September 1950) Annuaire vol 43-I (1950)

PART I

Theoretical Approaches to CIL and Its Interpretation

1

The Illusion of Gold-Digging: Interpretation of State Practice

PAULINE WESTERMAN

1 Introduction

Customary international law (CIL) is particularly vulnerable to the accusation that it is no more than 'mere assertion', a creation of the courts, if not downright fantasy.[1] Yet it is in CIL that one finds the strongest claim to objectivity in international law. It is expressed in the doctrine that one of the elements of CIL is state practice, which represents the 'objective' element of CIL. It is thought to supplement the 'subjective' or 'psychological' element of CIL: *opinio juris*.[2] Elsewhere, I have analysed *opinio juris* and concluded that it is much less 'subjective' than is commonly assumed.[3] Here, I will argue that state practice is much less 'objective' than is commonly assumed.

I will argue that the notion of state practice as a set of 'material facts' that should be 'identified' and from which customary norms can be 'induced' is grounded in obsolete epistemology. The identification of state practice is more adequately described as a selection of what deserves to be *counted* as state practice. I will argue that the starting point for this selective process is *opinio juris*. *Opinio juris* does not come after the fact,

The author thanks Andreas Follesdal and Kostiantyn Gorobets for their helpful comments on an earlier draft

[1] DH Joyner, 'Why I Stopped Believing in Customary International Law' (2019) 9 Asian JIL 31.

[2] For good – but not uncritical – expositions of the two-element doctrine, see P Haggenmacher, 'La doctrine des deux éléments du droit coutumier dans la pratique de la Cour internationale' (1986) 1 RGDIP 1; K Wolfke, 'Some Persistent Controversies Regarding Customary International Law' (1993) 24 NYIL 1; M Akehurst, 'Custom as a Source of International Law' (1975) 47 BYBIL 1, 37.

[3] See P Westerman, '*Opinio Juris*: Test, Filter, Ideal or Map?' in K Gorobets, A Hadjigeorgiou and P Westerman (eds), *Conceptual (Re)Constructions of International Law* (Edward Elgar 2022) 127.

as a subjective feeling of obligation that is superadded to a set of otherwise objective facts. *Opinio juris* is the indispensable conceptual framework without which habits and usages cannot even be 'seen' as state practice.

2 Gold-Digging

It is unclear what the adjectives 'objective' and 'subjective' refer to. To the elements themselves or to the ways in which these elements are studied? The latter option is not very plausible, for why may the convictions of states (*opinio juris*) not be dealt with in an objective manner? Any sociologist can tell you that it is possible to examine convictions and beliefs. And even if that would not be the case, why would one officially announce that half of the process of CIL identification is carried out in a 'subjective' manner?

No, apparently these adjectives refer to the elements themselves and not to the investigator. But then the question arises, why is state practice labelled an 'objective element'? In what sense can we say that acts, words, conventions and usages are objective elements? Can we speak at all about 'objective elements'? Are molecules and stars objective elements? And again, what is so subjective in *opinio juris* if we understand that notion as the conviction that a certain norm is a legal one? The more one thinks about it, the stranger it is.

The only way to make sense of the use of these terms is to take into account another dichotomous pair of words by means of which the two elements are distinguished: the 'normative' and the 'factual'. Apparently, the claim is that whereas *opinio juris* is the 'normative' element, state practice consists of 'facts'. There are three interrelated assumptions at stake here.

(1) The nature of the object that is investigated: facts.
Most authors understand practice as a heap of 'material facts'. State practice is called 'a sort of . . . raw material for custom',[4] an 'inert mass of accumulated usage'[5] or – in a modern version – a set of 'raw data'.[6]

[4] Wolfke (n 2) 4.

[5] HWA Thirlway, *International Customary Law and Codification* (AW Sijthoff 1972) 47, quoted in ILA Committee on Formation of Customary (General) International Law, 'Final Report of the Committee: Statement of Principles Applicable to the Formation of General Customary International Law' (London Conference, 2000) 30.

[6] AE Roberts, 'Traditional and Modern Approaches to Customary International Law: A Reconciliation' (2001) 95 AJIL 757, 757, 781, 788. Even Hakimi, despite her rich

(2) The method to be followed: induction.
The account of state practice as a heap of social facts gives rise to the idea that the analysis of state practice can be conducted as any inquiry into 'facts'. They can be collected as 'data', which should be 'described' and which forms the starting point of an inductive process of reasoning that moves from the described facts upwards to general statements about the rules that are followed.

(3) The aim of the investigation: identification.
The assumption is that state practice should be investigated in such a way that possible candidates for CIL can be 'identified'. The term 'identification' suggests that CIL is thus *found* rather than *constructed.*

The combination of these three related claims can be captured by the metaphor of gold-digging: the gold of CIL can be found by digging the inert material mass of sand and clay, and by bringing it upwards to the surface, after which it can be identified by sieving the sand.

Several authors have criticised this picture by criticising assumption (2). They think that an inductive description of the facts is only half of the work to be done. Roberts,[7] for instance, thinks that the 'descriptive accuracy' of an investigation of state practice should be complemented by a deductive method of searching for 'substantive normativity', starting with normative ideals and then descending to the formulation of rules. In a similar vein, Talmon[8] believes that we should make more room for deduction, especially where state practice is inconclusive, non-existent, contradictory or inconsistent with *opinio juris*. Finally, Merkouris[9] wants to complement the inductive method of rule identification with a deductive method of rule interpretation.

Although these authors have different objectives in mind, they are united in their view that describing practices is not enough to account for CIL, and that inductivism should be complemented by deductivism. They rightly point out that the problem of a merely inductivist investigation of state practice is both unrealistic and impossible, but they seek the solution of that problem by *adding* a normative or deductive approach. And through this search for an additional approach they leave intact the

conception of practice, describes claims and counterclaims as 'raw data'; M Hakimi, 'Making Sense of Customary International Law' (2020) 118 Mich L Rev 1487, 1493.

[7] Roberts (n 6).

[8] S Talmon, 'Determining Customary International Law: The ICJ's Methodology between Induction, Deduction and Assertion' (2015) 26 EJIL 417.

[9] P Merkouris, 'Interpreting the Customary Rules on Interpretation' (2017) 19 ICLR 126.

doctrinal picture of an initial investigation of state practice as a purely descriptive and inductive enterprise. Inductive 'identification' and deductive 'interpretation' are then seen as separate activities. Assumption (1) (practice as a collection of facts) as well as assumption (3) (identification of rules as the main aim of any investigation of state practice) remain untouched.

I will argue, however, that not only the assumption of induction (2), but the entire picture of gold-digging, is largely illusionary. I will start by addressing the assumption of induction (2) and take advantage of well-known insights that were developed in the philosophy of science. Consequently, I will criticise assumption (3), according to which identification is prior to interpretation. By using the insights of hermeneutics, I will argue that *opinio juris* is the starting point for any investigation of state practice and helps to define both state practice and CIL as a whole.

3 Loaded Perceptions: The Problem of Inductivism[10]

Let us put ourselves in the position of an international court[11] which is confronted with the task of deciding a case or of delivering an advisory opinion by distilling or identifying rules from a raw heap of facts. Such a court has to carry out two types of translation. In the first place, it should proceed from particular instances to general statements that deal with categories; in the second place, it has to proceed from facts to norms. The activity of such a court can be understood as similar to the interpretative activities of a domestic court which is asked to apply a given statutory rule to a concrete fact situation. Both courts are confronted with the task of translation; but they walk in opposite directions. Whereas an international court moves from particular fact situations to general norms, the domestic court moves in the opposite direction by applying general norms to concrete fact situations.

[10] I will refrain from discussing the problem of induction as the logical problem that general statements can never exhaustibly be verified by sense-data and that induction can therefore not be justified without having to rely on sense-data, which leads to infinite regress and circularity. See K Popper, *The Logic of Scientific Discovery* (Hutchinson 1972).

[11] We owe to Mendelson the important distinction between the various points of view from which we address CIL. M Mendelson, 'Formation of International Law and the Observational Standpoint' in ILA Committee on Formation of Customary (General) International Law, 'Report of 63rd Conference: Annex to the 1st Interim Report of the Committee' (Warsaw 1988) 935–72. This paper starts from the question of what courts (as 'third party decision-makers') do if they examine state practice.

The latter process of interpretation is beset by difficulties that are abundantly analysed in the literature on judicial interpretation and decision-making. But in one aspect these tasks are easier to accomplish than the inductive translation from particular facts into general norms, and that is that in interpretation one knows where to start. It is with a set of possible rules – general and normative statements – in mind that the facts are investigated. Did the defendant buy his knife before or not? Was the will drawn up in the presence of a notary or not? Rules guide the investigation and select the facts or the sets of facts that are relevant in the light of the rule. The rule highlights that part of factual reality which is possibly relevant. This is not to say that those parts that are not highlighted remain in obscurity forever. The outcome of interpretation may be downright undesirable and may provide reason to re-open the investigation and to search for other rules which may highlight other aspects which become relevant and which may generate a different outcome. This is what Llewellyn means when he talks about the necessary creativity of judges to erect alternative ladders through the legal material in order to arrive at the desired outcome. But alternative ladders also start with a rule that guides the investigation.[12]

Such starting points are absent if we consistently think of an inductive investigation of state practice. Then, it is supposed, we start with the facts and nothing but the facts. But which facts? There are a multitude of facts, events, gestures, movements, usages, conventions, declarations and resolutions, and we do not know how to make sense of such facts without any preconception in mind about what we hope or expect to find.[13]

This is obvious in even the most basic form of perception. As Hanson eloquently pointed out as early as 1958,[14] seeing involves recognising patterns. We can of course see black and white pixels and we can be sure everybody sees the same pixels. But as the well-known picture of rabbits

[12] See KN Llewellyn, *The Bramble Bush: The Classic Lectures on the Law and Law School; with a New Introduction and Notes by Steve Sheppard* (Oxford University Press 2008); F Schauer, 'Pitfalls in the Interpretation of Customary Law' in A Perreau-Saussine and JB Murphy (eds), *The Nature of Customary Law: Legal, Historical and Philosophical Perspectives* (Cambridge University Press 2007) 13–34.

[13] As Bradley remarked: 'Merely looking out into the world to see what nations have done and said does not itself reveal rules of international law.' CA Bradley, 'Customary International Law Adjudication as Common Law Adjudication' in CA Bradley (ed), *Custom's Future: International Law in a Changing World* (Cambridge University Press 2016) 34–61.

[14] NR Hanson, *Perception and Discovery: An Introduction to Scientific Inquiry* (MD Lund ed, Springer 2018).

and ducks illustrates, we can see these pixels in different ways, ordered in different patterns. And these ordering patterns are to a large extent informed by what we expect to see in a particular context as well as by our background knowledge. If I stare into the microscope, I might see beautiful colours but I do not really know what I see and I therefore see nothing at all. There is no simple observation, therefore, of 'what is there'. Our perception is loaded with preconceptions, conceptions, expectations and patterns that all lurk in the background. They should not be shunned and avoided, for if we were to succeed in discarding them, we would no longer know what we see. Or, as Heidegger succinctly put it: 'Only those who understand can hear.'[15]

If it is already difficult to make sense of dots and lines without any context that guides expectation and makes meaningful observation possible, how would we be able to understand things as elusive as 'acts', 'usages' and 'conventions'? I am not referring here to Hart's emphasis on an internal point of view. My claim is that even researchers who take an external point of view and regard people's doings like the movements of ants just have to start from *some* theory in order even to study such ants. As any sociologist or anthropologist knows, without a basic theoretical framework it would be impossible to select what kinds of phenomena are worth observing. If we add to this that international lawyers are supposed to investigate not only 'practice' (a complex phenomenon in itself) but 'state' practice, which is a legal notion, it is clear that the facts which are observed cannot possibly be considered as 'raw data' or 'raw material'.

4 Law as Theory and Object

Fortunately, that is not what legal scholars or courts do. Just like natural and social scientists, they start with a theoretical hypothesis that provides for the patterns that order the sense data in a meaningful way. Physics conceptualises light as either 'wave' or 'particle' and hence we 'see' light as waves or particles. Psychological concepts such as 'hysteria' and 'burn-out' are not merely different terms for the same phenomena but *constitute* different phenomena because they order facts in a different way.

So, too, courts and legal scholars start from a background theory. But there are three important differences between the background theories of social scientists and those of legal experts.

[15] 'Nur wer schon versteht, kann zuhören.' M Heidegger, *Sein und Zeit* (Max Niemeyer Verlag 1979) 164.

(1) Law as theoretical framework

As I have argued elsewhere,[16] legal research also starts from a theoretical framework, but, unlike social scientists who develop a theoretical framework that is independent from the object they investigate, the framework for legal research is the law itself. Legal notions and conceptions form the framework and pattern by means of which facts are ordered. Not only terms such as 'seabed' but also 'sovereignty' or 'specially affected' are notions that guide the investigation and furnish the patterns that enable us to see a point in the 'raw data'. Whereas in the social sciences there is a certain distance between theory and object, the peculiar feature of legal scholarship is that its theoretical framework and its object are identical. Of course, this does not apply to empirical legal studies or, for that matter, to philosophy of law, where the theoretical framework may (and should) be broader, but most doctrinal legal research revolves around the question of how certain novel social or technical developments or problems can be regulated such that they can be fitted into the legal system or in a way that is coherent with underlying principles, or, alternatively, how different legal arrangements from different legal orders can be integrated and harmonised. In all these studies, law is not only the object of research but also provides the theoretical framework consisting of legal concepts, standards and exemplars.

(2) Definitional concepts

The fact that the function of a theory is taken over by the law itself and that therefore the facts are examined by means of legal concepts entails another peculiarity, which has to do with the nature of legal concepts. Legal concepts are not descriptive but definitional. In law, such definitions are usually couched in terms of conditions, although one also encounters enumerative definitions.[17] When we say that some paper p is a 'contract', we say that this paper p meets the conditions that should be fulfilled in order to count as a contract. Legal general statements are of the form: For all X, if conditions a, b and c apply, they count as Y.

[16] P Westerman, 'Open or Autonomous? The Debate on Legal Methodology as a Reflection of the Debate on Law' in M van Hoecke (ed), *Methodologies of Legal Research: Which Kind of Method for What Kind of Discipline?* (Hart 2011) 87.

[17] In the Rome Statute, for instance, concepts such as 'crimes against humanity' are defined in part by enumerating instances and examples. See Rome Statute of the International Criminal Court (adopted 17 July 1998, entered into force 1 July 2002) 2187 UNTS 3.

This statement does not generate new knowledge but is a definition of Y.

If we start investigating state practices by means of such definitional concepts and apply the filter of the law to the facts, we examine that factual reality by enquiring into whether reality can be categorised into these definitions. We differentiate between items that do and items that do not, or only partially, fulfil the conditions that are contained in the general statement.

This strategy is applied at all levels. At the micro-level, we start for instance by investigating whether a certain contract x meets the conditions for 'contract' and can be considered a valid one; at the meso-level, we might ask whether conditions for 'sovereignty' are met; and at the most abstract level, we inquire into the degree to which a certain usage counts as 'practice'. Definitional concepts are very useful in a deductive process in which particular instances are examined for their conformity to the conditions and thus 'put to the test', but they are emphatically not the result of generalisations from particular facts. They are the result of our decision or of convention that defines a concept in terms of conditions. Their existence cannot be tested by reference to empirical facts but by referring to these conditions. That is why Kelsen could say that 'the existence of a legal norm is its validity'.[18] Contracts, sovereign states and practices exist insofar as they meet the conditions.

(3) No falsification by facts

This difference between descriptive and definitional concepts implies a third difference as well. Whereas scientific general statements can be refuted or falsified by recalcitrant facts, that is not the case in legal research. Scientific theory does not merely contain general statements such as 'if light has a wavelength of 400 nm we call it "violet"'. If that were the case, science would be just like legal scholarship and would proceed by definitional concepts based on convention. But although science makes use of conventions, and although observations on colours cannot be conducted without such conventions on numerical values, its general statements express new – hypothesised – correlations: hypotheses like 'violet flowers attract more butterflies than red ones', which can be falsified when a species of butterflies is discovered preferring red

[18] H Kelsen, *General Theory of Law and State* (A Wedberg tr, Harvard University Press 1945) 48.

> flowers. In legal research, it is not the theory that is falsified but the facts that are proven to be deficient. If we encounter papers that fulfil only half of the conditions for contracts, we do not think that our general statement is falsified; we just say that those papers are not 'proper' or valid contracts.

Is there then no sense in the idea that rules can be inferred by means of induction? Could we not say, 'Here is a contract which is signed and there is a contract which is not signed, so maybe signature is not a decisive condition'?

That can happen indeed. In international law (IL), the conditions for validity are often not clearly defined, are ambiguous or contested, and indeed it is possible to adjust our set of conditions somewhat to match reality, but that can be done only in the presence of other features that qualify a certain item as a suitable candidate for being examined as a potential 'contract'. If none of the conventional conditions are fulfilled, we do not even start investigating whether a paper counts as a contract or whether we should adjust our notion of contract in light of such divergent practices. We may for instance investigate the practices around marriage and see how in different cultures marriages are conducted and eventually end up with a wider concept of marriage than we initially had in mind. But such practices at least should have a credible claim to be considered as 'marriages'. If they do not even remotely look like marriages, we would not take the trouble to contemplate them as serious candidates for being considered as marriage.

This also applies to concepts such as 'sexual slavery'. They do not have a claim to validity, of course, but it should be possible to claim or suggest that the term might be appropriate to the case at hand. Further investigation may lead to limitation or expansion of the concept (and may even be extended to such an extent that it borders on 'marriage'), but again there should be some shared features in order to conduct such an investigation in the first place.

To say that rules cannot be *inferred* from facts is not the same as saying that rules cannot *emerge* out of facts. I think that this is very well possible and discernible in all those instances in which patterns of behaviour slowly develop into rules.[19] But we should make a difference between

[19] See GJ Postema, 'Custom, Normative Practice, and the Law' (2012) 62 DLJ 707, 707–38; K Gorobets, 'Practical Reasoning and Interpretation of Customary International Law' in P Merkouris, J Kammerhofer and N Arajärvi (eds), *The Theory, Practice, and Interpretation of Customary International Law* (Cambridge University Press 2022).

ontological views on how rules are formed and epistemological views on how they can be identified.[20]

In investigating state practice, legal decision-makers necessarily see the practices, usages and customs through the filter of rules and definitional concepts that they already have in mind. It is not necessary that these rules have an unambiguous status or are already legally valid. As Hakimi remarked, it is more to the point to refer to them as 'normative positions which may not be fully supported'.[21] But whether they are formally valid, endorsed by a majority, soft law or only half-baked rules in the making, they nevertheless function in the same way as theoretical hypotheses do in the sciences: they guide our perceptions and investigations by selecting the items that are 'relevant' and have 'legal salience'.[22]

At this point one may wonder, how is it possible to distil and identify rules if all we can do is to investigate the facts by means of . . . rules? The apparent circularity of *opinio juris*, much criticised on the ground that it presupposes the existence of law in order to identify law, seems to be repeated also in the examination of state practice! And indeed, circles abound. Any examination of practices or facts presupposes the guidance of rules. But which rules should be selected? In order to decide on the appropriate filter, the facts should be consulted. And how can the facts be consulted? By the guidance of rules. This treadmill is a well-known feature of interpretation and is called the hermeneutical circle.

According to Heidegger, such circles should not be shunned, as they reflect the structure of our existence.[23] But even without such metaphysics, it is important to see that it would be a misunderstanding to discard such circles as mistaken methodology or faulty logic. The preconceptions which are necessary to select that which is meaningful may be seen as 'prejudice', but it is a kind of prejudice which is essential for any understanding.[24] It is therefore worthwhile to be open about the inevitability of such circles. Instead of sweeping them under the carpet it is better to acknowledge them and to make clear where such circles arise and which points they cover. If we talk, therefore, about the identification

[20] Mendelson (n 11) 249. See also Bradley (n 13). A similar distinction is elaborated by Eugen Ehrlich, who distinguished between rules of conduct and norms for (juridical) decision. See E Ehrlich, *Fundamental Principles of the Sociology of Law, with an Introduction by Roscoe Pound* (Walter L Moll tr, first published 1936, Routledge 2017) esp ch XIX.

[21] Hakimi (n 6) 1511.

[22] ibid 1521.

[23] Heidegger (n 15) 153.

[24] HG Gadamer, *Wahrheit und Methode* (4th edn, JCB Mohr 1975) 255.

of rules by examining state practice, we should acknowledge that such an examination can be carried out only if we have standards, rules and normative positions in mind as a background theory. This does not imply that we can only discover what we already have in mind. After the initial selection of the relevant material, its weight should still be assessed. But to represent this 'material' as a heap of objective facts is a mischaracterisation.

5 Common Law?

Schauer and Bradley suggested that this process is very similar to common law adjudication.[25] They rightly point out that the examination of state practice is not the kind of inductivist enterprise that is commonly and officially announced. They propose that the identification of rules by an investigation of state practice should be regarded as an attempt to construct chains of precedents. Schauer refers to the fact that different chains of precedents can be constructed, just as Llewellyn pointed out that different ladders can be built by means of which it is possible to motivate different outcomes.

At first sight, one may question the wisdom of the term 'precedents'. State practice comprises not only precedents but acts, usages and conventions of all kinds. It is only in the eyes of a judicial decision-maker that such acts can be labelled as 'precedents': events that preceded a new case and might have a bearing on the ways in which a new case should be resolved. But this is not necessarily a problem. Both authors start from the perspective of the adjudicator and in such a perspective state practice is examined in the light of the theoretical framework of the law. The clear advantage of this comparison with common law adjudication is therefore that it openly concedes that the adjudicator runs in the hermeneutical circle. It makes clear that the examination of state practice is not just an investigation of raw material facts but presupposes a selective filter of possibly relevant legal perspectives, from which acts and usages are indeed regarded as 'precedents' for the case at hand. The plausibility of the perspectives is judged by means of a further investigation of the facts, which necessarily presupposes a theoretical background perspective, etc.

However, it seems to me that this account, although much more realistic than official objectivist inductivism, assumes too much: it

[25] Bradley (n 13); Schauer (n 12).

presupposes that it is clear what counts as precedent. In domestic common law adjudication that may be indeed the case, at least to a certain degree. The legal material is to some extent clearly defined, although here, too, the weight of the precedents may vary. Yet, it is within the domain of this legal material that the interpreter can choose to construct different chains of precedents leading to the decision in the new case.

In CIL, the boundaries of the legal material are less clearly demarcated. The questions to be answered are therefore not only how to construct different chains of precedents. Before those questions can arise, a prior question must be answered and that is whether a certain usage may count as precedent: is a certain act, text, omission weighty enough to count? This is clear for instance from the wording of the 1969 *North Continental Shelf* case, in which it is argued that despite the fact that the principle of equidistance is used by the majority of states and in numerous cases, there are 'several grounds which *deprive them of weight as precedents in the present context*'.[26] State practice is not examined in order to decide on the applicable chain of precedents and cannot merely be regarded as a matter of choice between various applicable chains. The court that examines state practice does so in order to find out which instances might qualify to be labelled 'precedents'. Only after that can their respective weight be ascertained and the connecting chains constructed.

6 The Double Function of *Opinio Juris*

Surprisingly, this prior question is usually answered by referring to *opinio juris*. In the *Asylum* case between Colombia and Peru (1950), for instance, the ICJ asserts that all the instances of granting asylum, mentioned by Colombia, simply do not count as precedents:

> The facts which have been laid before the Court show that in a number of cases the persons who have enjoyed asylum were not, at the moment at which asylum was granted, the object of any accusation on the part of the judicial authorities. In a more general way, considerations of convenience or simple political expediency seem to have led the territorial State to recognize asylum without that decision being dictated by any feeling of legal obligation.
>
> If these remarks tend to reduce considerably the value as precedents of the cases of asylum cited by the Government of Colombia, they show, none the less, that asylum as practised in Latin America is an institution which, to a very great extent, owes its development to extra-legal factors.

[26] *North Sea Continental Shelf Cases* (*Germany/Netherlands; Germany/Denmark*) (Judgment) [1969] ICJ Rep 3, 75 (emphasis added).

> The good-neighbour relations between the republics, the different political interests of the governments, have favoured the mutual recognition of asylum apart from any clearly defined juridical system.[27]

Institutions that arose in an extra-legal context lack legal relevance and do not count as 'precedents'. In the *Nicaragua* case, too, state practice is examined by reference to *opinio juris*, where it is argued that intervention is not undertaken with a sense of a legal right:

> The United States authorities have on some occasions clearly stated their grounds for intervening in the affairs of a foreign State for reasons connected with, for example, the domestic policies of that country, its ideology, the level of its armaments, or the direction of its foreign policy. But these were statements of international policy, and not an assertion of rules of existing international law.[28]

The reader might observe that these passages show exactly what is expressed by the official doctrine, which requires the presence of both an objective and a subjective element. *Opinio juris* is explicitly invoked.[29]

I would, however, say that the influence of *opinio juris* is much stronger than is officially conceded. The official claim is that there is first an – independent – examination of state practice, and that that practice can only be regarded as CIL if it is accompanied by *opinio juris*. What we see here, however, is that without *opinio juris* a recurrent and widespread usage simply does not count as legally relevant state practice. It counts as mere 'convention', as comity, etiquette or rules that are followed merely with a view to 'expediency' or 'international policy'. *Opinio juris* is required in order to 'see' something as relevant practice instead of merely a heap of facts or usages.

Opinio juris, therefore, indeed 'counts twice':

(1) A usage/act counts as 'practice' if carried out with a sense of legal obligation (*opinio juris*).
(2) A practice counts as an element of CIL if carried out with a sense of legal obligation (*opinio juris*).

Opinio juris is a condition not only for 'identifying' CIL, but also for differentiating those usages that might be seen as legally relevant practice ('precedents') and those which are not.[30]

27 *Asylum (Colombia v Peru)* (Judgment) [1950] ICJ Rep 266, 276–77.

28 *Military and Paramilitary Activities in and against Nicaragua (Nicaragua v USA)* (Merits) [1986] ICJ Rep 16 [207].

29 ibid.

30 To make matters worse, the argument in paragraph 77 of the *North Sea Continental Shelf* judgment runs that not only for CIL but also for *opinio juris* both elements are required.

This second function is usually not recognised in the official accounts of state practice as an objective element but it is in line with what I remarked on above about the necessity of a theory. In order to 'see' something as practice, the law functions as the indispensable theoretical searchlight – a searchlight which is only deemed fit if it has passed the test of *opinio juris*! That is why torture or pollution, although they are clearly practices that are widespread, uniform and consistent, do not 'count' as practices. That is why granting asylum can be regarded as legally irrelevant and as mere friendliness towards neighbours, as is maintained in the *Asylum* case. The objective element is therefore not only connected to the subjective element:[31] state practice cannot even be investigated without *opinio juris*. *Opinio juris* is the starting point for any meaningful investigation of state practice.

Of course, this is not to say that state practices cannot be normatively meaningful without *opinio juris*. As I noted above, we should be careful to distinguish the (ontological) formation of normative rules as emerging in and from practices from the (epistemological) identification of such rules. I am now just referring to how the courts in their investigation of state practice identify legally meaningful and relevant normative positions that might qualify as precedents in a certain case. And in order to do so, the *opinio juris* plays a major role as a theoretical searchlight.

7 A Practice of Claims

It seems then that my reading leads to an even more incongruous result than official doctrine. There, *opinio juris* is already troublesome because of its circularity. As is pointed out repeatedly, *opinio juris* identifies a rule of CIL by reference to the conviction of states that they are under an

Probably this is a mistake. In paragraph 77 it is stated: 'The essential point in this connection – and it seems necessary to stress it – is that even if these instances of action by non-parties to the Convention were much more numerous than they in fact are, they would not, even in the aggregate, suffice in themselves to constitute the *opinio juris*; for, in order to achieve this result, two conditions must be fulfilled. Not only must the acts concerned amount to a settled practice, but they must also be such, or be carried out in such a way, as to be evidence of *a belief that this practice is rendered obligatory by the existence of a rule of law requiring it*. The need for such a belief, i.e., the existence of a subjective element, is implicit in the very notion of the *opinio juris sive necessitatis*. The States concerned must therefore *feel that they are conforming to what amounts to a legal obligation*. The frequency, or even habitual character of the acts is not in itself enough.' (emphasis added).

[31] See Haggenmacher (n 2).

obligation to comply with that same rule. My contention seems to be even more bewildering than this: only those acts, usages and conventions that are carried out with a sense of legal obligation (*opinio juris* 1) count as state practice, as a set of potentially meaningful precedents, which can only give rise to CIL if coupled with *opinio juris* (2). There is not one circle; there are two – or more specifically, there is a spiral.

However, as I have pointed out elsewhere,[32] the circularity is not so devastating if we understand *opinio juris* not as a conviction or a belief that one is under a legal obligation but as an articulated and publicly accessible claim.[33] These claims are usually couched in general and descriptive terms: 'this is the rule/law/principle we maintain and cherish'. Because of this particular descriptive form we might easily mistake them for descriptions of facts (we *are* under this legal obligation) and then circularity is indeed vicious. But in fact they are declarative statements: statements that *constitute* the law by means of a declarative form.[34] They are not expressions *of* legality but claims *to* legality.[35]

If we understand that state practice can only be – and is only – investigated by means of such claims to legality that form the searchlight for the investigation of practices, a number of confusions can be clarified. In the first place, it has already been remarked that a lot of the ICJ's judgements refer, not to state practice as it is traditionally defined,[36] but to resolutions, declarations and the like. In a fascinating article Choi and Gulati[37] presented statistics of the kind of evidence found by the ICJ under the banner of 'state practice'. They found that acts and practices were hardly investigated at all, and the official sources of state practice

[32] See Westerman (n 3).

[33] That is why Anthony d'Amato has a point in emphasising articulation. See A d'Amato, *The Concept of Custom in International Law* (Cornell University Press 1971).

[34] In a similar vein, see M Mendelson, 'The Formation of Customary International Law' (1998) 272 RdC 155, 176. For an analysis of such declarative propositions, see JR Searle, *Expression and Meaning: Studies in the Theory of Speech Acts* (Cambridge University Press 1979) 17.

[35] See Westerman (n 3).

[36] External conduct of States with each other as well as 'diplomatic acts and correspondence; conduct in connection with resolutions adopted by an international organization or at an intergovernmental conference; conduct in connection with treaties; executive conduct, including operational conduct 'on the ground'; legislative and administrative acts; and decisions of national courts'. see ILC, 'Identification of Customary International Law: Text of the Draft Conclusions Provisionally Adopted by the Drafting Committee' (30 May 2016) UN Doc A/CN.4/L.872, art 6(2).

[37] SJ Choi & M Gulati, 'Customary International Law: How Do Courts Do It?' in CA Bradley (ed), *Custom's Future: International Law in a Changing World* (Cambridge University Press 2016) 117.

(diplomatic correspondence, domestic legislation, etc.) in only a small minority of cases. Instead, in an overwhelming majority of cases treaties and other 'aspirational and forward-looking documents' were cited. The authors find that amazing: states enter into treaties in the absence of CIL and it would therefore be strange to cite treaties as proof of the CIL.

Choi and Gulati confirm empirically the uneasiness expressed by Mendelson more than two decades ago, who observed, while commenting on the *Nicaragua* case (Merits):

> And even if we grant, for the sake of argument, that the resolutions represented the *opinio juris*, where then is the practice which, the Court seemed to be saying, is an independent element? If we say that the resolutions constitute verbal practice, then we are guilty of double-counting them – both as the objective and as the subjective elements.

And he adds to this:

> It might be responded that all that is needed is for the act of practice to be accompanied by *opinio juris*; so that what is required is not two completely separate elements, but both combined; however, *to count the act of voting for the resolution as practice still looks rather like pulling oneself up by one's own bootstraps.*[38]

And indeed it is. This is exactly the case. To lift oneself up by one's own bootstraps accurately describes the hermeneutic circle.

8 Interpretation Prior to Identification and Application

The observation that the identification of CIL is circular is hardly novel. Koskenniemmi had already observed that 'doctrine about customary law is indeterminate because circular. It assumes behaviour to be evidence of the *opinio juris* and the latter to be evidence of which behaviour is relevant as custom.'[39] However, as we have seen, 'behaviour' and 'evidence' are not as unproblematic as even Koskenniemi assumes. As Bodansky correctly asserts,[40] if it were only behaviour that is investigated, sociologists would be much better equipped. Legal investigation revolves around texts: an abundance of claims to legality such as resolutions, conventions and treaties. They form the object of investigation.

[38] Mendelson (n 34) 381–82 (emphasis added).

[39] M Koskenniemi, *From Apology to Utopia* (Cambridge University Press 2006) 437.

[40] D Bodansky, 'Customary (And Not So Customary) International Environmental Law' (1995) 3(1) IJGLS 105, 105–19.

And they figure at the two levels that we distinguished in Section 7. First of all, they are investigated in order to determine the legally relevant precedents, and secondly they are investigated in order to choose between potentially applicable precedents in order to apply them to a particular case. Both activities are usually conducted in one big sweep. In the judgments of the courts it is just pointed out which texts are considered legally relevant, weighty or convincing. They may be labelled differently, as either 'state practice' or '*opinio juris*', but they are all just texts the relevance of which is assessed and weighed.[41]

It is not possible to weigh precedents and to apply rules without prior interpretation. That interpretation can be grammatical or historical, but most importantly it is teleological. The texts should be interpreted as having a point. This is noticeable both in the attempt to determine the precedents and in the way in which chains of such precedents are constructed. To begin with the latter: it is obvious that in order to make a choice between different chains of precedents, as in common law adjudication, they should first be constructed as a chain. That can be done by discovering analogies or some aspects these precedents have in common. But this discovery of shared aspects can be conducted only by constructing an underlying principle or rationale. There *are* no shared features between 'books', 'electricity' and 'personal data'. We can only *construct* their shared features as 'goods' to which property law can be applied. And usually this construction is carried out by hypothesising an underlying aim or rationale. Do we follow all those solemn prohibitions of weapons and conclude by analogy that nuclear weapons should be prohibited as well? Or do we follow all – equally solemn – declarations of sovereignty and conclude that such a prohibition of nuclear weapons is not part of CIL?

The same applies, however, also to the first round in which different official acts and texts are examined in order to establish the legally relevant precedents. Here, too, there are numerous candidates, and they can be linked together in different chains, each focusing on different shared features and different underlying principles. Those texts, rules and claims which are not constructed as precedents are denied

41 The unity of the two elements is also observed by R Müllerson, 'The Interplay of Objective and Subjective Elements in Customary Law' in K Wellens (ed), *International Law, Theory and Practice* (Kluwer 1998) 161–78; O Elias, 'The Nature of the Subjective Element in Customary International Law' (1995) 44 ICLQ 501, 501–20; and, of course, Haggenmacher (n 2).

legal relevance and figure as 'technical rules' or as rules of etiquette, comity and friendliness. These 'legally irrelevant' rules are obviously not *found* but *interpreted* as lacking legal relevance, and they are interpreted by reference to texts that embody claims to legality. Postema adequately described the process of such interpretation of practices and compared this to discerning a pattern: 'the pattern is likely to be salient because it is meaningful within the practice, rather than meaningful because it is salient'.[42] The degree to which customs can be integrated in such a pattern is therefore decisive, according to Postema.

Although I distinguished for analytical reasons between the two rounds of legal interpretation in which legally relevant material is (a) determined and (b) applied, we should not think of determination and application as sequential in time. As noted above, they are usually carried out in one big sweep: both are the result of interpretation in the light of *opinio juris*, and they are intricately connected. The more successful the attempt in the first round to deny legal relevance to normative positions and, consequently, the narrower the selection of legally relevant material, the easier the task to choose a preferred ladder in the second round of application. Or, to put it differently, those normative positions that fail to be elevated to the status of 'legally relevant' state practice do not need to be examined as candidates for CIL. That is why the double-counting of *opinio juris* does not come to the surface. *Opinio juris* is usually already applied in the first round of determining relevant precedents and need not be re-emphasised in the determination of CIL.

It is important to see that both the determination of relevant precedents and the choice between rival chains of precedents presuppose interpretation of the normative material as material that is patterned around its point or *telos*. The degree to which a claim can be fitted into a pattern is to a large extent dependent on how we construct that *telos*. As Heidegger in his more lucid moments pointed out, it is not possible to identify something as something ('Etwas als etwas') without understanding it as something 'in order to' ('Um-zu').[43] Precedents, and also candidate-precedents, are constructed as parts of a Dworkinian chain-novel,[44] or at least – more modestly – as threads weaving a plot in a story.

42 Postema (n 19) 715.
43 Heidegger (n 15) 149.
44 R Dworkin, *Law's Empire* (Harvard University Press 1986) 228–38.

We should not think of this *telos* as a set of intentions, the honesty of which can be examined on the basis of diplomatic correspondence between officials. Interpretation is different from grasping intentions at face value. It may very well be the case that the states which signed a treaty had no serious intention at all of furthering the aim of the treaty. They might simply have thought about the reputational costs of making reservations to that treaty, or they were mistaken in thinking that they would not be burdened too much, or had already seen gaps in the treaty that would allow them an exit. If we interpret such texts in terms of intentions, many of those texts can indeed be disregarded as specimens of 'cheap talk'.[45]

However, as Ricœur pointed out, a text (any text, whether novel or academic publication or treaty) gains a certain distance from its drafter or writer. It is this distance that harbours the possibility for the interpreter to discern and to reconstruct several meanings of such texts. According to Paul Ricoeur, 'what must be interpreted in a text is a proposed world which I could inhabit and wherein I could project one of my ownmost possibilities'.[46]

This does not merely apply to my interpretation of literary works; it also relates to how legal texts can be understood.[47] Interpretation is an activity to understand not only what exists but also what is possible.[48] In fact, legal texts – as well as communiqués – are also *written* with an eye to such possible readings. The importance of textual subtleties can only be understood on the basis of this distantiation. If it were a matter of just unravelling intentions, such care for texts would be unnecessary. But they are highly important in view of the fact that texts live a life of their own. Even if such texts do not reflect the serious intentions of the signatories and are indeed no more than 'cheap talk', they can be read as elements of a purposive pattern, that can be constructed as meaningful by the interpreter.

[45] JL Goldsmith and EA Posner, *The Limits of International Law* (Oxford University Press 2005).

[46] P Ricœur, *Hermeneutics and the Human Sciences: Essays on Language, Action, and Interpretation* (JB Thompson ed, Cambridge University Press 2016) 104.

[47] For a nice application of Ricœur's insights, see the dissertation by P Phoa, *EU Law as a Creative Process: A Hermeneutic Approach for the EU Internal Market and Fundamental Rights Protection* (Europa Law 2021).

[48] ibid; Ricœur (n 46).

9 Conclusion: Possible Worlds

If we take seriously the notion of interpretation as delineating possible meanings, that means that different chains and patterns are conceivable that order the textual material in different ways. Depending on the choice of such patterns, a certain text is interpreted as a more or a less weighty claim, as a legally binding rule, as a normatively binding standard, as a technical standard or as just a convenient habit.

We should not think that there is one correct pattern. As I argued in my earlier article,[49] *opinio juris* should be understood in its plural form. There are different *opiniones juris*: official claims that propose different ordering patterns and which function as maps. The main function of such maps is not merely to represent reality. Maps typically highlight some elements at the expense of others. The cyclist map ignores the highways; underground maps emphasise the underground stations and may even be extremely unrealistic in the sense that they distort the physical distance between stations. The value of such maps does not depend on their realism but on the use – the 'point' – of such a map. The investigation of state practice, but also of CIL as a whole, can best be seen as a map drawn on a transparent sheet that is laid over the abundance of official documents and texts, by means of which this legal material is ordered in different ways.

All this implies that the claim cannot be justified that there is an objective examination of state practice and a neutral 'identification' of rules that precedes their interpretation. The transparent sheet cannot be removed without risking being plunged into a bewildering multitude of incomprehensible texts. But, and this is important, this does not imply that judgments are completely arbitrary. The courts are not 'objective', but neither are they 'subjective'. They do not deal exclusively with the factual, but nor are they condemned to the realm of normative ideals. Their judgments are never completely apologetic or utopian, because the interpretation of legal texts is not exclusively limited to what *is*, nor to what *ought* to be. The task of courts is to choose a path among possible worlds.

This implies a somewhat nuanced answer to the common objection against CIL as mere fantasy. It seems exaggerated to speak of judicial discretion in the strong sense of the word, according to which the judge is simply not bound by any rules. In fact, even in the advisory opinions

[49] See Westerman (n 3).

where the ICJ is just required to answer very open questions, there is always plenty of legal material that may or may not support the opinion. Courts do not fantasise. But neither are they unreservedly bound by that material. The texts are not determinate strongholds. Their weight is (co-)determined by the patterned transparent sheets. The plurality of these sheets leaves room for choice.[50]

[50] See the empirical study by SA Lindquist and FB Cross, 'Empirically Testing Dworkin's Chain Novel Theory: Studying the Path of Precedent' (2005) 80 NYUL Rev 1156.

2

Addressing the Chronological Paradox of CIL

From Good Faith to *Opinio Juris*, and *Opinio Juris* to New Customary Rules

HENRIQUE MARCOS

1 Introduction

Most social groups have rules[1] about how the people in that group should behave. In many cases, these rules develop from custom; they are called 'customary rules'. New customary rules arise from two elements: (i) the repeated practice of certain acts by the people in a group (*diuturnitas*); and (ii) a shared expectation that this practice will continue. This expectation leads people to sense or feel that they should act in a certain way. That is, people continue to engage in a particular practice because they believe they are obligated to do so (*opinio juris sive necessitatis*, or simply *opinio juris*). By contrast, practice without a sense of obligation leads to habits rather than customary rules.[2]

The author is grateful to Jaap Hage, Wagner Menezes, and Antonia Waltermann for discussing the initial ideas that inspired the research underlying this chapter; to Eloá Figaro, Sarah McGibbon, Paula Miranda da Cruz, Nevitton Vieira Souza, and the participants at the second TRICI-Law conference for their comments on an earlier version of the chapter; and especially to Pauline Westerman, Kostiantyn Gorobets, and Marina Fortuna for their valuable comments on this final version. The content remains the sole responsibility of the author. The research underlying this chapter was partially funded by the CAPES Foundation (Brazil).

[1] This chapter follows Wittgenstein's broad understanding of 'rule' as covering not only rules *sensu stricto* but also principles and other kinds of legal and non-legal rules such as norms, postulates, and standards. L Wittgenstein, *Philosophical Investigations* (GEM Anscombe tr, 3rd edn, Blackwell 1986) paras 207–32; H-J Glock, *A Wittgenstein Dictionary* (Blackwell 1996) 324–25.

[2] R Mangabeira Unger, *Law in Modern Society: Toward a Criticism of Social Theory* (Free Press 1976) 49; T Treves, 'Customary International Law' (MPEPIL 2006) <https://opil.ouplaw.com/display/10.1093/law:epil/9780199231690/law-9780199231690-e1393> accessed 27 March 2024; HLA Hart, *The Concept of Law* (3rd edn, Oxford University Press 2012) ch III.

Customary rules have become less important in domestic law, but the opposite is true in international law. International lawyers frequently rely on customary international law (CIL), and many of the most important rules of international law have come from CIL. The prohibition of genocide, torture, slavery, and piracy are relevant examples.[3] We can also see the importance of CIL for topics not yet regulated by treaties and topics addressed by treaties that are not universally ratified. The Law of the Sea Convention[4] is a good example of this. The Convention has helped codify CIL rules already in place and blended them with treaty rules, smoothing some of the differences between CIL and non-CIL rules.[5]

As a source of international law, CIL is not only important but also complex. Like international law in general, CIL results from a bottom-up process, where subjects of the law are also its makers. To complicate matters further, CIL develops informally and by implication. In CIL, unlike treaty law, there is no standard way for states to gather and decide on creating new rules. Instead, CIL rules seem to appear out of nowhere; they are just here, and it is sometimes unclear how long they have been with us.[6]

Another complication that affects CIL is the well-known chronological paradox. Despite its name, the paradox is not merely chronological: it raises a broad conceptual issue that threatens the coherence of (customary) international law. The paradox lies in the fact that for a new CIL rule to be created states must believe that the law already requires them to act in a certain way (*opinio juris*), but until the rule is created they are not legally required to do so as the rule establishing such a requirement has yet to exist.[7]

Since there does not seem to be any way out of the chronological paradox's vicious circle, the making of a new CIL rule would seem

[3] MH Mendelson, 'The Formation of Customary International Law' (1998) 272 RdC 155.

[4] United Nations Convention on the Law of the Sea (adopted 10 December 1982, entered into force 16 November 1994) 1833 UNTS 3.

[5] M Lee, 'The Interrelation between the Law of the Sea Convention and Customary International Law' (2006) 7 SDILJ 405.

[6] J d'Aspremont, *The Discourse on Customary International Law* (Oxford University Press 2021) ch 1.

[7] DH Levine, 'The Chronological Paradox in Customary International Law (Or, the Virtue of Sloppy Timing in a Messy World)' (PhD thesis, Georgetown University 2005); D Lefkowitz, '(Dis)Solving the Chronological Paradox in Customary International Law: A Hartian Approach' (2008) 21 CJLJ 129; V Jeutner and F Paddeu, 'Three Paradoxes of Customary Law' (Logic of International Law conference, Maastricht University 2022).

impossible, or, at the very least, our understanding of CIL would appear incoherent. Given that we know CIL rules *do* exist, their creation is not impossible, so we must entertain the possibility that our understanding of CIL is incoherent.[8] This is critical, as the legitimacy of a legal system depends in part on its coherence. If legitimacy is what makes us want to carry out our legal obligations, then coherence – the intelligibility of such obligations – is a requirement for legitimacy. After all, we can only effectively comply with what we understand.

Given that CIL rules are being used more and more against states, the chronological paradox is both a theoretical and a practical problem.[9] If the paradox is true (and, thus, our understanding of CIL is incoherent), states may be less inclined to follow CIL rules, which would be a blow to international law. Given how critical the paradox is, there is reason to think that the International Law Commission (ILC) would have directly addressed it in its 2018 report on identifying CIL.[10] Unfortunately, this was not the case. Ignoring the paradox's significance is problematic, as it casts a large shadow over CIL. In a landscape where CIL is a primary source of international law, practitioners should not be left stumbling in the dark.[11]

This chapter tries to shed some light on this topic by addressing the paradox in a way that ensures the coherence, and thus legitimacy, of (customary) international law. It does so by offering an interpretation of CIL that accounts for the creation of CIL rules through distinct, non-paradoxical steps. The chapter argues that the belief in a legal obligation (*opinio juris*) derives from the general principle of good faith. Good faith leads to legal obligations, which compel a subgroup of states to engage in specific behaviour. Then, as a result of this subgroup's repeated behaviour, a new CIL rule develops, obligating the entire community of states

[8] For this chapter, coherence means the possibility of intelligible argument. See S Haack, 'Coherence, Consistency, Cogency, Congruity, Cohesiveness, &c.: Remain Calm! Don't Go Overboard!' (2004) 35 NLH 167. See also Y Radi, 'Coherence' in J d'Aspremont and S Singh (eds), *Concepts for International Law: Contributions to Disciplinary Thought* (Edward Elgar 2019).

[9] J Tasioulas, 'Customary International Law and the Quest for Global Justice' in A Perreau-Saussine and JB Murphy (eds), *The Nature of Customary Law* (Cambridge University Press 2007) 307, 321–22.

[10] ILC, 'Draft Conclusions on Identification of Customary International Law, with Commentaries' (30 April–1 June and 2 July–10 August 2018) UN Doc A/73/10.

[11] P Merkouris, 'Interpreting the Customary Rules on Interpretation' (2017) 19 ICLR 126. See also L Blutman, 'Conceptual Confusion and Methodological Deficiencies: Some Ways that Theories on Customary International Law Fail' (2014) 25 EJIL 529.

to follow that behaviour. In elucidating the shift from good faith to legal obligations and from legal obligations to CIL rules, this chapter draws on interpretivism, social ontology, and contemporary research on constitutive rules.

In terms of structure, the chapter is divided into four sections. Following this introductory section, Section 2 discusses CIL and the chronological paradox. Section 3 examines constructivism in legal interpretation. Section 4 then focuses on the application of rules and on constitutive rules, explaining the role of good faith and how constitutive (meta)rules create new CIL rules. Section 5 concludes the chapter by reaffirming earlier conclusions.

2 CIL and Its Paradox

Article 38(1)(b) of the Statute of the International Court of Justice (ICJ)[12] states that CIL rules evince general practices that are accepted as law. The Statute thus refers to the two constituent elements of customary rules mentioned in Section 1 – namely, (i) the existence of a general practice in the form of repeated acts (*diuturnitas*), and (ii) performance of these acts in the belief that they are required by law (*opinio juris*).

Scholarship traditionally considers practice (*diuturnitas*) to refer to the practice of states. There have been fruitful discussions about the contribution of non-state actors to CIL.[13] For instance, the ILC has recognised that '[i]n certain cases, the practice of international organizations also contributes to the formation, or expression, of rules of customary international law'.[14] For the purposes of this chapter, the question of whether non-state actors' behaviour qualifies as 'practice' is beside the point; although an interesting debate, it has no bearing on the chapter's explanation of how CIL rules are created. Thus, although the chapter addresses state practice, it can also be read as encompassing non-state practice.

Acceptance as law (*opinio juris*) means that states believe a specific action is required under the law. In other words, states believe that a particular practice is legally obligatory. It should be pointed out that the term 'obligation' is used in this chapter to designate a basic normative

[12] Statute of the International Court of Justice (adopted 26 June 1945, entered into force 24 October 1945) 33 UNTS 993.

[13] S Droubi and J d'Aspremont (eds), *International Organisations, Non-State Actors, and the Formation of Customary International Law* (Manchester University Press 2020).

[14] ILC (n 10) 130 (Conclusion 4.2).

or deontic concept.[15] When we say that a particular behaviour is obligatory or required, or that someone must act or is responsible for acting, we mean that there is an obligation to act in a certain way. Some obligations, such as the obligation to pay taxes, are imposed by the law and legal rules. These are legal obligations. However, there are also non-legal obligations, like the obligation to honour a promise made to a friend. It is worth noting that obligations can be used as a basis from which to derive prohibitions or permissions.[16] A prohibition against using force, for example, is an obligation not to use force. Being permitted to use force in self-defence is tantamount to not being prohibited from using force in self-defence (a non-obligation not to use force in self-defence). Thus, while continuing to refer only to obligations, we use the term broadly to cover permissions and prohibitions, too.

When it comes to CIL, states act in the belief they are bound by a legal obligation (*opinio juris*). By belief, we to refer to a general acceptance of something as being the case.[17] Different beliefs move us in different ways. Some beliefs are about things we know for sure, while others are about things we only vaguely sense or feel. No matter how strong or weak, these are all beliefs. Besides, believing in something does not mean we have to think about it or do it all the time. For example, most of us believe that the moon is not made of cheese, but we do not usually think about it. Let it be said that there is nothing controversial about attributing beliefs to states: following Cassese, we can say that it is humans acting on behalf of states who believe that certain acts are obligatory.[18]

Opinio juris allows us to distinguish practices that are merely habitual from those that create normative expectations in the community and

[15] Duties being here treated as a kind of obligation; see J Hage, *Foundations and Building Blocks of Law* (Eleven International Publishing 2018) ch VI.

[16] SO Hansson, 'The Varieties of Permission' in DM Gabbay and others (eds), *Handbook of Deontic Logic and Normative Systems* (College Publications 2013) 204–06.

[17] E Schwitzgebel, 'Belief', *The Stanford Encyclopedia of Philosophy* (Winter edn, 2021) <https://plato.stanford.edu/entries/belief/> accessed 1 April 2022.

[18] A Cassese, *International Law* (2nd edn, Oxford University Press 2005) 4. See also A Waltermann, 'Why Non-Human Agency?' in A Waltermann and others (eds), *Law, Science, Rationality* (Eleven International Publishing 2020) 51. Also, the cognitive sciences teach us that human brains do not have a single, top-level decision-maker. So, when we assign a belief held by a group of humans to a state, we are simply going a step further than when we assign mental acts to humans rather than parts of their brains. See DC Dennett, *Consciousness Explained* (Little Brown 1991) 102–03; J Hage, 'Are the Cognitive Sciences Relevant for Law?' in B Brożek, J Hage, and N Vincent (eds), *Law and Mind: A Survey of Law and the Cognitive Sciences* (Cambridge University Press 2021) 17, 40–41.

consequently lead to the creation of CIL rules.[19] It should be borne in mind that what we are referring to here is the belief that a practice is required by law. States feel compelled to perform these acts because they consider them to be legally obligatory, not for any other, non-legal reason, no matter how strong it may be. As stated in Section 1, the chronological paradox suggests that CIL is caught in a vicious circle: to create a new CIL rule, states must believe that the law obligates them to act in a certain way (*opinio juris*), yet until this CIL rule is created the act in question is not required by law.[20]

To add colour to this explanation, let us imagine that a group of wealthy states begins donating vaccines to developing states during a pandemic. Suppose this practice continues to the point where states believe that they are under a legal obligation to donate vaccines. Lawyers then identify a new CIL rule, according to which wealthy states are obligated to donate vaccines to developing states during pandemics. The problem is that if this new 'vaccine donation CIL rule' exists simply because states believe the practice to be legally obligatory, then the rule cannot as such impose the obligation to donate vaccines. For it actually to be a legal obligation, a legal rule imposing the obligation is needed. As Bradley puts it: 'If State practices do not become binding as CIL until the States involved act out of a sense of legal obligation, how do the States develop that sense of legal obligation in the first place?'[21] In our example, if wealthy states are legally obligated to donate vaccines only by virtue of a CIL rule, how did they come to believe that the law obligates them to donate vaccines in the first place?

The paradox is disconcerting, because if it correctly accounts for the creation of new CIL rules, then CIL is fated to chase its tail. Such circular reasoning is problematic: it uses its conclusion as a premise, while giving us no reason to accept its premise other than that we already believe its conclusion. We have to assume that the law requires specific behaviour on the part of states (there must be a legal obligation) before we can conclude that a given CIL rule exists. But to assume that the law requires such behaviour of states (i.e. that there is indeed a legal obligation), we

[19] Hart (n 2) ch I. See also GJ Postema, 'Custom in International Law: A Normative Practice Account' in A Perreau-Saussine and JB Murphy (eds), *The Nature of Customary Law* (Cambridge University Press 2007).

[20] Levine (n 7); Lefkowitz (n 7); Jeutner and Paddeu (n 7).

[21] CA Bradley, 'Customary International Law Adjudication as Common Law Adjudication' in CA Bradley (ed), *Custom's Future: International Law in a Changing World* (Cambridge University Press 2016) 34.

need a pre-existing CIL rule commanding such behaviour (i.e. we need a CIL rule to impose that legal obligation).

Gény gives a straightforward (but unsatisfactory) answer to the paradox. He says that states are wrong to think they are legally required to act: their *opinio juris* is mistaken.[22] That is, states have – or feign – a false view about what is happening,[23] whereas there is no obligation at all. Gény says that when this mistake is made repeatedly by a lot of states, it generates mutual expectations that turn into a legal obligation. Gény's response admittedly short-circuits the paradox, but in avoiding one problem it falls into another, for if states are mistaken, then CIL is incoherent and its entire structure based on a delusion. As exposed in Section 1, such a workaround falls short of what this chapter sets out to do, which is to address the paradox in a way that preserves the coherence, and thus the legitimacy, of (customary) international law.

Some authors have made intriguing attempts to re-imagine *opinio juris* as more than just a description of the law, arguing that it helps to create the law. To put it differently, these authors claim that *opinio juris* goes beyond a descriptive stance on the existence of legal obligations, because it also plays a prescriptive role in determining the content of these legal obligations. In Westerman's words: '*Opinio juris* can better be regarded as a map, which represents the law by selecting and highlighting those aspects that are deemed important. It describes and prescribes at the same time.'[24] When states believe that a certain act is legally obligatory, they are not simply describing a pre-existing reality. Their belief is effectively building reality as we know it. This – the constructive role of our collective beliefs – is a topic central to social ontology; as a field of study, it investigates how the combined action of our minds can shape the world around us. According to social ontology, our minds are not (just) describing reality; they are projecting meaning onto it.[25] For example, when people believe that a river marks the frontier between two communities, they are not only acknowledging that fact but also creating it. If it

[22] PE Benson, 'François Gény's Doctrine of Customary Law' (1983) 20 CYIL 267, 276.

[23] Tasioulas (n 9) 321.

[24] P Westerman, 'Test, Filter, Ideal or Map?' in K Gorobets, A Hadjigeorgiou and P Westerman (eds), *Conceptual (Re)Constructions of International Law* (Edward Elgar 2022) 127. See also O Elias, 'The Nature of the Subjective Element in Customary International Law' (1995) 44 ICLQ 501.

[25] J Searle, *The Construction of Social Reality* (Free Press 1995) 31; J Searle, *Mind, Language, and Society: Philosophy in the Real World* (Basic Books 1999) 85; J Searle, *Making the Social World: The Structure of Human Civilization* (Oxford University Press 2010) 25.

were not for people collectively believing that the river is a frontier, it would be just another watercourse.

The depiction of *opinio juris* as a belief with both descriptive and prescriptive functions does not contradict traditional views on CIL. In fact, the ILC's explanation of acceptance as law (*opinio juris*) corresponds to social ontology's account of collective acceptance. The ILC explains that acceptance as law implies there is a 'subjective' or 'psychological' dimension to the 'binding character of the practice in question', in the sense that 'the practice must be undertaken with a sense of legal right or obligation.'[26] According to social ontology, collective acceptance is when the members of a social group come to share and maintain a relevant social attitude (a 'we-attitude') towards a certain practice.[27] Like the constructive role of beliefs in the river-frontier example mentioned above, when states believe they have an obligation to engage in a particular practice, this belief is both descriptive and prescriptive. It should be added that participants must be committed to what they believe, though their belief can range from enthusiastic endorsement to simply going along with the group.[28] As a result, the lines between passive acceptance and active support or desire are frequently blurred.

3 Constructive Interpretation

In Section 2, we discussed the two constituent elements of CIL, dissected the chronological paradox, and began to discuss how our collective beliefs can shape the social world. We saw that the crux of the paradox lies in the manner in which a new CIL rule is created: how can the existence of a CIL rule be dependent on a condition (belief in a legal obligation – *opinio juris*) that appears to be itself dependent on an already existing CIL rule? The challenging feature of the chronological paradox is thus the transition from the first point in time when a CIL rule does not yet exist to a second point in time when it does. To understand the transition between these two points, we must first understand how CIL rules are identified.

The identification of a CIL rule involves gathering evidence that its two constituent elements – repeated practice (*diuturnitas*) and a belief in legal obligation (*opinio juris*) – are present. Such evidence is sought in prior

26 ILC (n 10) 138.

27 R Tuomela, 'Collective Acceptance, Social Institutions, and Social Reality' (2003) 62 AJES 123.

28 Searle (n 25) 57.

pronouncements and empirical data relating to state behaviour. Through observation of relevant materials (wherever these materials are found), the aim is to determine whether a specific CIL rule exists. If sufficient evidence of the two constituent elements is found, a new CIL rule is said to exist. If the evidence is insufficient, there is (as yet) no new CIL rule.

The search for corroborative materials should not be thought of as 'gold-digging' for evidence.[29] Far from being based on neutral observation, the identification of CIL rules is a highly interpretive activity. As philosophers have long recognised, no evidence is 'given' neutrally, because all observation is theory-laden:[30] the theoretical framework of the observer/interpreter determines the meaning of what they observe. Likewise, how people choose, see, and judge evidence is affected by the theories they hold.[31] In a legal context, as explained by Hart, 'situations do not await us neatly labelled, creased, and folded; nor is their legal classification written on them to be simply read off by the judge.'[32] On the contrary, evidentiary materials call for purposeful interpretation: it is the responsibility of the interpreter to determine the import of the words and actions.[33]

The question therefore arises as to what role and purpose interpretation has in relation to CIL rules. There are at least two possible answers to this question, for legal interpretation may be of two kinds: descriptive or constructive. The former simply describes what the law is and what rules exist. The latter not only tells us what the law is but also creates the law and its rules. The descriptivist viewpoint has 'realist'[34] undertones, because it presupposes the existence of a legal reality independent of the interpreter, whose task is therefore merely to point out answers that are

[29] See Chapter 1.

[30] On the (widely rejected) idea that experience gives points of certainty that can be used as absolute bases for knowledge, see JR O'Shea, 'What Is the Myth of the Given?' (2021) 199 Synthese 10543.

[31] NR Hanson, *Patterns of Discovery* (Cambridge University Press 1965) 4; PK Feyerabend, 'Science Without Experience' (1969) 66 Journal of Philosophy 791; TS Kuhn, *The Structure of Scientific Revolutions* (2nd edn, University of Chicago Press 1970) 35. See also RW Proctor and EJ Capaldi, *Psychology of Science: Implicit and Explicit Processes* (Oxford University Press 2012) 1–10.

[32] HLA Hart, 'Positivism and the Separation of Law and Morals' in Hart, *Essays in Jurisprudence and Philosophy* (Oxford University Press 1983) 63.

[33] HG Gadamer, *Truth and Method* (J Weinsheimer and DG Marshall trs, 2nd edn, Continuum 2004) 383.

[34] This chapter uses the term 'realism' not in the sense of legal realism but to express the idea that true statements are true because they reflect the content of an independently existing reality. See M Devitt, *Realism and Truth* (2nd edn, Princeton University Press 1997) ch 2.

already there. By contrast, the constructivist viewpoint is based on the premise that legal interpretation is more than just a search for answers; it considers the interpreter to be engaging in an act of creation when assigning meaning to what they interpret.[35]

This chapter discounts the descriptivist point of view for a number of reasons,[36] one of which is that descriptivism ignores the fact that observation is theory-laden. As previously stated, all observation, including interpretation, is coloured by the observer's theoretical bias. Consequently, observation (or interpretation) can never be purely descriptive; it always has, to some extent, a constitutive role. Furthermore, the descriptivist viewpoint is unable to account for the necessary role argumentation plays in the interpreter's efforts to solve 'hard cases'.[37] Consider the discussions currently taking place over whether there is a customary rule that allows states to intervene in the territories of other states to stop human rights violations;[38] whether there is a level of gravity below which small-scale armed attacks are not considered acts of aggression under international law;[39] and whether it is illegal for states to conduct military exercises or manoeuvres in foreign exclusive economic zones.[40] The answers to these questions are not a 'given', but rather depend on the quality of the interpreters' arguments. In other words, the ideas of those who interpret the law shape the contents of international law and international legal rules.

Dworkin took a similar constructivist approach to legal interpretation in saying that interpretation is a creative process in which meaning is imposed on the object of interpretation to make it the best instantiation of a given form or genre.[41] However, he did not think interpreters should be able to

[35] P Lorenzen, *Constructive Philosophy* (University of Massachusetts Press 1987) ix.

[36] For a comprehensive argument against the descriptivist view, see J Hage, 'Construction or Reconstruction? On the Function of Argumentation in the Law' in C Dahlman and E Feteris (eds), *Legal Argumentation Theory: Cross-Disciplinary Perspectives* (Springer 2012) 125; J Hage, 'Legal Reasoning and the Construction of Law' (2012) i-Lex 81.

[37] R Dworkin, *Taking Rights Seriously* (Harvard University Press 1978) 81. See also G Dorota, 'Hard Cases' (2013) 2 UMSLR 240.

[38] J Vidmar, 'The Use of Force as a Plea of Necessity' (2017) 111 AJIL 302.

[39] T Ruys, 'The Meaning of "Force" and the Boundaries of the *Jus ad Bellum*: Are "Minimal" Uses of Force Excluded from UN Charter Article 2(4)?' (2014) 108 AJIL 159; O Corten, *The Law Against War: The Prohibition on the Use of Force in Contemporary International Law* (2nd ed, Hart 2021) ch 2.

[40] S Yee, 'Sketching the Debate on Military Activities in the EEZ: An Editorial Comment' (2010) 9 Chinese JIL 1.

[41] R Dworkin, *Law's Empire* (Harvard University Press 1986) 52. See also DO Brink, 'Originalism and Constructive Interpretation' in W Waluchow and S Sciaraffa (eds), *The Legacy of Ronald Dworkin* (Oxford University Press 2016) 273.

interpret sources however they wished. Although interpretation must allow for innovation to ensure that the object as interpreted best serves its purpose, its scope is limited by the object's history.[42] Thus, legal interpretation is Janus-faced, looking both backwards and forwards.[43] While based on the observation of pre-existing materials, it is also creative in that it is not a mere reproduction of those materials; rather, it creates something new by giving them meaning. This is equally true of CIL interpretation, for once evidence of the two constituent elements of CIL has been established, CIL interpretation fulfils a constructive role by shaping and determining its content.

It is important to note that we can still talk about 'interpreting' CIL even when the evidence of its two constituent elements is not in textual form. True, interpretive activity in the legal sphere is often directed at pieces of text, as when we extract rules from the text of a treaty. This, for instance, happens when we read Article 8 of the Rome Statute[44] to determine the content of the rule punishing aggression. But interpretation goes beyond textual hermeneutics. It is possible to distinguish between two types of interpretation – (i) source interpretation, which is the interpretation of (formal and material) sources of law; and (ii) rule-to-case interpretation, which is the classification of a case according to the conditions under which a given rule is applicable to it.[45] In both cases, interpretation may be directed at unwritten materials. For example, when lawyers identify a new CIL rule on the basis of empirical evidence (source interpretation), or determine, on the basis of visual evidence of armed conflict, that the crime of aggression has been committed (rule-to-case interpretation), they are relying on unwritten materials.

Both the ICJ and the ILC believe that CIL is susceptible to interpretation. In *Nicaragua*, the ICJ held that rules derived from CIL could be distinguished from those derived from international treaties by 'reference

[42] GJ Postema, *Legal Philosophy in the Twentieth Century: The Common Law World* (Springer 2011) 425; R Porto Macedo Júnior, *Do Xadrez à Cortesia: Dworkin e a Teoria do Direito Contemporânea* (Saraiva 2013) 219.

[43] A Peczenik, *Scientia Juris: Legal Doctrine as Knowledge of Law and as a Source of Law* (Springer 2005) 6.

[44] Rome Statute of the International Criminal Court (adopted 17 July 1998, entered into force 1 July 2002) 2187 UNTS 3.

[45] On interpretation (or classification) of rules in relation to cases, see J Hage, *Reasoning with Rules: An Essay on Legal Reasoning and Its Underlying Logic* (Springer 1997) 95–97. See also J Raz, 'Why Interpret?' (1996) 9 Ratio Juris 349; F Perin Shecaira, 'Sources of Law Are Not Legal Norms' (2015) 28 Ratio Juris 15.

to the methods of interpretation and application.'[46] Likewise, in *North Sea Continental Shelf* Judge Tanaka asserted that '[c]ustomary law ... requires precision and completion about its content. This task, in its nature being interpretative, would be incumbent upon the Court.'[47] The ILC has taken a similar line: when commenting on materials that may be consulted to help identify CIL, it stated that specific 'texts may assist in collecting, synthesizing or interpreting practice relevant to the identification of customary international law'.[48] It furthermore explained that '[e]ach of the forms [of state practice] listed is to be interpreted broadly to reflect the multiple and diverse ways in which states act and react'.[49] Therefore, it cannot be considered controversial to claim that CIL is interpretable.[50]

To conclude this discussion of the interpretive nature of identifying CIL rules, it is crucial to keep in mind that there is no absolute separation in how evidence for the two CIL elements is interpreted. Although the ICJ held in the *Asylum* case that *diuturnitas* and *opinio juris* should be determined separately,[51] this view has gradually been replaced by one that allows evidence of both constituent elements to be extracted from the same act. D'Aspremont discerned signs of this change in the *Gulf of Maine* and *Nicaragua* cases.[52] The most recent rebuttal of the ICJ's initial position came from the ILC in its 2018 Draft Conclusions. When defining what materials may serve as evidence of repeated practice and the belief that such practice is legally required, the ILC acknowledged that one and the same act may provide evidence of both.[53]

46 *Military and Paramilitary Activities in and against Nicaragua (Nicaragua v United States of America)* (Merits) [1986] ICJ Rep 14 [178].

47 *North Sea Continental Shelf* (Judgment, Dissenting Opinion of Judge Tanaka) [1969] ICJ Rep 172 [182].

48 ILC (n 10) 142.

49 ibid 134.

50 Merkouris (n 11); O Chasapis Tassinis, 'Customary International Law: Interpretation from Beginning to End' (2020) 31 EJIL 235; K Gorobets, 'Practical Reasoning and Interpretation of Customary International Law' in P Merkouris, J Kammerhofer and N Arajärvi (eds), *The Theory, Practice, and Interpretation of Customary International Law* (Cambridge University Press 2022) 370.

51 *Colombian-Peruvian Asylum Case* (Judgment) [1950] ICJ Rep 266 [276].

52 D'Aspremont (n 6) ch 2. See also *Military and Paramilitary Activities in and against Nicaragua (Nicaragua v United States of America)* (Merits) [1986] ICJ Rep 14; *Delimitation of the Maritime Boundary in the Gulf of Maine Area* (Judgment) [1984] ICJ Rep 246.

53 ILC (n 10) 133, 140–41.

4 The Formation of CIL Rules

This section will break down the formation of CIL rules into distinct steps. It is a process that begins with the principle of good faith, which leads to legal obligations, and these legal obligations in turn contribute to the development of a new CIL rule. But before we can discuss these steps, some general ideas must first be addressed – namely, rule applicability and application, constitutive rules, and rules about rules (metarules). Although these matters might not seem directly related to the chronological paradox, their elucidation is important to further discussion of the paradox. Given that problems are best solved when broken down into their most basic parts and then put it back together again, this section will focus on deconstructing and rebuilding the problem.

4.1 Rule Applicability and Rule Application

Section 3 distinguished between two types of interpretation: source interpretation, which, through an examination of formal and material sources, written and unwritten, allows us to determine the existence and content of legal rules; and rule-to-case interpretation, which, in situations where a rule already exists, allows us to determine whether that rule is applicable – and applies – to a particular case. When examining evidence of the existence of a CIL rule that holds states responsible for internationally wrongful acts, we are engaging in source interpretation.[54] When we then go on to consider whether that rule is applicable to a specific case in which Uganda commits a wrongful act against the Democratic Republic of the Congo (DRC), we are engaging in rule-to-case interpretation.[55]

To say that a rule is applicable is not to say that it actually applies to a specific case.[56] In the example given above, there is a distinction to be drawn between admitting that the state responsibility rule is applicable to the case between Uganda and the DRC and concluding that this rule

[54] The ILC's formulations on state responsibility reflect CIL. See ILC, 'Draft Articles on Responsibility of States for Internationally Wrongful Acts, with Commentaries' (23 April–1 June and 2 July–10 August 2001) UN Doc A/56/10; F Lusa Bordin, 'Reflections of Customary International Law: The Authority of Codification Conventions and ILC Draft Articles in International Law' (2014) 63 ICLQ 535.

[55] *Armed Activities on the Territory of the Congo (Democratic Republic of the Congo v Uganda)* (Judgment) [2022] ICJ Rep 1.

[56] Hage (n 45); J Hage and A Waltermann, 'Logical Techniques for International Law' in D Krimphove and G Lentner (eds), *Law and Logic: Contemporary Issues* (Duncker und Humblot 2017) 125; H Marcos, A Waltermann and J Hage, 'From Sovereignty to International Cooperation: Lessons from Legal Logic and Social Ontology' (2021) Maastricht

indeed applies to that case. If Uganda's action against the DRC is wrongful, then the rule is applicable. If an international court decides that the rule applies to this case, Uganda is not only responsible for its actions but also obligated to make reparations to the DRC. In other words, a rule *is applicable* to a case when the conditions for its application are met; a rule *applies* when its consequences take effect in a case.[57]

In practice, it is often hard to differentiate between the two types of interpretation and between a rule's applicability and its application to a specific case. We tend to look at a source, decide whether a rule is applicable to a case, and conclude that it applies to the case, all in one go. For present purposes, however, it is relevant to distinguish between these different notions. One way to grasp the differences between the stages of interpretation is to remember that a rule and its source are distinct. For example, the ILC's report on state responsibility[58] is distinct from the rules holding states accountable for wrongful acts that are derived from that document (and other sources). We can further distinguish between applicability and application by framing rules as a conditions–conclusion formula.[59] For instance, the CIL rule on state responsibility can be simplified as follows:

Conditions: 'X and Y are states' and 'X commits a wrongful act against Y' – Conclusion: 'X is obligated to make reparations to Y'

In this formula, 'X' and 'Y' are variables for states like Uganda and the DRC. The conjunction 'and' means that all conditional blocks must be satisfied for a case to meet that rule's conditions. The dash separates the conditions from the conclusion, and the inverted commas mark out the conditional and conclusion blocks. If both Uganda and the DRC are states and Uganda has committed a wrongful act against the DRC, then when this rule applies, it obligates Uganda to make reparations to the DRC.

Faculty of Law Working Paper Series 2021/01 <www.maastrichtuniversity.nl/maastricht-faculty-law-working-paper-series-2021> accessed 15 April 2024.

57 On the different kinds of rule application, see L Duarte d'Almeida, 'What Is It to Apply the Law?' (2021) 40 Law Philos 361.

58 ILC (n 54).

59 While it is possible to formulate a rule as a statement, we should not conclude that rules are statements. See J Hage, 'Consistency of Rules and Norms' (2000) 9 ICTL 219; H Marcos, 'A Study on Defeasibility and Defeaters in International Law: Process or Procedure Distinction against the Non-discrimination Rule' in W Menezes, A Nunes Filho and PH Reis de Oliveira (eds), *Tribunais Internacionais e a Garantia dos Direitos Sociais* (Academia Brasileira de Direito Internacional 2021) 199, 208.

Before moving on, it is essential to note that the application of a rule presupposes interpretation. It is only after we have extracted a rule from its source (source interpretation) and inferred its applicability to a case (rule-to-case interpretation) that the rule will apply. Rule application, like interpretation, is a constructive exercise. When rules apply to cases, they create legal consequences. So, when the state responsibility rule applies to Uganda and the DRC's case, this is not a mere description of the fact that Uganda must make reparations to the DRC; the rule's application to the case puts Uganda under an obligation to make reparations to the DRC.

4.2 Constitutive Rules

As explained in Section 2, social ontology studies how our collective beliefs shape the world around us. We gave the example of a river, which can mark the frontier between two communities only if people believe it does. If no one held such a belief, the river would simply be a stretch of water. Rules are similar in that they exist only because people believe in them. Interestingly, unlike the river-frontier, which has a physical presence in the natural world, rules are abstract. Rules have no corporeal form that we can touch, but they still exist because people collectively believe they do.[60] Let us develop these ideas in the following paragraphs.

Anything that exists can be called an 'entity', and anything that exists because of people can be called a 'social entity'.[61] A frontier is a social entity. A business, a state, and an international organisation are all examples of social entities. Lawyers, judges, obligations, and rules are all social entities. All of these things exist because of people. There would be no borders, businesses, states, international organisations, lawyers, judges, and, most importantly, no obligations or rules if people did not exist.

Social entities can be separated into two levels.[62] At the first level are what we may call 'basic social entities' – that is, entities that directly

[60] B Smith, 'John Searle: From Speech Acts to Social Reality' in B Smith (ed), *John Searle* (Cambridge University Press 2003) 19.

[61] Some authors prefer to use 'object', 'being', or 'existent' instead of 'entity.' See B Rettler and AM Bailey, 'Object', *The Stanford Encyclopedia of Philosophy* (Winter edn, 2017) <https://plato.stanford.edu/entries/object/> accessed 2 April 2022.

[62] The terminology 'basic social entities' and 'rule-based entities' used in this chapter reflects the influence of Hage's work on legal logic and social ontology. See J Hage and B Verheij, 'Reason-Based Logic: A Logic for Reasoning with Rules and Reasons' (1994) 3 ICTL 171; Hage, *Foundations and Building Blocks of Law* (n 15); J Hage, 'Constructivist Facts as the Bridge between Is and Ought' (2022) 1 IJSL 1. Following Anscombe, basic entities and

depend on people's beliefs. We often find these basic social entities in simple groups. For instance, if two tribal groups use a river as a frontier to separate their respective territories, that frontier is a basic social entity. Its existence is directly dependent on a belief held by the members of a group. A rule stating that the eldest descendant of a deceased tribe leader becomes the new leader is another example of a basic social entity.

At the second level we find entities that are not directly grounded in people's beliefs. Although they again exist because of what people believe, it is only in an indirect way, for these entities are based on other entities and are only secondarily grounded in a group's collective beliefs. Suppose, for example, that when Chief Umoro dies, his firstborn son, Raoni, becomes the leader of his tribe, the Kayapo, by virtue of a rule according to which the deceased tribe leader is succeeded by the eldest descendant. Raoni's position as the new leader is thus a direct result of that rule and is only indirectly grounded in the Kayapo's collective beliefs.

These second-level entities are the result of rule application. Let us call them 'rule-based entities'. To understand how rules can lead to the existence of social entities, we must first consider a few aspects of how rules work. To begin with, rules are not limited to the law;[63] Language, etiquette, games, and inferences rely frequently on rules, too. Consider the conceptual rule qualifying a plane figure with three straight sides and three angles as a triangle; or the etiquette rule dictating that guests should offer to lend a hand to the host; or the chess rule permitting the bishop to move diagonally in any direction; or the inference rule allowing 'Q is true' to be deduced from the premises 'P implies Q' and 'P is true'. These are not legal rules in the strict sense, but they are still rules.

Most rules operate tacitly in the background without our being aware of them.[64] Consider chess: we think about the rules telling us how to move each piece only if we are still learning the game; once we know how to play, we focus on choosing the best moves and strategies to win. Even

rule-based entities may also be called 'conventional' and 'institutional' entities, respectively. See GEM Anscombe, 'On Brute Facts' (1958) 18 Analysis 69; N MacCormick and O Weinberger (eds), *Institutional Theory of Law: New Approaches to Legal Positivism* (Springer 1986).

63 F Schauer, *Playing by the Rules: A Philosophical Examination of Rule-Based Decision-Making in Law and in Life* (Oxford University Press 1991) 10.

64 Wittgenstein (n 1) para 219; R Brandom, *Making It Explicit: Reasoning, Representing, and Discursive Commitment* (Harvard University Press 1994) 649–50.

though we no longer think about the rules, they are still there in the background and affect how the game is played. As Wittgenstein pointed out, a person who follows rules does not usually think about or check them; when following a rule, they may even be unaware that they are doing so.[65]

We often focus on how rules regulate behaviour (rules tell us our obligations, permissions, and prohibitions), but some rules also constitute social practices. Philosophers call them 'constitutive rules'.[66] The rules for games are a good example: It is only thanks to its rules that we can play a game like chess; without them, chess would not exist. Legal rules are similarly constitutive; for example, together they may create a certain kind of political system that determines how people are put into power. Another way in which constitutive rules operate is by making something count as something else.[67] Chess rules make certain positions on the board count as checkmate. The rule according to which the eldest descendant becomes the new leader makes the eldest descendant count as the new leader when the incumbent dies. In this respect, constitutive rules can create social entities. For example, there is no such thing as checkmate without the rules of chess, so checkmate is a rule-based entity. The same goes for Raoni: he is the leader of the Kayapo tribe because of the rule that makes the eldest descendant of the deceased tribe leader the new leader.

Some second-level rule-based entities exist through the application of other rules called 'metarules'.[68] A metarule is a rule about rules, meaning that a rule forms part of its conditions or conclusion. Certain metarules, when applied, create entities that are also rules. There are many examples in present-day legal systems. Think of the domestic rules enacted when parliament passes a bill into law or the international rules created when state representatives ratify treaties. These rules of law are directly based on the metarules that give members of parliament or state representatives the power to make rules of law. Second-level rules are still indirectly based on what people collectively believe, for they would not exist if it were not for people.

[65] Wittgenstein (n 1) paras 207–32; Glock (n 1) 324–25.

[66] Searle (n 25) 97. See also J Hage, 'Two Concepts of Constitutive Rules' (2018) 4 Argumenta 21; C Roversi, 'In Defence of Constitutive Rules' (2021) 199 Synthese 14349; Hage, 'Constructivist Facts as the Bridge between Is and Ought' (n 62).

[67] Smith (n 60).

[68] Hage calls them 'rule-based rules'. See Hage, *Foundations and Building Blocks of Law* (n 15) 87; Hage, 'Constructivist Facts as the Bridge between Is and Ought' (n 62).

4.3 The CIL Metarule

This section argues that CIL rules exist as rule-based entities. It will explain that individual CIL rules are created through a metarule – the CIL metarule, or 'M' for short. But before discussing M, it is worth reiterating that, unlike Gény, this chapter does not suppose that states are mistaken in their *opinio juris*. On the contrary, it assumes they are correct in believing themselves to be under a legal obligatio. So, both the belief and the obligation to which the belief relates are taken as accurate. The rationale behind this assumption is simple: as pointed out in Section 2 when discussing Gény's answer to the chronological paradox, if the belief held by states is wrong, then CIL is built on a delusion and is therefore incoherent. The alternative is that the belief is correct and that states have a legal obligation. After all, if we believe something (that today is Monday, for example) and that belief is correct, then what we believe is a fact (today is in fact Monday).

M's conditions are the two elements needed to identify a CIL rule: the practice (*diuturnitas*) and the belief that this practice is legally obligatory (*opinio juris*). If M's conditions are satisfied, M is applicable. If M applies, M leads to the consequence that a particular CIL rule exists. Let us call this generic CIL rule 'R'. If 'Φ' stands for engaging in a named act or activity, such as 'not using force', 'donating vaccines', or 'granting immunity to heads of state', we can write M as the following conditions–conclusion formulation:

Conditions: 'states generally Φ' and 'states are under the legal obligation to Φ' – Conclusion: 'there is a CIL rule R obligating states to Φ'

When M applies to a case, M gives rise to a CIL rule R. But R must still be interpreted in light of M's application to a case (rule-to-case interpretation).[69] It is important to note that R is not derived directly from the formulation of M, but is the result of M's application. Knowledge of R comes only from lawyers interpreting M's application to a specific case. This frequently occurs when lawyers debate possible interpretations in cases where a court recognises that a specific CIL rule applies to the disputants.

How is it that M can lead to the creation of new CIL rules if no one has ever talked about M before? As previously stated, the truth is that many rules control what we do without us even realising it.[70] According to

[69] See Section 3.
[70] See Section 4.2.

Wittgenstein, obeying a rule is a matter of practice, whereas understanding a rule is to know what counts as acting by it.[71] In 1920, Descamps implicitly described how M works when he said that CIL rules are 'established by the continual and general usage of nations, which has consequently obtained the force of law'.[72] Despite not mentioning M or discussing constitutive (meta)rules, Descamps is unknowingly referring to M in this explanation of how a new CIL rule is created. As Russell stated, anyone who engages in a practice has some knowledge of the logical rules behind that practice, but this knowledge is in most cases implicit.[73]

M works behind the scenes, much like many other rules that make up our world. As mentioned in Section 4.2, most rules operate implicitly in the background, and no conscious effort is required for their interpretation or application. Chess exists only because of its rules, but most people do not think about the rules when they play. In international law, the metarules that empower state representatives to ratify treaties and that make treaties legal sources are similar; whenever a rule from a specific treaty is recognised, both of these metarules are interpreted and applied, even if only implicitly. The same goes for M.

We should also consider the ICJ's decision in *North Sea Continental Shelf*. When deciding if the equidistance principle was based on custom, the ICJ said: 'It would in the first place be necessary that the provision concerned should, at all events potentially, be of a fundamentally norm-creating character, such as could be regarded as forming the basis of a general rule of law.'[74] This passage is important because it shows a rule-creating aspect of the standards used to find a CIL rule, which d'Aspremont calls the 'third element' for identifying CIL.[75] In relation to the present discussion, M is an example of such standards with rule-creating dimensions.

Framing M in terms of a conditions⇒conclusion formula helps to show the chronological paradox at work. For M to be applicable, states must Φ and be obligated to Φ. The consequence of M is that a CIL rule R will emerge, obligating states to Φ. The paradox is that for states to be

[71] Wittgenstein (n 1) para 201; Glock (n 1) 327.

[72] Advisory Committee of Jurists, 'Procès-Verbaux of the Proceedings of the Committee' (Permanent Court of International Justice 1920) 322.

[73] B Russell, *Our Knowledge of the External World: As a Field for Scientific Method in Philosophy* (Routledge 2009) 49.

[74] *North Sea Continental Shelf* (Judgment) [1969] ICJ Rep 3 [72].

[75] D'Aspremont (n 6) ch 3.

obligated to Φ in the first place, we would need a CIL rule R obligating states to Φ. Let us recall the earlier example of a hypothetical CIL rule obligating wealthy states to donate vaccines. If wealthy states donate vaccines because of an obligation to donate vaccines, M is applicable. If M applies, M constitutes a CIL rule R that obligates wealthy states to donate vaccines. But how can wealthy states be obligated to donate vaccines if the rule that obligates them comes into existence only once M applies?

The answer is that this depiction of CIL needs to be revised. While M does constitute a CIL rule R that imposes an obligation to Φ, the initial obligation to Φ is imposed neither by M nor by R. There are two alternative explanations for the origin of the obligation to Φ.

4.3.1 First Explanation

The first explanation is straightforward. The obligation to Φ is a basic social entity with deontic content that comes directly from what states believe. A subgroup of states creates an obligation to Φ when these states believe they have an obligation to Φ. (This is similar to how groups of people create social entities by believing in them.[76]) Since this subgroup of states believes that they are obligated to Φ, they engage in Φ. If states generally are engaging in Φ because they are obligated to Φ, M is applicable. If M applies, M constitutes a CIL rule R, the effect of which is that all states have an obligation to Φ.[77]

This first explanation raises two problems. The first concerns the distinction between 'is' and 'ought'.[78] It is unclear why states ought to Φ because of a social entity in which they have only recently started to believe. In other words, how can a social entity that exists as a matter of social fact ('is') be used to judge what states are obligated to do ('ought')? There have been some intriguing philosophical attempts to bridge the is/ought gap through reference to deontic entities.[79] It could be argued that states ought to Φ because a deontic entity has imposed on them an obligation to Φ. Deontic entities are social entities that are factual and normative at the same time. Although belonging to the sphere of what is,

[76] See Section 4.2.

[77] We will discuss persistent objectors later in Section 4.3.2.

[78] As first explained by Hume, the is/ought problem arises when we derive an 'ought judgement' from premises based on 'is' and vice versa. D Hume, *A Treatise of Human Nature* (Floating Press 2009) 715–16.

[79] See Hage, *Foundations and Building Blocks of Law* (n 15) ch IX; Hage, 'Two Concepts of Constitutive Rules' (n 66). See also J Searle, 'How to Derive "Ought" From "Is"' (1964) 73 Philosophical Review 43.

they can be used to judge what ought to be. As a result, they can bridge the gap between what is and what ought to be. So, an 'ought judgement' like 'states ought to Φ' could be derived from a factual entity that imposes an obligation to Φ, on condition that this factual entity is deontic.

The second problem with this first explanation is that it does not clarify how there can be a legal obligation to Φ before a legal rule imposes that obligation. As explained in Section 2, the paradox stems from the prerequisite that for a new CIL rule to be created states must believe that the law obligates them to act in a certain way (*opinio juris*). Yet, according to the first explanation, the obligation to Φ is a basic social entity sourced in states' collective beliefs. Thus, a legal rule does not impose this obligation. However, it could be argued that the obligation to Φ acquires the status of a legal obligation due to the longstanding practice of engaging in Φ, which reinforces shared expectations within the international community. This argument follows Descamps's explanation of CIL rules as rules set up by the continued use on the part of states, which, over time, would give these obligations the force of law.[80]

If we agree that deontic entities can bridge the is/ought gap and that the legal nature of obligations can be derived from a longstanding practice, then this first explanation works. But we must admit that it can be challenged by those who contend there is an absolute separation between 'is' and 'ought', and by those who maintain that a legal rule must impose an obligation for that obligation to be legal. To address these challenges, an alternative explanation of the paradox is needed.

4.3.2 Second Explanation

The second explanation deals with the two problems the first explanation left unsolved by putting the legal obligation to Φ in the context of the general principle of good faith. Good faith is of fundamental importance to all contemporary legal orders, making it a general principle of law under Article 38(1)(c) of the ICJ Statute.[81] In fact, Grotius stated in *De Jure Belli ac Pacis* that good faith was one of the most significant legal standards. He also mentions how Aristotle and Cicero saw it as the foundation of all human interaction.[82] The general principle of good

[80] Advisory Committee of Jurists (n 72) 322.

[81] Statute of the International Court of Justice (n 12). On good faith as a general principle of law, see R Kolb, *Good Faith in International Law* (Hart 2017); S Reinhold, 'Good Faith in International Law' (2013) 2 UCLJLJ 40.

[82] H Grotius, *The Rights of War and Peace* (Richard Tuck ed, Liberty Fund 2005) bk III, ch XXV, s I.1.

faith has a broad, value-oriented scope, allowing us to derive a variety of legal by-products from it. In similar vein, the ICJ declared in *Nuclear Tests* that good faith governs 'the creation and performance of legal obligations, whatever their source'.[83] So it is safe to say that good faith is the basis for many rules of international law, including (meta)rules on how to interpret and apply legal rules.[84]

One of the by-products of the general principle of good faith is that it protects legitimate expectations by prohibiting states from acting inconsistently with such expectations (or obligating states to act consistently with them).[85] There have been several precedents affirming the legal protection of legitimate expectations. In *Certain German Interests in Upper Silesia*, for instance, the Permanent Court of International Justice held that Germany could not act against good faith by frustrating expectations.[86] In the Megalidis award, the arbitral tribunal considered the prohibition on frustrating the object of a treaty before it enters into force to be linked to the protection of legitimate expectations, thereby acknowledging this prohibition as an expression of good faith.[87] We can find similar references to protecting legitimate expectations in the *Preah Vihear* and *North Sea Continental Shelf* judgments.[88] In the recent *Obligation to Negotiate Access to the Pacific Ocean* case, however, the ICJ ruled otherwise:

> [R]eferences to legitimate expectations may be found in arbitral awards concerning disputes between a foreign investor and the host State that

[83] *Nuclear Tests (Australia v France)* (Judgment) [1974] ICJ Rep 253 [46].

[84] K Schmalenbach, 'Article 26' in O Dörr and K Schmalenbach (eds), *Vienna Convention on the Law of Treaties: A Commentary* (2nd edn, Springer 2018) 473.

[85] B Cheng, *General Principles of Law as Applied by International Courts and Tribunals* (Cambridge University Press 1994) s 5.C; Reinhold (n 81) 54. As explained in Section 2, a prohibition on acting is equivalent to an obligation not to act. We might wonder if the general principle of good faith is not itself this rule on legitimate expectations. As pointed out above, good faith leads to many legal by-products. Some of them are tied to prohibiting states from acting inconsistently, but others are focused on legal interpretation and rule application. We can also think of *pacta sunt servanda*, *rebus sic stantibus*, and the prohibition of *abus de droit*, which are also derivatives of good faith. In any case, it is theoretically possible to perceive good faith as a rule protecting legitimate expectations. But in this chapter we formulate it as a general principle which has as a corollary the rule that protects legitimate expectations by prohibiting acts inconsistent with such expectations. This theoretical choice allows for a simple conditions⇒conclusion formulation, as will become clear.

[86] *Case Concerning Certain German Interests in Polish Upper Silesia* (Merits) [1926] PCIJ Rep 5 Series A No 7.

[87] 'A. A. Megalidis v Turkey' [1932] 4 ADPILC 395.

[88] *Case Concerning the Temple of Preah Vihear (Cambodia v Thailand)* (Merits, Separate Opinion of Vice-President Alfaro) [1962] ICJ Rep 39; *North Sea Continental Shelf* (Judgment, Separate Opinion of Judge Fouad Ammoun) [1969] ICJ Rep 101.

> apply treaty clauses providing for fair and equitable treatment. It does not follow from such references that there exists in general international law a principle that would give rise to an obligation on the basis of what could be considered a legitimate expectation.[89]

Consequently, there is some controversy over whether there is a general rule of international law protecting legitimate expectations. But that does not affect the second explanation's account of how the legal obligation materialises. The legal obligation to Φ emerges from the general principle of good faith, particularly from a rule that obligates states to Φ if the practice of engaging in Φ generates legitimate expectations. Let us call this rule 'L'. We can formulate it like this:

Conditions: 'X is a state' and 'X engages in Φ' and 'X engaging in Φ generates legitimate expectations' – Conclusion: 'X is obligated to Φ'

The ICJ's statement in *Obligation to Negotiate Access to the Pacific Ocean* puts us in a predicament. If we were to ignore its pronouncement, we could say that L is a rule of international law that creates an international legal obligation enforceable under international law, full stop. However, this is not the line taken in this chapter, which therefore contemplates that L may not be a general rule of international law. Even so, it is still possible to say that L leads to a legal obligation in a broad sense, because L is a by-product of the general principle of good faith.

According to the ICJ in *Obligation to Negotiate Access to the Pacific Ocean*, L alone does not create an obligation under general international law. Nonetheless, L can still create an enforceable obligation if a source can be found in a specific provision of international law. As pointed out by Judge ad hoc Daudet, invoking good faith to protect legitimate expectations is effective only when it comes with a clear legal underpinning.[90] Even if L's obligation may not be directly enforceable under general international law, it is still a legal obligation because it results from good faith, which is a general principle of law. This is precisely why states feel they have a legal obligation even before a CIL rule exists. The obligation materialised in L is legal because it follows from the general principle of good faith. Even though the ICJ says that L is not a rule of general international law, this does not mean that L does not constitute law. If we can trace L back to a specific provision of

[89] *Obligation to Negotiate Access to the Pacific Ocean (Bolivia v Chile)* (Merits) [2018] ICJ Rep 507 [162].

[90] *Obligation to Negotiate Access to the Pacific Ocean (Bolivia v Chile)* (Merits, Dissenting Opinion of Judge ad hoc Daudet) [2018] ICJ Rep 607 [45].

international law (source interpretation), the obligation in L becomes enforceable under international law.

Saying that L is 'outside' general international law may even support the second explanation's account of CIL. This is because this claim would match Fitzmaurice's explanation about 'outer rules' being the basis for the coherence of international law:

> The system of international law cannot be clothed with force by a principle that is part of the system itself; for unless the system already had force, that principle itself would have no validity, and there would be a *circulus inextricabilis* or *viciosus*.[91]

If we try to solve the problem posed by the chronological paradox without using elements that are not part of international law, we might run into a problem similar to the 'this sentence is false' self-reference antinomy: if 'this sentence is false' is false, then it is true; if it is true, then it is false.[92] One way of dealing with such antinomies is to follow Tarski, who suggested separating elements into distinct, hierarchically arranged sets to prevent them from looping back on themselves.[93] Accordingly, if L lies above international law, then L is a legal rule *about* international law, but not *of* international law. This arrangement allows us to avoid the chronological paradox, because we are outside international law when adducing L. However, we are still within the law when L applies, because L is still part of a legal set. In other words, we are outside of international law but within the general framework of the law.[94]

We are now in a position to understand how a CIL rule R is created according to the second explanation. Suppose that a state S1 engages in Φ and that S1's engaging in Φ generates legitimate expectations among states S2, S3 … Sn that S1 will continue to Φ. Thus, L is applicable. If L applies, L imposes on S1 the obligation to Φ. L's obligation is legal because it comes from the principle of good faith, a general principle of law. Now, imagine that, in addition to S1, a large group of other states also start to Φ. Their action creates legitimate expectations among the

91 See G Fitzmaurice, 'The Law and Procedure of the International Court of Justice, 1954–9: General Principles and Sources of International Law' (1959) 35 BYIL 183, 195.

92 G Priest, 'The Structure of the Paradoxes of Self-Reference' (1994) 103 Mind 25.

93 On Tarski's escape from the self-reference antinomy, see M Gruber, *Alfred Tarski and the 'Concept of Truth in Formalized Languages'* (Springer 2016).

94 This ensures that L and M are a part of the same activity or 'language game'. Wittgenstein (n 1) para 23. On international law and language games, see A Carty, 'Language Games of International Law' (2012) 13 Melb JIL 1.

rest of the international community. L applies to each of these states, such that any state that engages in Φ is now obligated to Φ. So, M becomes applicable as states generally engage in Φ and (due to L) these states are obligated to Φ. If M applies, it creates a CIL rule R that imposes on all states the obligation to Φ.

There are two main differences between L and R. The first is that L applies only to states that are actively engaging in Φ. This means that, under L, only states that are actively engaging in Φ are obligated to Φ. Conversely, R applies to all states (not just those that are engaging in Φ). R obligates all states to Φ. In other words, L applies individually, and R applies universally. Nonetheless, an exception to R can be made for persistent objectors.[95] The ILC explains that if a state objects to a CIL rule while it is still being created, the rule does not apply to that state as long as it maintains its objection.[96] So, R does not apply to any objecting states. The exception to the exception is when R is a peremptory rule of international law (*jus cogens*),[97] in which case it will also apply to persistent objectors. The second difference between L and R is shown by the ICJ's decision in the *Obligation to Negotiate Access to the Pacific Ocean* case. While L imposes a legal obligation to Φ, that obligation might not be enforceable within general international law. Conversely, when M applies and creates R, the obligation to Φ that R imposes is perfectly enforceable as this obligation is now sourced in (customary) international law. Because R is a CIL rule, it is fully enforceable by international courts and legal officials.

A simple illustration may help to clarify this explanation, highlighting how M, L, and R can address the chronological paradox. Let us go back to our vaccine donation example. Suppose a subgroup of wealthy states began donating vaccines to developing states during a pandemic. These wealthy states donate vaccines without any prior obligations. But these donations create legitimate expectations in developing states that vaccines will continue to be provided by wealthy states. L is thus applicable. If L applies, it imposes a legal obligation on that subgroup of wealthy states to continue donating vaccines to developing states. Because of the legal obligation imposed by L, that subgroup of wealthy states continues to donate vaccines. Suppose that an increasing number

[95] On exceptions see J Hage, A Waltermann and G Arosemena Solorzano, 'Exceptions in International Law' in L Bartels and F Paddeu (eds), *Exceptions and Defences in International Law* (Oxford University Press 2018) 11.

[96] ILC (n 10) 152.

[97] ibid.

of wealthy states start to adopt this practice. Due to L's application to each of these states, this practice becomes a general, legally obligatory practice. So, the two CIL elements (*diuturnitas* and *opinio juris*) are satisfied. M is now applicable. If M applies, a CIL Rule R is created, imposing on all wealthy states the obligation to donate vaccines to developing states. R, unlike L, is an enforceable rule of general international law.

5 Final Remarks

This chapter argued that CIL rules result from applying a constitutive metarule. A constitutive metarule is a metarule (a rule about rules) that creates another rule when applied. When the constitutive CIL metarule (which we call M) applies, it creates an individual CIL rule (referred to as R). This chapter has proposed two alternative explanations for how a belief in a legal obligation (*opinio juris*) can arise prior to the imposition of such an obligation by a CIL rule. In doing so, it assumes in both cases that states are correct in believing they are legally obligated. So there is not just a belief in a legal obligation; there actually is a legal obligation.

The first explanation presented the obligation as a basic social entity based directly on what states believe. Some may be satisfied with this explanation. However, others might criticise it for failing to bridge the gap between 'is' and 'ought'. It could also be argued that this first explanation does not clarify how this basic social entity can impose a *legal* obligation. For these reasons, this chapter laid aside this first explanation and went on to develop an alternative explanation.

The second explanation addresses the chronological paradox by breaking down the creation of a new CIL rule R into three non-contradictory steps:

Step 1: A subgroup of states starts to act in a certain way. Their behaviour leads to legitimate expectations that they will continue acting that way. This subgroup of states is now obligated to continue acting pursuant to a rule derived from the principle of good faith (we call this rule L). However, because this obligation arises from a rule (L) outside general international law, its enforceability is questionable.

Step 2: The practice of this subgroup of states spreads among other states to the point where it becomes a general practice accepted as law. So, the two CIL elements – *diuturnitas* and *opinio juris* – are present. Therefore, the CIL metarule, M, is now applicable.

Step 3: M applies, thus creating a specific CIL rule, R. This CIL rule R imposes an obligation to act on all states except for persistent objectors (unless R is a *jus cogens* rule, in which case it applies even to persistent objectors).

The creation of a new CIL rule as a three-step process allows us to unravel the apparent circularity of the chronological paradox. It also allows the creation of CIL rules to be explained in such a way as not to jeopardise the coherence (and legitimacy) of (customary) international law.

Some of the claims made in this chapter might seem controversial, because it is unusual to think of CIL rules as being created through the application of a (meta)rule. We are more inclined to think that it is a matter of finding already formed CIL rules rather than creating them. But that intuition is not incompatible with the contention made in this chapter. For when we find CIL rules, we are doing more than just describing; we are giving meaning to the things being interpreted. In the case of CIL, these things are the proof of practice (*diuturnitas*) and belief in a legal obligation (*opinio juris*). We should consider the CIL metarule as an unspoken rule that operates behind the scenes. Even if its action is unannounced, this metarule helps international lawyers interpret the law to identify individual CIL rules. The point is that for lawyers in their daily work the three steps set out above occur simultaneously, giving the impression that CIL rules are paradoxical. By looking at CIL analytically, however, we have been able to pinpoint these separate steps and show that CIL is not flawed by circular reasoning.

Like the rules of chess, the CIL metarule operates in the background. When experts play chess, they do not have to keep referring to the rules and reminding themselves that, for example they are using the checkmate rule: when they look at the chessboard, they know it is checkmate. The same is true in international law, with the important difference, however, that law is an argumentative activity.[98] Unlike chess, it is not an activity where all the rules are laid down categorically. On the contrary, the law involves deploying and disputing the very rules that constitute it. Part of what it means to be a lawyer is the ability to understand and question the law itself. In this respect, one of the goals of legal philosophy is to make the implicit background rules of legal activity explicit.

[98] Dworkin (n 41) 13. See also Brandom (n 64) 649–50.

3

Interpreting the Plural Sources of CIL

HARLAN GRANT COHEN

1 Introduction

When faced with the inevitable task of interpreting customary international law (CIL), what should a court do, and what should it consider? Should the court engage in an 'inductive' process of sifting through available evidence of state practice and *opinio juris*, or a deductive process designed to reason logically from principles embedded in the rule? Should the court invoke something like the rules of treaty interpretation with their focus on good faith, ordinary meaning, context, and object and purpose? How should it weigh available evidence of state practice, *opinio juris*, and prior interpretations – both its own and that of others? How concerned should the court be about fitting its interpretation into the broader corpus of international law?

This is where international law doctrine – particularly concerning sources – falls short. Figuring out how to interpret and apply custom requires a theory of custom. What is customary international law? Why is it worthy of being followed? How does custom acquire normative and legal authority? These are difficult and contentious questions we (and certainly courts) usually try to avoid.[1] The doctrine of sources does not

The author is indebted to Marina Fortuna and the organizers of the December 2021 TRICI-Law conference, where an earlier version of this chapter was first presented. Thanks also go to Dan Bodansky, Evan Criddle, Andreas Follesdal, Kostia Gorobets, Fleur Johns, David Lefkowitz, Nahuel Maisley, Steve Ratner, Nicole Roughan, and Oisin Suttle for helping to work through the ideas expressed in this chapter and to Sarah Burns for helping to round it into shape.

[1] See M Fortuna, 'Different Strings of the Same Harp: Interpretation of Customary International Rules, Their Identification and Treaty Interpretation' in P Merkouris, J Kammerhofer, and N Arajärvi (eds), *The Theory, Practice and Interpretation of Customary International Law* (Cambridge University Press 2021) (observing that 'hardly

answer them. Article 38 of the Statute of the International Court of Justice (arguably) lists the formal sources of international law – treaties, customary international law, and general principles. Its formulation 'international custom, as evidence of a general practice accepted as law'[2] has been interpreted as implying a two-element test, requiring evidence of both state practice and *opinio juris*.[3] But it provides no account of why those elements would, together, create law or be deserving of normative authority. The International Law Commission (ILC) also studiously avoided these questions in its Draft Conclusions on Identification of Customary International Law.[4]

This is perhaps not surprising. These theoretical questions are difficult and contentious. International actors disagree over the answers, sometimes deeply. And Article 38 and the two-element test might best be seen as an attempt to bridge such theoretical disputes. It encodes formal sources that we agree count as international law, without encoding why. Focused on method rather than theory, the doctrine provides a discursive convention – an agreed-upon framework for structuring claims about rules that is capacious enough to accommodate a range of views on where they come from. It acts as a normative compromise that allows us to operate on the basis of overlapping consensus while leaving room for a certain amount of normative pluralism. If Article 38 and the two-element test count as a rulebook,[5] it is a rulebook on how to argue.

Questions about interpretation, however, reveal the instability of this compromise. We simply cannot answer questions about how rules should be interpreted without some theory as to why certain interpretations would or would not be legitimate. And for an interpretation to be legitimate it must be able to trace its legitimacy to that of the international law source being interpreted and/or the legitimacy of the particular interpreter. Figuring out both requires looking behind the list of sources

any theoretical account of customary international law can coherently explain what it is, how it emerges and how it develops').

[2] Statute of the International Court of Justice (adopted 26 June 1945, entered into force 24 October 1945) 33 UNTS 993, art 38(1)(b).

[3] See ILC, 'Draft Conclusions on Identification of Customary International Law, with Commentaries' (30 April–1 June and 2 July–10 August 2018) UN Doc A/73/10, 121, 124.

[4] ibid 124 ('[T]he draft conclusions do not address, directly, the processes by which customary international law develops over time . . . They do not . . . deal systematically with how such rules emerge, change, or terminate.').

[5] See generally M Hakimi, 'Making Sense of Customary International Law' (2020) 118 Mich L Rev 1487 (rejecting the rulebook approach to CIL).

in Article 38 and asking why we treat each one as a source of normative authority. It requires us to focus on the normative stories we tell.

Such an inquiry, though, reveals that there is not just one story explaining why custom should be a source of law, but multiple stories, each legitimated in very different ways. In fact, if we started not with Article 38 but with our accounts of international law's legitimacy, we would find, as I argue below, that what we call 'custom' may represent or draw from at least three different sources of law,[6] which I will refer to as 'Negotiated Law', 'Legislated Law', and 'Adjudicated Law'.[7] Although we refer to nontreaty rules derived from each as 'custom',[8] they draw on different sources of legitimacy, operate according to different logics, dictate different methods of interpretation, and favour different methods for resolving disputes. Answering questions about any of those aspects of the rule thus requires us first to figure out the sort of custom we are talking about. The types of justification we start with dictate the answer to a range of other questions we might have about the rules emanating from them. And those debating how custom should be interpreted, I argue, are often arguing about different sources of law. Their disagreement is not over how custom should be interpreted, but over the ultimate authority of particular international law rules.

Some readers may bristle at the suggestion that these are distinct 'sources' of law. Do we really need to upend our categories of treaty, custom, and general principles? To the extent, though, that the rules seem to be emanating from entirely distinct sources of legitimacy and operating according to contradictory logics, it is hard to describe them as the

[6] I am not the first to suggest that what we call 'customary international law' may, in fact, reflect more than one source or type of international law rules. See generally D Bodansky, 'Prologue to a Theory of Non-Treaty Norms' in MH Arsanjani and others (eds), *Looking to the Future: Essays on International Law in Honor of W. Michael Reisman* (Brill 2010); D Bodansky, 'Does Custom Have a Source?' (2014) 108 AJIL Unbound 179. In fact, the three sources of custom identified here bear some resemblance to Bodansky's categories of common law, declarative law, and the behaviour of states (Bodansky, 'Does Custom Have a Source' 180). The list is also not exclusive. A more exhaustive account would need to include a variety of potential natural law sources as well.

[7] While built on somewhat different explanations, these sources also very roughly coincide with notions of traditional custom, modern custom, and international common law proffered by others. See generally AE Roberts, 'Traditional and Modern Approaches to Customary International Law: A Reconciliation' (2001) 95 AJIL 757. One advantage of this account of international law's sources is that it may help explain the divergence between those categories.

[8] As will be explained in Section 2, these sources of justification cut across our formal sources. For our purposes here, though, we will focus primarily on custom.

same in any way other than form. As already noted, formal lip service to the features in Article 38 may play a role in anchoring discussions, but it is unlikely to capture deeper agreement about where these rules come from or what they represent.[9] These three models are meant to capture the true sources of these rules' authority.[10] That said, even if one is unwilling to embrace the idea of plural sources of custom, recognizing that there may be different types of custom may help clarify the stakes involved in debates over interpretation and in interpretive choices.

This chapter starts in Section 2 with a reconstruction of international law's sources built not on the forms described in Article 38 but instead on the legitimating stories we tell. Section 2 lays out three such stories and the types of law they describe. These three types of law – Negotiated Law, Legislated Law, and Adjudicated Law – each draw on distinct notions of legitimacy, follow distinct logics, and instantiate distinct values. Section 2 describes the very different notions of 'custom' emanating from each of these sources. Section 3 looks at each of these three new sources from the standpoint of interpretation. How are each of these sources interpreted? Section 3 explains how the justificatory story told about each of these sources flows through interpretation, requiring different approaches attentive to different concerns. Again, interpreting 'custom' will require very different approaches and operations depending on its ultimate source and justificatory logic. Finally, Section 4 shifts the vantage point to courts. How should courts approach the task of interpreting each of these sources? Each type of custom, this section argues, dictates not only its own interpretive rules but the specific role of the court in applying them and the weight to be given to the court's judgments in the future. The hope is that this reconstruction of international law's sources, including the identification of different types of custom, can put old arguments about custom and its interpretation in a new light, explain the intractability of certain fights, anchor phenomena that others have observed, and clarify the real stakes behind differing methods of interpretation.

[9] See Bodansky, 'Does Custom Have a Source?' (n 6) 180–81 ('Should we follow the example of Ptolemaic astronomers, who added epicycle upon epicycle to their descriptions of planetary motion, in their efforts to save the geocentric system? Or should we seek a paradigm shift, a new way of understanding the sources of international law?'). No one will be surprised if, like Bodansky, I favour the latter.

[10] To be clear, what I am exploring here is why people *think* certain rules have normative authority – the justifications they articulate. I leave to the side both whether these reasons are good and worthy of authority and whether they actually explain the operative authority of these rules.

2 Three Models of Custom

Article 38 largely describes international law's forms – written agreements, customary practices, accepted principles. What if we defined international law's sources instead according to their sources of legitimacy? What if we started by asking why we give international law rules normative force at all, listening more carefully to the explicit and implicit legitimating stories we tell? This section lays out three prominent stories we tell that cut across form, but for the purposes of this volume explains why nontreaty rules[11] might carry the force of law. Each of the stories produces a different model of law – Negotiated Law, Legislated Law, and Adjudicated Law – drawing legitimacy from different sources, instantiating different values, and following its own logic.

2.1 This Argument Never Ends . . .

Negotiated Law, as a model, is imagined as the product of settlements hashed out over time. These are hard-fought rules, subject to back-and-forth wrangling between states that might range in form and forum from negotiations around a table to jawboning in the media to conflict on the battlefield.[12] The rules that emerge represent a form of compromise, a pragmatic accommodation of different interests. Particularly successful rules reflect a common acceptable balance between states' freedom to take action now and the stability and predictability necessary to pursuing their interests generally.[13] But all of these rules are open-ended and tentative; they leave space for further negotiation and wrangling as circumstances and interests shift.[14] Negotiated Law, to use the words of Myres McDougal, is the product of 'a process of continuous interaction,

[11] See Bodansky, 'Prologue to a Theory of Non-Treaty Norms' (n 6).

[12] See Hakimi (n 5) 1493; see also MH Mendelson, 'The Formation of Customary International Law' (1998) 272 RdC 155, 189–91 ('Out of this constant process of claim and response rules emerge, are strengthened, or are superseded.'). For more on this model and other places where we might find it, see HG Cohen, 'International Law's *Erie* Moment' (2013) 34 MJIL 249, 257–70.

[13] GJ Postema, 'Custom, Normative Practice, and the Law' (2012) 62 DLJ 707, 726 ('Customs are relatively stable points or nodes in the network of expectations.').

[14] See Hakimi (n 5) 1495 ('[B]ecause the CIL process is continuous, a position's status or content within CIL can be transitory and elusive.'); Postema (n 13) 710 ('As such it is flexible, open to *reformulation* and *reformation*, and inviting rather than silencing *scrutiny*.').

of continuous demand and response'.[15] Upheld by a level of consensus among states, these rules shift as that consensus shifts.

Negotiated Law might be seen as a solution to international law's inherent fragmentation. How do we know what is expected of us and how do we guarantee that others know what we expect of them when the law's meaning is not revealed in a document but trapped inside our respective heads?[16] We know what we think it requires, but does anyone else agree? The only way to forge common expectations and to guarantee commitment to them is to talk – a lot.[17] Actors need to constantly explain where their acts fit within the community's rules, why their acts should be seen as conforming, why someone else's acts fail to meet their understanding of the rule. Constant communication, through words and acts, is the structure on which the law remains elevated, the container in which it is held. Without that jostling, the law would collapse or float away into the ether.

This model of the law finds its clearest form in descriptions of 'traditional' custom and the ways that the iterative practice of states can slowly over time produce settlement over rules. It is a model of customary law that Gerald Postema describes as emerging from discursive normative practice.[18] It is the anti-formalist, anti-rulebook model of custom described by Monica Hakimi.[19] But this model also describes traditional bilateral treaty agreements, whose legitimacy emanates from the particulars of the negotiated deal and whose rules are interpreted in light of subsequent practice and agreement between parties.[20]

15 MS McDougal, 'The Hydrogen Bomb Tests and the International Law of Sea' (1955) 49 AJIL 356, 357. Negotiation here may thus be more implicit than explicit. Rules emerge from a constant give-and-take ('negotiation'), but the results need not take the form of an explicit agreement.

16 For a rich account that seeks to move beyond this 'separation thesis', see C Turner, 'Interconstituted Legal Agents' (2022) University of Georgia School of Law Research Paper 2022-07, <https://papers.ssrn.com/sol3/papers.cfm?abstract_id=4049942> accessed 27 May 2022.

17 See generally J Brunnée and SJ Toope, *Legitimacy and Legality in International Law: An Interactional Account* (Cambridge University Press 2010).

18 Postema (n 13) 709 and passim.

19 See Hakimi (n 5) 1493–96.

20 See Vienna Convention on the Law of Treaties (adopted 23 May 1969, entered into force 27 January 1980) 1155 UNTS 331, art 31(3)(a) and (b). See also K Gorobets, 'Peaks and Valleys: Contemplating the Authority of International Law' in K Gorobets, A Hadjigeorgiou, and P Westerman (eds), *Conceptual (Re)Constructions of International Law* (Edward Elgar 2022) 171 (noting the commonality between CIL and bilateral treaties). General principles, the third sources mentioned in Article 38, generally are not described this way. Their

Whether taking the form of traditional custom or 'conventional' treaties, Negotiated Law derives its purported authority from notions of consent, autonomy, pragmatism, and the lessons of experience.[21] It elevates values of flexibility and supports efforts at renegotiation. States have fought and have accepted these results. They will continue to fight and test their resiliency. Rules that emerge from this process have proven to 'work'; rules that do not will be challenged. And the (perhaps only) theoretical ability to participate in this ongoing process of contestation and acceptance serves to legitimate the normative authority of settlements that emerge.[22] Rules are legitimated as much by the promise of future process as by the process that produced them.

2.2 But We Agreed . . .

But there are other stories we tell about both custom and treaties that sound far less like negotiated settlements than like forms of international legislation. In these stories, rules are propounded, proposed, and then accepted by some proportion of the community, whether by affirmative acts or by common, silent acquiescence. Rather than the iterative, open-ended, continuous process of acceptance reflected by Negotiated Law, this model assumes a moment in which a rule with particular elements is proffered, and a moment, or series of moments, in which affirmation is collected. Obviously, as with Negotiated Law, these justificatory stories are more metaphor than description.

What rules are described this way? The paradigmatic examples of international law rules described as Legislated Law are products of the ILC – both multilateral treaties, like the Vienna Convention on the Law of Treaties (VCLT), and reports on custom, like the draft articles on state responsibility. As many have noticed, the particular codifications of rules in these ILC products are often treated as fixed points. After they are issued, the relevant question is how they are received. If states' responses can generally be described positively (or at least not negatively), the rule as described by the ILC is taken as the rule of international law.[23] Only if

legitimacy is instead usually described either as a concomitant of rule of law principles or as derivative of their acceptance at the national law level.

21 Hakimi (n 5) 1525 ('CIL derives what legitimacy it has not from any secondary rules but from the process through which it is developed and used.').

22 ibid 1524–26.

23 As Stefan Talmon observes: 'In none of the cases where the Court has found a (draft) article of the ILC to reflect customary international law did it enquire whether the

the ILC's efforts have failed to receive requisite acceptance (whatever that means)[24] are investigations begun into traditional custom's elements of state practice and *opinio juris*.

But these stories of quasi-legislation are far more ubiquitous. Efforts at universalizing treaties have commonly been described this way, whether the Genocide Convention, the UN Charter's rules on the use of force, or the Rome Statute's codification of international criminal law. But key nonbinding declarations of international law rules have been described this way as well. This is, for example, how the International Court of Justice (ICJ) treats the UN General Assembly Declaration on Friendly Relations[25] in the *Nicaragua* decision.[26] The Stockholm Declaration[27] often receives similar treatment with regard to the prevention of trans-boundary environmental harm.[28] And sometimes customary international law, more broadly, is described and justified this way. Certainly, the way post-decolonization states were required to accept the full customary international *acquis* has this feel.[29] What was proffered in return for recognition was not participation in an ongoing process of

Commission was actually codifying international law or whether it was not perhaps progressively developing international law. In all cases, the ILC has served as a kind of pseudo-witness for a rule having acquired the status of customary international law.' S Talmon, 'Determining Customary International Law: The ICJ's Methodology between Induction, Deduction and Assertion' (2015) 26 EJIL 417, 437.

24 One might compare here the more critical reception of the Draft Articles on the Responsibility of International Organizations to that of the much more successful Articles on the Responsibility of States for Internationally Wrongful Acts. See K Daugirdas, 'Reputation and the Responsibility of International Organizations' (2014) 25 EJIL 991, 992; ILC, 'Draft Articles on the Responsibility of International Organizations' (2011) UN Doc A/66/10; ILC, 'Draft Articles on Responsibility of States for Internationally Wrongful Acts, with Commentaries' (23 April–1 June and 2 July–10 August 2001) UN Doc A/56/10.

25 Declaration on Principles of International Law Concerning Friendly Relations and Co-operation among States in Accordance with the Charter of the United Nations, UNGA Res 2625 (XXV) (24 October 1970).

26 *Military and Paramilitary Activities in and against Nicaragua (Nicaragua v United States of America)* (Merits) [1986] ICJ Rep 14, eg [264].

27 Stockholm Declaration on the Human Environment in 'Report of the United Nations Conference on the Human Environment' (Stockholm 5–16 June 1972) (16 June 1972) UN Doc. A/CONF. 48/14, at 2 and Corr. 1.

28 See J Vessey, 'The Principle of Prevention in International Law' (1998) 3 ARIEL 181, 182 (observing that 'the Stockholm Declaration contains the most widely cited version of the principle'); *Legality of the Threat or Use of Nuclear Weapons* (Advisory Opinion) [1996], ICJ Rep 226 [27], [29].

29 See R Mohamad, 'Some Reflections on the International Law Commission Topic "Identification of Customary International Law"' (2016) 15 Chinese JIL 41; ILA, Committee on the Formation of Customary (General) International Law, 'Statement of

jawboning and negotiation, but instead a supposedly set canon of established international law rules. But more generally, this model of Legislated Law seems implicit in how many people talk about customary international law in a modern world of 200 states. The old rough-and-tumble model, perhaps a fit for a small clique of states, seems neither practicable nor fair in this broader community. [30] Instead, proposed rules are tested by surveying reactions: where a sufficient number of states seem to have accepted the rule, it reflects custom; where a sufficient number object, the rule is rejected.

Deriving rules more from multilateral documents than from traditional state practice, Legislated Law seems to describe some of the phenomena others have described as 'modern' custom.[31] But Legislated Law focuses less on the normative content of the rule than on the justificatory story told. Human rights and humanitarian concerns are often described in ways that sound more like Legislated Law than Negotiated Law,[32] but they are often the rules most likely to be the subjects of universalizing treaty negotiations or attempts to declare custom. This is what these rules have in common with subjects like treaty interpretation or state responsibility, which are arguably less value-driven but seem to be derived in similar ways.

Crucially, this type of Legislated Law is a very different source from traditional notions of custom best described as Negotiated Law. Whereas Negotiated Law derives its authority from its flexible, open-ended, rough-and-tumble process and the battle-tested nature of current settlements, Legislated Law derives its authority from particular imagined moments of proposal and ratification. Whereas Negotiated Law elevates a type of specific consent associated with settlements, Legislated Law relies on a more democratic type of consent associated with voting. The

Principles Applicable to the Formation of General Customary International Law' (2000) 24–25.

30 As has been oft noted, the traditional model of Negotiated Law favours action over inaction and the powerful, better-resourced states more able to monitor activity and defend their interests. The vast majority of states are rendered (or kept) voiceless – rule-takers rather than rule-makers. Legislated Law, with its emphasis on formal processes of articulation and a more democratic notion of ratification, shifts that power more towards the majority.

31 See Roberts (n 7). See also Talmon (n 23) 429.

32 Choi and Gulati note, for example, that international courts seem more likely to look to treaties and international organization declarations when assessing customs related to human rights and international humanitarian law. See SJ Choi and M Gulati, 'Customary International Law: How Do Courts Do It?' in CA Bradley (ed), *Custom's Future: International Law in a Changing World* (Cambridge University Press 2016) 117, 145.

open-ended, never-ending give-and-take of Negotiated Law (supposedly) promises any state the ability to participate in shaping or reshaping the rule over time; the fixed point of Legislated Law guarantees a type of majority rule, freed from the whim of powerful states. And whereas Negotiated Law celebrates flexibility and renegotiation; Legislated Law promotes the stability and predictability of recognized rules.

2.3 *Use Your Best Judgment . . .*

Finally, we have a model of Adjudicated Law. This is law produced or articulated through judicial or judicial-like decision-making. This justificatory story emphasizes the value of neutral, reasoned articulation of the rules, removed from power politics. This model comes closest to notions of common law and, like common law, looks to third-party decision-makers to fill the inevitable gaps in prior agreements and practice.[33] It imagines delegation to courts as a type of preemptive hand-tying, requiring states to live up to the principles of their agreements, even as their politics might suggest otherwise. In this model, courts are there not just to resolve disputes[34] but to apply the law. The law, not the wishes of the parties, prevails.[35]

Various international courts and court-like bodies – the European Court of Human Rights, the Inter-American Court of Human Rights, the World Trade Organization Appellate Body, the UN Human Rights Committee – have told such stories about themselves to justify interpretations less deferential to state views. Some investment tribunals have as well.[36] These stories may or may not resonate with all of those bodies' stakeholders. But Adjudicated Law also describes a range of rules that

[33] See eg I Ehrlich and RA Posner, 'An Economic Analysis of Legal Rulemaking' (1974) 3 JLS 257, 258, 261.

[34] See EA Posner and JC Yoo, 'Judicial Independence in International Tribunals' (2005) 93 CLR 1.

[35] See N Grossman, 'Solomonic Judgments and the Legitimacy of the International Court of Justice' in N Grossman and others (eds), *Legitimacy and International Courts* (Cambridge University Press 2018) 43; see also LR Helfer and AM Slaughter, 'Why States Create International Tribunals: A Response to Professors Posner and Yoo' (2005) 93 CLR 901, 942.

[36] To be clear, courts and court-like bodies are not the only ones who can or might articulate this view of the law. Based on reasoned articulation, many legal 'experts' may claim this authority, whether they are self-designated (scholars?) or given a specific formal role (UN special rapporteurs).

exist only in and for courts. International criminal tribunals could not rely on state practice to develop rules of *mens rea* or forms of liability; a type of common law articulation, attentive to commonly held principles of justice, was all that was available. International courts also need to be attentive to concerns about procedural fairness and fairness to parties, irrelevant outside the courtroom, producing procedural or evidentiary rules distinct to adjudication.

Justifying or legitimating this kind of court-made law requires recourse to different values. Adjudicated Law derives its authority from implied or explicit delegation; the authority of the decision-maker; the power of reasoned exposition; and neutral, even-handed consideration. In contrast to Negotiated Law, which emphasizes values like pragmatism, open-endedness, flexibility, and continued negotiation, Adjudicated Law emphasizes uniformity of treatment,[37] even-handedness, finality, and justice.[38]

2.4 Talking With, and Yet Past, One Another . . .

To put it another way, in Negotiated Law authority flows from the collective results of innumerable dyads of negotiating actors, who come to settle on particular rules; in Legislated Law authority flows from common, collective will; and in Adjudicated Law authority flows from judge or court (see Table 1). Putting form aside and focusing on these justifications, it becomes clear these are really different, and in some ways irreconcilable, sources. A particular rule might be traceable to multiple potential sources, but interpreting that rule requires identifying the right one.

This is not to suggest that identifying that source is easy or obvious. We each may slip between them as we talk about a rule. And while certain rules may often be associated with one source or another, disagreements over the ultimate source of these rules are common, reflected in the types of justifications used.[39] Meant to provide common rules across a range of states and cultures, international law is deeply pluralistic, accommodating significant disagreement even over the ultimate source of the law's

[37] For more on the role of uniformity in Adjudicated Law, see n 80 and accompanying text.

[38] See Cohen, 'International Law's *Erie* Moment' (n 12) 259–66.

[39] Some may also take categorical approaches, believing that all customary international law rules, for example, can and should be associated with only one of these sources. Such a categorical approach to the justificatory source should and likely will result in an equally categorical approach to interpretation.

Table 1 *Justification-based sources of international law*

	Negotiated Law	Legislated Law	Adjudicated Law
Underlying logic	Product of settlements hashed out over time	Broad (precisely how much unclear) acquiescence to some stated proposition	Product of reasoned elaboration and application by experts
Justification	Specific consent, autonomy, pragmatic experience, flexibility	Common consent, certainty, predictable planning	Delegation, expertise, neutrality, finality, justice
Examples	Traditional custom, bilateral treaties such as BITs	Articles on State Responsibility, VCLT, Genocide Convention	Regime-specific precedents, general public international law (PIL) precedents

authority. Such disagreements may help explain some of the most difficult and intractable fights over rules. Take, for example, fights over a potential 'unwilling or unable' standard for self-defense against non-state actors. Those supporting such a rule often draw from a Negotiated Law model, arguing that the rules must pragmatically respond to reality and focusing on the rules being hashed out by those taking these actions; under this model those states responding to attacks by non-state actors are a specially affected group, whose actions and interactions help define the resulting rule.[40] For many of those opposed, the argument seems derived from a Legislated Law model; looking to fixed points like the UN Charter, they question whether the 'unwilling or unable' standard is what was agreed on or whether, now proffered, sufficient states have accepted it.[41] Others focus on Adjudicated Law, placing heavy weight on the ICJ's

[40] See eg SA Yeini, 'The Specially-Affecting States Doctrine' (2018) 112 AJIL 244. See also generally AS Deeks, 'Unwilling or Unable: Toward a Normative Framework for Extraterritorial Self-Defense' (2012) 52 VJIL 483.

[41] See KJ Heller, 'Specially-Affected States and the Formation of Custom' (2018) 112 AJIL 191 (developing such an account).

prior reasoned articulation of customary international law of self-defense;[42] for them, ignoring the ICJ's views would violate notions of rule of law, coherence, predictability, and fairness.

Immunity presents another good example. Disagreements over whether states or officials should retain their immunity in the face of alleged international crimes seem fuelled by competing models of where those rules would come from. While a majority of the ICJ looks to state practice,[43] others look to quasi-legislative moments like Nuremberg,[44] or seek to reason from broader principles of international law.[45] These disagreements are often coded as doctrinal or interpretative, but they seem to run much deeper; those arguing over immunity are actually arguing over the ultimate source of those rules.

And while these three models do reflect different sources of international law, they are not hermetically sealed. Rules can over time be translated from one source to another – a rule developed through Negotiated Law may over time be rearticulated as a form of Legislated Law. This process is most explicit with many ILC products[46] but may happen more implicitly as particular rules becomes canonized through repetition in declarations, judgments, and treatises.[47] As some have noted, when rules seem to become 'established' in this way, they take on new characteristics and are interpreted in a different way, as explained

[42] See eg KJ Heller, 'The Law of Neutrality Does Not Apply to the Conflict with Al-Qaeda, and It's a Good Thing, Too: A Response to Chang' (2011) 47 TILJ 115, 140; ME O'Connell, 'Remarks: The Resort to Drones under International Law' (2011) 39 Denv J Intl L & Pol'y 585, 594–95.

[43] See *Jurisdictional Immunities of the State (Germany v Italy; Greece intervening)* (Merits) [2012] ICJ Rep 99; *Arrest Warrant (Democratic Republic of the Congo v Belgium)* (Jurisdiction and Admissibility) [2002] ICJ Rep 3.

[44] See *The Prosecutor v Omar Hassan Ahmad Al Bashir* (Judgment in the Jordan Referral re Al-Bashir Appeal) ICC-02/05-01/09-397-Corr (6 May 2019) [103].

[45] See *Jurisdictional Immunities* (n 43) Dissenting Opinion of Judge Cançado Trindade 331.

[46] Particularly intriguing here is the ILC's citation in the final Draft Articles on State Responsibility to the ICJ's decision in *Gabčíkovo Nagymaros, Gabčíkovo-Nagymaros Project (Hungary v Slovakia)* (Merits) [1997] ICJ Rep 7, a decision which favourably cited the ILC's first draft report on the subject, a draft which was itself a distillation of state practice. See J d'Aspremont, 'Canonical Cross-Referencing in the Making of the Law of International Responsibility' in S Forlati, M Mbengue, and B McGarry (eds), *The Gabčíkovo-Nagymaros Judgment and Its Contribution to the Development of International Law* (2020) 22.

[47] Think here, for example, of how, regularly repeated, Daniel Webster's particular formulation of the customary international law of anticipatory self-defense – 'a necessity of self-defense, instant, overwhelming, leaving no choice of means, and no moment for deliberation' – is now interpreted almost as text, with each word parsed as if deliberately chosen.

in Section 3. Alternatively, a customary international law rule developed through adjudication can become an input into the process of negotiation, its development and articulation moved out of the realm of judicial reasoning and into Negotiated Law's 'bid and barter' system.[48]

3 Interpretive Paths

Negotiated Law, Legislated Law, and Adjudicated Law each have their own sources of legitimacy and operate according to attendant logics. Each reflects a coherent story as to why a rule developed and operating in a particular way should carry normative authority, why it deserves to be treated as law. For interpretations of those rules to benefit from those rules' legitimacy, they must be able to fit within those same stories. What legitimates the rule should also legitimate interpretation. This means that interpretation will look different, involving different processes and considerations, depending on the asserted source of the rule. These divergent methods of interpretation also help explain why the interpretability of custom remains so controversial: those taking opposing views may simply be focused on different sources, all unfortunately labelled 'custom'.

3.1 *Interpreting Arguments*

Negotiated Law, or traditional custom, is what scholars likely have in mind when they argue that customary international law cannot be interpreted.[49] As explained in Section 2.2, Negotiated Law imagines the law as a product of a constant, never-ending discursive dance between states. Every interaction involves claims about the nature, scope, and application of the rule that may or may not be accepted by others.[50] In the Negotiated Law model, rules are constantly being made and remade through arguments and actions. Even when relatively stable, the rule is not static; whether it will change or remain the same are both determined

[48] See, for example, Ezgi Yildiz and Umut Yüksel's investigation of the role of ICJ judgments in maritime boundary negotiations. E Yildiz and U Yüksel, 'Limits of Behavioral Approaches: Lessons from the Field of Maritime Boundary Making' (2022) 23 GLJ 413–30.

[49] See eg T Treves, 'Customary International Law' para 2 (2006) MPEPIL <https://opil.ouplaw.com/display/10.1093/law:epil/9780199231690/law-9780199231690-e1393> accessed 27 March 2024; M Bos, *A Methodology of International Law* (Elsevier 1984).

[50] 'Claims are advanced and interpretations and defenses of actions are offered; exchanges of interpretations are made with other parties; counterclaims or challenges are advanced; arguments are offered, reviewed, assessed, and answered.' Postema (n 13) 728.

by the arguments states have made, are making, or will make.[51] As Postema writes: 'No one, not even the entire community, has unchallengeable, final say on what the norms of the practice are.'[52] Authoritative interpretation is an inapposite concept. Interpretations of the rule melt into the process of argumentation, becoming a 'bid' for what the rule is that can be accepted, modified, or rejected as states dance or wrestle (depending on the mood) over the rule.[53]

This, though, does not mean that Negotiated Law is not interpreted. On the contrary, it is and must be constantly interpreted. As Orfeas Chasapis Tassinis observes, deriving rules from practices requires more than just observation.[54] It requires the 'imposition of meaning'[55] on those observations, a process that requires theorizing and categorizing[56] – in other words, interpretation. But in Negotiated Law this theorizing goes in both directions.[57] Practices are themselves arguments, reflecting views on what rules do or should require.[58] Actors committed to being part of a rule-based community must assess how and where their actions will fit within others' expectations of what the rules mean and require.[59] In the

[51] ibid 726 ('custom following is never a matter of rote repetition'). Başak Etkin beautifully evokes the image of the river to describe this reality, in which flux is the constant and defining state of customary international law. B Etkin, 'The Changing Rivers of Customary International Law: The Interpretative Process as Flux' (2022) 11(5) ESIL Reflections <https://esil-sedi.eu/esil-reflection-the-changing-rivers-of-customary-international-law-the-interpretative-process-as-flux/> accessed 16 December 2022.

[52] Postema (n 13) 728. See also Hakimi (n 5) 1494 ('No one entity is entitled to assess the various claims on an issue, weed out the outliers, and finally settle CIL's normative content.'); MJ Durkee, 'Interpretive Entrepreneurs' (2021) 107 VLR 431, 442 (describing interpretation of international law as 'decentralized').

[53] Etkin (n 51) ('While interpretation is done in an active sense by an actor invested with the authority to interpret the rule, be it for instance a court or a state, change (as an umbrella term for modification, evolution and beyond as used in this paper) is the result of that process, and all of these phenomena contribute to the rule's flux.')

[54] OC Tassinis, 'Customary International Law: Interpretation from Beginning to End' (2020) 31 EJIL 235, 243 ('Observation is then itself theory-laden.').

[55] A Marmor, *Interpretation and Legal Theory* (2nd edn, Hart 2005) 25.

[56] See Chapter 1.

[57] See Etkin (n 51) ('[T]he direction of fit is doubled, as the interpreting authority, while trying to fit world to word, also fits word to world.').

[58] K Gorobets, 'Practical Reasoning and Interpretation of Customary International Law' in P Merkouris, J Kammerhofer, and N Arajärvi (eds), *The Theory, Practice and Interpretation of Customary International Law* (Cambridge University Press 2021) 382 ('This is precisely why, even when states do not explicate their position regarding actions of other states, this may still contribute to formation of a new, or sustaining an existing, practice.'), also 375 (observing that 'state practices are not only the *containers* but also the *content* of rules one wants to interpret').

[59] This is precisely why, even when states do not explicate their position regarding actions of other states, this may still contribute to the formation of a new, or sustaining of an

model of Negotiated Law, actors' interactions are structured by their understanding of the rules. Interpretation is embedded in every action and interaction.[60]

This, though, is where interpretation of Negotiated Law diverges from the more textual methods of interpretation. Negotiated Law is intersubjective. Its meaning is a function, not of a particular formulation, written or unwritten, but of the networked expectations of members of the community. The questions one must ask in interpreting the law are not 'what does this rule mean?' but 'what do others think the rule is and how would others apply it to my potential conduct?' As Postema writes 'Caught in the net of interactions, one must know not only what others have done, but also how they understand what they have done, what they expect one to do, and so how they expect one to understand what one has done and what they have done.'[61]

Nor does Negotiated Law imagine any interpretation as an end point. Instead, interpretation and action are embedded in an ongoing dance, a give-and-take over the rules. For Negotiated Law, interpretation is thus both a form of second-person thinking – a prediction of what others think the rule is – and a first-person assertion – a proffer of a desired interpretation going forward.[62]

The ever forward-looking nature of this enterprise also means that interpretation is somewhat open-ended and tentative, an attempt to discern the space open for action, the negative space between prior negotiations. While actors must determine what actions are definitively forbidden, they do not need to determine the four corners of a particular rule. Quite the contrary, interpretation should foster the same values of flexibility, pragmatism, and renegotiation that the rules themselves are thought to promote. Interpreting away the rules' frayed edges may make future negotiations more difficult.

existing, practice. Even an absence of reaction may, under certain circumstances, be deciphered by other participants in a practice meaningfully either as endorsement or at least as acquiescence. Gorobets, 'Practical Reasoning' (n 58) 382.

60 ibid ('From this perspective, customary rules do not and cannot exist separately or detached from practices that sustain them.'). See also J d'Aspremont, 'The Multidimensional Process of Interpretation: Content-Determination and Law-Ascertainment Distinguished' in A Bianchi, D Peat, and M Windsor (eds), *Interpretation in International Law* (Oxford University Press 2015) 111, 114 ('all practices and discourses about international law having an interpretive dimension').

61 Postema (n 13) 728.

62 See Chapter 1 (where Westerman describes a 'practice of claims' in which *opinio juris* is understood best 'not as a conviction or belief' but 'as an articulated and publicly accessible claim'). See also d'Aspremont (n 60) 113.

All of this, as I will explain in Section 4 (and have explained elsewhere[63]), is a difficult, perhaps impossible, task for courts, whose mandate and institutional role may conflict with the logic and legitimacy of Negotiated Law. But courts are not the paradigmatic interpreters in this model.[64] Instead, they are sometime interlopers, used more for ad hoc dispute settlement than for rule development: 'authoritative determinations analogous to umpires' rulings are the exception'.[65] In Negotiated Law, interpretation is part of the daily life of living in an international community, practiced in every interaction, by all members of the community.[66]

3.2 *Interpreting Agreement*

The interpretation of Legislated Law, by contrast, comes much closer to the textual methods familiar to treaty law. Partly, this is because Legislated Law is often tied to texts – broad multilateral treaties, codification efforts, international organization declarations, judicial opinions, even treatises. Even if these are not directly binding, they nonetheless establish commonly accepted baselines that can be interpreted. But the analogy to treaties runs deeper. Legislated Law is meant to create common baselines and consensus around rules. It is meant to supersede the uncertainty and power politics of Negotiated Law/traditional custom. And it is meant to foster predictability and encourage planning. Predictability is both the point and the justification. Legislated Law is also legitimated by notions of ratification, in which states are imagined to have agreed, at least implicitly, to a specific rule. This notion of ratification, in turn, requires greater attention to what specifically was ratified.

Scholars endorsing the interpretability of custom often seem to have the model of Legislated Law in mind. It should perhaps not be surprising

63 Cohen, 'International Law's *Erie* Moment' (n 12); HG Cohen, 'Methodology and Misdirection: Custom and the ICJ' (*EJIL:Talk!*, 1 December 2015) <www.ejiltalk.org/methodology-and-misdirection-a-response-to-stefan-talmon-on-custom-and-the-icj/> accessed 27 May 2022.

64 FV Kratochwil, *Rules, Norms, and Decisions: On the Conditions of Practical and Legal Reasoning in International Relations and Domestic Affairs* (Cambridge University Press 1989) 102.

65 ibid.

66 'In the international system, which does not have the benefit of much judicial assistance, the norms are interpreted, elaborated, shaped, reformulated, and applied in large part in the course of debate about the justification for contested action.' A Chayes and AH Chayes, *The New Sovereignty: Compliance with International Regulatory Agreements* (Harvard University Press 1995) 122.

that many of their examples involve customary rules said to be reflected in multilateral treaties, ILC codification efforts, or declarations of international organizations. (Such efforts themselves have often been described as more legislative than contractual.[67]) Panos Merkouris, for example, focuses in on the customary rules of interpretation and the ways they are interpreted in parallel with the VCLT.[68] But Legislated Law's justificatory stories seem also to run just below the surface of these arguments, which often attempt to distinguish between the period when rules are forming and the period after they 'come into existence'[69] or are 'established'. It imagines identification of a rule and interpretation as separate temporal stages (even if just for the purposes of theorizing).[70] This sort of description does not fit well with notions of Negotiated Law, in which the process never ends, rules are always debatable, and complete agreement over the rule is ephemeral at best.

Whereas interpreting Negotiated Law involves prediction and thus looks to the future (how will others respond?), interpreting Legislated Law is backward-looking, requiring excavation of what actually has been agreed, with help from ordinary meaning, context, and object and purpose. Along with other applicable rules from the VCLT, interpreting Legislated Law is also a good fit for the principle of systemic integration.[71] Imagined as the product of a concerted attempt at codification, it makes sense to imagine these rules as part of a more cohesive international law fabric. It makes sense to interpret them against the backdrop of other international rules, particularly other rules imagined to be similarly established within the international community.

3.3 *Interpreting Decision*

Interpretation of Adjudicated Law can look somewhat similar – in part, because judges often prefer to rely on state-created, rather than judge-made, law and may try to squeeze the latter into the rhetoric of the former whenever possible.[72] But following the alternative logic and justifications

[67] See eg B Clark, 'The Vienna Convention Reservations Regime and the Convention on Discrimination Against Women' (1991) 85 AJIL 281, 361.
[68] See P Merkouris, 'Interpreting the Customary Rules on Interpretation' (2017) 19 ICLR 126.
[69] ibid 128, 136.
[70] See Tassinis (n 54) 244–46.
[71] Vienna Convention on the Law of Treaties (n 20) art 31(3)(c).
[72] Cohen, 'International Law's *Erie* Moment' (n 12).

of Adjudicated Law, interpretation will look somewhat different. For one, designed to resolve disputes with some finality, Adjudicated Law is specifically meant to fill gaps, rather than leave them open. This contrasts interpretation of Adjudicated Law most starkly with Negotiated Law. Negotiated Law's open-ended interpretations are pushed aside in favour of binary ones, in which one side wins and one side loses, or one side's view of the law is right and the other's is wrong. But Adjudicated Law goes beyond mere dispute settlement. Adjudicated Law imagines courts playing a systemic role: Adjudicated Law should not just resolve present disputes but avoid future ones as well. This requires developing rules for prospective application: rules that states can rely on, and interpretations they can predict. But how are those gaps to be filled where the rules before them seem to run out? Adjudicated Law might be seen as a mandate, perhaps even an obligation, to find and apply broader principles of law that can fill the gaps. '[A]s Judge Higgins pointed out, it is "an important and well-established principle that the concept of *non-liquet* . . . is no part of the Court's jurisprudence".'[73]

Adjudicated Law thus dovetails well with some of the instances Stefan Talmon identifies, in which the ICJ uses deduction rather than induction to discern the content of customary international law. Talmon notes the ICJ's deduction from 'axiomatic principles such as sovereignty, sovereign equality or territorial sovereignty'[74] in cases like the *Jurisdictional Immunities of the State*, or 'general and well-recognized principles' in cases like *Corfu Channel*.[75] He also observes that the 'ICJ deduces rules from general considerations concerning the function of a person or organization'[76] in cases like *Reparations for Injuries*, *South West Africa*, and *Arrest Warrants*. But the logic of Adjudicated Law is visible in instances of what Talmon calls 'assertion' as well. In those decisions, regardless of evidence, the ICJ often justifies its interpretation on assertions of common knowledge.[77]

Courts also derive some of their authority to apply these rules from their respect for procedural and substantive fairness. They draw legitimacy from their ability to treat parties equally before the law and from their promise to treat like cases alike. These become especially weighty in

[73] *Legality of the Threat or Use of Nuclear Weapons*, Dissenting Opinion, in Talmon (n 23) 423.
[74] Talmon (n 23) 423.
[75] ibid 424.
[76] ibid 425.
[77] ibid 434–40.

international criminal law contexts, in which fairness and due process become matters of human rights. Predictability, for example, merges with the legality principle of *nullum crimen sine lege*. All of this creates incentive and pressure for courts to look to their own prior judgments and to adopt some notion of precedent.[78] Whatever pressure they feel to have their decisions cohere with the broader corpus of international law will face countervailing pressure to guarantee that their current interpretation coheres with their own prior interpretations.

At the same time, as Adjudicated Law relies on explicit or implicit delegation for its legitimacy, judges will also have to be attentive to their specific mandate in interpreting the rules. When they understand their mandate broadly as international courts within an international legal system, treating like cases alike may point to the work of other courts interpreting similar rules. When they understand their mandate more narrowly as extending only to a specific regime, they may feel pressure to hew closely to their own decisions even where courts outside the regime have decided differently.

In sum, though, the interpretative process of adjudicative law will focus much more on reasoned gap-filling and court-specific predictability. Adjudicated Law should make it easier for actors to know what to expect, both to avoid the courtroom and once inside it.

4 The Quandary of Courts

Negotiated Law, Legislated Law, and Adjudicated Law are thus best seen as distinct sources, with their own legitimating logics, favoring different interpretive techniques. These differences highlight the problem for courts of interpreting custom (or really any source of international law). Although ostensibly focused on one formal source in Article 38 – custom – courts are faced with a choice between divergent paths, a fork in the road, that will dictate the factors they should consider and the weight they should give them. These choices can be stark, resulting in contradictory interpretations of what custom requires. As such, courts need a theory, whether explicit or implicit, of what 'custom' is and where it comes from before they can interpret any particular rule before them.

[78] HG Cohen, 'Theorizing Precedent in International Law' in A Bianchi, D Peat, and M Windsor (eds), *Interpretation in International Law* (Oxford University Press 2015) 268, 282–83.

The challenge for courts can be illustrated well by the problem of coherence. We might want courts to worry about coherence,[79] but coherence with what? The different possible sources described here – Negotiated Law, Legislated Law, and Adjudicated Law – point to different concepts of coherence favoring different outcomes in specific cases. Here, we can go in the opposite order, moving from the source easiest for courts to interpret to the hardest.

Courts will have the easiest time with Adjudicated Law. Adjudicated Law maps what courts do (or at least imagine themselves doing) well: asking judges (or other decision-makers) to resolve arguments about the meaning and requirements of the law by reasoning their way to definitive answers. It leans on their (perceived) instincts, talents, and expertise.

For the court engaged with Adjudicated Law, the demands of coherence will point first and foremost to what might be called 'courtroom coherence'. Courts working within an Adjudicated Law model need to worry that like cases be treated alike and that litigants be able to predict the rules that will apply to them. These are core factors legitimating a court's authority to explicate and develop legal rules, which only become heightened in international criminal cases where they may merge with human rights and due process. Courtroom coherence grows out of the model's emphasis on legitimacy of reasoning and expertise. Both of those would be undercut if rules were interpreted differently in each case: if the court's legal reasoning is so solid, why can it not convince itself? If the court is so expert in the law, why does it have so much trouble finding the right rule? But courtroom coherence also draws from Adjudicated Law's emphasis on justice and binary choices of right and wrong, winner and loser. It becomes much harder to argue that one answer is the just one in any given case if that answer's justice seems so unclear over time.[80]

In sum, Adjudicated Law's emphasis on courtroom coherence and the expectations of litigants before them should lead courts to favour interpretations concordant with their own prior rulings, to follow a form of precedent, even at the expense of developments elsewhere in international

[79] Coherence is arguably a factor in the legitimacy of their judgments. See TM Franck, 'Legitimacy in the International System' (1988) 82 AJIL 705, 712.

[80] One can arguably see the results of the opposite in perceptions of the International Criminal Court, where regular disagreements between its judges have undercut its legitimacy. For some discussion, see D Guilfoyle, 'Lacking Conviction: Is the International Criminal Court Broken? An Organisational Failure Analysis' (2019) 20 Melb JIL 401.

law or renegotiation or clarification by states. When investment tribunals do just this, rightly or wrongly, Adjudicated Law seems to be the model they have in mind.

Legislated Law, drawing on a story of ratification, common understanding, and the demands of cooperation and planning, also favour the coherence that comes from predictable rules. Focused, though, on the quasi-legislative nature of international agreement, Legislated Law will favour transsubstantive, transforum predictability – the coherence of systemic integration. Legislated Law is meant to avoid the uncertainty of Negotiated Law and the ex-post justice of Adjudicated Law by creating clear frameworks for action that can be interpreted in common ways with as little friction between them as possible. Legislated Law values coordination over conflict, settled rules over settlement. Fragmentation undercuts these goals and may even seem illegitimate. A court placing its own precedent ahead of the will of the international community becomes a judicial despot. Legislated Law will thus favour common rules for all, accepted by all, which can integrate rules across courts and regimes into a single doctrine of international law.

In a vacuum then, courts applying Legislated Law would still be expected to hew to prior rulings. But that expectation would be based on the assumption that the court was correct in its prior interpretation, not on notions of litigant fairness. A single court's interpretation should remain revisable in the face of evidence of other courts having arrived at a different interpretation or in light of developments elsewhere in international law. Legislated Law argues in favour of transjudicial dialogue and drawing from one set of rules to another, whether environmental law into trade or human rights into humanitarian law.

Negotiated Law presents the most difficult problems for courts. As noted in Sections 2.3 and 2.4, the logics of Negotiated Law and of courts are in some opposition.[81] Courts are asked to decide in favour of one party or another, to decide that one actor was right and the other was wrong; Negotiated Law prefers negotiated settlements that leave room for future negotiation and wrangling. Courts are asked to provide justice; Negotiated Law is looked to provide a modicum of peace. Courts lean on delegated responsibility to the law; Negotiated Law leans on the autonomy of parties to order their affairs. To some extent, courts are faced with a problem like Heisenberg's: deciding a case based on Negotiated Law

[81] For more, see Cohen, 'International Law's *Erie* Moment' (n 12); Cohen, 'Methodology and Misdirection' (n 63).

risks transforming it, giving its rules a level of certainty that wrangling within that model would not have produced.

If courts are to be attentive to Negotiated Law, if they believe that Negotiated Law is the true source of the rules before them, then they must be very careful not to overstep their role. Courts should be minimalist in their decision-making and treat their decisions as ad hoc and revisable. They should revisit state practice in each new case regarding the rule at issue to see whether their prior interpretation has been vindicated or rejected.[82] Here, the coherence sought is negotiating-table coherence. The goal for courts interpreting Negotiated Law is to maintain states' expectations about the shape of the negotiating space, about what has been negotiated and what has not. A court should not be able, like an interloper, to stick its nose in ongoing negotiations (which in this model are all the time and endemic) and throw things in favour of one side or another.

An analog to these problematic, divergent choices can be seen in the WTO Dispute Settlement Understanding (DSU). While largely a matter of treaty interpretation, the problem is the same. DSU 3.2 provides that:

> The dispute settlement system of the WTO is a central element in providing security and predictability to the multilateral trading system. The Members recognize that it serves to preserve the rights and obligations of Members under the covered agreements, and to clarify the existing provisions of those agreements in accordance with customary rules of interpretation of public international law. Recommendations and rulings of the DSB [Dispute Settlement Body] cannot add to or diminish the rights and obligations provided in the covered agreements.[83]

In other words, WTO panels and the Appellate Body should stick to negotiated agreements, and only those agreements, but provide security and predictability (a justification for precedent), all while taking account of customary rules of interpretation of public international law, which of course might require looking at other, external agreements and general

[82] See Etkin (n 51) ('One cannot adjudicate the same custom twice.'). Recognizing that decisions of international courts are only 'subsidiary means for the determination of such rules', the ILC nods in this direction as well. ILC (n 3) 149 ('It needs to be borne in mind, moreover, that judicial pronouncements on customary international law do not freeze the law: rules of customary international law may have evolved since the date of a particular decision.'). Whether courts pay any attention is a different matter.

[83] Understanding on the Rules and Procedures Governing the Settlement of Disputes, Annex 2 to the 1994 Agreement Establishing the World Trade Organization (1947) 1869 UNTS 401, art 3.2.

international law.[84] The impossibility and incompatibility of doing all of those at the same time is evident in the Appellate Body's attempts to interpret rules regarding antidumping duties and zeroing, where the Appellate Body, seeking courtroom predictability, adopted a doctrine of precedent, policed by a cogent reasons standard.[85] Simple, the Appellate Body thought, we will apply the same zeroing rule regardless of plaintiff and regardless of defendant. But to the United States, this position regarding both the rule and the Appellate Body's authority was simply wrong. In response, the United States declared war on the body, drawing on a Negotiated Law model to argue that zeroing was a gap in the agreements purposely left for future negotiation and explicitly questioning the Appellate Body's authority to fill it.[86]

Fair and equitable treatment in investment law provides another example. Faced with a question about the scope and meaning of the concept,[87] an arbitral panel is left with a series of choices:[88] if it wants to be true to the Negotiated Law model, it will adopt a minimalist view of role and precedent, see its interpretations as mere proffers, and be extraordinarily attentive to state responses to these decisions, including attempts to renegotiate bilateral investment treaties. This, though, would come at the cost of doctrinal coherence or courtroom coherence. If the panel instead worries most about its authority as court-like tribunal and about courtroom coherence, it will strive to treat like cases alike and stick to its own precedent, potentially at the cost of both systemic integration and negotiating space. If, though, the panel is concerned about systemic or doctrinal coherence, it might eschew the consistency of its own opinions in favour of looking to *jurisprudence constante* or *acquis*, or even beyond to foster systemic integration by looking to rules about the environment, human rights, and sovereignty. In this case, the panel could

[84] See Vienna Convention on the Law of Treaties (n 20) art 31(3)(c). See also Merkouris (n 68).

[85] See HG Cohen, 'Culture Clash: The Sociology of WTO Precedent' in A Frese and J Schumann (eds), *Precedent as Rules and Practice: New Approaches and Methodologies in Studies of Legal Precedents* (Nomos 2021) 112; N Ridi, 'United States: Anti-dumping Measures Applying Differential Pricing Methodology to Softwood Lumber from Canada' (2020) 114 AJIL 735.

[86] See Cohen, 'Culture Clash' (n 85) 114–22.

[87] The question is usually complicated by its entanglement of treaty and customary international law, though, as noted in Section 2, from the perspective of interpretation those may not be as different as is usually thought.

[88] See similar discussion in A Roberts, 'Power and Persuasion in Investment Treaty Interpretation: The Dual Role of States' (2010) 104 AJIL 179.

Table 2 *Justification-based sources of international law: summary*

	Negotiated Law	Legislated Law	Adjudicated Law
Underlying logic	Product of settlements hashed out over time	Broad (precisely how much unclear) acquiescence to some stated proposition	Product of reasoned elaboration and application by experts
Justification	Specific consent, autonomy, pragmatic experience, flexibility	Common consent, certainty, predictable planning	Delegation, expertise, neutrality, finality, justice
Examples	Traditional custom, bilateral treaties such as BITS	Articles on State Responsibility, VCLT, Genocide Convention	Regime-specific precedents, general PIL precedents
Coherence?	Negotiating table coherence, predictability of negotiating space	Doctrinal coherence, transsubstantive and transforum predictability, common rules for all	Courtroom coherence, treating like cases alike

rely neither on Negotiated Law bases of legitimacy nor on its delegated authority. Instead, it would have to rely on the authority of the international community. Systemic integration might be achieved, but only at the cost of treating like cases alike, respecting specific negotiated deals, and respecting space for future deals (see Table 2).

Coherence, ironically, thus represents a fragmented choice. Different courts will take different views on these issues, but these decisions are always contested and contestable. What is often only recognized by critics, though, is that these choices are foundationally not about coherence or methods of interpretation, but about justifications of authority. Even if only implicit, the legitimating source of a rule must be identified before the proper interpretative tools can be deployed.

5 Conclusion

Debates over the proper interpretation of customary international law reveal the limits of doctrinal consensus. Methods of interpretation draw on the authority of the particular interpreter and the authority of the rules being interpreted. As such, the choice of methods must be sensitive to our accounts of each. But surfacing those accounts by teasing out the stories we tell to justify customary international law rules reveals the deep theoretical disagreements buried beneath our doctrine of sources. Multiple, competing, perhaps even contradictory concepts of customary international law are in common use; what we call 'custom' might emanate from any of those sources of authority. It is no wonder that we disagree on how to interpret it. Interpretive debates reflect the varied sources we have agreed to group under the label of 'custom' and the deep normative pluralism undergirding the agreed formal sources of international law. Competing justificatory accounts of customary international law that formal doctrine seeks to ignore resurface in these debates. Interpretation becomes the battleground on which our justificatory accounts of custom are forced into combat.

4

Interpretation Dynamics in CIL

An Entropic Approach

ELENI MICHA

A throw of the dice never, even when truly cast in the eternal circumstance of a shipwreck's depth, will abolish chance.

Stéphane Mallarmé, French poet, 1842–98

The tossing of a dice – the symbol of chance, uncertainty and unpredictability.

Jiří Kylián, Czech former dancer and choreographer, b. 1947

1 Uncertainty and Change: The Dynamic Character of CIL

The uncertain character of CIL has been discussed time and time again among academics and practitioners. To most of them, the uncertain character of CIL entails a twofold defect: first, uncertainty is perceived with respect to the identification of the rule, since we may not know whether there is a valid legal rule,[1] and second, uncertainty is perceived with respect to the content of the rule, since we may not know the precise meaning of the rule.[2]

Thus, uncertainty is viewed as the basic reason for the lack of coherence and consistency attributed to CIL rules. In turn, it is argued that uncertainty is a doctrinal issue discussed among scholars but not among judges. However, judges will inevitably deal with uncertainty, even indirectly, when they have to assess the meaning of the rule to apply in the case at

[1] See eg M Jovanovic, *The Nature of International Law* (Cambridge University Press 2019) 228–33; J Kammerhofer, *Uncertainty in International Law: A Kelsenian Perspective* (Routledge 2010) 3–4, 59.

[2] Such cognitive questions lie at the heart of the epistemological debate concerning CIL's uncertainty. See J Kammerhofer (n 1) 3–4. Yet there is not necessarily a strong connection between certainty and knowledge. AP Martinich and A Stroll, 'epistemology', *Encyclopedia Britannica* (26 August 2022) <www.britannica.com/topic/epistemology> accessed 10 January 2023.

hand. Uncertainty will in this respect lead to unpredictability (and, consequently, even greater uncertainty) when different legal meanings taken from a range of probabilities are assigned to a CIL rule. But if uncertainty is taken to mean ambiguity – i.e. different interpretive approaches to an applicable rule – then, by induction, there can be no evolution of CIL, which leads to rigidity and denial of change. Yet, not only is such an inference irrational but it does not even correspond to existing judicial practice.[3] Therefore – and to hark back to H. L. A. Hart once again[4] – the quest for certainty is of vital importance in attempting to soften the shadows of uncertainty.

At the same time, uncertainty in terms of unpredictability, although seen as a 'necessary evil' by its discussants, ought to be avoided in order to strengthen state compliance with judicial rulings.[5] Understandably, therefore, both practitioners and scholars, albeit through different paths, have tried and are still struggling to manage uncertainty in international law in order to better apprehend the nature of CIL and how it functions.[6] To this end and inasmuch as uncertainty cannot be eliminated, it can be argued that 'reduced' uncertainty is preferable as the 'lesser of two evils'.[7]

Vital questions also arise regarding the way CIL develops. One such question is, how does interpretation of CIL rules functions in a complex environment with a multiplicity of actors generating 'polycentric disputes',[8] if indeed the interpretation process applies to CIL at all? And where international courts interpret CIL, what kind of change can be

[3] P Merkouris, 'Interpreting Customary International Law: You'll Never Walk Alone' in P Merkouris, J Kammerhofer and N Arajarvi (eds), *The Theory, Practice, and Interpretation of Customary International Law* (Cambridge University Press 2022) 4.

[4] HLA Hart, The Concept of the Law (1st edn, Cambridge University Press 1961) esp 12–13.

[5] A Guzman, 'A Compliance-Based Theory of International Law' (2002) 90 CLR 1823; A D'Amato, 'Legal Uncertainty' (2010) Faculty Working Papers 108 <http://scholarlycommons.law.northwestern.edu/facultyworkingpapers/108> accessed 10 January 2023.

[6] Jovanovich (n 1) 232 n.

[7] Use of probabilistic reasoning to frame and manage risk, and thus uncertainty, by predicting a number of possible outcomes and adopting preventive measures seems to offer a way out of the uncertainty gap. S Townley, 'The Rise of Risk in International Law' (2018) 18 CJIL 593; M Ambrus, R Reyfuse and W Werner (eds), *Risk and the Regulation of Uncertainty in International Law* (Oxford University Press 2017) 3–10. Yet such an approach is based upon a fragmented view of international law, as the various legal regimes function according to their own rules and procedures, hence the need for a 'different modelling for framing and regulating their inherent uncertainties'. See Jovanovich (n 1) 3.

[8] The concept of a polycentric policy dispute was introduced by LL Fuller, who described a situation of interacting points of influence among a large number of parties that generates a polycentric problem, which, he argued, is beyond the limits of adjudication. LL Fuller and KI Winston, 'The Forms and Limits of Adjudication' (1978) 92 Harv L Rev 353.

expected with respect to the application of CIL? Is there a 'spontaneous' change like a Grotian moment,[9] or a slow-developing process that rarely leads to change in CIL rules? And is it likely to contribute to the progressive development of CIL or to its decline?

Providing answers to these questions is of crucial importance to understanding the proper function of CIL, given that uncertainty is a fact of life, and as such characteristic of the international legal system, too. Yet, what seems to be missing from the entire discourse on uncertainty is a focus on how CIL functions. Although a number of theories have been formulated, extensively discussed, and even strongly debated,[10] there are no persuasive answers that would explain when and how changes in CIL occur, the significance of CIL inertia in resisting these changes, and the effects these changes may produce with respect to a certain time and place. In other words, the dynamics of CIL, as the driving force behind its evolution, remain essentially unexplored.[11]

Providing answers to these questions requires in-depth understanding not only of the structure of CIL but also of the processes that occur in and out of CIL during its operation as a social system. In this respect, the discussion on uncertainty is closely connected to the complexity of the law. When lawyers refer to the complex nature of legal problems, they are pointing out not only the density of the legislation and its lack of simplicity but also the difficulty of understanding the meaning of the law. Thus, issues of indeterminacy, uncertainty and, often, unpredictability arise when multiple meanings become available through interpretation of the law.

The present chapter is divided into four parts. Section 2 focuses on the dynamic character of CIL and what dynamic complexity entails for the system of CIL. In Section 3 we discuss how complexity science may throw light on the functioning of CIL and explore CIL's construction as a social

9 A Grotian moment occurs when a fundamental change within the international system, acting as an accelerating agent, enables CIL to form rapidly and with less state practice instead of the ordinary long-term process. See M Scharf, 'Hugo Grotius and the Concept of Grotian Moments in International Law' (2022) 54 CWR J Int Law 17. See also T Sparks and M Somos, 'Grotian Moments: An Introduction' (2021) 42 Grotiana 179.

10 PH Verdier and E Voeten, 'Precedent, Compliance, and Change in Customary International Law: An Explanatory Theory' (2014) 108 AJIL 389.

11 The word dynamics comes from the Greek *denames*, meaning force. Authors who have dealt with the dynamic character of CIL have mostly treated the subject through the lens of political science. See the insightful work of P Diehl and C Ku, *The Dynamics of International Law* (Cambridge University Press 2010) esp 1–27, in which, through the lens of international relations, the authors offer an explanation of how and why international law evolves with a view to closing the gap between international law and international relations.

system. In Section 4 we demonstrate the force that sets the CIL system in motion and gives it its dynamic character: this section attempts to construct a physically based representation of the interpretation process in the CIL system. Since the present analysis regards interpretation of CIL as a process, we introduce the concept of entropy, a fundamental concept of nature, to explain the functioning of CIL as a complex social system. In Section 5, focussing on the interpretative authority of international criminal courts, we will uncover the various phases of the interpretation process followed by those courts in their case law. The analysis will, thus, adopt an entropic approach to interpretation in order to explain the progressive development of CIL.

2 The Theoretical Foundations of CIL's Dynamic Character: A Study in Physics

It has been rightly maintained that complex laws are the inevitable price of human society that is itself complex.[12] But what exactly is complexity in relation to CIL, and why is it something we only acknowledge 'when we see it'?[13]

To begin with, complexity concerns the dynamic expression of a whole – that is, a system comprising a hierarchy of multiple interacting components. As described in the natural sciences, complexity usually implies the existence of a hierarchical, multi-component system in which each component is networked and interacts with a multiplicity of other components at all hierarchical levels. Accordingly, complexity includes a process that distributes/re-distributes energy throughout the system; owing to the multiplicity of local and remote connections at all levels, this causes the system to evolve in an apparently simple but formally unpredictable manner.[14] In other words, the multiplicity of actors and the large number of issues generated between them are the main characteristics of a complex system. The prime example of such a 'polycentric situation' is a human society,: it involves a great number of interacting social forces

[12] E Kades, 'The Laws of Complexity and the Complexity of Laws: The Implications of Computational Complexity Theory for the Law' (1997) Faculty Publications 646 <https://scholarship.law.wm.edu/facpubs/646> accessed 25 January 2023.

[13] The expression 'I know . . . when I see it' was famously used by US Supreme Court judge Potter Stewart in 1964 when referring to hard-core pornography, which lay outside the Constitution's protection of obscenity. *Jacobellis v Ohio* (378 U.S. 184).

[14] To a layman, a complex problem might seem equivalent to a complicated problem; however, this is far from the truth since the two concepts are qualitatively different. See Section 3.

that create various network structures, which in turn interact with their environment. Such a scheme is prone to change in order to adapt to new realities, especially when the existing law cannot address them.

The present analysis looks at CIL as the outcome of social processing within a constantly evolving international milieu, as originally perceived by G. Scelle.[15] It will show that this dynamic character of CIL is inherent to its social identity, since complexity serves as a frame of reference for CIL. Thus, CIL is not considered as a self-referential system, but a communicative, flexible and adaptive network analogous to physical systems.[16] In turn, interpretation, as the main function of the judiciary, will be treated as an internal property of the CIL system that initiates changes according to the particular circumstances of each individual case. In this context, interpretation plays a cardinal role in ensuring legal security.[17] Such an approach cannot of course confer on CIL the consistency and coherence it is alleged to lack, but it can explain how legal interpretation works in a complex social environment like that of CIL.

Such an approach to CIL may raise objections. Pre-emptively addressing these provides an opportunity to make a number of clarifications and further delimit the scope of the present analysis. To begin with, there is no doubt that the transfer of concepts and definitions from one discipline to another is subject to many risks. One example is the possible misinterpretation of the phenomenological basis and semantics of concepts deriving from different scientific areas. This would undermine a common effort to ask the right questions and seek the proper answers: the interpretative tools of different disciplines are by nature distinct and those of one may not fully apply, or be transposable, to the conceptual constructs of another. By way of illustration, a deterministic approach to the law does not fully correspond to how determinism functions in physics. Determinism in the natural sciences

[15] G Scelle, *Manuel de droit international public* (Domat-Montchrestien 1948) 9–10 and esp 577–78.

[16] On interpretation as a self-referential construction that 'invents [its] own origin and regulates [its] own functioning', see J d'Aspremont, 'Bypassing the Authority of International Law: The Virtue of Modern Self-Referentiality' (21 September 2017; forthcoming in G Hernandez and G Jokubauskaite (eds), *Constructing Authority in International Law*) <https://papers.ssrn.com/sol3/papers.cfm?abstract_id=3040975> accessed 1 February 2023. On the basic characteristics of complex adaptive systems, see B Parsons, 'Using Complexity Science Concepts When Designing System Interventions and Evaluations' (*InSites*, April 2010, revised March 2012) <https://insites.org/wp-content/uploads/559c709812d66-InS.10.CASConcpts.pdf> accessed 1 February 2023.

[17] According to Scelle, legal security is achieved through the judicial function. See Scelle (n 15) 662–64. See also Section 4, where it will be argued that these conclusions are mirrored in the process of CIL interpretation by international criminal tribunals.

implies exact knowledge, a mathematical description of natural processes. Complicated, multiparametric physical systems involving interdependent physical processes subject to different random effects may evolve in totally unpredictable ways depending on the initial conditions.[18] Prime examples of such chaotic systems are the weather, the geomagnetic field and celestial dynamics. By contrast, the law associates determinism with strict predictability through causation; in other words, an event is causally determined if, and only if, a set of prior events has taken place. Accordingly, the law 'argues' that future events can be predicted with reference to prior events. The assessment of CIL is a mirror image of this construction.

If, on the other hand, we oversimplify the way things work, we tend to underestimate the complexity of both nature and society and risk producing unwarranted assumptions that do not correspond to reality – an outcome that often occurs to the detriment of both disciplines.[19] Trying to find all the answers to the questions presented is a most ambitious undertaking that cannot be realized within the restricted limits of the present chapter. Instead, our analysis will merely try to define a basis for elaborating a functional model to explain how judicial interpretation of CIL works as the main force for the motion and, accordingly, the development of CIL. The ensuing analysis will further explore the mechanics of CIL by placing a special focus on international criminal justice.

The findings of international criminal courts and tribunals are of interest mainly due to the strong ties that international criminal law maintains with CIL. As one of the sources of international criminal law, CIL has been applied not only to fill gaps in the characterization of 'criminal conduct' as a war crime or a crime against humanity, but also to introduce new crimes for future mass atrocities that allegedly contravene the principle of legality. In this regard, much attention has been given to the case law of the ICTY – in contrast to the ICC, whose statutory foundations in the Rome Statute has had the effect of reducing the role of CIL, since the latter constitutes a secondary source of law for the ICC.[20]

[18] This deterministic view of nature is chaotic (deterministic chaos). Chaos, as perceived in natural sciences, is not to be confused with disorder and decay. On the contrary, it describes dynamic systems that evolve over time depending on their initial conditions and the precision with which these conditions can be measured. Thus, determinism is related to a probabilistic view of things but not to strict predictability. See M Cattani and others, 'Deterministic Chaos Theory: Some Basic Concepts' (2017) 39(1) RBEF e1309-1.

[19] RP Crease, 'Comment: The Quantum Moment' (2013) 26(3) Physics World 25.

[20] Y Tan, *The Rome Statute as Evidence of Customary International Law* (Brill 2021) 1–27; WA Schabas, *The International Criminal Court: A Commentary on the Rome Statute* (2nd edn, Oxford University Press 2016) 519–23; L van den Herik, 'The Decline of Customary

This is not to say that CIL has lost its importance; instead, it functions as both a source of international criminal law (ICL) and an interpretative instrument for the purpose of clarifying or filling gaps in the text of the Rome Statute, which 'is not in all aspects an authoritative account of the current state of the law'.[21] For there is persistent debate over possible breaches of the legality principle,[22] which creates even more uncertainty than that which interpretation of the relevant CIL rules seeks to remove.

3 CIL as a Complex Social System: The Shared Understanding of CIL

As the outcome of 'social constraint',[23] CIL is distinguished by its diversity and adaptability to a constantly changing societal environment, thus reflecting the maxim *ubi societas, ibi jus*. It is this dynamic character of CIL that makes it a complex system and, in particular, a complex social system.

The idea of explaining societal functions and interconnections in terms of complexity has its roots in systems theory as proposed by Talcott Parsons in the 1950s and much later by Niklas Luhmann at the beginning of the 1990s. Concurrently, system dynamics was introduced by Jay Forrester in the mid1950s as an aspect of systems theory, though in a different setting. Whereas Luhmann held that social systems, including the law, are closed ones tending to (re)produce themselves, Forrester, an engineer, introduced a methodology and a mathematical model for understanding and solving complex problems, initially in the corporate domain but later also in non-corporate areas where the focus was on the world's socioeconomic system.[24] Notwithstanding the influence of Luhmann's theory on the law, the author of the present study argues that CIL is an open system whose interacting elements also interact with its environment.[25]

International Law as a Source of International Criminal Law' in C Bradley (ed), *Custom's Future: International Law in a Changing World* (Cambridge University Press 2016) 230–52.

[21] C Stahn, *A Critical Introduction to International Criminal Law* (Cambridge University Press 2019) 95.

[22] A Bufalini, 'The Principle of Legality and the Role of CIL in the Interpretation of the ICC Statute' (2015) 14 LPICT 233.

[23] The term, from the French *contrainte sociale*, belongs to Scelle, who argued that sociability (*sociabilité*) describes the true nature of contemporary international society. Scelle (n 15) 577–78.

[24] JW Forrester, *World Dynamics* (2nd edn, Wright-Allen 1973).

[25] C Mesjasz, 'Complexity of Social Systems' (2010) 117 Acta Phys Pol A 706, 707–08; S Wheatley, *The Idea of International Human Rights Law* (Oxford University Press 2019) 45–48; A Siegenfeld and Y Bar-Yam, 'An Introduction to Complex Systems Science and

In short, complexity theory as developed to explain social behaviour rests upon the findings of sociology, which viewed societal institutions as autopoietic, dynamic and chaotic. However, the concept of complexity originated in the physical sciences is not defined, as sociologists or lawyers would expect, according to their normative background. As a result, the concept of *complexity* is often confused with the concept of *complicatedness.* A complicated system is one made of an intricate arrangement of many individual components and can be understood by explaining the function of each of its constituent parts. On the other hand, complexity concerns the dynamic, evolutionary behaviour of a system and is manifested by dynamically emergent properties that arise from interactions between its constituent parts; complex systems can be understood only by interpreting the multiple interactions between their multiple components.[26] Besides, the exchange of energy within and through a system's boundaries is of critical importance in comprehending the functioning of open complex systems. Accordingly, 'complexity' refers to the capacity of a 'living', dynamic system to change, adapt and evolve and should not be confused with complicatedness, which refers to a collection of discrete elements that can be de-assembled and re-assembled. Thus, a complicated problem is usually difficult to solve, although it may be simple in its structure, whereas a complex problem may be understood by studying how the whole system operates.[27]

Therefore, to consider CIL a complex system is to acknowledge that human society is part of nature and functions in compliance with its fundamental laws. As pointed out in Section 2, the construction of an adequate model of CIL is essential to understanding how complexity works in this area of international law. To be functional, such a model must be

Its Applications' [2020] Complexity <https://onlinelibrary.wiley.com/doi/epdf/10.1155/2020/6105872> accessed 1 March 2023.

[26] Although complex systems may be complicated, this is not their inherent characteristic. A car and an aircraft are examples of complicated systems, since they can be dismantled and their parts put back together again. As far as legal systems are concerned, the large number of laws and the ambiguity of their content does not necessarily mean that there are many interactions between the system's components. See D Bourcier and P Mazzega, 'Toward Measures of Complexity in Legal Systems', *ICAIL '07: Proceedings of the11th International Conference on Artificial Intelligence and Law* (June 2007) <https://dl.acm.org/doi/10.1145/1276318.1276359> accessed 27 May 2024.

[27] For a digest of the distinctions between the two concepts, see JM Kamensky, 'Managing the Complicated vs. the Complex' (IBM Center for the Business of Government, Fall/Winter 2011) <www.businessofgovernment.org/sites/default/files/JohnKamensky.pdf> accessed 1 March 2023.

representative of the society it simulates or, in mathematical terms, be isomorphic to the physical setting of CIL. To clarify, isomorphic models are not identical to the entities they represent; instead, they are structured in such a way as to preserve the arrangements and binary relationships between the elements of those entities. Let us give an illustration from elementary algebra: adding together two numbers and then multiplying the sum by a third number gives the same result as multiplying each natural number by the same third number and then adding together the products (distributive property); so these sets of numbers are isomorphic, since one set can be mapped onto the other set of numbers.[28] In the present analysis, isomorphism can aptly represent the two-way relationships developed between the elements of the 'complex CIL system'. Accordingly, and for the purposes of this study, the CIL model will comprise a network of multiple, connected (interacting) states, each engaged in two-way, one-to-one interaction with international criminal tribunals.[29]

At this point, it is necessary to clarify that the current CIL social order is shaped by various actors, both state and non-state, operating at the international or transnational level. International and regional organizations, general or specialized, play a significant role in building the 'practice' endorsed by states; armed groups originating from various environments contribute to building 'practice', often through their involvement in conducting military operations; judicial institutions even forge state practice through compliance mechanisms.[30]

[28] WL Hosch, 'isomorphism', *Encyclopedia Britannica* (15 July 2009) <www.britannica.com/science/isomorphism-mathematics> accessed 1 March 2023.

[29] Modelling a complex social system, like CIL, will inevitably entail a simplified representation of reality, since, especially at this early stage of research, it is not possible to depict all possible interactions, direct and indirect, between the agents of the system (see Figure 1). See C Castellano, S Fortunato and V Loretto, 'Statistical Physics on Social Dynamics' (2009) 81 RMP 591; M Boon and T Knuuttila, 'Models as Epistemic Tools in Engineering Sciences' in AWM Meijers (ed), *Philosophy of Technology and Engineering Sciences* (Elsevier 2009) 695–703.

[30] It is important to note that these developments are also recognized by the ILC in 'Draft Conclusions on Identification of Customary International Law, with Commentaries' (30 April–1 June and 2 July–10 August 2018) UN Doc A/73/10. Yet the ILC emphatically states that, as a constituent element of customary international law, general practice refers primarily to the practice of states and only secondarily to the practice of international organizations. As far as other non-state actors are concerned, their practice can play only an indirect role 'to the extent that *States have endorsed or reacted* [to these practices]' (Conclusion 4, emphasis added). For text accompanying n. 35 for a characteristic example of states' reactions. On the behaviour of non-state actors regarding CIL and how they affect transnational behaviour, see also RB Baker, 'Customary International Law: A Reconceptualization' (2016) 41 BJIL 458.

An illustration of the diversity of actors who join other actors in the field of CIL can be found in the recent *Ongwen* case before the ICC.[31] The ICC stressed that human communities shape their own concept of property according to their customary rules and principles. For the ICC, the content of such 'communal property' must be taken into account when considering the material element (*actus reus*) of ownership in relation to the war crime of pillaging within the context of a non-international armed conflict.[32]

Such a kaleidoscope of actors renders the system of CIL even more complex, adding components and interactions that call for further study in respect of their input and output. The diversity of actors may also lead to the emergence of multiple clusters;[33] new relationships will arise between the agents of the system, and the feedback the agents receive from one another but also from their environment will probably lead to new processes and patterns of behaviour. This two-way feedback will reflect shared or opposing views of the law.[34] Such movement entails exchange of energy between the various components of the system and may influence its evolution. Yet, one thing is certain: a complex CIL system is dynamic, since it can change in response to changing circumstances over time.

The United Kingdom's position on air strikes in Syria in 2013 and 2018 is illustrative of the interactions between the diverse actors within the complex CIL system and between CIL and its environment, since it reveals how CIL is assessed and functions. In deciding to join with the United States and France in their efforts to reduce Syria's chemical weapons capability, the UK

[31] *Prosecutor v Dominic Ongwen*, ICC-02/04-01/15 (4 February 2021).

[32] ibid [2766]. Customary practices regarding land ownership adopted by indigenous peoples have been taken into account not only by the ICC but also by human rights judicial bodies. As a result, possession of land by indigenous communities should suffice for official recognition of ownership even if a title of ownership is missing. *Mayagna (Sumo) Awas Tingni Community v Nicaragua* (Merits, Reparations and Costs) IACHR Series C No 79 (2001) [151].

[33] A cluster is defined as a group of states that, on occasion, operate coherently towards a specific objective.

[34] The concept of shared understanding of the law draws upon the theory of interactional law as conceived and developed by J Brunnée and S Toope, 'International Law and the Practice of Legality: Stability and Change' (2018) 49 VUWLR, 429, 433–37. The present author similarly considers that 'the law is grounded in a society's shared understanding' and further argues in favour of a dynamic CIL system, capable of change and subsequent evolution, while acknowledging the need to safeguard its predictable character. See also van Aaken's view on the role of states and international courts in the interpretation process from the perspective of veto player theory. A van Aaken 'Interests, Strategies and Veto Players: The Political Economy of Interpreting Customary International Law' (2022) ESIL Reflections 11(2) <https://esil-sedi.eu/wp-content/uploads/2022/09/ESIL-Reflection-Anne-van-Aaken_final-version.pdf> accessed 2 April 2022.

Department of Defence argued in favour of a right to humanitarian intervention as the legal basis for its actions.[35] It is significant to note that in 2013 the UK did not take part in the air strikes since the British parliament rejected the government's motion for intervention. In both 2013 and 2018, however, the UK tried to establish a general doctrine of intervention applicable in situations of humanitarian necessity and to give the doctrine the force of customary law.

What is significant here is the reaction of several states to the UK's position on the right of humanitarian intervention. Those actors and the various interactions between them and the UK form a cluster (often ephemeral) within the CIL system. Systems do not function in a vacuum, but operate within a specific environment which affects them through the exchange and redistribution of energy. In a complex legal system, like that of CIL, the flow of information regarding the meaning of the law is defined to be the energy source of the system (see Section 4).

The UK's complex system lies within the environment of the United Nations; that environment affects the UK through the UN Security Council's decision on air strikes against Syria.[36] Although the air strikes were not qualified as an act of aggression, it seems that there was no agreement with the UK as to the customary law status of humanitarian intervention, since no state referred directly to a right of humanitarian intervention in accord with the UK's reasoning.[37] It is interesting to note that the states which rejected the proposal by the Russian Federation to condemn the air strikes – eight out of fifteen – did not openly disagree with the UK on the need to alleviate humanitarian suffering nor on the need to

[35] UK Government, 'Chemical Weapon Use by Syrian Regime: UK Government Legal Position' (Policy paper, 29 August 2013) <www.gov.uk/government/publications/chemical-weapon-use-by-syrian-regime-uk-government-legal-position/chemical-weapon-use-by-syrian-regime-uk-government-legal-position-html-version> accessed 7 March 2023. Yet, like its allies, the UK relied on the customary law status of the prohibition on the use of chemical weapons that most states accepted. For present purposes, we do not consider whether the UK's position was valid according to the interpretation of CIL current at the time.

[36] A system's environment encompasses factors beyond its natural boundaries that affect it through the exchange of energy/information. See K Bailey, *Social Entropy* (State University of New York Press 1990) 51.

[37] None of the four states that abstained referred to this issue. UNSC 8233rd meeting (14 April 2018) UN Doc S/PV.8233 (Provisional) <https://documents-dds-ny.un.org/doc/UNDOC/PRO/N18/108/91/PDF/N1810891.pdf?OpenElement> accessed 30 April 2022. See M Milanovic, 'The Syria Strikes: Still Clearly Illegal' (*EJIL:Talk!*, 15 April 2018) <www.ejiltalk.org/the-syria-strikes-still-clearly-illegal/> accessed 30 April 2020; C Henderson, 'The UK Government's Legal Opinion on Forcible Measures in Response to the Use of Chemical Weapons by the Syrian Government' (2015) 64 ICLQ 179.

ensure compliance with the prohibition on the manufacture and use of chemical weapons. The absence of such feedback could signify that a shared understanding on the content of humanitarian intervention by the states was wanting.

The principal characteristic of the complex environment of CIL is the diversity of the components' internal activity, explained by the fact that they possess a considerable degree of freedom:[38] it is the discretionary power of the judiciary that confers such diversity on the agents of the system. Under the influence of Hersch Lauterpacht, the International Criminal Court underlined that the 'constant presence of judicial discretion in matters of customary international law [entails] the "constant necessity of making a choice . . . between conflicting and equally legitimate principles of interpretation"'.[39] In the context of an international organization (the UN in the UK example), the multiple interactions between states and other actors even accelerate the process of international standard-setting. In this respect, the UK example mirrors the model of an open system that can adapt to changing circumstances thanks to the degrees of freedom that its agents possess. In turn, when making choices, international courts cannot ignore the statements made by state leaders – nor their silence – within an international organization; thus, the courts can adapt to the developing needs of the international community.[40]

Accordingly, there may be a two-level complexity in the structure of a CIL system, with a number of complex CIL sub-systems operating within the main system (see Figures 1 and 2).

The result is a network, in which a broad array of interactions link the system's various actors, the nodes of the system.[41] Therefore, understanding the binary relationships between states and international courts as a one-to-one correspondence constitutes the first crucial step in explaining the function of CIL as a complex system, and in turn its dynamic character.

[38] PH Schuck, 'Legal Complexity: Some Causes, Consequences and Cures' (1992) 42 DLJ 9.

[39] *Prosecutor v Uhuru Muigai Kenyatta*, ICC-01/09-02/11 (18 October 2013) [102]–[103], citing Hersch Lauterpacht, *The Development of International Law by the International Court* (Cambridge University Press 1996) 395–96.

[40] *Prosecutor v Uhuru Muigai Kenyatta*, ICC-01/09-02/11 (18 October 2013), separate further opinion of Judge Eboe-Osuji [12].

[41] These may be 'short path lengths' and/or 'high clustering coefficients' (i.e. the links between two or three neighbouring nodes). F Schweitzer, 'Sociophysics' (2018) 71 Physics Today 2, 40. With regard to a CIL complex system, see also Figure 2 (public domain map available at <www.freeworldmaps.net> accessed 20 March 2022)

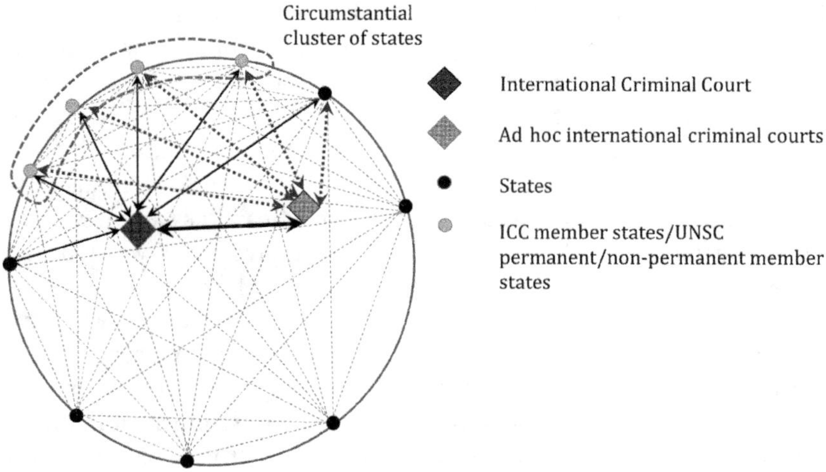

Figure 1 A one-to-one, binary relationship

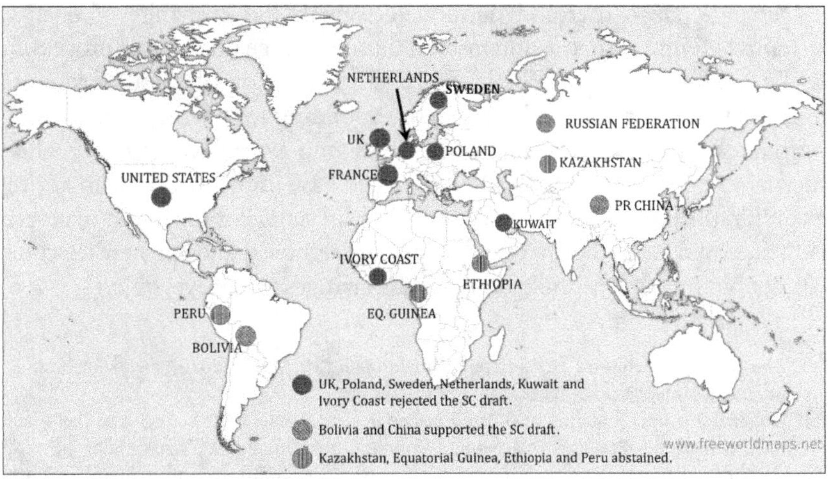

Figure 2 Security Council draft resolution proposed by the Russian Federation

4 The Mechanics of CIL: A Manifestation of Entropy

Having designed our CIL complex system with its basic units and interacting constituent parts (states, international courts, international organizations and other non-state actors as agents), we shall now proceed to explore the forces that cause it to react and stimulate its evolution. We will refer to these dynamic processes as the 'mechanics' of CIL and its 'laws of motion'.[42] It is the relationship between the force that excites a system and the motion it causes that defines the dynamic response of the system, causing it to change, if necessary adapt and subsequently evolve.[43] This is true of the CIL system, which is prone to change, to adapt whenever required and, therefore, to evolve. In this respect, the CIL is not a deterministic system. This fundamental characteristic of CIL constitutes both its strength and its weakness, since unpredictability is the offspring of change, whereas predictability – or, better, foreseeability – is an essential requirement of our legal universe.[44]

In order to account for these conflicting characteristics, we will have recourse to the concept of entropy as applied by information theory. Rooted in the field of thermodynamics and statistical mechanics, information entropy is the measure of the number of possible ways in which information is distributed in a system. A neologism derived from Greek, the term and concept of entropy was introduced by Rudolf Clausius in the mid nineteenth century[45] to describe a thermodynamic property of all physical systems. To the German physicist, entropy was related to transformation and change, since thermodynamics deals with the exchange of energy between different physical systems and the work done during this process.[46]

The melting of an ice cube is the classic illustration of what entropy is, given that heat is a form of energy corresponding to a definite amount of mechanical work: when heated, ice turns into water, leading to higher internal energy (entropy) as the molecules have more freedom to move around in the liquid than in the ice cube's solid state. For the liquid to revert back to a solid state, thermal energy must be removed and the new ice cube will not be the same as the old one. Thus changes are irreversible.

42 D Goodstein, 'mechanics', *Encyclopedia Britannica* (21 August 2020) <www.britannica.com/science/mechanics> accessed 2 April 2022.

43 The German mathematician and philosopher Leibniz (1646–1716) conceived the word dynamics from the Greek word δύναμις (*denames*), meaning 'force', 'strength' or 'power', which in turn comes from the Greek word δύναμαι (*denamai*), meaning 'I can' or 'I am able'.

44 On the 'paradox of custom as a source both dynamic and stabilizing', see O Corten and others, *A Critical Introduction to International Law* (Éditions de l'Université de Bruxelles 2019) 311–14; P Staubach, *The Rule of Written International Law* (Routledge 2018) 56–63.

45 The German physicist and mathematician Clausius (1822–88) synthesized 'entropy' (*entrepein* in Greek) from the terms 'energy' and 'trope' (i.e. direction of motion); it literally means to turn about, to change.

46 Thus, entropy was defined as the thermodynamic state of a physical system according to the distribution of its internal thermal energy. See GWF Drake, 'thermodynamics', *Encyclopedia Britannica* (15 May 2023) <www.britannica.com/science/thermodynamics> accessed 10 April 2022.

In turn, this led to the 'second law of thermodynamics', which is one of the most fundamental axioms of nature and essentially states that entropy cannot decrease. Later, Ludwig Boltzmann linked entropy with probability in relation to the thermal motion of particles in systems with large numbers of agents (like gases composed of large numbers of molecules), thus introducing the discipline of statistical mechanics.[47] In other words, the second law of thermodynamics is explained as the system's tendency towards more probable states. Consequently, entropy tends to maximize when the internal thermal energy is evenly distributed among the agents of a system – that is, when all probabilities (expectations) tend to be the same and no energy can be extracted from the system.

Information entropy offers an analogous definition: here, entropy is the measure of the amount of uncertainty represented by the probability distribution of unavailable information in a system.[48] The entropic state of a physical or informational system cannot be reversed unless an outside force removes internal energy from the system, but that will always be at the expense of increasing entropy elsewhere and in the Universe at large. Consequently, entropy is the sum of the probabilities of all possible microstates (configurations) of a physical or informational system.[49]

As already explained, entropy defines the thermodynamic state of a physical system, which may be reversible or irreversible depending on the ability of the system to exchange energy with its environment (i.e. with other systems).[50] In closed/isolated systems that cannot exchange energy

[47] It was thus clear that the second thermodynamics law was essentially statistical; thus, entropy can be measured to give us the total number of possible states of particles distributed within a given system. See J Sethna, 'What Is Statistical Mechanics?' in *Statistical Mechanics: Entropy, Order Parameters and Complexity* (2nd edn, Oxford University Press 2021) 6.

[48] ET Jaynes, 'Information Theory and Statistical Mechanics' (1957) 106 Phys Rev 620, 622. As successfully argued, 'the purpose of probability theory is to help us in forming plausible conclusions in cases where there is not enough information available to lead to certain conclusions; thus detailed verification is not expected.' (ibid 622).

[49] It is crucial to note that entropy is *always* a property of the whole (i.e. a system) but *not* of the microstates that form the system. As a probabilistic concept, entropy 'does not focus on individuals or small sub-sets, [but] presupposes a macroscopic view of the [physical] phenomena'. D Koutsoyiannis and GF Sargentis, 'Entropy and Wealth' (2021) 23 Entropy 1356.

[50] In a social context, entropy has been applied to indicate disorder, social disintegration and possibly the decay of society, largely due to its ability to increase. As a natural property, however, entropy is an objective concept and not a subjective one with negative implications for the future of humanity. E Michaelides, 'Entropy, Order and Disorder' (2008) 2 Open Thermodyn J 7. In this respect, entropy constitutes the driving force of evolution, since in a state of uncertainty there is a plurality of options, which in turn

with their environment, entropy is irreversible; although it cannot decrease, entropy can remain constant, in which case the system is said to rest in thermodynamic equilibrium.[51] In short, isolated systems are incapable of changing and, thus, evolving. If a system is not isolated and can exchange energy with its environment, then it cannot remain in equilibrium and must evolve. Human societal constructs are by nature open systems, as they are embedded in, and continuously interact with, other human societal constructs: their internal energy is subject to continuous redistribution, putting them in a state of perpetual non-equilibrium resulting in continuous change and evolution.

The definition of entropy in statistical mechanics is, to all intents and purposes, identical to that introduced by Claude Shannon in information theory/communication science in 1948.[52] It applies to social systems, and most certainly to legal network systems such as CIL. There, the exchange of information assumes the role of the exchange of energy in inducing excitation and response of the system. In non-technical parlance, Shannon entropy quantifies the expected value of information in a message:[53] the more information is transmitted/received, the less uncertainty results and the less information entropy in the system, causing the possible outcomes of the exchange of information to be highly predictable. Flipping coins or rolling dice provide characteristic examples of measurable Shannon entropy – namely, the difference between the information contained in the message and the part of information provided by the message (i.e. the coin or the dice). Before we flip a coin, we are uncertain about what will happen when it is flipped. After the coin is flipped, the uncertainty immediately drops to zero since we now know the response (i.e. heads or tails). This, in turn, means that we have gained information on the content of the message. As a measure of uncertainty of a random variable,

entails freedom to choose among the most probable outcomes. See Koutsoyiannis and Sargentis (n 49) 1364.

51 Although the concept of equilibrium is crucial in structuring a system, it has been misinterpreted as the self-maintenance of order in a system and the non-randomness of the system's variables. However, drawing an analogy between equilibrium and regularity has been correctly characterized as arbitrary, since in a state of equilibrium there can be no change in a closed or isolated system except where an external force acts upon parts of the system. See Britannica, The Editors of Encyclopedia, 'equilibrium', *Encyclopedia Britannica* (21 July 2022) <www.britannica.com/science/equilibrium-physics> accessed 12 May 2022.

52 C Shannon, 'A Mathematical Theory of Communication' (1948) 27 BSTJ 379 and 623.

53 O Rioul, 'This Is IT: A Primer on Shannon's Entropy and Information' in B Duplantier and V Rivasseau (eds), *Information Theory* (Progress in Mathematical Physics vol 78, Springer 2021).

this definition of entropy is probabilistic in nature; accordingly, the information exchanged is a measure of that entropy's reduction.[54]

Transposing this fundamental physical process to CIL allows us to make some very interesting observations. The CIL system's elements – namely, states and courts – exchange information regarding the meaning of CIL; states respond through their practice and courts by interpreting rules. The greater the number of probable meanings assigned to the rules in question, the greater the entropy of the CIL system; conversely, when there are fewer probable meanings, there is less uncertainty as to the content of the rule and thus minimal entropy. To this end, legal interpretation plays a fundamental role in reducing the entropy of the CIL system by providing the information that was originally not available (i.e. the concrete meaning of the CIL rule). In particular, the exchange of information about the most probable, or even precise, content of a CIL rule creates a network of binary relations between the courts that transmit the message contained in the information and the states that receive it. When international courts like the ICC form binary relations with states, this creates a one-to-one connection between them, since they are the sole components of the complex CIL system concerned.[55] The transmission of the precise content of a CIL rule to states by international courts through the interpretation process shapes the connections between the courts and the states, for courts receive feedback from the states, regardless of whether the states comply with the court's judgment.

Having said this, the analysis will now focus in Section 5 on what we call an entropic approach to the interpretation of CIL and how it is reflected in the jurisprudence of the ICC and other international criminal tribunals.

5 Modelling the Interpretation of CIL: What Do International (Criminal) Courts Say?

Traditionally, the function of the judicial power – that is, courts and tribunals *stricto sensu* – is to state the law (i.e. not only to decide which legal rules are applicable but also to determine their content in

[54] JP Sethna (n 47) 99.

[55] Based on mathematics and computer science, a binary relation is represented by a line connecting the two entities. There are three types of binary relations: one-to-one, where one entity is related to another entity; one-to-many, where one entity is related to many other entities; and many-to-many, where each entity is related to many other entities. A characteristic example of a many-to-many binary relation is a university student enrolled in many courses with each course having many students enrolled in it. For present purposes we are referring to a one-to-one binary relation between international criminal courts and individual states in a simplified form (see Figure 1).

a concrete case).[56] The legal reasoning that unfolds during the process of interpreting a CIL rule has a concretizing function (i.e. to give a concrete meaning to a CIL rule, the content of which is by definition general).[57] Legal interpretation is an exercise akin to the solving of a mathematical problem; when judges seek to determine the content of a rule in a particular case, they apply their skills to solve the problem by either settling the dispute or establishing the guilt of an accused individual.

In the case of CIL interpretation, courts determine the content of a rule by searching for states' shared understanding of the rule. Such was the approach taken by the International Criminal Court when its Appeals Chamber dealt with the thorny issue of immunity for heads of state having committed international crimes under the Rome Statute in Sudan. As Judges Eboe-Osuji, Morrison, Hofmanski and Bossa in their concurring opinion openly stated, 'the consistent and repeated rejection of immunity (even for Heads of State) in sundry instruments of international law since World War II ... has resulted in *a general understanding of customary international law* in that way'.[58]

[56] The judicial function is the main feature of the judicial authority. Literally, *juris dictio* means to state what the law is. Scelle (n 15) 694–95. Notwithstanding the debate over the susceptibility of CIL rules to the same form of interpretation as treaty law, the arbitration tribunal in the *Lake Lanoux* case of 1957 clarified that 'international law does not sanction any absolute and rigid method of interpretation'. See *Lake Lanoux (France v Spain)* (1957) 12 RIAA 281. See also M Herdegen, 'Interpretation in International Law' (MPEPIL 2020) <https://opil.ouplaw.com/display/10.1093/law:epil/9780199231690/law-9780199231690-e723> accessed 26 April 2024. Accordingly, the present author argues that interpretation has an entropic character since it gives meaning to CIL rules by transmitting information about their content. On the discussion regarding the role of the international judiciary, see also GI Hernández, 'Interpretative Authority and the International Judiciary' in A Bianchi, D Peat and M Windsor (eds), *Interpretation in International Law* (Oxford University Press 2015) 166–85.

[57] Merkouris and Mileva have argued that interpretation of a CIL rule performs an evolutive function in addition to the concretizing one. See P Merkouris and N Mileva, 'Introduction to the Series: Customary Law Interpretation as a Tool' (2022) 11(2) ESIL Reflections <https://esil-sedi.eu/esil-reflection-introduction-to-the-series-customary-law-interpretation-as-a-tool/> accessed 20 May 2022. The present author believes that there is no clear-cut distinction between these two functions of legal reasoning; in practice, they are intertwined with each other, like ivy on an oak tree, and shape the content of a CIL rule through evolutive interpretation. The content-determination process of interpretation is an inherent part of adjudication. On the content-determination process and its distinction from the law-ascertainment process of interpretation, see J d'Aspremont, 'The Multidimensional Process of Interpretation: Content-Determination and Law-Ascertainment Distinguished' in A Bianchi, D Peat and M Windsor (eds), *Interpretation in International Law* (Oxford University Press 2015) 111, 117–18.

[58] *Prosecutor v Al-Bashir*, ICC-02/05-01/09-397-Anx1 (6 May 2019) [66] (emphasis added). It has been said that this judgment 'has added another important layer of jurisprudence,

Yet, interpreting CIL rules in a criminal law context runs the grave risk of overstepping the principle of legality, which is one of the basic pillars of international criminal justice. Since international criminal courts are not permitted to 'expand uncritically the scope of [international] crimes',[59] they are confronted with a challenge when called upon to determine the content of a CIL rule with a view to characterizing it as a core international crime.

In the *Kupreskic* case, the ICTY adopted an interpretation with interesting reasoning when, following extensive analysis, it defined the content of the residual category of 'inhumane acts' as crimes against humanity.[60] Based on the notion of 'humane treatment' included in Common Article 3 of the Geneva Conventions 1949 and international human rights standards, the ICTY ruled that it is possible to 'identify a set of basic human rights' whose violation could amount to a crime against humanity. Bearing in mind that Common Article 3 had already been recognized as having *erga omnes* effect and that basic rules protecting human rights have the force of customary law, the ICTY defined the notion of inhumane act as a rule having 'less broad' customary law content.[61] The flexibility with which the ICTY handled the issue of CIL interpretation is particularly revealing, albeit not always plain to see. The case of *Krstic* is also indicative, since the ICTY recognized the concretizing function of CIL, which had delimited the *actus reus* of the crime of genocide so as to include only acts of physical destruction, a limitation accepted both by the ICTY and the ICTR in their respective statutes.[62]

Most significantly, the Appeals Chamber of the International Criminal Court followed the same path in one of its most recent judgments in the *Ntaganda* case,[63] although not in order to directly downsize the CIL rule;

[although] it will not silence the raging academic and political debate'. See A Mudukuti, 'Prosecutor v. Omar Hassan Ahmad Al-Bashir, Judgment in the Jordan Referral re Al-Bashir Appeal' (2020) 114 AJIL 103. See also *Prosecutor v Uhuru Muigai Kenyatta* (n 40) [7], [12].

59 *Prosecutor v Ongwen* (n 31) [2741].

60 *Prosecutor v Kupreskic* (Judgment) ICTY-95-16-T (14 January 2000) [562]–[566].

61 ibid [566]. See also *Prosecutor v Kordic and Cerkez* (Judgment) ICTY-95-14/2-T (26 February 2001) [269]–[270]; *Prosecutor v Kordic and Cerkez* (Judgment) ICTY-95-14/2-A (17 December 2004). In the *Ongwen* case, the ICC followed the same interpretive approach when it had to decide if the act of forced marriage could be qualified as another inhumane act, and subsequently as a crime against humanity, according to Article 7(1)(k) of the Rome Statute (Statute of the International Criminal Court (adopted 17 July 1998, entered into force 1 July 2002) 2187 UNTS 3). See *Prosecutor v Ongwen* (n 31) [2741], [2747].

62 *Prosecutor v Krstic* (Judgment) ICTY-98-33-T (2 August 2001) [580].

63 *Prosecutor v Ntaganda*, ICC-01/04-02/06 OA5 (15 June 2017).

instead, the its aim was to ensure consistency with international humanitarian law (IHL), in both its customary and its treaty forms. Such an outcome can be achieved either by interpretation of its terms or by identifying additional elements to the crime in question. In particular, the Appeals Chamber came to an 'unprecedented' conclusion when it accepted that additional elements originating from CIL can be included as an element of the war crimes listed in Article 8(2)(b) or (e) of the Rome Statute as part of examining the 'established framework of international law'.[64] Although not openly stated, it is clear from the Court's analysis that if an element external to the Rome Statute is added to the war crimes enumerated as other serious violations of the law of war, such an element can and will be interpreted, irrespective of whether it derives from customary or treaty IHL. Besides, the Court explicitly ruled that 'the "established framework of international law" within article 8 (2) (b) and (e) of the Statute permits recourse to customary and conventional international law regardless of whether any lacuna exists.'[65] In short, the ICC recognized the interpretability of CIL and rejected allegations of possible violation of the legality principle.[66] This is a novel approach, not only for ICL but for the function of the judiciary in general. As successfully argued by Scelle back in 1948, jurisprudence '*assouplit et adapte*' (softens and adjusts) legal rules in accordance with evolving social needs. Since the judicial function grows out of the social environment through natural evolution, its technique has a dynamic character. In this respect, jurisprudence, fulfilling the law, is part of the judicial order.[67] The interpretation process as just described allows CIL, thanks to its equally dynamic character, to adjust to changes in its social environment. The reactions of the acting agents in the CIL system (i.e. states, non-state actors and international criminal courts) provide feedback into the system, driving it to change and evolve.

[64] ibid [52]–[55]. See also F Pocar, 'Symposium on the Rome Statute at Twenty: Transformation of Customary Law through ICC Practice' (2018) 112 AJIL Unbound 182.

[65] *Prosecutor v Ntaganda* (n 63) [53].

[66] ibid [54]. On the interpretability of CIL, see P Merkouris, 'Interpreting the Customary Rules on Interpretation' (2017) 19 ICLR 139. For an early, yet meaningful, discussion regarding the contribution of international case law to the interpretation of CIL, see KS Gallant, 'International Criminal Courts and the Making of Public International Law: New Roles for International Organizations and Individuals' (2010) 43 J Marshall L Rev. 607.

[67] Scelle (n 15) 16–17, 662–64, 676–78. According to the French jurist, the judicial function aims towards establishing a legal order ('*ordonnancement juridique*') that describes the legal relations/connections between public and private persons. Scelle's systemic approach to international law dates back to 1948.

Entropy is thus at a low level, since uncertainty over the content of the CIL rule has been reduced.

This dynamic process was analysed by Judge Antonio Cassese when, as president of the Special Tribunal for Lebanon (STL), he delivered an interlocutory decision on the applicable law in the *Ayyash* case.[68] In explaining the role of the interpreting judge, Cassese recalled the constructive function of interpretation as being 'to give consistency, homogeneity and due weighting to the different elements of a diverging or heterogeneous set of provisions'.[69] This approach to interpretation is founded upon the context of the rule, both internal and external. In particular, it was stressed that 'the rules of interpretation that evolved in international custom and were codified or developed in the 1969 Vienna Convention on the Law of Treaties . . . must . . . be held to be applicable to *any internationally binding instrument, whatever its normative source*'.[70]

As CIL is unwritten law, it falls upon the courts to elucidate relevant rules in their context – in other words, to contextualize the CIL rules.[71] Thereby, CIL can be interpreted according to the general principles of judicial interpretation with a view to 'apply[ing] legal norms consistently'.[72] The constructive approach, adopted by the STL, is inextricably linked to teleological interpretation. Taking the form of the effectiveness principle, contextual interpretation aims to 'harmonise the various provisions in light of the goal pursued by the legislature'.[73] In giving concrete meaning to a CIL rule, it reconciles the various meanings of the CIL rule. Subsequently, entropy is reduced, as harmonization counteracts uncertainty by revealing the most probable meaning of a CIL rule. In this respect, a CIL rule will consequently reflect the shared understanding of international actors regarding the content of the rule.

For the STL, such an interpretive approach corresponds to the reality of a dynamic society that changes over time, thus leading to the progressive development of the law. Recalling Jeremy Bentham, the presiding judge,

[68] *Interlocutory Decision on the Applicable Law: Terrorism, Conspiracy, Homicide, Perpetration, Cumulative Charging* STL-11-01/I (16 February 2011).

[69] ibid [23]–[24]. On Judge Cassese's contribution regarding the construction of international criminal law through custom, see M Fan, 'Custom, General Principles and the Great Architect Cassese' (2012) 10 JICJ 1063.

[70] *Interlocutory Decision* (n 68) [26] (emphasis added).

[71] ibid [19]–[20]. For present purposes, 'contextualize' means 'to provide information about the situation in which something happens'. See 'contextualize' (*The Britannica Dictionary*) <www.britannica.com/dictionary/contextualize> accessed 30 May 2022.

[72] *Interlocutory Decision* (n 68) [26].

[73] ibid [30].

the late Antonio Cassese, clarified that CIL also develops through a 'continuing and prospective evolution' in order 'to adjust [the Court's] decision to the special circumstances [of a particular case]'.[74] Progressive development does not preclude the application of the legality principle, 'as long as this application was foreseeable'.[75] To the extent that international actors – state and non-state – are affected by that interpretation, they will react by providing feedback to the Court's interpretative approach.[76]

At this point, some clarification is needed: obtaining feedback from states in ICL cases is not of the same nature as in other international law interstate cases such as those before the ICJ. Feedback from states in ICL cases involving CIL interpretation can assume different shapes and forms. Take, for example, Articles 86–87 and 97 of the Rome State on the obligation of state parties to cooperate and consult with the ICC during the investigation, prosecution and enforcement stages. Here, the triggering of a mechanism of non-compliance with the Court's judgments constitutes proof of feedback by a member state. Let us elaborate on the facts and the Court's reasoning to comprehend how entropy changes in this case.

The judgments against South Africa and Jordan, parties to the Rome Statute, concerning non-execution of the arrest warrant against Omar al-Bashir, are examples of such a complex case. The ICC ruled that both states had violated their obligations deriving from the Rome Statute, since they had not arrested and surrendered Sudan's head of state al-Bashir to the Court for having committed war crimes, crimes against humanity and genocide.[77] Pursuant to a UN Security Council referral of the situation in

[74] ibid [106], [135].

[75] ibid. The ICC has equally ruled in the *Ongwen* case and in relation to Article 7(1)(k) of the Rome Statute that judicial interpretation 'must be consistent with the essence of the offence and *in a manner which could have been reasonably foreseen*'. *Prosecutor v Ongwen* (n 31) [2741] (emphasis added). Yet debate over the strict application of the legality principle remains intense, with those opposed arguing in favour of flexibility of the rules in order to fight impunity. See JL Corsi, 'An Argument for Strict Legality in International Criminal Law' (2018) 49(4) GJIL 1321.

[76] According to Sur, the subjects of international law provide feedback when they accept a judicial interpretation; in so doing, they lend authenticity to this interpretation. S Sur, 'La créativité du droit international' (2012) 363 RdC 9. Such was the interpretative stance of the ICC in the *Ntaganda* case when the Court rejected the defence submissions on introducing status requirements as additional elements to the war crimes of Article 8(2)(b)(xxii) and (e)(vi) of the Rome Statute. The Court thereby transmitted information on the customary law context of war crimes based on the intention of the drafters of the Rome Statute; such intention demonstrated the drafters' shared understanding of the provisions. *Prosecutor v Ntaganda* (n 63) [47]–[48].

[77] *Prosecutor v Al-Bashir*, Decision under Article 87(7) of the Rome Statute on the Non-compliance by South Africa with the Request by the Court for the Arrest and Surrender of

Darfur to the ICC, the latter issued two arrest warrants for al-Bashir in 2009 and 2010 calling upon all state parties to cooperate with the Court in accordance with their obligations under the Rome Statute.[78] After rejecting the objections of South Africa and Jordan invoking the immunity rule for heads of state, the Court explained that there was no CIL norm on immunity that shielded active heads of state accused of having committed core international crimes.[79] The most interesting conclusion of the ICC Pre-Trial Chamber was its decision to refer the non-compliance issue to the Assembly of States Parties and the UN Security Council. However, it did so only for Jordan, not for South Africa, reasoning that the former was aware of its obligations but 'chose not to execute [them]',[80] whereas the latter was not. The second Pre-Trial Chamber (PTC II) maintained a different approach towards South Africa based on two main reasons: firstly, there was genuine interaction with South African authorities regarding the state's obligation to co-operate with the Court and, secondly, South Africa's violation of its obligations had also been recognized by the country's domestic courts.[81] The Appeals Chamber overturned the decision for Jordan and decided not to refer the situation to the Assembly of States Parties and the UN Security Council. It held that Jordan had not refused to consult with the court in defiance of its obligation deriving from Article 97 of the Rome Statute. On the contrary, its *note verbale* qualified as a request for consultations with the Court and was proof of good faith with regard to the problem of the execution of the arrest warrant.[82]

We draw particular attention to the feedback of the Court based on the different legal reasoning of the PTC II and the Appeals Chamber. Although not directly connected to interpreting CIL, each legal reasoning is important insofar as it portrays how interpretation works as a means of keeping the entropy of the CIL system at a low level. Further evidence of that is the Appeal Chamber judgment concluding that the different treatment of

Omar Al-Bashir, ICC-02/05-01/09-302 (6 July 2017); *Prosecutor v al-Bashir*, Decision under Article 87(7) of the Rome Statute on the Con-compliance by Jordan with the Request by the Court for the Arrest and Surrender or Omar Al-Bashir, ICC-02/05-01/09-309 (11 December 2017).

78 Rome Statute (n 61) arts 86ff.

79 Although strongly criticized for these judgments by part of academia, the ICJ had already been receptive to the idea that the immunity rule cannot justify impunity when the accused is a head of state. *Case Concerning the Arrest Warrant of 11 April 2000 (Democratic Republic of Congo v Belgium)* [2002] ICJ Rep 3.

80 *Prosecutor v Al-Bashir* (n 77) (11 December 2017) [53].

81 *Prosecutor v Al-Bashir* (n 77) (6 July 2017) [136].

82 *Prosecutor v Al-Bashir*, ICC-02/05-01/09 OA2 (6 May 2019) [204].

Jordan and South Africa was due to abuse by PTC II of its discretionary power. When state parties rejected the Court's interpretation regarding their obligations under the customary rule of immunity, the entropy of the system increased, as there were many possible interpretive (and conflicting) outcomes. When the Appeals Chamber overturned the PTC II's judgment, the CIL entropy had been reduced to a minimum as there was only one possible interpretive outcome for the CIL rule on immunity. This shows that the process of ICC feedback to states proves to be particularly influential for complex systems, since it keeps the entropy at a low level.

International case law can also affect state behaviour by triggering a change in state practice.[83] The feedback process leads the CIL system to adapt through a learning process that relies on information from its own agents as well as its environment. In other words, the topology of the CIL system (i.e. the structure of the CIL network and the frequency and intensity of interactions between its agents) is indicative of its inherently dynamic character and its ability to evolve as a real social phenomenon.

6 Concluding Remarks: A 'Low Entropy' Mode of Interpretation for CIL

The present chapter has attempted to show how the interpretation of CIL operates in accordance with the fundamental rules of nature. Since human systems are affected by various kinds of complexity, we turned to the findings of complexity science to describe CIL as a complex adaptive system forming societal bonds between the various state and non-state agents involved in international criminal justice.

In modelling CIL as an epistemic tool, we have sought to explain the mechanical behaviour of CIL when international criminal tribunals and, in

[83] A characteristic example is the European Court of Human Rights and the profound influence of its judgments upon the shaping of state policies, through the adoption of national legislation and/or administrative practice. See Verdier, and Voeten (n 10) 420; L Helfer and E Voeten, 'International Courts as Agents of Legal Change: Evidence from LGBT Rights in Europe' (2014) 68 IO 77. In the area of international criminal law, the notion of positive complementarity as a state policy to address core crimes through the adoption of domestic measures and the initiation of national proceedings, is of particular importance with respect to the feedback provided by member states to the Rome Statute. See Annual Report of the Office of the Prosecutor (2022) <www.icc-cpi.int/sites/default/files/2022-12/2022-12-05-annual-report-of-the-office-of-the-prosecutor.pdf> accessed 1 June 2022; Final Report of the ILA Committee on positive complementarity in international criminal law (2022) <www.ila-hq.org/en/committees/complementarity-in-international-criminal-law> accessed 1 June 2022.

particular, the ICC interpret its rules. To this end, we introduced entropy, as the internal property of a complex system that stimulates changes according to the flow of information transmitted both between its component elements and between the latter and the system's environment.

For the CIL complex system, legal interpretation is the source of information provided by the international courts when they concretize abstract CIL rules by attributing the most probable meaning to those rules. Such an entropic mode of interpretation reduces uncertainties over the content of the rules, triggers changes in the CIL system and, thus, encourages the system to develop further and thereby evolve. The extent of the changes that will occur depends on the feedback such interpretation draws from the agents of the CIL system.

Adopting such an approach to the interpretation of CIL helps us redefine our perceptions as lawyers regarding the quest for certainty and predictability in international law. Thus, we have argued that chance does not correspond to the unknown and the uncertain that Czech choreographer J. Kylian considered to be epitomized in the tossing of the dice; rather, throwing a dice is all about probabilities.

In the field of international criminal justice, reducing uncertainties is especially vital to the unity and progressive development of international criminal law. Recent interpretation by the ICC has displayed low entropy. Were the Court to follow such an entropic interpretation in the future, this could lead to the transformation of CIL and in turn to a unified approach in ICL. It remains to be seen whether the international judiciary will seize the opportunity to 'activate' entropic interpretation to stimulate changes in the complex CIL system.

PART II

Methods of CIL Interpretation in International Courts

Tools of the Trade

5

The Application of Logic and Reason in CIL Identification and Interpretation

WILLIAM THOMAS WORSTER

1 Introduction

The process of identifying and interpreting norms of customary international law, while appearing to be primarily based on an inductive analysis of state practice and *opinio juris*, is sometimes a deductive exercise based on logic and reason. Logic permeates every decision in international law. Illogic might also be present as well, of course, but in terms of identifying, interpreting, and applying law, we tend to claim that we do it logically and, perhaps, even scientifically. Logic manifests itself inherently throughout the process and can be identified in all steps of reasoning in identifying, interpreting, and applying customary international law. Logic, however, can constitute the application of either an inductive or deductive inference. This chapter will focus on situations in which the International Court of Justice (ICJ) and Permanent Court of International Justice (PCIJ) applied a deductive approach, identifying or interpreting norms of customary international law without seeming to consult state practice and *opinio juris*. Specifically, it will consider whether norms that can be reasonably inferred or deduced from existing rules, or that are simply logical for the operation of the international legal system, can be identified as norms of customary international law under a complementary, supplementary, or distinctive interpretive approach.

One initial observation is necessary at the outset regarding proving customary international law. In customary international law, the process of constituting or prescribing a norm, while analytically distinct from proving the existence of the norm with evidence, is often blurred with it. That is to say, we usually claim that a norm of customary international law has been created when we can prove the existence of sufficient state practice and *opinio juris*. We might concede that the norm could have existed prior to our discovery of it, but we would likely still insist that the norm came into being when a critical mass of state practice and *opinio juris*, the evidence of the norm, coalesced. In addition, we do not usually distinguish between the ascertainment of the existence of a rule of customary international law and the interpretation of the rule's content. Generally, those operations are combined into one act of ascertaining the content of the rule through evidence at the level of its identification. In the International Law Commission (ILC) study on customary international law, the special rapporteur was careful to observe that the study was undertaken to state the rules on the *identification* of customary international law.[1] As will be discussed further, the ICJ as well, implicitly, distinguishes between these operations.[2] Thus, the proof of the norm and its creation, constitution, or prescription, as well as the development and identification of content, while they are casually unified into one act of discovery and confirmation through evidence, can be distinguished.

Part of the reason for mixing these questions into a casual unified approach is that we do not clearly state whether the state practice–*opinio juris* analytical framework is a question of law or a question of fact. Surely, it cannot be a question of fact, because we are not trying to establish acts that trigger the application of the law, but then why do we collect a sampling of evidence and consider its reliability and sufficiency, as if we were proving a fact? Surely, it is a question of law, but then why do we not simply allow the court to inform itself as it sees fit, *jura novit curia*? The difficulty is that it is law, but the content and existence of the law is established by facts. The ILC special rapporteur was well aware of this difficulty and was careful to note that he did not use the expression

[1] ILC, 'Draft Conclusions on Identification of Customary International Law, with Commentaries' (30 April–1 June and 2 July–10 August 2018) UN Doc A/73/10.

[2] See *Delimitation of the Maritime Boundary in the Gulf of Maine Area (Canada v US)* (Judgment) [1984] ICJ Rep 246 [111]–[112] (after rejecting the existence of detailed rules under customary international law, suggesting that a better approach is to clarify the content of the existing rules: 'A body of detailed rules is not to be looked for in customary international law . . . It is therefore unrewarding . . . to look to general international law to provide a readymade set of rules . . . A more useful course is to seek a better formulation of the fundamental norm, on which the Parties were fortunate enough to be agreed, and whose existence in the legal convictions not only of the Parties to the present dispute, but of all States, is apparent from an examination of the realities of international legal relations. The Chamber therefore wishes to conclude this review of the rules of international law on the question to which the dispute between Canada and the United States relates by attempting a more complete and, in its opinion, more precise reformulation of the "fundamental norm" already mentioned.')

'evidence' in the sense of establishing a fact.[3] But this conclusion also means that the court is perhaps freer to use various forms – perhaps conflicting forms – of logical inferences throughout the process of identifying customary international law than it might if it was establishing facts.

2 Forms of Logic and Reasoning

What does it mean to use 'logic' or 'reason' to identify customary international law? A fully detailed explanation of logic is outside the scope of this chapter,[4] but essentially it involves the process of drawing inferences, either through induction or deduction.[5]

Induction is usually described as drawing inferences from examples of empirical phenomena to create a general theory explaining those phenomena. The assumption is that a sample of instances will produce observable phenomena that will always be the case,[6] based on a statistical syllogism that the overall population of cases resembles the sample pool.[7] This inference to a theory will be more or less accurate depending on the quantity and quality of the evidence.[8] In terms of collecting evidence, the approach uses a sampling pool of data and generalization to an explanation.[9] However, the process of sampling and generalization is usually predicated on the sample pool being

[3] ibid, Conclusion 3, Comment (1), n 680 ('The term "evidence" is used here as a broad concept relating to all the materials that may be considered as a basis for the identification of customary international law, not in any technical sense as used by particular courts or in particular legal systems.')

[4] For a more detailed discussion of forms of logic, see W Worster, 'The Inductive and Deductive Methods in Customary International Law Analysis: Traditional and Modern Approaches' (2014) 45 GJIL 445.

[5] cf the use of logic in treaty interpretation described in 'Appendix 4: Fiore's Draft Code' (1935) 29 AJIL Supp 1212, 1218–19, citing P Fiore, *International Law Codified and Its Legal Sanction* (Edwin M. Borchard tr, Baker Voorhis 1918) (identifying various logical interpretative techniques, including intent of the parties, context, systematicity, and teleology, which provide a means for an inference to meaning).

[6] G King, R Keohane, and S Verba, *Designing Social Inquiry: Scientific Inference in Qualitative Research* (Princeton University Press 1994) 8.

[7] ibid.

[8] See J Vickers, 'The Problem of Induction', *The Stanford Encyclopedia of Philosophy* (Winter edn 2022) <http://plato.stanford.edu/entries/induction-problem/> (accessed 10 September 2022); K Popper and D Miller, 'A Proof of the Impossibility of Inductive Probability' (1983) 302 Nature 687.

[9] A Giddens and others, *Essentials of Sociology* (WW Norton 2010) 28.

random.[10] Of course, random sampling could include sampling with an equal probability of selecting a sample, sampling a number of cases from the same pool rather than a single instance (cluster sampling), or deliberately placing samples into certain subpools and randomly drawing from them (stratified sampling).[11]

Deduction, on the other hand, begins with premises, which are either established (themselves through induction or deduction) or presumed to be true, and then proceeds to infer a conclusion that must follow.[12] Its strength is that, again, if the premises are true, the conclusion is not subject to falsification.[13] It is not based on sampling instances or developing theories to explain those cases. There are many forms of deductive reasoning that could be characterized as logical, but several are relevant for this chapter. Talmon, for example, identified normative, functional, and analogical deductions in the case law of the ICJ.[14] These logical inferences are based on, respectively, deducing the content of rules from other rules or principles, the functions of an organization or actor, or by drawing an analogy from existing rules to a situation not initially covered by the rule.[15]

Having surveyed the basic forms and approaches of logic, this chapter will now turn to their application in identifying rules of customary international law.

3 The Use of Logic and Reasoning in the Analysis of Customary International Law

Traditionally, we say that the identification of customary international law is a process of inductive reasoning from manifestations of state practice and expressions of *opinio juris*,[16] but the various steps in customary international law analysis are also infused with a considerable

[10] C Sanders Peirce, *Philosophical Writings of Peirce* (Justus Buchler ed, Dover 1955) 152; Giddens and others (n 9) 28–30.

[11] See generally DS Yates and others, *The Practice of Statistics* (3rd edn, WH Freeman 2008).

[12] J Kammerhofer, 'Uncertainty in the Formal Sources of International Law: Customary International Law and Some of Its Problems' (2004) 15 EJIL 523, 542.

[13] See E Adam, 'A Logic of Conditionals' (1965) 8 Inquiry 166.

[14] S Talmon, 'Determining Customary International Law: The ICJ's Methodology between Induction, Deduction and Assertion' (2015) 26 EJIL 417, 423–26.

[15] ibid.

[16] See G Schwarzenberger, *The Inductive Approach to International Law* (Stevens & Sons 1965) 22, 47, 51, 65–66, 71; G Schwarzenberger, 'The Inductive Approach to International Law' (1947) 60 Har L Rev 539.

degree of deductive logic – including both the processes to discover secondary rules and those used to discover primary rules.[17] The chamber of the ICJ in the *Gulf of Maine* case stated that customary international law 'can be tested by induction based on the analysis of a sufficiently extensive and convincing practice, and not by deduction from preconceived ideas'.[18]

But the ICJ does not necessarily follow a truly inductive process. We do not randomly identify states to examine. Instead, we select which states to sample based on a specially interested states analysis and/or a (geographic, historical, etc.) diversity of states. In either case, the states chosen are not selected by random draw, but are chosen for their 'representativity'. In addition, induction usually establishes a prior standard for determining when the sampled cases would be sufficient,[19] and sets the standard of proof accordingly,[20] yet the ICJ has not articulated a clear standard of proof for customary international law. More importantly, a truly inductive logical approach must find the rule negated by even one instance of contrary practice,[21] and yet, in the *Nicaragua* case, the ICJ was explicit that perfect conformity was not required.[22] And in the *Gulf of Maine* case cited above, the ICJ chamber added that, while induction is one approach to identifying customary international law, there was also 'a limited set of norms for ensuring the coexistence and vital cooperation of the members of the international community'.[23] For these reasons, and others, many scholars have argued that a 'modern'

[17] But see M Hakimi, 'Making Sense of Customary International Law' (2020) 118 Mich L Rev 1487, 1510 ('The lack of secondary rules in CIL does not mean that "anything goes". It means that what goes is not determined by secondary rules. The status of a given normative position within CIL depends instead on how global actors interact with it over time.').

[18] *Gulf of Maine* (n 2) [111]. See also *Continental Shelf (Libya/Malta)* (Judgment) [1985] ICJ Rep 13 [27].

[19] See R Rudner, 'The Scientist *qua* Scientist Makes Value Judgments' (1953) 20 Philos Sci 1, 2 ('since no hypothesis is ever completely verified, in accepting a hypothesis the scientist must make the decision that the evidence is *sufficiently* strong or that the probability is *sufficiently* high to warrant the acceptance of the hypothesis').

[20] See I Levi, *Hard Choices: Decision Making under Unresolved Conflict* (Cambridge University Press 1986) 43–46; F Plumpton Ramsey, 'Truth and Probability' in F Plumpton Ramsey and RB Braithwaite (eds), *The Foundations of Mathematics and Other Logical Essays* (Martino Fine Books 1931) 156.

[21] See eg K Popper, 'Science: Conjectures and Refutations' in JA Curd and M Cover (eds) *Philosophy of Science: The Central Issues* (WW Norton 1998) 3–10.

[22] *Military and Paramilitary Activities in and against Nicaragua (Nicaragua v US)* (Judgment) [1986] ICJ Rep 14 [186].

[23] *Gulf of Maine* (n 2) [111]. See also *Continental Shelf (Libya/Malta)* (n 18) [27]. D Anzilotti, *Corso di diritto internazionale* (3rd edn, Athenaeum 1928) 67 (observing

approach (or 'human rights approach') to customary international law in fact applies deductive logic.[24]

That being said, the actual logical reasoning applied by courts is often opaque. Sometimes it can appear that a court has deduced the existence of a rule when it may have applied an inductive approach. For example, in *Maclaine Watson*, the House of Lords (as per Lord Templeman) concluded that imposing liability on the states that constituted the International Tin Council when that organization dissolved would not be logical: 'An international law or a domestic law which imposed and enforced joint and several liability on 23 sovereign States without imposing and enforcing contribution between those States would be devoid of logic and justice.'[25] This sentence suggests a deductive approach. However, Templeman continued to explain that: 'No plausible evidence was produced of the existence of such a rule of international law before or at the time of the Sixth Agreement in 1982 or thereafter.'[26] Therefore, although it might at first appear that he was asserting a rule, he was in fact concluding that such a rule was not logical or just because it had not been proven to exist. Of course, it might be that rules of customary international law are logical, as deduced from certain values rather than induction from practice, but that the same rule would result from either deduction or induction, and deduction only buttresses the conclusion from induction.[27]

that that 'constructive rules' were simply logical and necessary in the international legal system) (English translation in G Gaja, 'Positivism and Dualism in Dionisio Anzilotti' (1992) 3 EJIL 123). Though Anzilotti acknowledged the existence of rules of this type, he linked them to general principles of law and distinguished them from treaty law or customary international law. See Anzilotti, *Corso* 67 ('Constructive rules and general principles of law are close concepts'). Therefore, Anzilotti's constructive rules would not fall within the category of logical customary international law described by the ICJ in the *Gulf of Maine case*.

24 See J Wouters and C Ryngaert, 'The Impact on the Process of the Formation of Customary International Law' in MT Kamminga and M Scheinin (eds), *The Impact of Human Rights Law on General International Law* (Oxford University Press 2009) 111; AE Roberts, 'Traditional and Modern Approaches to Customary International Law: A Reconciliation' (2001) 95 AJIL 757, 758; ILA Committee on Formation of Customary (General) International Law, 'Final Report of the Committee: Statement of Principles Applicable to the Formation of General Customary International Law' (2000) Principle 19, Comment (a); MH Mendelson, 'The Formation of Customary International Law' (1998) 272 RdC 155; JI Charney, 'Universal International Law' (1993) 87 AJIL 529, 544–45; FL Kirgis Jr, 'Custom on a Sliding Scale' (1987) 81 AJIL 146.

25 *Maclaine Watson v Department of Trade* [1989] 3 All ER 523 (HL) 529.

26 ibid 554.

27 The language that courts use to describe their logical steps is not always consistent; see eg *R v Bow St Metropolitan Stipendiary Magistrate, ex p Pinochet Ugarte* [*Pinochet III*] [1999] 2 WLR 827 (HL) [58] (describing an inductive step as deduction).

3.1 *The Foundations of Customary International Law as a Source of International Law*

The very existence of customary international law as a source of international law is largely a result of a logical deduction. In the early jurisprudence of the PCIJ and other bodies, no effort was made to establish consistent state practice and *opinio juris* for the existence of custom as a source of law,[28] and instead the PCIJ and other authorities deduced the existence of custom.[29] Similarly, when the International Law Association sought to complete its study on customary international law, it acknowledged that it would draw on the practice of states to identify the rules of customary international law, though that was not simply an exercise in using custom to support the existence and rules of custom itself.[30] In the ILC study on customary international law, the special rapporteur relied almost exclusively on the case law of the ICJ, among other courts and tribunals, and cited to little state practice or *opinio juris* as expressed by states on point.[31] Of course, those cases that were cited might or might not have cited to state practice or *opinio juris* in turn. These approaches do not make the conclusions wrong; after all, reliance on prior judicial decisions is a valid subsidiary source for the content of any of the formal sources.[32] But such reliance on prior cases demonstrates that the identification of customary international law as a source of international law is not entirely established by state practice and *opinio juris* alone and is likely a logical deduction from the behaviour of states.

In turn, the very constitution of customary international law by state practice and *opinio juris* alone is also not clearly based on a logical inductive examination of state practice and *opinio juris*.[33] Instead, the requirement of state practice and *opinio juris* is primarily derived from

[28] See *The Case of the S.S. 'Lotus' (France v Turkey)* [1927] PCIJ Series A No 10; *North Sea Continental Shelf (Germany v Denmark; Germany v Netherlands)* (Judgment) [1969] ICJ Rep 3, 42, 44; *Continental Shelf (Libya/Malta)* (n 18) [27]–[30]; *Jurisdictional Immunities of the State (Germany v Italy)* (Judgment) [2012] ICJ Rep 99 [55].

[29] *Lotus* (n 28) 28–30.

[30] ILA Committee on Formation of Customary (General) International Law, 'Final Report' (n 24) para 6.

[31] Eg ibid fns 689–98 (discussing the 'Requirement of practice' with almost exclusive reference to ICJ case law and one reference to the practice of international financial organizations).

[32] See Statute of the International Court of Justice (adopted 26 June 1945, entered into force 24 October 1945) 892 UNTS 119, art 38(1)(d).

[33] See eg PE Benson, 'François Gény's Doctrine on Customary Law' (1983) 20 Can YIL 267 (arguing that it was Gény who first articulated the elements of practice and *opinio juris*, based on principles of natural law).

the PCIJ and ICJ Statutes, upheld by legal tradition and reaffirmed by, inter alia, the ICJ.[34] From the language of the Statutes, it is not completely clear that customary international law is formed by state practice and *opinio juris* as elements.[35] There is certainly space to argue that these aspects are factors or perhaps even evidentiary measures for custom.[36] In fact, the process of identifying rules of customary international law often treats state practice and *opinio juris* more like factors or evidence than truly as elements.[37] Nonetheless, they are commonly understood to be elements.[38]

3.2 The Deduction of Customary International Law without Resort to the Elements

Both the ICJ and PCIJ have suggested that some rules of customary international law might not be established by the elements of state practice and *opinio juris*.[39] As noted above, the ICJ chamber in the *Gulf of Maine* case took note of some norms in international law that were not proved through induction but by their role in 'ensuring ... coexistence and vital cooperation'.[40] The ICJ seems to be saying that there are some rules that are established through an inductive inference from state practice and *opinio juris*, but that there are other rules that

[34] See eg *Lotus* (n 28); *North Sea Continental Shelf* (n 28) 44; *Continental Shelf (Libya/Malta)* (n 18) [27]–[30]; *Jurisdictional Immunities of the State* (n 28) [55]; ILC, 'Draft Conclusions' (n 1).

[35] Compare Statute of the International Court of Justice (n 32) art 38(1)(b) ('international custom, as evidence of a general practice accepted as law' merely evidenced by practice and *opinio juris*), *with* European Union Guidelines on Promoting Compliance with International Humanitarian Law (IHL) [2005] OJ C327/04 [7] ('Customary international law is formed by the practice of States which they accept as binding upon them.').

[36] See Case of the *S.S. 'Wimbledon' (UK, France, Italy and Japan v Germany)* [1923] PCIJ Series A No 1, 25 (inferring *opinio juris* from widespread and consistent practice); *Nottebohm (Liechtenstein v Guatemala) (second phase)* (Judgment) [1955] ICJ Rep 4, 22; *North Sea Continental Shelf* (n 28) Dissenting Opinion of Judge Lachs 231, Dissenting Opinion of Judge Sørensen 246–47.

[37] See Roberts (n 24) 758; ILA Committee on Formation of Customary (General) International Law, 'Final Report' (n 24) [10](c) ('undoubtedly it is often difficult or impossible to separate the two elements'); B Cheng, 'United Nations Resolutions on Outer Space: "Instant" International Customary Law?' (1965) 5 IJIL 23, 36 ('international customary law has in reality only one constitutive element, the *opinio juris*').

[38] See ILC, 'Draft Conclusions' (n 1), Conclusion 3(2): 'Each of the two constituent elements is to be separately ascertained. This requires an assessment of evidence for each element.'

[39] See also C Tomuschat, 'Obligations Arising for States without or against Their Will' (1993) 241 RdC 195, 292–304, 307.

[40] *Gulf of Maine* (n 2) [111].

are not.[41] This approach is not isolated. In the *Corfu Channel* case, the ICJ relied on 'elementary considerations of humanity' to identify rules of customary international law.[42] We could interpret this passage in an alternate way: that some rules of customary international law, while constituted by state practice and *opinio juris*, can be proved to exist by simply being logical for coexistence, vital cooperation or principles of humanity. And yet, the ICJ has also held quite clearly that customary international law norms cannot simply be deduced from 'humanitarian considerations' or 'moral principles'.[43]

The ICJ takes several approaches to deducing the existence of customary international law. The first approach – what Talmon terms 'normative deduction' – is to infer the existence of a rule from other rules. For example, the ICJ has relied on the contents of treaties to prove the existence of customary international law.[44] While it identified the right of self-determination in the *Namibia* advisory opinion, it used the UN Charter to interpret the rule as applying for all peoples.[45] In a similar fashion, it has looked to UNGA resolutions to prove customary international rules.[46] However, in both instances one could argue that the ICJ

41 See also E Benvenisti, 'Customary International Law as a Judicial Tool for Promoting Efficiency' in E Benvenisti and M Hirsch (eds), *The Impact of International Law on International Cooperation: Theoretical Perspectives* (Cambridge University Press 2004) 85, 86 ('The ICJ has, in fact, the authority to invent the custom.').

42 *Corfu Channel (UK v Albania)* (Judgment) [1949] ICJ Rep 4, 83.

43 *South West Africa (Liberia v South Africa)* (Judgment) [1966] ICJ Rep 6, 34, [49]–[50].

44 See *Gulf of Maine* (n 2) [112] ('The Chamber [will] attempt a more complete and, in its opinion, more precise reformulation of the "fundamental norm" already mentioned. For this purpose it will, *inter alia*, draw also upon the definition of the "actual rules of law . . . which govern the delimitation of adjacent continental shelves – that is to say, rules binding upon States for all delimitations" which was given by the Court in its 1969 Judgment in the *North Sea Continental Shelf* cases') (citing *North Sea Continental Shelf* (n 28) 46–47 [85]); *Armed Activities on the Territory of the Congo (DR Congo v Uganda)* (Judgment) [2005] ICJ Rep 168 [161]–[162], [213]–[214], [244] (finding customary international humanitarian law by relying on the role of the Hague Convention Respecting the Laws and Customs of Land Warfare, and customary international law on the 'principle of permanent sovereignty over natural resources' by relying on UNGA resolutions); *Jurisdictional Immunities of the State* (n 28) [54] (citing the European Convention on State Immunity (signed 16 May 1972, entered into force 11 June 1976, 4 October 1979 in UK) 1495 UNTS 182, and the UN Convention on Jurisdictional Immunities of States and Their Property (adopted 2 December 2004, not yet in force) UN Doc A/59/508).

45 *Legal Consequences for States of the Continued Presence of South Africa in Namibia (South West Africa) Notwithstanding Security Council Resolution 276 (1970)* (Advisory Opinion) [1971] ICJ Rep 16, 31 [52] (regarding the right to self-determination).

46 See *Military and Paramilitary Activities in and against Nicaragua* (n 22) [191]–[193], [264] (recognizing that the text of UNGA Resolution 2625 (XXV) (Friendly Relations

was not identifying a new rule of customary international law, but was instead using the UN Charter and UNGA resolutions to clarify the content of a rule through systemic interpretation. In the *Territorial and Maritime Dispute*, Nicaragua and Colombia agreed that customary international law would apply to the case because Colombia was not a party to the UN Convention on the Law of the Sea (UNCLOS), and agreed that the provisions in UNCLOS regarding the baselines and entitlement to maritime zones, exclusive economic zone (EEZ), and continental shelf reflected customary international law,[47] though they disagreed over the content of the rules concerning the continental shelf beyond 200 nautical miles.[48] It is possible to argue that the ICJ was merely affirming that Nicaragua had an obligation toward the other states parties to UNCLOS to comply with Article 76 when it referred to the 'interrelated' nature of ocean space.[49] However, it did explicitly cite to obligations *inter partes* between states not parties to the dispute. In fact, it argued that UNCLOS created a new 'legal order', so Nicaragua was under this obligation in a dispute with a state not a party to UNCLOS.[50] Thus, the failure of Nicaragua to comply with the procedural requirements of UNCLOS meant it had not established its continental margin vis-à-vis Colombia, a state not a party to UNCLOS.[51] Judge Robinson criticized this conclusion, arguing that the procedural condition was not part of customary international law and could not be applied.[52] What is not entirely clear in these cases is whether the ICJ was using the existence and content of treaties to prove the existence of a custom or clarifying the content of the rule.[53]

Declaration) correctly stated customary international law); *Armed Activities on the Territory of the Congo* (n 44) [162] ('These provisions [of the Friendly Relations Declaration] are declaratory of customary international law.').

47 *Territorial and Maritime Dispute (Nicaragua v Colombia)* (Judgment) [2012] ICJ Rep 624 [114].

48 ibid [115].

49 ibid 126. See also *Questions of the Delimitation of the Continental Shelf between Nicaragua and Colombia beyond 200 Nautical Miles from the Nicaraguan Coast (Nicaragua v Colombia)* (Preliminary Objections) [2016] ICJ Rep 100 [82].

50 *Territorial and Maritime Dispute (Nicaragua v Colombia)* (n 47) [126].

51 ibid [129].

52 *Nicaragua v Colombia Delimitation of the Continental Shelf* (n 49) Declaration of Judge Robinson [16].

53 See *Military and Paramilitary Activities in and against Nicaragua* (n 22) [218], [220]; *Legality of the Threat or Use of Nuclear Weapons* (Advisory Opinion) [1996] ICJ Rep 226, 257 [78]–[79]; *Maritime Delimitation and Territorial Question between Qatar and Bahrain (Qatar v Bahrain)* (Merits) [2001] ICJ Rep 40 [185]; *Armed Activities on the Territory of the Congo* (n 44) [217]; *Territorial and Maritime Dispute between Nicaragua*

The ICJ also deduces rules of customary international law from other customary international rules. In the *Burkina Faso/Mali Frontier Dispute*, it held that *uti possidetis* was customary international law because 'it is logically connected with the phenomenon of the obtaining of independence'.[54] While this phrase might even suggest deduction of the rule from facts, actually the ICJ was deducing the customary rule of *uti possidetis* from the other customary rules governing independence. In the *Qatar and Bahrain Maritime Delimitation*, the ICJ set aside evidence of practice as inconclusive and instead deduced that 'low-tide elevations cannot be equated with islands ... or other land territory' as they are understood under prevailing rules on territorial sovereignty.[55] Thus, in these cases another norm of customary international law formed the framework for assessing the norm at issue. And while it is debatable whether the ICJ was identifying a new rule or clarifying an existing one, it appears to apply a teleological interpretation of other rules of customary international law. This approach should not be too shocking, because domestic courts sometimes take the same approach. In the case of *A* v. *Attorney-General*, the Swiss Federal Criminal Court held that the accused was covered by the same immunity enjoyed by a head of state because, as minister of defence, he was a member of the unusual collegiate body – the HCE, or Haut Comité d'État (High State Council) – that discharged presidential authority. The Federal Criminal Court did not examine state practice and *opinio juris* to determine whether a collegiate presidential council would enjoy the same immunities, but reasoned that logically it would, based on the purposes of head-of-state immunity.[56]

However, the ICJ has also deduced the existence of customary rules from other customary rules, not by logically deriving the rules from other rules but by analogy. In this approach, the ICJ is more clearly focused on applying customary international law rules that apply in other situations to a case where they clearly do not, and thus is more likely identifying a new rule rather than clarifying an existing one. For example, in the *Libya and Malta Continental Shelf* case, the ICJ identified a customary

and Honduras in the Caribbean Sea (Nicaragua v Honduras) (Judgment) [2007] ICJ Rep 661, 696 [113].

54 *Frontier Dispute (Burkina Faso/Mali)* (Judgment) [1986] ICJ Rep 554, 565–66 [20]–[23].

55 *Maritime Delimitation and Territorial Question between Qatar and Bahrain* (n 53) [204]–[208].

56 *A v Office of the Attorney General of Switzerland*, File no BB.2011.140 (25 July 2012) [5.3.1.]–[5.4.2] ('The HCE was created to replace the presidency and assume its duties') (translation by TRIAL, Track Impunity Always), reprinted in ILDC 1933 (CH 2012).

rule permitting 200 nautical miles of continental shelf by drawing an analogy with the exclusive economic zone.[57] However, this approach is not without criticism. In the *Arrest Warrant* case, the ICJ deduced the existence of immunities from arrest for a foreign minster by considering the functions of the office.[58] Unlike the situation of a head of state mentioned above, which clearly benefitted from a rule of immunity and needed clarification, this case asked whether the official had any immunities at all. Judge Van den Wyngaert critiqued the approach of identifying the new rule by deduction, calling it 'a mere analogy with immunities for diplomatic agents and Heads of State' without proper reliance on evidence of state practice and *opinio juris*.[59]

The ICJ also deduces customary international law from legal principles. There are at least two versions of this approach. One possibility, a more conservative one, is to deduce the existence of certain principles from treaties or other customary law and then take one more step and deduce the existence of rules from those principles. This is the approach that Talmon terms 'triangular reasoning'.[60] For example, in the *Corfu Channel case*, the ICJ identified the principle underlying the Hague Convention VIII of 1907 (i.e. the obligation to notify ships of minefields).[61] The treaty did not specifically apply to the situation of peacetime, and yet the Court stated that such a duty also applied in peacetime.[62] Similar to the practice of deduction by analogy, this practice appears to be focused on identifying new rules of customary international law.

[57] *Continental Shelf (Libya/Malta)* (n 18) [34].

[58] *Arrest Warrant of 11 April 2000 (DR Congo v Belgium)* [2002] ICJ Rep 3, 20–22 [51]–[54].

[59] ibid, Dissenting Opinion of Judge van den Wyngaert 146 [14]. Talmon also notes a functional deduction from the functions of a person or organization; see Talmon (n 14) 423–26. However, the two cases he cites, *Reparations* and *South West Africa*, are not truly customary international law, but rather the functional interpretation of treaty instruments. See *Reparation for Injuries Suffered in the Service of the United Nations* (Advisory Opinion) [1949] ICJ Rep 174, 180–85; *International Status of South West Africa* (Advisory Opinion) [1950] ICJ Rep 128, 136, 159, 162, 172.

[60] See *Gulf of Maine* (n 2) [114] (identifying the approach to delimiting a single maritime boundary).

[61] *Corfu Channel* (n 42) 22; *Corfu Channel (UK v Albania)* Memorial of the UK (30 Sept 1947) 37–38 [63]–[65] <www.icj-cij.org/sites/default/files/case-related/1/1489.pdf> accessed 1 April 2022.

[62] *Corfu Channel* (n 42) 22 ('certain general and well-recognized principles, namely: elementary considerations of humanity, even more exacting in peace than in war; the principle of the freedom of maritime communication; and every State's obligation not to allow knowingly its territory to be used for acts contrary to the rights of other States').

One method for reasoning the existence of customary international law from abstracted principles, themselves potentially drawn from other treaties and customary law, is the necessity of the rule. As the ICJ said in the *Gulf of Maine* case, some rules are 'vital' or 'ensur[e]' international cooperation and coexistence, and in the *Gabčikovo-Nagymaros Project* case the ICJ stated that the rule was 'require[d]'.[63] The ICJ has stated that the reason for this view is that it should be reluctant to find customary international law restraining state action '[w]hen the stakes are not as high',[64] – that is to say, when the rules would be less necessary. That being said, the ICJ has been willing to deduce rules that are not absolutely necessary. Some rules are merely 'important'[65] and perhaps even 'logically connected' to other principles.[66] In fact, some rules are simply reasonable expectations from other principles, such as the 'elementary considerations of humanity' cited in both the *Nicaragua* case[67] and the *Corfu Channel* case.[68]

The ICJ also occasionally applies an even more liberal approach, not necessarily identifying a treaty or customary law from which to draw legal principles before deducing the existence of customary international law. This is the case in *Jurisdictional Immunities*, where the ICJ noted the important principle of sovereignty and its derivatives sovereign equality and territorial sovereignty,[69] and in *Certain Documents*, when the ICJ took note of the principles protecting the integrity of legal proceedings.[70]

63 *Gabčikovo-Nagymaros Project (Hungary v Slovakia)* (Judgment) [1997] ICJ Rep 7 [104] ('the stability of treaty relations requires that the plea of fundamental change of circumstances be applied only in exceptional cases.')

64 Kirgis (n 24) 148 ('When the stakes are not as high, international decision makers have not been as quick to find restrictive customary rules.') (citing *Fisheries Jurisdiction Case (UK v Iceland; Germany v Iceland)* (Merits) [1974] ICJ Rep 3, 175).

65 *Jurisdictional Immunities of the State* (n 28) [57] ('The Court considers that the rule of State immunity occupies an important place in international law and international relations.')

66 *Frontier Dispute (Burkina Faso/Mali)* (n 54) [20]–[23] (concluding that *uti possidetis* is customary international law because 'it is logically connected with the phenomenon of the obtaining of independence'); *Jurisdictional Immunities of the State* (n 28) [57] ('[the rule of State immunity] derives from the principle of sovereign equality of States').

67 *Military and Paramilitary Activities in and against Nicaragua* (n 22) [215], [218] (beginning with 'elementary considerations of humanity' to arrive at the conclusion that Common Article 3 of the Geneva Conventions was customary international law).

68 *Corfu Channel* (n 42) at 22.

69 *Jurisdictional Immunities of the State* (n 28) [57]; *Asylum Case (Colombia/Peru)* (Judgment) [1950] ICJ Rep 266, 274–77.

70 *Questions Related to the Seizure and Detention of Certain Documents and Data (Timor-Leste v Australia)* (Provisional Measures, Order) [2014] ICJ Rep 147 [27].

Such practice can even be identified in the *Lotus* case, where the ICJ stated that '[a] corollary of the principle of the freedom of the seas is that a ship on the high seas is assimilated to the territory of the State the flag of which it flies, for, just as in its own territory, that State exercises its authority, upon it, and no other State may do so',[71] and in the *Pulp Mills* case the ICJ observed that 'a precautionary approach may be relevant in the interpretation and application of the' treaty and then stated that the treaty 'has to be interpreted in accordance with [what] ... may now be considered a requirement under general international law to undertake an environmental impact assessment'.[72] Perhaps the ICJ could have identified treaties and other custom that evidenced such principles as applicable, but that step was omitted.

In other cases, the ICJ does not deduce the existence and content of a customary rule from a treaty or other source of law, nor deduce principles from those sources, but instead deduces customary rules from the logic and reasoning, the underlying purpose, of the rule itself. As such, the particulars of the rule applicable in a given case might be merely characterized as explaining the content of the rule in more detail, rather than identifying an entirely new rule. In the *Western Sahara* and *Wall* advisory opinions, the ICJ deduced from the existence of the rule of self-determination under customary international law that its full scope of application was *erga omnes*,[73] again with little regard to state practice and *opinio juris*.

One the one hand, the ICJ appears to use deduction of rules quite often, yet, on the other hand, insists that it does not simply deduce rules.[74] A possible explanation is twofold. First, in many of these cases the ICJ is not necessarily deducing the existence of new rules but rather interpreting the content, scope, and application of existing rules. For example, in the *Arrest Warrant* case, one could characterize the rule as being immunity for certain high state officials, with head of state being a clearly established example and foreign minister a less clear example. The ICJ did not discover a new rule of immunity of foreign ministers, but

[71] *Lotus* (n 28) 25.

[72] *Pulp Mills on the River Uruguay (Argentina v Uruguay)* (Judgment) [2010] ICJ Rep 13 [61], [160]–[164], [204].

[73] *Western Sahara* (Advisory Opinion) [1975] ICJ Rep 12, 31 [55] (self-determination as a right of peoples); *East Timor (Portugal v Australia)* (Judgment) [1995] ICJ Rep 90, 102 [29] (interpreting the right of self-determination to have an *erga omnes* character); *Legal Consequences of the Construction of a Wall in the Occupied Palestinian Territory* (Advisory Opinion) [2004] ICJ Rep 136, 172 [88].

[74] See *South West Africa* (n 43) [49]–[50].

instead clarified that the scope of high state official immunities covered them. State practice and *opinio juris* was not necessary for these narrow cases, because there was already well-established state practice and *opinio juris* for the functional category in which foreign ministers fall. In a similar manner, the extension of customary international humanitarian law to cyber operations might not call for supplementary evidence of state practice and *opinio juris*, because there is already solid evidence that these rules apply to armed conflict through whatever mode it is manifested.[75] This view can be justified by recalling the distinction between the identification and the interpretation of customary international law. Where the ICJ is identifying a new and distinct rule, perhaps it must locate state practice and *opinio juris*, but when it is merely interpreting the content of the rule, it is freer to use other legal interpretative techniques such as analogy and the context of other legal rules. That being said, the line between identifying a new rule and clarifying the content of the rule is so fine that the distinction is admittedly difficult to draw, potentially opening the door to more flexible interpretative techniques. Given the ICJ's affirmations of the state practice-*opinio juris* rule, we could conclude that when it applies deduction in this manner, it is presuming what state practice and *opinio juris* it would expect to find, had it looked.

Second, we can also recall the distinction between the formation of customary international law and evidence for the formation. Several authorities have argued for the use of deduction when determining whether there is sufficient evidence for customary international law. The ICJ could be deducing the probable existence of certain rules and then lowering the threshold of evidence to establish the rule (perhaps even reducing it to zero in clearly obvious cases), rather than deducing

[75] See eg M Schmitt (ed), *Tallinn Manual 2.0 on the International Law Applicable to Cyber Operations* (2nd edn, Cambridge University Press 2017); German Federal Foreign Office, German Federal Ministry of Defence, and German Federal Ministry of the Interior, Building and Community, 'On the Application of International Law in Cyberspace' (Position paper, March 2021) <www.auswaertiges-amt.de/blob/2446304/32e7b2498e10b74fb17204c54665bdf0/on-the-application-of-international-law-in-cyberspace-data.pdf> accessed 1 April 2022 (agreeing with the authors of *Tallinn Manual 2.0*, even though '[t]he fact that cyberspace as a domain of warfare was unknown at the time when the core treaties of IHL were drafted does not exempt the conduct of hostilities in cyberspace from the application of IHL'; and concluding that other rules of customary international law (eg the obligation of states not to allow their territory to be used for acts contrary to the rights of other states, rules on attribution of conduct) applied to cyber operations without the need to submit state practice and *opinio juris*).

the existence of customary international without any regard to state practice and *opinio juris*. In essence, some norms are simply more obvious,[76] because they are logical or necessary for international cooperation. In his dissent in the *North Sea Continental Shelf* cases, Judge Lachs stated that deduction is an alternative to induction when the norms are difficult to prove.[77] Certainly, the ICJ appeared to take this approach in the *Asylum*,[78] *Nicaragua*,[79] and *Qatar/Bahrain Maritime Delimitation* cases.[80]

However, the ICJ does not confirm that either of these explanations is correct. More often, it dispenses with a lengthy explanation, or perhaps any explanation at all, of the evidence on which it based its decision, leaving obscurity over whether deduction was the sole basis for the rule, a supplementary basis, or a reduction in the burden of proof through inductive means.[81] For example, in the *Arrest Warrant* case the ICJ simply stated 'it is firmly established that'.[82] Use of the term 'established' can probably be assimilated to 'proved', although even if it was a synonym for 'constituted', the ICJ is still referencing confidence in its existence, which is an evidentiary matter. In the *Gulf of Maine* case, the ICJ expressly stated that there were two classes of rules of customary international law, proved by induction and by deduction.[83] In the *Corfu Channel* case, the ICJ quite clearly drew on considerations of humanity as the reason for its conclusion, not as a basis for deducing the scope of another rule of law.[84] If it truly was simply a lower evidentiary burden, one would expect the ICJ to use different phrasing to describe what it was doing. While we might attempt to overlook the *Corfu Channel* approach

76 See Mendelson (n 24) 292.

77 *North Sea Continental Shelf* (n 28) Dissenting Opinion of Judge Tanaka 179, also Dissenting Opinion of Judge Sørensen 246; *Legality of the Threat or Use of Nuclear Weapons* (n 53) Dissenting Opinion of Judge Higgins 591 [36]; *Corfu Channel* (n 42) Separate Opinion of Judge Azevedo 83.

78 *Asylum Case* (n 69) 274–77, Dissenting Opinion of Caicedo Castilla 370 [17].

79 *Military and Paramilitary Activities in and against Nicaragua* (n 22) [202], [206]–[207] (using deduction when there is inconsistent state practice and *opinio juris*).

80 *Qatar v Bahrain Maritime Delimitation and Territorial Question* (n 53) [204]–[208].

81 See T Treves, 'Customary International Law' (MPEPIL 2006) <https://opil.ouplaw.com/display/10.1093/law:epil/9780199231690/law-9780199231690-e1393>; Mendelson (n 24) 292 (arguing that *opinio juris* is not necessary in obvious cases).

82 *Arrest Warrant* (n 58) [51], also Separate Opinion of Judge Koroma 61 [6]; *Questions Related to the Obligation to Prosecute or Extradite (Belgium v Senegal)* (Judgment) [2012] ICJ Rep 422, 457 [99].

83 *Gulf of Maine* (n 2) [111].

84 *Corfu Channel* (n 42) 42.

because it emerged during an era when international law might not have been well developed, the *Gulf of Maine* case was decided in 1984.

Most likely, the best explanation is that, in principle, state practice and *opinio juris* are required in all cases. However, when a norm is necessary (or at least logical or sensible) for the international legal system, or a parallel treaty is in place that governs the parties, or the question is really just a clarification of the scope of an already existing general rule of customary international law, then the ICJ can deduce that it is safe to presume state practice and *opinio juris*, and an inductive analysis with evidence is not necessary. The rule is simply very obvious in such cases. Other, more novel, situations demand stronger evidence of state practice and *opinio juris*. While the distinction between these two approaches is more likely a spectral one, reducing the need for compelling evidence in proportion to the reasonableness that the rule exists, the ICJ in *Gulf of Maine* identifies the two ends of the spectrum. Thus, the ICJ is not necessarily inventing customary international law from whole cloth by pure deduction, assertion, or arbitrariness, but instead identifying rules that are more likely than not to exist, and more likely than not to have certain content, when operating within an environment of other rules of international law.

3.3 Deduction of Customary International Law within the Application of the Elements

Of course, this analysis means that the ICJ still makes use of inductive reasoning. In many cases, it does apply state practice and *opinio juris* as elements that are used to identify legal rules. Following from Section 3.2, where logic and reason could be justifications for an abridged inductive analysis, this section discusses the assessment of evidence for customary international law in the inductive process, and again we find the use of logic throughout the process.

Initially, it could be that the states disputing a matter might simply agree on the existence of a rule of customary international law.[85] If they stipulated this rule, then it would govern the dispute and, especially if

[85] See *Jurisdictional Immunities of the State* (n 28) [57] (Germany did not object to Italy's characterization of the acts of the German armed forces in World War II as constituting violations of international law); *Certain Questions of Mutual Assistance in Criminal Matters (Djibouti v France)* (Judgment) [2008] ICJ Rep 177 [112] (neither France nor Djibouti objected to the application of the Vienna Convention on the Law of Treaties as a matter of customary international law, even though neither was a party to the convention).

used as the basis for a decision by the ICJ, would control the outcome. This outcome would stand, even if the norm of customary international law later appeared to be unfounded in state practice or *opinio juris*. After all, some of the votes of the ICJ on questions of the existence of a rule of customary international law have been rather close.[86] For its part, the European Court of Justice has also taken the position that the parties must contest the existence of a customary international law rule or it can be presumed to exist.[87] Pellet and Gaja have both argued that acceptance of a rule of customary international law is not required by states, so whether states accept the existence of such a rule in a dispute between them is not a requirement.[88] The question in this chapter, however, is the reverse. While acceptance is not a prerequisite for the existence and application of the rule, in the sense that refusal could block creation and application of the norm, acceptance does appear to be constitutive of the norm, at least insofar as the norm is applied in the dispute and serves as precedent for disputes that follow. Pellet argues that acceptance is not constitutive, but instead merely eases the burden of establishing the existence of the rule in the dispute.[89] Here again, the distinction between the existence of a rule and the evidence of a rule appears.

In a similar fashion, for some states the views of their foreign ministry might preclude any ascertainment of customary international law. A state's internal determination by its foreign ministry on the existence of the customary rule might be determinative that a rule exists under customary international law, be it in operationalizing its foreign policy or for settling a dispute of international character within its domestic legal system.[90] Again, such a determination might not be supported by adequate state practice and *opinio juris*. Such a decision by a domestic court might in turn be used elsewhere as evidence of the existence of the norm. The ILA concluded that the differing views of the executive or

[86] See *Reservations to the Convention on the Prevention and Punishment of the Crime of Genocide* (Advisory Opinion) [1951] ICJ Rep 15, 24–25 (seven judges voting in favour of the norm, five voting against), also Joint Dissenting Opinion of Judges Guerrero, McNair, Read and Hsu Mo 32.

[87] See Case C-366/10 *Air Transport Association of America and ors v Secretary of State for Energy and Climate Change* [2011] EU:C:2011:864 [105]–[106].

[88] See A Pellet, 'The Normative Dilemma: Will and Consent in International Law-Making' (1989) 12 Aus YIL 3, 37; G Gaja in A Cassese and JHH Weiler (eds), *Change and Stability in International Law-Making* (De Gruyter 1989) pt I, ch I ('Custom and Treaties) 16.

[89] See Pellet (n 88).

[90] See eg *R v Bottrill, ex p Kuechenmeister* [1947] 1 KB 41 (Court of Appeal, England and Wales).

legislature on a customary international law norm would have different weight, but that neither was necessarily excluded.[91] However, when the question of the norm is raised within a domestic situation, the executive's position might be binding on a court.

When states disagree over the existence of a rule, then the ICJ may take a more scientific inductive approach, but this approach should not blind us to the use of deductive logic within the application of induction. The dispute serves to frame the question about the rule and, as such, already impacts the form of the rule, as states suggest competing hypotheses and the decision-maker needs to adopt one or the other hypothesis.[92] Important to note, however, is that the competing hypotheses are themselves not necessarily the outcome of inductive logic but could be based on deduction from other principles or aims. Evidence of state practice and *opinio juris* that does not support one or the other hypothesis can be disregarded.[93] In this regard, Judge Van den Wyngaert's dissent in the *Arrest Warrant case* is important, for there she challenged the framing of the hypothesis by the ICJ:

> In technical terms, the dispute was about an arrest warrant against an incumbent Foreign Minister ... In a more principled way ... [i]t was about the question what international law requires or allows States to do as 'agents' of the international community ...
>
> The Court has not addressed the dispute from this perspective and has instead focused on the very narrow question of immunities ...[94]

Whether there is any presumption in favour of or against the formation of a rule of customary international law is also deduced logically. In principle, we might apply the *Lotus* presumption against states binding themselves, but the ICJ has suggested that UNGA resolutions on point can create a presumption in favour of customary

[91] ILA Committee on Formation of Customary (General) International Law, 'Final Report' (n 24) Principle 9, Comment (e) ('It can happen, particularly in countries where there is a separation of powers, that the position of the judiciary (or of the legislature) conflicts with that of the executive. This is a matter of what *weight* is to be attached to the various instances of the State's practice.').

[92] See *Jurisdictional Immunities of the State* (n 28) [62]–[63].

[93] See *Jurisdictional Immunities of the State (Germany v Italy)* Memorial of the Federal Republic of Germany (12 June 2009) <www.icj-cij.org/sites/default/files/case-related/143/16644.pdf> accessed 10 April 2022 [55], Counter-Memorial of Italy (22 December 2009) <www.icj-cij.org/sites/default/files/case-related/143/16648.pdf> accessed 10 April 2022 [4.3], Rejoinder of Italy (10 January 2011) <www.icj-cij.org/sites/default/files/case-related/143/16652.pdf> accessed 10 April 2022 [4.19].

[94] *Arrest Warrant* (n 58) Dissenting Opinion of Judge ad hoc Van den Wyngaert [5]–[6].

international law.[95] Instead of a presumption, it might simply be that UNGA resolutions are weighty evidence.[96] Also consider in the *Navigational and Related Rights* case, where the ICJ found the existence of particular customary international law because Nicaragua failed to object to a long-undisturbed practice.[97] It is difficult to understand how the ICJ believed a *Lotus* presumption against custom had been overcome in *Navigational and Related Rights* with such weak *opinio juris* and – as it admits – not well-substantiated practice. In essence, the ICJ used logic to interpret the meaning of silence.

Logical deduction is also largely the basis for determining the types and forms of evidence that the ICJ and other authorities accept for the purpose of identifying customary international law. As a preliminary matter, the limitation of practice to acts of states, rather than international organizations or other actors, is largely traditional. The ILC special rapporteur cited little actual practice of states to support his conclusion that international organizations contribute to customary international law '[i]n certain cases' and that we should approach the question with 'caution'.[98] In addition, whether actors within a state engage the state's role in constituting customary international law is often assessed by analogy to either the Draft Articles on State Responsibility rules on attribution[99] or the Vienna Convention on the

95 *Legality of the Threat or Use of Nuclear Weapons* (n 53) [70]–[71] ('[UNGA resolutions] can, in certain circumstances, provide evidence important for establishing the existence of a rule or the emergence of an *opinio juris*.'); ILA Committee on Formation of Customary (General) International Law, 'Final Report' (n 24) [6], Principle 29 ('Resolutions of the General Assembly expressly or impliedly asserting that a customary rule exists constitute rebuttable evidence that such is the case.'). But see *Voting Procedure on Questions Related to Reports and Petitions Concerning the Territory of South West Africa* (Advisory Opinion) [1955] ICJ Rep 84, Separate Opinion of Judge Klaestad, Separate Opinion of Judge Lauterpacht.

96 See *Accordance with International Law of the Unilateral Declaration of Independence in Respect of Kosovo* (Advisory Opinion) [2010] ICJ Rep 403 [80]; *Armed Activities on the Territory of the Congo* (n 44) Separate Opinion of Judge Elaraby 331 [16], Separate Opinion of Judge Kooijmans 322 [63].

97 *Dispute Regarding Navigational and Related Rights (Costa Rica v Nicaragua)* (Judgment) [2009] ICJ Rep 213 [140]–[141].

98 ILC, 'Draft Conclusions' o (n 1), Conclusion 4(2), also Comments (4), (6), (7), (8). Note that the special rapporteur did not cite to the *Reservations to the Genocide Convention* case for the role of UN Secretary-General practice as depositary, which would have been a natural reference, though the ICJ did not rely on state practice or *opinio juris* for this secondary rule. See *Reservations to the Convention on the Prevention and Punishment of the Crime of Genocide* (Advisory Opinion) [1951] ICJ Rep 15, 24–25.

99 See ILC, 'Draft Conclusions' (n 1) Conclusion 5, Comment (2) n 699 (citing ILC, 'Draft Articles on Responsibility of States for Internationally Wrongful Acts with

Law of Treaties rules on capacity to bind the state.[100] There is no clear classification of which acts are 'practice',[101] and states often suggest which acts qualify as practice in yearbooks or digests on practice.[102] Indeed, sometimes the ICJ appears to reduce the evidentiary burden for proving customary international law by invoking strong, convincing authorities such as the ILC.[103] One would imagine that a state would need to bring quite compelling evidence to convince the ICJ to determine that a provision in the Draft Articles on State Responsibility was not customary international law. Beyond these basic conditions, the ICJ and other authorities do not perform any inductive analyses of the secondary rules on the nature and quality of the practice being 'sufficiently widespread and representative, as well as consistent'.[104] Again, we can note

Commentaries' (23 April–1 June and 2 July–10 August 2001) UN Doc A/56/10, arts 5–6). See also ILA Committee on Formation of Customary (General) International Law, 'Final Report' (n 24) Principles 7, 8, 9.

100 Vienna Convention on the Law of Treaties (adopted 23 May 1969, entered into force 27 January 1980) 1155 UNTS 331.

101 See ILC, 'Draft Conclusions' (n 1); ILC, 'Report to the United Nations General Assembly' pt II 'Ways and Means for Making the Evidence of Customary International Law More Readily Available' (1950) YILC II 368–72 [31]: 'Evidence of the practice of States is to be sought in a variety of materials. The reference in article 24 of the Statute of the Commission to "documents concerning State practice" (*documents établissant la pratique des États*) supplies no criteria for judging the nature of such "documents". Nor is it practicable to list all the numerous types of materials which reveal State practice on each of the many problems arising in international relations.'

102 See eg UNGA Res 2099(XX) 'Technical Assistance to Promote the Teaching, Study, Dissemination and Wider Appreciation of International Law' (20 December 1965) UN Doc A/RES/2099(XX); CoE Committee of Ministers Res (68)17, 'Model Plan for the Classification of Documents Concerning State Practice in the Field of Public International Law' (June 28, 1968), as amended by Recommendation 97(11).

103 See *Gabčikovo-Nagymaros Project* (n 63) [51]–[53] (referring to the work of the ILC); *Difference Related to Immunities from Legal Process of a Special Rapporteur of the Commission on Human Rights* (Advisory Opinion) [1999] ICJ Rep 62, 87 [62]; *Wall Advisory Opinion* (n 73) [140]; *Diallo Case (Guinea v DR Congo)* (Judgment) [2007] ICJ Rep 582, 599 [39]; *Application of the Convention on the Prevention and Punishment of the Crime of Genocide (Bosnia and Herzegovina v Serbia and Montenegro)* (Judgment) [2007] ICJ Rep 47, 202, 209 [385], [401]; *Application of the Convention on the Prevention and Punishment of the Crime of Genocide (Croatia v Serbia)* (Judgment) [2008] ICJ Rep 413, 459 [127]. It is here that Hakimi's argument (see Hakimi (n 17) 1510) might be reconsidered within the framework of secondary rules, rather than refuting secondary rules.

104 See ILC, 'Draft Conclusions' (n 1), Conclusions 7, 8(1). See also *North Sea Continental Shelf* (n 28) 42–43; *Military and Paramilitary Activities in and against Nicaragua* (n 22) [186]; *Fisheries Jurisdiction Case (UK v Iceland; Germany v Iceland)* (n 64) 116, 131, 138; *Asylum Case* (n 69) 277–78.

the lack of inductive analysis also on the part of the ILC special rapporteur in reaching his conclusions on these points.[105]

After offering competing hypotheses, the ICJ must weigh the evidence. There does not appear to be any inductive analysis on the burden of proof or weight of evidence for customary international law.[106] The ICJ has only issued very vague statements that evidence is weighed and contradicted.[107] The Special Tribunal for Lebanon used the expression 'beyond any shadow of doubt' when considering whether a customary rule had been proven, though it did not indicate whether this was the burden of proof it applied or whether this was merely a rhetorical flourish.[108]

Having produced a final pool of data on the basis of all of these logical steps, the ICJ will perform an inductive inference to identify the applicable rules (or least says that it will). The usual approach, in line with an inductive logic, is to employ a sampling survey. The actual sampling conducted by the ICJ is not random or following typical scientific approaches for induction.[109] For example, the practice is not simply

[105] ILC, 'Draft Conclusions' (n 1) Conclusion 8, Comment (3) n 714 (citing *Ure v The Commonwealth of Australia* (Federal Court of Australia, 4 February 2016) FCAFC 8 [37]); ILC, 'Draft Conclusions' (n 1) Conclusion 8, Comment (7) (citing *Military and Paramilitary Activities in and against Nicaragua* (n 22) [186]).

[106] See ILA Committee on Formation of Customary (General) International Law, 'Final Report' (24) Principle 3, Comment ('What is suggested here is something analogous to (but not the same as) the well-known distinction in the law of evidence between the admissibility of evidence and its weight (convincingness).'); *Fisheries Case (UK v Norway)* (Judgment) [1951] ICJ Rep 116, Dissenting Opinion of Judge Reed 191.

[107] See *Jurisdictional Immunities of the State* (n 28) [72]; *Prosecutor v Ayyash and ors*, STL-11-01/I (Interlocutory Decision on the Applicable Law, 16 February 2011) [91]; *Lotus* (n 28) 26 ('In the Court's opinion, the existence of such a rule has not been conclusively proved.'); *Air Transport Association of America* (n 87) [106] ('insufficient evidence exists to establish ... the principle of customary international law'); *Van v Public Prosecutor* (Singapore Court of Appeal, 20 October 2004) SGCA 47 [88] ('Any customary international law rule must be clearly and firmly established before its adoption by the courts', yet relying on only one report:, 'Question of the Death Penalty: Report of the Secretary-General' (2 July 2012) UN Doc A/HRC/21/29. See also AM Weisburd, 'Customary International Law: The Problem of Treaties' (1988) 21 VJIL 1; A D'Amato, 'Custom and Treaty: A Response to Professor Weisburd' (1988) 21 VJIL 459, 473; A D'Amato, 'A Brief Rejoinder' (1988) 21 VJIL 489.

[108] *Prosecutor v Ayyash* (n 107) [86] ('However significant these judicial pronouncements may be as an expression of the legal view of the courts of different States, to establish beyond any shadow of doubt whether a customary rule of international law has crystallised one must also delve into other elements.').

[109] Consider, for example, the discussion of the representativity of states selected for sampling: *North Sea Continental Shelf* (n 28) Dissenting Opinion of Judge Lachs 227; ICRC, JM Henckaerts and L Doswald-Beck (eds), *Customary International Humanitarian Law* (Cambridge University Press 2005) vol 2, xliv–xlv, li; Treves (n 81) [35].

quantified based on the number of states in alignment, but certain acts by certain states might be weighted more heavily.[110] For example, the judges in the *Legality of the Threat or Use of Nuclear Weapons* advisory opinion disagreed, not about the methodology but about relative significance of the practice.[111] In both situations, the judges are applying logic to the value of practice.

Some cases will result in insufficient or inconsistent evidence. Talmon has observed that in such cases the ICJ might simply deduce the existence of the rule. He reads the *Gulf of Maine* case to say that the lack of evidence could lead the ICJ to rely on a deductive approach.[112] The present author, however, considers that the chamber in the *Gulf of Maine* case might have only identified a certain class of norms that are reasonable as to their content and, as a result, imposed a lower burden of proof.[113] That is to say that the determination of the content of the rule preceded the identification of method,[114] whereas Talmon reads the chamber judgment as holding that the method of proof came first, and that only when it failed was an alternate method adopted.

Lastly, although it is agreed that, in principle, one applies inductive reasoning to infer the existence of a rule from examples of practice and *opinio juris*, the precise form of the inference remains somewhat unclear. The inference could be an enumeration of cases and inverse inference, concluding that the frequency of a certain characteristic in the sampled population is the same as in the general population.[115] The inference

[110] See *Military and Paramilitary Activities in and against Nicaragua* (n 22) [186]; Treves (n 81) para 30 ('Particularly significant are manifestations of practice that go against the interest of the State from which they come, or that entail for them significant costs in political, military, economic or other terms, as it is less likely that they reflect reasons of political opportunity, courtesy etc.').

[111] *Legality of the Threat or Use of Nuclear Weapons* (n 53) Dissenting Opinion of Judge Schwebel [78], Dissenting Opinion of Judge Higgins 583 [9]–[10].

[112] Talmon (n 14) 421–24. He also cites the *Reparations* case for support when practice is limited or nonexistent: *Reparations Advisory Opinion* (n 59) 182, Opinion of Judge Alvarez 190, Dissenting Opinion of Judge Krylov 218; and other ICJ cases for support when practice is too inconsistent: *Continental Shelf (Libya/Malta)* (n 18) [44]; *North Sea Continental Shelf* (n 28) 45; *Maritime Delimitation and Territorial Question between Qatar and Bahrain* (n 53) [205].

[113] Anzilotti (n 23) 67.

[114] See B Schlütter, *Developments in Customary International Law: Theory and the Practice of the International Court of Justice and the International Ad Hoc Criminal Tribunals for Rwanda and Yugoslavia* (Brill 2010) 326–29; R Kolb, 'Selected Problems in the Theory of Customary International Law' (2003) 50 NILR 129.

[115] See generally R Carnap, *The Continuum of Inductive Methods* (Chicago University Press 1952); J Williamson, 'Inductive Influence' (2007) 58 BJPhS 689; HE Kyburg Jr, 'Belief,

might instead be a predictive inference. This approach attempts to use past examples of actions to predict likely behaviour in the future,[116] or uses past practice to identify an underlying characteristic that gives cause to the behaviour and predicts behaviour when that characteristic is present.[117] Or, in a similar approach, the investigator could engage in universal (hypothetical) inference, proposing a rule that applies to the general population, due to it being exhibited in the sample pool.[118] In the usual adversarial approach, a court practices Bayesian confirmation, where it identifies which of the hypotheses is the better explanation for the evidence,[119] though it is certainly possible that a court or other authority could develop its own hypothesis. Some language from the ICJ suggests that it is applying Bayesian confirmation of a universal inference. For example, in examining the evidence in *Jurisdictional Immunities* case, the ICJ merely observed that practice had not been contradicted with other evidence of practice.[120] In any event, one cannot use the sample pool merely to describe the likely state practice exhibited and *opinio juris* held by states; it must identify what custom has been prescribed.[121] These inductive approaches can only result in descriptive outcomes, and one must still make a normative inference from the descriptive outcome.

4 Conclusion

This chapter has analysed the presence of logic and reasoning throughout the ICJ's approach to customary international law. Logical reasoning takes several forms, primarily deductive or inductive. While the ICJ argues that it applies inductive reasoning, the reality is that at multiple

Evidence, and Conditioning' (2006) 73 Philos Sci 42; P Maher, 'A Conception of Inductive Logic' (2006) 73 Philos Sci 513; T Seidenfeld, 'Direct Inference and Inverse Inference' (1978) 75 J Philos 709–30.

[116] See R Carnap, *Logical Foundations of Probability* (Chicago University Press 1950) 207.

[117] See generally C Howson, *Hume's Problem: Induction and the Justification of Belief* (Oxford University Press 2000); Carnap (n 115); S Okasha, 'What Did Hume Really Show About Induction?' (2001) 51 Philos Q 27.

[118] See Carnap (n 115); E Eells & B Fitelson, 'Measuring Confirmation and Evidence' (2000) 97 J Philos 663; D Christensen, 'Measuring Confirmation' (1999) 96 J Philos 437; Kyburg (n 115).

[119] See generally P Horwich, *Probability and Evidence* (Cambridge University Press 1982); RD Rosenkrantz, 'Does the Philosophy of Induction Rest on a Mistake?' (1982) 79 J Philos 78, 78–97; P Teller, 'Goodman's Theory of Projection' (1969) 20 BJPhS 219, 219–38.

[120] *Jurisdictional Immunities of the State* (n 28) [72].

[121] See Kammerhofer (n 12) 544–45.

steps in its analysis it also applies deductive reasoning. This approach is clearly apparent when the ICJ assesses the fundamental rules of customary international law, such as the existence and nature of the state practice and *opinio juris* elements. The ICJ does appear, at least in some cases, to deduce the existence of customary international law as a logical or necessary conclusion from other treaty or customary norms, or by analogy to similar norms, or even perhaps from legal principles. But the ICJ also uses deductive logic when it applies the (primarily) inductive approach. It determines how the elements will be evidenced, evaluated, and weighted.

However, the ICJ is also not very transparent in the logical reasoning it applies. While we might be tempted to conclude that customary international law has no secondary rules at all aside from appeals to deductive logic, the ICJ continues to affirm its adherence to the two-element, inductive approach. A possible solution is to distinguish between the existence and constitution of customary international law from its evidence. And it might also be helpful to observe that the ICJ is, after all, not proving facts, but law, where courts traditionally have more freedom with less demanding standards of evidence. These deductive steps might simply be methods for establishing some fundamental secondary rules but also lowering the threshold for inductive analysis when certain primary rules would make logical sense.

Ultimately, we return to the question posed at the outset of this chapter – that is, whether the identification and interpretation of customary international law is a question of fact or law. If it is a question of law, which seems reasonable, then the ICJ has a much more flexible guide in informing itself of the law, *jura novit curia*. Talmon concludes that this amounts to an 'assertion' of customary international law,[122] and Hakimi has even argued that there are no secondary rules at all.[123] But the analysis of the ICJ discussed above is not completely untethered from the logic of state practice–*opinio juris* and the various interpretive techniques meant to give content to rules generally. Thus, it is too extreme to say that the ICJ merely asserts rules on the basis of no secondary rules. Instead, it draws on and is constrained by an argumentative framework where it must identify rules with reference to what states do and what they think as a basis, and can give content those rules through deductions and analogies.

[122] Talmon (n 14) 423–26.
[123] Hakimi (n 17) 1510.

6

The Interpretation of 'Direction or Control' in Investor–State Arbitration

The Case of State-Owned Enterprises

PAULA BALDINI MIRANDA DA CRUZ

1 Introduction

In this chapter I explore how the interpretation of customary international law can be shaped by the underlying premises and political values of a system. My argument focuses on how investor–state arbitration has interpreted the customary international law rule establishing that the actions of state-owned enterprises will be attributed to the controlling state, as expressed in Article 8 of the Articles on the Responsibility of States for Internationally Wrongful Acts (ARSIWA).[1]

International lawyers use the term 'state-owned enterprise' to refer to corporate entities that are not part of a state but are still owned or controlled by a state. State-owned enterprises pose challenges for international law because, although they are formally independent and autonomous entities, their corporate and operational ties with states can make it hard to distinguish their activities and goals from those of the states that own or control them. This sometimes nebulous relationship between states and state-owned enterprises has generated international concern that states might use state-owned enterprises to cover reprehensible and even illegal activities.[2]

This chapter was produced in 2022 as part of the author's PhD research. The views expressed herein are personal to the author and do not necessarily reflect those of any organization with which she is or has been affiliated.

[1] UNGA Res 56/83 (12 December 2001) UN Doc A/RES/56/83, annex.

[2] On general cautiousness towards state-owned enterprises, see generally A Musacchio and SG Lazzarini, *Reinventing State Capitalism: Leviathan in Business, Brazil and Beyond* (Harvard University Press 2014); FMM Barnes, 'International Investment Law and State-Owned Entities: Recurrent Key Issues and Future Directions' in LE Sachs, L Johnson and

Without a specific international legal regime for state-owned enterprises, discussions on state involvement in the international activities of these entities should be grounded on general international law, including the customary rules on attribution that are expressed in the ARSIWA. Investment arbitration tribunals have generally agreed on the applicability of customary international law on state responsibility to cases that deal with attribution to states of actions that violate treaty protections.[3] However, they have approached these cases from several different perspectives and standards (Section 2). I argue that such variation arises from the specific characteristics of investment law – namely, a cautious approach towards state-owned enterprises, coupled with an individualized application of the 'effective control' test. These two elements have pushed tribunals towards interpreting Article 8 of the ARSIWA in an individualized way that calibrates general international law standards in the light of common investment law practices, the rules specifically agreed by the states involved, and the specific needs and circumstances of the parties (Section 3).

2 The Interpretation of Control in International Law and Investment Arbitration

The ARSIWA were developed by the International Law Commission (ILC) as a way of codifying and developing the international law on state responsibility. Although the ARSIWA themselves do not constitute a binding instrument, many of their provisions, including Article 8, are considered to reflect customary international law.[4] The ARSIWA themselves are rather a subsidiary instrument[5] that describes these provisions in a way that is considered authoritative. It is worth mentioning here that despite the subsidiary nature of the ARSIWA as a source of international

J Coleman (eds), *Yearbook on International Investment Law & Policy 2018* (Oxford University Press 2019) 432.

[3] *InfraRed Environmental Infrastructure GP Limited and ors v Spain* (Decision on the Continuation of the Stay of the Enforcement of the Award) ICSID Case No ARB/14/12 (27 October 2020) [122].

[4] Specifically in relation to Article 8 of the ARSIWA, see eg *Application of the Convention on the Prevention and Punishment of the Crime of Genocide (Bosnia and Herzegovina v Serbia and Montenegro)* (Merits) [2007] ICJ Rep 43 [398] ('On this subject the applicable rule, which is one of customary law of international responsibility, is laid down in Article 8 of the ILC Articles on State Responsibility').

[5] See Statute of the International Court of Justice (adopted 26 June 1945, entered into force 24 October 1945) 33 UNTS 993, art 38(1)(d).

law, the recognized authority of the rules expressed in the ARSIWA has led international lawyers (including myself in this chapter) to broadly refer to these rules as binding.

According to Article 8 of the ARSIWA, the conduct of a non-state actor, including a state-owned enterprise, is attributable to a state if such entity 'is in fact acting on the instructions of, or under the direction or control of, that State in carrying out the conduct'.[6] As I describe below, the interpretation of the term 'control' has been a subject of discussion in international law. The ILC, in its commentary to the ARSIWA, emphasized that there were different ways of interpreting the term 'control'.[7] It is therefore up for those applying Article 8 to determine how to interpret and apply it in light of the circumstances of each case. As noted by the ILC:

> It is clear then that a State may, either by specific directions or by exercising control over a group, in effect assume responsibility for their conduct. Each case will depend on its own facts, in particular those concerning the relationship between the instructions given or the direction or control exercised and the specific conduct complained of.[8]

Although the 'effective control' test of the International Court of Justice's (ICJ) is referred to as the standard test for attributing actions of state-controlled entities to states, it has been shaped to different circumstances. Although there are many possible approaches, tribunals have been generally consistent and applied similar tests when faced with similar sets of circumstances (Section 2.1). This effort for consistency contrasts with broader variations in approaches seen in the context of investment tribunals ruling on the attribution to states of the actions of state-owned enterprises (Section 3.2).

2.1 'Control' in International Law

The best-known test for determining whether a state has enough control to be held responsible over the actions of other entities is the 'effective control' test set by the ICJ. In all cases where the ICJ has discussed the issue of attribution to states of actions committed by other entities, it has

[6] UN Doc A/RES/56/83, annex (n 1) art 8.

[7] ILC, 'Draft Articles on Responsibility of States for Internationally Wrongful Acts with Commentaries' (23 April–1 June and 2 July–10 August 2001) UN Doc A/56/10, commentary to art 8, paras (4)–(5).

[8] ibid para (7).

found that states could only be held responsible for the actions of actors that they effectively controlled. In the case of *Military and Paramilitary Activities in and against Nicaragua (Nicaragua* v. *USA)*, the ICJ established what it considered to be the threshold of control for attribution of conduct to states based on the rule expressed in Article 8. Nicaragua had turned to the Court claiming that the United States was responsible for supporting armed actions by a non-state armed group known as the Contras in Nicaraguan territory. The Court concluded that the United States should be held responsible for supporting the Contras. However, it also found that it could not hold the United States responsible for illegal actions committed by the Contras in their armed operations because, although the United States played a relevant role in the Contras' operations, it did not have effective control over them.[9] The ICJ later reiterated its understanding that attribution under Article 8 of the ARSIWA would require evidence that a state has effective control over the actions of a non-state actor in the *Armed Activities in the Congo* case[10] and in the *Bosnia* v. *Serbia* case.[11]

Other tribunals read the ICJ's interpretation of control as the standard customary law test for attribution of conduct under Article 8 of the ARSIWA.[12] However, the solution found by the ICJ was not the only possible one. For example, those operating in specialized fields of international law have found that it was sometimes necessary to adopt a lower threshold of control in light of the legal and practical circumstances of the cases they were handling.

This flexibility is illustrated by the International Criminal Tribunal for the Former Yugoslavia (ICTY), which attributed the conduct of armed forces to states by making use of what became known as the 'overall control' test. In the *Tadić* case, the ICTY acknowledged the 'effective control' test developed by the ICJ, but found that its high threshold was incompatible with the strict hierarchy under which military operations take form. According to the ICTY: 'The requirement of international law for the attribution to States of acts performed by private individuals is

[9] *Military and Paramilitary Activities in and against Nicaragua (Nicaragua v United States of America)* (Merits) [1986] ICJ Rep 14 [115]–[116].

[10] *Armed Activities on the Territory of the Congo (New Application: 2002) (Democratic Republic of the Congo v Rwanda)* (Jurisdiction) [2006] ICJ Rep 6 [160].

[11] *Bosnia v Serbia* (2007) (n 4) [399].

[12] See eg *Responsibilities and Obligations of States Sponsoring Persons and Entities with Respect to Activities in the Area* (Advisory Opinion) ITLOS Reports 2011, 10 [169].

that the State exercises control over the individuals. The *degree of control* may, however, vary according to the factual circumstances of each case.'[13]

Following this logic, the ICTY concluded that the 'effective control' test set by the ICJ was suited for situations where it was necessary to determine whether the actions of a private individual (or group of individuals) are attributable to a state. In these cases, the ICTY stressed, there must be evidence that such an individual received from a state specific instructions to act as its de facto agent.[14] However, such detailed examination would not be necessary when the state already has authority over an individual or group that operates under an organized hierarchy. Organized and hierarchical structures, such as military units, operate under more predictable, preexisting logics and strategies and therefore do not require a threshold as high as the one expressed by the ICJ in *Nicaragua* v. *USA*. The ICTY clarified that:

> Normally a member of the group does not act on his own but conforms to the standards prevailing in the group and is subject to the authority of the head of the group. Consequently, for the attribution to a State of acts of these groups it is sufficient to require that the group as a whole be under the overall control of the State.[15]

The ICJ responded specifically to the *Tadić* test in its *Bosnia* v. *Serbia* judgment, suggesting that the approach taken by the ICTY in this case was 'unpersuasive' and dismissing the possibility of applying it in the context of state responsibility.[16] The ICTY, however, kept following its own test as set in *Tadić*,[17] with defenders of this approach arguing that both tests can coexist because they are designed to deal with different circumstances.[18]

The peculiarities of state-owned enterprises may also justify a specific approach to establish that a state controls them. In its commentary to Article 8 of the ARSIWA, the ILC discussed the attribution of conduct of enterprises that are owned and controlled by the state as an example of a situation

[13] *The Prosecutor v Duško Tadić* (Judgment) ICTY-94-1-A (15 July 1999) [117] (emphasis in original).

[14] ibid [118].

[15] ibid [120].

[16] *Bosnia v Serbia* (n 4) [404]ff.

[17] *The Prosecutor v Prlić and ors* (Judgment vol 1) ICTY-04-74-A (29 November 2017) [238]. See also *The Prosecutor v Aleksovski* (Judgment) ICTY-95-14-1-A (24 March 2000) [130]ff; *The Prosecutor v Delalić and ors* (Judgment) ICTY-96-21-A (20 February 2001) [47].

[18] See generally A Cassese, 'The *Nicaragua* and *Tadić* Test Revisited in Light of the ICJ Judgment on Genocide in Bosnia' (2007) 4 EJIL 649.

that could warrant a threshold different from that used in ICJ case law. According to the ILC, the conduct of a state-owned enterprise should be attributed to the state pursuant to Article 8 of the ARSIWA when there is 'evidence ... that the State was using its ownership interest in or control over a corporation specifically in order to achieve a particular result'.[19]

The ILC's commentary relied on an example from the case law of the Iran–US Claims Tribunal (IUSCT) on the attribution of the conduct of state-owned enterprises. The IUSCT, a tribunal created as part of a set of measures to manage the political crisis between the United States and Iran arising from the 1979 hostage crisis and the subsequent freezing of Iranian assets by the United States, decided several cases that involved the attribution to the state of the actions of state-owned enterprises. These decisions were grounded on interpretation of Article VII(3) and (4) of the Claims Settlement Agreement, which provided for the attribution to Iran and the United States respectively of the acts of the entities they controlled.

In most cases, the IUSCT attributed the actions of state-owned enterprises to the state only if there was proof that the latter was using its controlling stake to direct the actions of the enterprise.[20] However, in cases such as *Foremost Tehran* v. *Iran* the tribunal's decision on attribution rested on the corporate characteristics of an enterprise – namely, 'the identity of its shareholders and the composition and behaviour of its board of directors, which must be examined together',[21] rather than on the specific interactions between the state and the corporations.[22] The reason for such variation was the position taken by the minority of judges, as stated in Judge Khalilian's opinion in the case of *SEDCO* v. *Iran*:

> Until now, the majority has taken the position, in its past Awards, that the term 'control' in Article VII (paras. 2, 3, 4) involves a qualitative predominance and, in the words of Chamber Three, 'control over management'....

[19] ILC, 'Draft Articles on Responsibility of States for Internationally Wrongful Acts with Commentaries' (n 7) commentary to art 8, para (6).

[20] See eg *International Technical Products Corporation and ITP Export Corporation, Its Wholly Owned Subsidiary v Iran and Its Agencies, the Islamic Republic Iranian Air Force and the Ministry of National Defense, Acting for the Civil Aviation Organization* (Award No. 196-302-3) IUSCT Case No 302 (28 October 1985) [113].

[21] *Foremost Tehran, Inc, Foremost Shir, Inc, and ors v Iran, the Ministry of Economic Affairs and Finance, and ors* (Award No 220-37/231-1) IUSCT Case Nos 37 and 231 (11 April 1986) [47]. See also *PepsiCo, Inc v Iran, Foundation for the Oppressed, Zamzam Bottling Company, and ors* (Award No 260-18-1) IUSCT Case No 18 (13 October 1986) [61]–[62].

[22] *Foremost Tehran v Iran* (n 21) [49].

> Nonetheless, it is worth noting, as a digression, that this same Tribunal has elsewhere correctly given the meaning of 'control' as set forth in paragraph 3, since it has held that two conditions must be met, before there can be a finding of control.[23]

The ILC, when examining the IUSCT case law, focused on the majority cases where the tribunal looked for evidence that the state had used its corporate power to push the state-owned enterprise towards adopting specific actions.[24] The ILC found these majority cases representative, not only of the IUSCT practice for dealing with state-owned enterprises but of the position of international law in general.[25]

These examples show how there are multiple ways of interpreting and applying Article 8 of the ARSIWA. The term 'control', in the way that it is used in the ARSIWA, or even the 'effective control' terminology used by the ICJ, are polysemic terms – they do not encompass a single type of relationship between states and non-state entities. It is up to those applying Article 8 to examine whether each situation they face meets the conditions for attribution under that provision. However, this case-by-case approach does not mean that Article 8 should be interpreted indiscriminately or inconsistently. In fact, all bodies examined in this section have sought a consistent application of Article 8 when dealing with similar sets of facts. Consistency in these cases is achieved not by applying the exact same text, but rather through constant judicial dialogue. This logic can be seen in the intense dialogue between ICJ and the ICTY about whether there should be a single control test, and if so, which should be the correct one. Both concluded that there were different possible interpretations for the term 'control' and that the test that each of them had been applying so far was the correct one for the specific circumstances they were facing.[26] Similarly,

[23] *SEDCO Inc v National Iranian Oil Company and Iran* (Award No 419-128/129-2) IUSCT Case Nos 128 and 129 (30 March 1989) [10].

[24] See ILC, First Report on State Responsibility, UN Doc A/CN.4/490/Add.5 (22 July 1998), para 213. The cases examined by the ILC for these purposes were *Schering Corporation v Iran* (Award No 122–38-3) IUSCT Case No 38 (16 April 1984); *Otis Elevator Company v Iran and Bank Mellat (formerly Foreign Trade Bank of Iran)* (Award No 304-284-2) IUSCT Case No 284 (29 April 1987); *Eastman Kodak Company v the Government of Iran* (Award No 329-227/12384-3) IUSCT Case No 227 (11 November 1987); *SEDCO v National Iranian Oil Company* (n 23) Dissenting and Concurring Opinion of Judge Khalilian; Flexi-Van Leasing, Inc v Iran (Award No 259–36-1) IUSCT Case No 36 (13 October 1986).

[25] ILC, First Report on State Responsibility, UN Doc A/CN.4/490/Add.5 (22 July 1998), para 213.

[26] *Bosnia v Serbia* (n 4) [405] ('It should be first observed that logic does not require the same test to be adopted in resolving the two issues, which are very different in nature . . . Thus, it is on the basis of its settled jurisprudence that the Court will determine whether the

in the IUSCT the judges that were in the minority in cases such as *SEDCO* engaged in internal judicial dialogue when dissenting from its own case law.[27]

2.1.1 Control Tests in Investment Arbitration

Investment tribunals have followed a tendency similar to that of their counterparts in other fields of international law. However, there is a key difference between the bodies examined in Section 2.1 and investment arbitration tribunals. Unlike the former which are permanent institutions with a stable composition of judges, investment arbitration is a fragmented dispute settlement system. Although investment arbitration is developed on the basis of common principles and goals, cases are grounded on agreements that are negotiated and drafted individually, each with its own particularities. Neither these agreements nor the tribunals that settle the disputes arising from them have formal ties with each other. There is also no formal obligation to follow precedent, meaning that tribunals may rely on previous case law when appropriate, but are not forced to follow it.[28] As a result, the findings made by a tribunal in one case do not bind other tribunals, making it hard to make definitive affirmations about the field.

With that caveat made, investment tribunals have generally acknowledged the ICJ's 'effective control' test as the standard approach for holding states responsible for the actions of non-state actors. In the case of *Marfin* v. *Cyprus*, for example, the tribunal stressed that investment arbitration jurisprudence had consistently upheld the ICJ test and

Respondent has incurred responsibility under the rule of customary international law set out in Article 8 of the ILC Articles on State Responsibility.'); *Prlić* (n 17) [238] (noting that 'the ICJ refrained from taking a position on whether the Overall Control Test employed by the Appeals Chamber in *Tadić* was correct' and that it saw no 'cogent reason why the Appeals Chamber should depart from its well-settled precedent regarding the Overall Control Test').

27 *SEDCO v National Iranian Oil Company* (n 23) Dissenting and Concurring Opinion of Judge Khalilian [10] (arguing that the majority judgment in this case does not agree with most of the IUSCT case law).

28 On precedent and the use of case law in investment arbitration, see generally AR Sureda, 'Precedent in Investment Treaty Arbitration' in C Binder, U Kriebaum, A Reinisch, and S Wittich (eds), *International Investment Law for the 21st Century: Essays in Honour of Christoph Schreuer* (Oxford University Press 2009) 830; C Schreuer and M Weiniger, 'A Doctrine of Precedent?' in PT Muchlinski, F Ortino, and C Schreuer (eds), *The Oxford Handbook of International Investment Law* (Oxford University Press 2008) 1188.

that there was no reason to depart from it.[29] As a consequence, the tribunal found that Cyprus could not be held responsible for treaty violations allegedly committed by a private bank, because although Cyprus had sometimes interfered in the bank's administration and guided some of its decisions, there was no evidence that Cyprus had effective control over the bank's alleged violations.[30]

Arbitral tribunals' attitudes towards the ICJ test vary, however, when the cases concern state responsibility for the actions of a state-owned enterprise. While many cases have followed the ICJ's threshold of effective control, others have adopted much lower standards. Cases can be divided into three groups:

1. those applying the 'effective control' standard set by the ICJ;
2. those that consider the 'effective control' standard too high for cases involving state-owned enterprises and instead determine that states that cleared or authorized an action by a state-owned enterprise are responsible for those actions; and
3. those that presume that states are responsible for the actions of any enterprise in which they hold more than 50 percent of the shares.

Cases applying the ICJ's 'effective control' standard include *Jan de Nul* v. *Egypt*, where the tribunal examined whether actions of an Egyptian agency with distinct legal personality were attributable to the state of Egypt. The tribunal focused strictly on international rules on attribution and followed general standards for the interpretation of ARSIWA Articles 4, 5, and 8,[31] making specific reference to the ICJ's effective control test.[32] Such an approach was also followed by the tribunals in *Hamester* v. *Ghana*, *White Industries* v. *India*, and *Tulip Real Estate* v. *Turkey*.[33]

In several other cases the tribunals adopted much lower thresholds of control. In the *Bayindir* v. *Pakistan* case, the tribunal had to determine whether Pakistan should be held responsible for clearing actions of the National Highway Authority (NHA) that violated investment protections

[29] *Marfin Investment Group Holdings SA, Alexandros Bakatselos, and ors v Cyprus* (Award) ICSID Case No ARB/13/27 (26 July 2018) [674]–[675].

[30] ibid [679].

[31] *Jan de Nul NV and Dredging International NV v Egypt* (Award) ICSID Case No ARB/04/13 (6 November 2008) [157].

[32] ibid [173].

[33] *Gustav F W Hamester GmbH & Co KG v Ghana* (Award) ICSID Case No ARB/07/24 (18 June 2010) [159]; *White Industries Australia Limited v India* (Award) (30 November 2011) [8.1.18]; *Tulip Real Estate Investment and Development Netherlands BV v Turkey* (Award) ICSID Case No ARB/11/28 (10 March 2014) [306]–[308].

owed to the claimant. The tribunal was aware that state clearance met neither of the thresholds set in the ICJ's effective control test and the ICTY's overall control test, but chose nevertheless to attribute the NHA's conduct to Pakistan under Article 8 of the ARSIWA.[34] The tribunal summarized its logic in the following way:

> [T]he Tribunal is aware that the levels of control required for a finding of attribution under Article 8 in other factual contexts, such as foreign armed intervention or international criminal responsibility, may be different. It believes, however, that the approach developed in such areas of international law is not always adapted to the realities of international economic law and that they should not prevent a finding of attribution if the specific facts of an investment dispute so warrant.[35]

The tribunal unfortunately did not go further into clarifying what were the 'specific facts of the investment dispute' that justified its departure from tests that were already established in international case law. Nevertheless, such interpretation was later followed by the tribunal in *Deutsche Bank* v. *Sri Lanka.* In this case, the tribunal found that the actions of a state-owned entity should be attributed to Sri Lanka on the basis of evidence that the entity was following a governmental directive when it started the program that led to the dispute.[36]

Most tribunals are not, however, so explicit on the reasons that led them to depart from the general 'effective control' test. Take, for example, the case of *Maffezini* v. *Spain.* The question that was raised before the tribunal concerned the attribution to the state of the actions of SODIGA, a state-owned company engaged in a joint venture with the claimant. In its analysis, the tribunal stressed that the applicable law to determine attribution was that of state responsibility, in particular the provisions contained in the (then) draft ARSIWA. However, its analysis followed very different lines from those in the ARSIWA or those used by other international law courts. The tribunal ruled that the actions of state-owned entities are presumed to be attributable to the state if that entity (1) was owned by the state, (2) was controlled by the state, or (3) performed state functions.[37] The tribunal then focused on what it described as a 'structural test',

[34] *Bayindir Insaat Turizm Ticaret Ve Sanayi AS v Pakistan* (Award) ICSID Case No ARB/03/29 (27 August 2009), [128]–[130].

[35] ibid [130].

[36] *Deutsche Bank AG v Sri Lanka* (Award) ICSID Case No ARB/09/2 (31 October 2012) [405](c), (d).

[37] *Emilio Agustín Maffezini v Spain* (Decision of the Tribunal on Objections to Jurisdiction) ICSID Case No ARB/97/7 (25 January 2000) [76]–[77].

through which the tribunal allowed itself to presume that any entity in which the government owned more than half of the shares would be operating under its control. Based on this test, the tribunal concluded that the Spanish state was responsible for SODIGA's actions because it owned 'no less than' 51 percent of its shares.[38]

The tribunals in *RFCC* v. *Morocco* and *Salini* v. *Morocco* approached 'control' in Article 8 from a similar perspective. Both cases arose from contracts between foreign investors and the Société Nationale des Autoroutes du Maroc (ADM), a state-owned enterprise responsible for many of Morocco's highways. In *RFCC* v. *Morocco*, the tribunal concluded that Morocco had control over ADM after examining the information on its corporate ownership and its administration contained in its bylaws.[39] In *Salini* v. *Morocco*, the tribunal went further with its suggestion of attributing to states the actions of all state-owned enterprises, which the tribunal defined as 'any commercial company dominated or predominantly controlled by the State or by State institutions, whether it has a legal personality or not'.[40] Years later, this approach was reiterated

[38] ibid [83] ('[I]n spite of the fact that the government chose to create SODIGA in the form of a private commercial corporation, it did so by providing that the Instituto Nacional de Industria would own no less than 51% of the capital. In fact, as of December 31, 1990, the percentage of governmentally owned capital of SODIGA had increased to over 88%, including the stock holdings of the Xunta de Galicia, also a state entity in charge of the executive power in the Autonomous Community of Galicia, several savings and loans associations (*cajas de ahorros*), other regional development agencies and the Banco Exterior de España.') and [89] ('In view of the fact that SODIGA meets both the *structural test of State creation and capital ownership* and the functional test of performing activities of a public nature, the Tribunal concludes that the Claimant has made out a prima facie case that SODIGA is a State entity acting on behalf of the Kingdom of Spain.' (emphasis added)).

[39] *Consortium RFCC v Morocco* (Decision on Jurisdiction) ICSID Case No ARB/00/6 (16 July 2001) [35]–[36].

[40] *Salini Costruttori SpA and Italstrade SpA v Morocco* (Decision on Jurisdiction) ICSID Case No ARB/00/4 (23 July 2001) [31] ('Neither the Convention nor the Bilateral Treaty gives the slightest indication of what should be understood by "Contracting State". The reference made to "any constituent subdivision" or "agency of a Contracting State" is of no importance in this regard, because ADM does not fulfil the conditions required by the Washington Convention to be a party to these proceedings. Generally, any commercial company dominated or predominantly controlled by the State or by State institutions, whether it has a legal personality or not, is considered to be a State-owned company. . . . In order to determine the degree of control and participation of a State in a company, the Tribunal, referring to an ICSID award rendered in a case between Emilio Agustin Maffezini and the Kingdom of Spain (ICSID Case No ARBI977), considers that it must take into account the international rules governing the liability of States. The assessment of the degree of State control and participation in a company is based on two criteria: the first, structural, in other words, related to the structure of the company and, in particular,

in the case of *Helnan* v. *Egypt*, where the tribunal attributed the actions of a corporation to Egypt based solely on the fact that it was owned by Egypt.[41]

In some cases, tribunals have also combined elements from different interpretations, tailoring their analysis of control to the circumstances of the case. In the case of *Karkey Karadeniz* v. *Pakistan*, the tribunal applied a test that included both corporate and effective control when applying Article 8 of the ARSIWA. The case concerned contracts signed by the claimant with a Pakistani corporation as part of a broader governmental plan to tackle the Pakistani energy crisis. The tribunal started its examination by pointing out that the company itself had acknowledged that it was 'owned and controlled by the government of Pakistan', suggesting that it would apply the criterion of corporate control to the 'control' threshold in Article 8 of the ARSIWA.[42] However, the tribunal then stressed that the evidence on record indicated that it was the government of Pakistan that had negotiated the contract and selected the corporation that was going to enter into it as a buyer.[43] Ultimately the tribunal's conclusion was that the company's 'acts related to the conclusion and execution of the Contract were directed, instructed or controlled by Pakistan, and are accordingly attributable to Pakistan, irrespective of the disclaimer contained in the RFP [Request for Proposal]'.[44]

The interpretation of the term 'control' in Article 8 of the ARSIWA will therefore vary depending on the specific circumstances of a case, the broader legal framework, and the rules which the tribunal is applying to the case. In this sense, investment arbitration tribunals dealing with questions of attribution of conduct of state-owned enterprises to states have followed similar patterns to the ones seen in other international law contexts. The use of the 'effective control' test by the ICJ in preference to a lower standard is a way to prevent it from overstepping its functions and ensuring that it does not meddle in states' domestic affairs. On the other hand, the ICTY employed a lower threshold justified by the fact that armed troops operate under the oversight of the state and follow a rigid hierarchy.

to its shareholders; the other, functional, related to the objectives of the company in question.').

41 *Helnan Inqsazternational Hotels A/S v Egypt* (Decision on Objection to Jurisdiction) ICSID Case No ARB/05/19 (17 October 2006) [92].

42 *Karkey Karadeniz Elektrik Uretim AS v Pakistan* (Award) ICSID Case No ARB/13/1 (22 August 2017) [572].

43 ibid [573]–[579].

44 ibid [582].

However, as shown by the IUSCT, the particularities of state-owned enterprises may warrant for a specific interpretation of the term 'control'. The control test applied by the majority of the IUSCT determined, first, whether the state was able to use its shares or other corporate or institutional mechanisms to control the actions of the enterprise. Secondly, the tribunal would look at whether the state had indeed used those powers to control the enterprise and have it perform the specific actions discussed in the case at hand. In investment law, tribunals applying Article 8 of the ARSIWA have employed three different tests, holding states responsible (1) only for the actions of state-owned enterprises they effectively controlled and specifically directed, adopting a test similar to that of the IUSCT; (ii) for any action they authorized; or (iii) for any action of the state-owned enterprises over which they held corporate control.

3 Investment Law Shaping the Concept of Control

In the absence of specific provisions on state responsibility for the actions of state-owned enterprises, the applicable rules are those contained in the ARSIWA, which is deemed to mostly reflect customary international law. However, the interpretation of such rules is shaped by the specific factual and legal context of each case. The factual context relates to the particularities of the relationship between the state and the entity, including the powers that the state holds as a shareholder and the specific interactions between the state and the enterprise in the circumstances of the case. The legal context comprises the characteristics of the field of international law and the instruments applicable to the relationship between the parties, including the legal principles that guide them, and how the stakeholders see and apply the rules contained in these instruments.[45]

In this section, I discuss two particularities of international investment law that may help explain why arbitrators adopt lower thresholds of control when applying Article 8 of the ARSIWA to the actions of state-owned enterprises. International investment law is a field that is

[45] For the sake of transparency, I want to clarify that my own views on how context plays into interpretation, and specifically legal interpretation, is mostly shaped by the works of Derrida, Gadamer, and Dworkin, especially J Derrida, *Specters of Marx: The State of Debt, the Work of Mourning and the New International* (Routledge 1994); HG Gadamer, *Truth and Method* (2nd rev edn, Continuum 2004); RM Dworkin, *Law's Empire* (Harvard University Press 1986). See also LL Streck, *Hermenêutica Jurídica e(m) Crise: Uma Exploração Hermenêutica da Construção do Direito* (Livraria do Advogado 2018); E Voyiakis, 'International Law, Interpretative Fidelity and the Hermeneutics of Hans-Georg Gadamer' (2011) 54 GYIL 385.

largely inspired by the goal of depoliticizing investment relations, which translates into discouraging states from participating directly in investments.[46] This underlying goal may push arbitrators to approach state-led investment initiatives cautiously (Section 3.1). On top of that, arbitrators have in other situations equated 'effective control' with corporate control, thus suggesting that investment tribunals interpret Article 8 of the ARSIWA much more flexibly than courts that operate in other fields of international law (Section 3.2). Ultimately, a tribunal will calibrate the threshold of the control by looking at the characteristics of the field, general international law standards, and the particularities of each case (Section 3.3).

3.1 Caution towards State-Led Initiatives in the Development of International Investment Law and Investment Arbitration

Investment arbitration is often guided by a general cautiousness towards state-led initiatives. International investment law was developed around the principle of investment neutrality, which assumes that state involvement in investment relations may generate political risks that harm foreign investment.[47] The term 'political risk' is not defined legally but is used in investment and business circles to refer to risks associated with political fluctuations such as changes of power and policy. Many of the protections contained in investment agreements are aimed at reducing political risks that foreign investors may face in the host state – for example, most-favored-nation and fair-and-equitable-treatment clauses. Most-favored-nation clauses prevent the host states' relationships with other states from interfering with investment relations by allowing foreign investors to claim most-favored-nation treatment.[48] Fair-

[46] On this, see generally KJ Vandevelde, 'Sustainable Liberalism and the International Investment Regime' (1997) 19 MJIL 373; KJ Vandevelde, 'The Liberal Vision of the International Law on Foreign Investment' in CL Lim (ed), *Alternative Visions of the International Law on Foreign Investment: Essays in Honour of Muthucumaraswamy Sornarajah* (Cambridge University Press 2016) 43.

[47] Vandevelde, 'The Liberal Vision' (n 46).

[48] An example of typical wording for such clauses can be found in Article 4 of the 2012 US Model Bilateral Investment Treaty: 'Most-Favored-Nation Treatment. 1. Each Party shall accord to investors of the other Party treatment no less favorable than that it accords, in like circumstances, to investors of any non-Party with respect to the establishment, acquisition, expansion, management, conduct, operation, and sale or other disposition of investments in its territory. 2. Each Party shall accord to covered investments treatment

and-equitable-treatment provisions require foreign investors to be treated 'fairly and equitably'[49] – terms that have been interpreted as a blanket protection for foreign investors against host state actions that seem to be politically motivated or 'irrational'.[50]

This logic of limiting state power also applies to investment arbitration. Investors often feel that the host states' domestic courts – the default forum for them to settle these disputes – may be biased against foreign investors or lack the expertise to deal with investment treaty claims. Even before clauses providing for arbitration as a means to settle disputes started to be introduced in investment treaties, states and investors were already reaching out to organizations such as the World Bank to request informal assistance to settle their disputes.[51] At the same time, the international dispute settlement options that existed then were limited and politically sensitive. To start a case against the host state, investors had to convince their home states to exercise diplomatic protection. This forced investors to spend significant time and political resources without any guarantee that the case would be picked up by their home states or lead to a desirable outcome.[52] Investment arbitration as a mechanism of dispute settlement that investors can use directly, without having to appeal to their state of origin, was thus considered a more politically neutral option than both domestic dispute settlement and diplomatic protection.[53]

In addition to depoliticizing the access of investors to international dispute settlement mechanisms, there is also the goal of depoliticizing the resolution of disputes themselves. Investment law often deals with subjects that are highly sensitive to states,[54] and one of the central goals of investment arbitration is to reduce state influence over litigation

no less favorable than that it accords, in like circumstances, to investments in its territory of investors of any non-Party with respect to the establishment, acquisition, expansion, management, conduct, operation, and sale or other disposition of investments.' '2012 U.S. Model Bilateral Investment Treaty <https://ustr.gov/sites/default/files/BIT%20text%20for%20ACIEP%20Meeting.pdf> accessed 15 January 2022.

[49] See eg 2012 US Model Bilateral Investment Treaty (n 48) art 5(1): 'Each Party shall accord to covered investments treatment in accordance with customary international law, including fair and equitable treatment and full protection and security.'

[50] See generally UNCTAD, 'Fair and Equitable Treatment: A Sequel' UNCTAD Series in International Investment Agreements II (2012) UN Doc UNCTAD/DIAE/IA/2011/5.

[51] A Broches, 'The Convention on the Settlement of Investment Disputes between States and Nationals of Other States' (1972) 136 RdC 344–45.

[52] ibid 344.

[53] JW Salacuse, *The Law of Investment Treaties* (3rd edn, Oxford University Press 2021) 535.

[54] ibid 495.

outcomes.[55] This includes, for example, prohibiting investors' home states from directly engaging in investment disputes, as provided in Article 27 of the ICSID Convention.[56]

The ICSID Convention also prevents states from making use of investment arbitration as investors themselves. The idea of having investor-states as parties to investment arbitration was raised and rejected during the negotiations of the ICSID Convention. Many of the states involved in negotiations feared that allowing states to access investment arbitration as investors would facilitate political capture of the system, which would defeat the purpose of creating a depoliticized system.[57] Article 25(1) of the ICSID Convention, which establishes ICSID jurisdiction, therefore excludes the possibility of interstate disputes:

> The jurisdiction of the Centre shall extend to any legal dispute arising directly out of an investment, between a Contracting State (or any constituent subdivision or agency of a Contracting State designated to the Centre by that State) and a national of another Contracting State …

Similarly, the early development of investment arbitration seems to have embedded in its discussions the idea that, although formally separate from states, state-owned enterprises would probably not be eligible claimants in investment arbitration because they operated under state control. Early ICSID drafts determined that, for jurisdictional purposes, state-owned enterprises should be equated to states.[58] The final draft of the ICSID Convention also allowed states to consent to foreign investors filing claims directly against their state-owned enterprises, therefore presuming that those enterprises were part of host states themselves.[59] Even today, there are investment treaties

[55] U Kriebaum, 'Evaluating Social Benefits and Costs of Investment Treaties: Depoliticization of Investment Disputes' (2018) 33 ICSID Rev 14.

[56] Convention on the Settlement of Investment Disputes between States and Nationals of Other States (adopted 18 March 1965, entered into force 14 October 1966) 575 UNTS 159.

[57] ICSID, *History of the ICSID Convention: Documents Concerning the Origin and the Formulation of the Convention on the Settlement of Investment Disputes between States and Nationals of Other States*, vol II-1 (ICSID 1968) 401.

[58] ICSID, *History of the ICSID Convention: Documents Concerning the Origin and the Formulation of the Convention on the Settlement of Investment Disputes between States and Nationals of Other States*, vol II-2 (ICSID 1968) 832 ('The competence of the Center shall extend to any legal dispute between a Contracting State (or any juridical person of public law controlled by that State) and a national of another Contracting State …') and 867 ('In this connection, Mr. Kpognon (Dahomey) suggested that, as far as the French text was concerned, words such as "personne morale de droit public" would achieve the desired purpose.').

[59] Convention on the Settlement of Investment Disputes (n 56) art 25(3).

with provisions limiting the protections afforded to state-owned investors and, as a consequence, their capacity to resort to investment arbitration.[60]

However, the creators of this dispute settlement system were aware that these preconceptions were subjective and could not reasonably justify a blanket prohibition against state-owned claimants making use of investment arbitration. When faced with the question of whether state-owned enterprises should be excluded from filing investment arbitration cases, Aaron Broches, former general counsel of the World Bank and one of the main sponsors of the ICSID Convention, acknowledged that they could play distinct roles in an economy, but seemed to believe that truly independent and market-oriented state-owned enterprises were an exception. In Broches's words, '[t]here would appear to be no reason why a state-owned enterprise, *if it elected to assimilate itself to a private enterprise rather than a government agency*'[61] should be treated differently from a privately owned corporation.

Most of the discussions on state-owned enterprises in investment law were, however, informal and were not translated into explicit treaty provisions. Broches's writings on the ICSID negotiations indicate that the drafters of these treaties may have thought that it was not necessary to add such a level of detail on state-owned enterprises, since they shared a 'common understanding' on the subject. This understanding was that although state-owned enterprises could not be automatically equated to states, most of them presented a risk for a free market economy because they operated under strict state supervision. This notion, however, covered only the political behaviour and characteristics of state-owned enterprises.

It is worth noting that this tendency to overgeneralize treaty terms on state-owned enterprises also prevails in modern investment treaties.

[60] See eg Agreement between the Government of the United Kingdom of Great Britain and Northern Ireland and the Government of the Republic of Panama for the Promotion and Protection of Investments (signed 7 October 1983, entered into force 7 November 1985) 2107 UNTS 300, art 1(d)(1) (excluding state-owned enterprises from the definition of investors); Treaty between the United States of America and the Republic of Senegal Concerning the Reciprocal Encouragement and Protection of Investment (signed 6 December 1983, entered into force 25 October 1990), annex (reservations to strategic sectors that are occupied by state-owned enterprises) <https://investmentpolicy.unctad.org/international-investment-agreements/treaty-files/2249/download> accessed 2 February 2022; Agreement for the Reciprocal Promotion and Protection of Investments between the Argentine Republic and the United Arab Emirates (signed 16 April 2018, not in force) arts 3(3) and 4(3) (most-favored-nation clause 'will depend on all the circumstances, including distinction between investors or investment').

[61] ICSID, *History of the ICSID Convention* (n 57) 11 para 30 (emphasis added).

With the exception of the EU–China Comprehensive Agreement on Investment, which specifically lists the entities covered by its provisions,[62] the few treaties that contain provisions on how to distinguish state-owned from other corporations or from states still do so in very broad terms, such as 'when it exercises any regulatory, administrative or other governmental authority'.[63]

While the legal instruments shaping international investment law do not provide much guidance on how to deal with legal questions involving state-owned enterprises, they show that stakeholders engaged in developing international investment law and investment arbitration were cautious towards recognizing rights of state-owned enterprises as investors. As stressed by the tribunal in *Maffezini* v. *Spain*, the overall framework of international investment law presumes that state-owned enterprises will, as a general rule, operate alongside states and even as part of their structure.[64] In the extreme, relying on such notions may lead to decisions such as the one taken by the tribunal in *Bayindir* v. *Pakistan*, which concluded that it could attribute to a state the actions of any enterprise that it owns, regardless of there being specific evidence showing that the state indeed exercised control over that entity.[65]

[62] China–EU Comprehensive Agreement on Investment (signed 22 January 2021) art 3bis ('1. Covered entity means, at all levels of government, the following entities ... (a) Enterprise in which a Party directly or indirectly, i. owns more than 50 per cent of the share capital; ii. controls, through ownership interests the exercise of more than 50 per cent of the voting rights; iii. holds the power to appoint a majority of members of the board of directors or any other equivalent management body; or iv. holds the power to control the decisions of the enterprise through any other ownership interest, including minority ownership; (b) Enterprise in which a Party has the power to legally direct the actions or otherwise exercise an equivalent level of control in accordance with its laws and regulations; (c) Any entity, public or private, including where relevant any subsidiary thereof, or a consortium, which in a relevant market in the territory of a Party is authorized or established formally or in effect by that Party as the sole supplier or purchaser of a good or service, but does not include an entity that has been granted an exclusive intellectual property right solely by reason of such grant; (d) Two or a small number of enterprises, public or private, including where relevant any subsidiary thereof, designated by a Party, formally or in effect, as the only suppliers or purchasers of a particular good or service in a relevant market in the territory of that Party.').

[63] See eg Treaty between the Government of the United States of America and the Government of the Republic of Rwanda Concerning the Encouragement and Reciprocal Protection of Investment (signed 19 February 2008, entered into force 1 December 2012) art 2(2)(a), <https://investmentpolicy.unctad.org/international-investment-agreements/treaty-files/2241/download> accessed 8 February 2022.

[64] *Maffezini v Spain* (n 37) [83] ('The fact that an entity is owned by the State gives rise to a rebuttable presumption that it is a State entity.').

[65] *Bayindir v Pakistan* (n 34) [128]–[130].

3.2 *Using 'Effective Control' as a Flexible Standard*

A second element shaping how investment arbitration approaches the attribution to states of state-owned enterprise actions is the flexibility with which investment tribunals have approached the term 'effective control'. Tribunals have relied on the terminology of effective control in various contexts and referring to different thresholds of control, including corporate control. In the context of investment arbitration, the term 'effective control' has been used to indicate that a tribunal must look at the facts of each case, rather than relying on general formulas that presume control.

The legal issue with regard to which the tribunals show the greatest flexibility in the interpretation of the standards of effective control is the determination of the nationality of foreign investors. As stated in Article 25(1) of the ICSID Convention, modern investment arbitration is supposed to be between a state and a national of another state. Therefore, a corporate foreign investor will be allowed to file an investment claim on its own only if it proves that it is a national of a state party to a relevant treaty. However, it is not easy to determine the nationality of an investor, since many host states require investments to be made through local subsidiaries that would not normally qualify as foreign investors. In general international law, the nationality of a corporate investor is determined on the basis of its place of incorporation,[66] which makes it impossible for foreign shareholders to file claims seeking relief for damages suffered through a local subsidiary. Aware that this would hamper the access of transnational companies to investment arbitration,[67] the drafters of the ICSID Convention included in Article 25(2)(b) the possibility for states to agree to treating local subsidiaries controlled by foreign corporations as foreign nationals:

> (2) 'National of another Contracting State' means: . . .
>
> (b) any juridical person which had the nationality of a Contracting State other than the State party to the dispute on the date on which the parties consented to submit such dispute to conciliation or arbitration and any juridical person which had the nationality of the Contracting State party to the dispute on that date and which, because of *foreign control*, the parties have agreed should be treated as a national of another Contracting State for the purposes of this Convention.[68]

[66] *Case Concerning the Barcelona Traction, Light and Power Company, Limited (New Application: 1962) (Belgium v Spain)* [1970] ICJ Rep 3, 70.

[67] C Schreuer and others, *The ICSID Convention: A Commentary* (Cambridge University Press 2009) 792.

[68] Emphasis added.

Many investment treaties thus include in their dispute settlement chapters provisions that also treat as foreign investors subsidiaries that are controlled by a national of a foreign state.[69] However, such provisions require proof that the claimant parent company has corporate control over the local subsidiary.[70] Although the most obvious form of corporate control would be to hold more than half of the subsidiary's shares, there are many ways of controlling a corporation – for example, through special voting rights, golden shares, or joint ownership, to name but a few. Perhaps to avoid being blindsided by looking only at majority shareholding, tribunals have treated as nationals of a state claimants that are under the 'effective' corporate control of an entity established in that state.[71]

Despite the use of terminology identical that used by the ICJ in the *Nicaragua* v. *United States* case, the test used by arbitral tribunals to determine the nationality of investors could not be more different from the one employed by the ICJ. Whereas the ICJ test focused on whether a state had de facto control over another entity's specific actions, the test used by arbitral tribunals to determine the nationality of investors involves an inquiry into the company's corporate control mechanisms. In the case of *Rompetrol* v. *Romania*, the tribunal examined the successive changes in the ownership of Rompetrol since 1993 to determine who had 'effective control of the corporate entities in question'.[72] The *Vivendi I* annulment committee adopted a similar approach to examine whether a transfer of control over one of the claimants could affect its nationality, stressing that a company could be considered a foreign national only if it was 'effectively controlled, directly or indirectly, by nationals of one of the contracting parties'.[73]

Neither of the tribunals in the cases of *Rompetrol* or *Vivendi I* referred or drew connections to *Nicaragua* v. *United States* or to

[69] That said, an agreement to this effect has in practice been considered as implied in treaties that contain an ICSID dispute settlement clause. See *Liberian Eastern Timber Corporation v Liberia* (Award) ICSID Case No ARB/83/2 (31 March 1986); *Cable Television of Nevis, Ltd and Cable Television of Nevis Holdings, Ltd v St Kitts and Nevis* (Award) ICSID Case No ARB/95/2 (13 January 1997) [5.17], [5.18].

[70] R Dolzer and C Schreuer, *Principles of International Investment Law* (Oxford University Press 2012) 53. See *Vacuum Salt Products Ltd v Ghana* (Award) ICSID Case No ARB/92/1 (16 February 1994) [36].

[71] See eg *The Rompetrol Group NV v Romania* (Decision on Respondent's Preliminary Objections on Jurisdiction and Admissibility) ICSID Case No ARB/06/3 (18 April 2008) [35]ff.

[72] ibid.

[73] *Compañía de Aguas del Aconquija SA and Vivendi Universal (formerly Aguas del Aconquija and Compagnie Générale des Eaux) v Argentine Republic (I)* (Decision on Annulment) ICSID Case No ARB/97/3 (3 July 2002) [50].

Article 8 of the ARSIWA. This raises the question of whether these two investment tribunals had the intention to apply and interpret the ICJ's effective control test through the lens of investment law when adopting such terminology. Nevertheless, the use of the term 'effective control' has led other tribunals to treat such case law as part of a common analytical framework. In *Pan American Energy and BP Argentina* v. *Argentina*, the claimants and the tribunal referred to case law on the determination of nationality and on attribution of conduct to justify the use of corporate control as a criterion to determine nationality.[74] The resulting award thus combined the case law on 'effective control', thereby creating another new test for attribution of conduct under these criteria.[75]

Investment tribunals therefore approach the interpretation of the term 'control' under Article 8 of the ARSIWA from a rather unique perspective. In the absence of a distinction between 'corporate nationality control' and 'control over non-state actor's conduct', the concept of 'effective control' ceases to be a specific threshold for control in the context of investment arbitration. Rather than using it as a reference to a threshold of control, investment tribunals seem to treat the 'effective control' standard as translating an obligation to examine each case individually and to evaluate different legal approaches to reach a solution that is appropriate to the specific circumstances of the case.

3.3 *Judicial Reasoning as a Compass for Determining a Threshold for Control*

The flexibility with which tribunals have approached the 'effective control test' is not exceptional in investment arbitration. As argued elsewhere,

[74] *Pan American Energy LLC and BP Argentina Exploration Company v Argentine Republic* (Decision on Preliminary Objections) ICSID Case No ARB/03/13 (27 July 2006) 198, 210, citing the following cases: *Vivendi and ors v Argentina (I)* (n 73); *Alex Genin, Eastern Credit Limited, Inc and AS Baltoil v Estonia* (Award) ICSID Case No ARB/99/2 (25 June 2001); *CMS Gas Transmission Company v Argentina* (Decision on Jurisdiction) ICSID Case No ARB/01/8 (17 July 2003); *Azurix Corp v Argentina (I)* (Decision on Jurisdiction) ICSID Case No ARB/01/12 (8 December 2003); *Enron Creditors Recovery Corporation (formerly Enron Corporation) and Ponderosa Assets, LP v Argentina* (Decision on Jurisdiction) ICSID Case No ARB/01/3 (14 January 2004); and *Siemens AG v Argentina* (Decision on Jurisdiction) ICSID Case No ARB/02/8 (3 August 2004) (on determination of nationality); and *Maffezini v Spain* (n 37); *Asian Agricultural Products Ltd (AAPL) v Republic of Sri Lanka* (Award) ICSID Case No ARB/87/3 (27 June 1990) (on attribution).

[75] *Pan American Energy LLC and BP Argentina Exploration Company v Argentina* (Decision on Preliminary Objections) ICSID Case No ARB/03/13 (27 July 2006) [221].

investment arbitration tribunals approach situations on a case-by-case basis, tailoring their legal solutions to the characteristics of the agreements at hand and the specific needs of the parties to the dispute.[76] Faced with the question of attribution of state-owned enterprise conduct to states based on Article 8 of the ARSIWA, investment tribunals will therefore determine what threshold of control to apply in each case by calibrating[77] standards used in general international law and the specific characteristics of the international investment law applicable to the case at hand.

An examination of the way in which investment arbitration tribunals applied Article 8 of the ARSIWA raises the question not only of the threshold of control that they apply but even more so the elements that they take into consideration to determine the threshold of control applicable to each case. A tribunal that rules on whether to attribute the actions of a state-owned enterprise to a state pursuant to Article 8 of the ARSIWA will have to consider whether the (very high) threshold of control set by the ICJ is appropriate to the circumstances of the case at hand,[78] including the rules agreed upon by the treaty parties; the common practices in the field;[79] the treaty parties' laws on state-owned enterprises;[80] and evidence of the involvement of the treaty party in the state-owned enterprise or in events related to the case.[81]

The highest threshold of control that a tribunal could adopt would be the one applied by the ICJ in the *Nicaragua* v. *United States* case, which holds states responsible only for actions that they have specifically

[76] E De Brabandere and P Baldini Miranda Da Cruz, 'The Role of Proportionality in International Investment Law and Arbitration: A System-Specific Perspective' (2020) 89 NJIL 471.

[77] On how investment tribunals deal with competing interests, see generally E De Brabandere, '(Re)calibration, Standard-Setting and the Shaping of Investment Law and Arbitration' (2018) 59 BCLR 2607.

[78] As stressed by Cassese (n 18) 665ff.

[79] See eg *Stadtwerke München GmbH and ors v Spain* (Award) ICSID Case No ARB/15/1 (2 December 2019) [134] (noting that the applicable treaty does not provide that state-owned companies should be treated differently from companies owned by private investors).

[80] See eg *Salini v Morrocco* (n 40) [31] (actions of state-owned enterprises attributable to the state when their activities were 'dominated or predominantly controlled by the State or by State institutions', which in this case could be determined by looking at whether the state held corporate control over the enterprise and whether the corporate objectives of the corporation matched those of the states).

[81] See eg *Deutsche Bank v Sri Lanka* (n 36) [405](c) and (d) (concluding that it was not necessary to examine control, as there was sufficient evidence that the state-owned entity had acted under the direct instruction of Sri Lanka, since it had no choice but to follow a directive from the government when starting the hedging program).

controlled by, for example, ordering or directing the state-owned enterprise to act in such a way. The lowest threshold would be to attribute to the state the actions of any entity in respect of which it has participatory decision-making power, regardless of whether it is indeed involved in the decisions taken concerning that entity. Between these two extremes there is a range of other possible thresholds that may be adopted depending on the context of a case. A tribunal may, for example, hold states responsible for the actions of non-state entities when they have evidence that the state formally cleared or authorized those actions. All of these approaches are in principle allowed by international investment law and investment arbitration, as arbitral tribunals have the power to interpret and apply international law to solve the conflict they have at hand.

Tribunals' powers to interpret and apply open-ended rules such as the one expressed in Article 8 of the ARSIWA is tied to an obligation to provide reasoning. Article 48(3) of the ICSID Convention requires tribunals to state the reasons upon which they have made their decisions. Article 34(3) of the UNCITRAL Arbitration Rules contains a similar obligation, which applies unless the parties have agreed otherwise. In ICSID proceedings, an arbitral award that lacks an account of the tribunal's reasoning may even be annulled pursuant to Article 52(1)(e) of the ICSID Convention. The amount of detail that a tribunal must give to fulfill its obligation to provide its reasoning will vary from case to case. As noted by the annulment committee in *Wena*, there is no single compulsory format in which the tribunal must present its reasons, and it can even leave its reasons implicit, 'provided that they can be reasonably inferred from the terms used in the decision'.[82] For example, we can assume that a tribunal dealing with Article 8 of the ARSIWA that applies the exact same threshold for control as the ICJ did in *Nicaragua* did so because it saw no specific reason to recalibrate the general international law standard. However, if a tribunal issues a decision that seems to depart from previous understandings, it should consider explaining why it decided to do so.[83]

Although tribunals enjoy considerable freedom when interpreting open-ended rules such as that expressed in Article 8, references to

[82] *Wena Hotels Ltd v Egypt* (Decision on Annulment) ICSID Case No ARB/98/4 (5 February 2002) [81]. See also *Perenco Ecuador Limited v Ecuador* (Decision on Annulment) ICSID Case No ARB/08/6 (28 May 2021) [166].

[83] On the need for tribunals to detail their reasoning when departing from previous jurisprudence in order to maintain coherence, see Dworkin's concept of 'chain novel' and law as integrity in Dworkin (n 45) 176ff and 229ff.

different approaches in a single award suggest that, in investment arbitration, the term 'effective control' refers more to a standard of evaluation than a specific threshold of control.[84] Take the tribunal in *Karkey Karadeniz*, for instance, which justified its decision on attribution on the basis of elements that refer to corporate control, de facto control, and specific instructions – namely (1) the state-owned had acknowledged that it was owned and controlled by the government of Pakistan; (2) the government of Pakistan had approved the contract related to the dispute; (3) the government of Pakistan was the guarantor of that contract; and (4) the buyer was not allowed to interfere in licenses granted in the contract, which was interpreted as a sign of bad faith.[85] The diverse interpretations, each unique to a particular award, demonstrate the elasticity the term 'effective control' has within this system.

In the absence of a specific threshold of control to be applied uniformly across cases, a correct application of Article 8 of the ARSIWA relies on judicial reasoning. Rather than simply looking at the case law for possible tests and picking one, investment arbitration tribunals must explain their reasons when ruling on what would be the correct threshold of control to be applied in the case before them. As tribunals are not limited in the reasoning that they need to present to justify their decision, they have the power and freedom to decide what elements they will consider relevant in each case and how they weigh each of those elements. However, those reasons must be clear and rational from the stance of international investment law.

4 Conclusion

Although the ICJ's effective control test is commonly described as a standard solution for applying Article 8 of the ARSIWA, the ICJ has itself recognized that this test cannot be applied universally.[86] Being a polysemic term, 'control' in Article 8 can only be interpreted in the light of the circumstances of a particular case. As a consequence,

[84] See eg *Maffezini v Spain* (n 37) [76]–[77]; *RFCC v Morocco* (n 39) [35]–[36]; *Salini v Morocco* (n 40) [31].

[85] *Karkey Karadeniz v Pakistan* (n 42) [573]ff.

[86] *Bosnia v Serbia* (2007) (n 4) [405] (commenting on the ICTY test, the ICJ stated that 'the degree and nature of a State's involvement in an armed conflict on another State's territory which is required for the conflict to be characterized as international, can very well, and without logical inconsistency, differ from the degree and nature of involvement required to give rise to that State's responsibility for a specific act committed in the course of the conflict').

tribunals applying Article 8 have each had to develop their own control tests according to the legal and factual particularities of the cases before them. The process of interpreting these tests required tribunals to dialogue with each other in order to determine what elements it was appropriate for them to rely on when interpreting control in the cases before them.

Investment tribunals have often interpreted Article 8 of the ARSIWA differently in each case. Rather than establishing a single threshold that would be applied in every case involving state-owned enterprises, arbitral tribunals gauge the ideal threshold of control on the basis of the characteristics and needs of each case. Each tribunal operates independently and therefore has the power to decide alone what factors it will take into consideration when it determines the level of control, such as (1) the importance of following general international law precedent; (2) the specific characteristics of the case at hand, including the parties' needs and the particularities of the treaty that they agreed upon; and (3) the legal principles that guide international investment law and common practices in investment arbitration. In this chapter, I have focused on the last of these elements and identified two characteristics of international investment law that play a relevant role in tribunals' interpretations of Article 8 of the ARSIWA in cases involving state-owned enterprises.

The first of these characteristics is the principle of investment neutrality that inspires international investment law and guides investment agreements. The principle of investment neutrality assumes that state participation or interference in investment relations may create political risks prejudicial to investment relations, and acts as a warning to stakeholders to approach any state-led initiative with caution. In practice, this caution guides the drafting of treaty provisions focusing on the protection of foreign investment and may lead tribunals to interpret provisions in ways that extend the scope of state liability for participating directly in foreign investment. The second characteristic is the fact that investment tribunals have used the term 'effective control' to refer to other levels of control besides the very high and stable threshold set by the ICJ in *Nicaragua* v. *United States*. This flexible approach towards effective control suggests that investment tribunals approach cases from a more individualized perspective and one that takes into consideration the principles that guide the field.

However, this individualized approach towards the application of Article 8 of the ARSIWA increases the burden laid upon tribunals to justify their decisions. Tribunals have the obligation to provide in their awards the reasons that led them to decide in a certain way. While there is no specific format for presenting these reasons, they must be clear to the reader and follow a rational line of thought. When calibrating the threshold of control that they are going to apply in each case, tribunals must therefore clarify what elements they considered relevant for such calibration, how they have weighted them, and why they concluded that the threshold applied is best suited for that specific case.

7

The Court of Justice of the EU and CIL Interpretation

Close Encounters of a Third Kind?

TAMÁS MOLNÁR*

the intellectual prison of custom seems to be gradually transformed into a large dance floor where (almost) every step and movement is allowed

Jean d'Aspremont, 'Customary International Law as a Dance Floor: Part I' (*EJIL:Talk!* 14 April 2014)

1 Setting the Scene

It is uncontested that the European Union (EU) – endowed with distinct international legal personality (pursuant to Article 47 of the Treaty on European Union (TEU)) and being a subject of international law – is bound by relevant norms of customary international law (CIL).[1] Rules of CIL form an integral part of the EU legal order, and the Court of Justice of the EU (CJEU) must use CIL at least as an interpretive tool.[2] The status of CIL within EU law

* The views expressed in this chapter are solely those of the author and its content does not necessarily represent the views or position of the European Union Agency for Fundamental Rights.

1 See the following rulings from the CJEU's consistent case law: Case C-286/90 *Anklagemyndigheden v Peter Michael Poulsen and Diva Navigation Corp* [1992] ECR I-6019 [9]; Case C-162/96 *A Racke GmbH & Co v Hauptzollamt Mainz* [1998] ECR I-3655 [24], [45]–[46]; Joined Cases C-402/05 P and C-415/05 P *Kadi and Al Barakaat International Foundation v Council of the European Union and Commission of the European Communities* [2008] ECR I-6351 [291]; Case C-366/10 *Air Transport Association of America (ATAA) & ors* [2011] ECLI:EU:C:2011:864 [101], [123]; Case C-364/10 *Hungary v Slovakia* [2012] ECLI:EU:C:2012:630 [44].

2 From well-established CJEU case law, see eg the recent *Front Polisario* rulings (Case C-104/16 P [88]–[89], Case T-279/19 [37], [91]–[92], and Joined Cases T-344/19 and T-356/19 [38], [143], [227]).

does not differ from that of international agreements which are binding on the EU,[3] as a result of which rules of universal CIL likewise prevail over conflicting secondary EU law.

As an international legal entity and an international actor, the EU can exert formative influence on the development of CIL rules, including through interpreting them. As Advocate General Szpunar pointed out, 'so far as customary international law concerns questions pertaining to matters falling within the mandate of international organisations, the practice of international organisations may also contribute to the formation or expression of rules of customary international law'.[4] He also expressed the need for CIL rules in principle – putting aside regional[5] and bilateral[6] custom – to be consistent globally and contain no notable contradictions.[7]

Still, the CJEU's interpretations of CIL norms and the interpretative methods and techniques it employs have received little attention in legal scholarship.[8] Indeed, critical analysis of the interpretation of CIL rules by international courts and tribunals has in general suffered similar neglect – not to mention the United Nations (UN) International Law Commission's awkwardness in addressing this matter in its Draft Conclusions on Identification of Customary International Law[9] – even

[3] A Rosas, 'The European Court of Justice and Public International Law' in J Wouters, A Nollkaemper, and E de Wet (eds), *The Europeanisation of International Law. The Status of International Law in the EU and Its Member States* (TMC Asser Press 2008) 71, 80; PJ Kuijper '"It Shall Contribute to … the Strict Observance and Development of International Law …": The Role of the Court of Justice' in A Rosas, E Levits, and Y Bot (eds), *The Court of Justice and the Construction of Europe: Analyses and Perspectives on Sixty Years of Case-Law/La Cour de Justice et la construction de l'Europe: Analyses et perspectives de soixante ans de jurisprudence* (TMC Asser Press/Springer 2013) 589; P Koutrakos, *EU International Relations Law* (2nd edn, Hart 2015) 228.

[4] Case C-641/18 *LG v Rina SpA, Ente Registro Italiano Navale,* Opinion of AG Szpunar (14 January 2020) ECLI:EU:C:2020:3 [123].

[5] See eg the customary practice of diplomatic asylum in Latin American countries (*Asylum (Colombia v Peru)* (Judgment) [1950] ICJ Rep 266).

[6] Consider eg a bilateral custom between Nicaragua and Costa Rica granting subsistence fishing rights to nationals inhabiting the banks of their boundary river (*Dispute Regarding Navigational and Related Rights* (*Costa Rica v Nicaragua*) (Judgment) [2009] ICJ Rep 213).

[7] Case C-641/18 *LG v Rina,* Opinion of AG Szpunar (n 4) [125].

[8] Some EU law scholars even purport that CIL is 'not to be assimilated with a source of EU law subject to interpretation from a European perspective' (E Neframi, 'Customary International Law and the European Union from the Perspective of Article 3(5) TEU' in P Eeckhout P and M Lopez-Escuerdo (eds), *The European Union's External Action in Times of Crisis* (Hart 2016) 217).

[9] ILC, 'Draft Conclusions on Identification of Customary International Law, with Commentaries' (30 April–1 June and 2 July–10 August 2018) UN Doc A/73/10, 117.

though the questions of both interpretation and customary law are classic topics in international law scholarship.[10]

The CJEU, including its Advocates General, generally finds and identifies rules of CIL in (codification) treaties to which the EU is not a party[11] and/or accepts them as customary norms on the basis of judgments of the International Court of Justice (ICJ)[12] and its predecessor, the Permanent

[10] P Merkouris, 'Interpreting the Customary Rules on Interpretation' (2017) 19 ICLR 129, 133; O Chasapis Tassinis, 'Customary International Law: Interpretation from Beginning to End' (2020) 31 EJIL 235, 235–37, 239–40; P Merkouris, 'Interpreting Customary International Law: You'll Never Walk Alone' in P Merkouris, J Kammerhofer, and N Arajärvi (eds), *The Theory, Practice, and Interpretation of Customary International Law* (Cambridge University Press 2022) 347; M Fortuna, 'Different Strings of the Same Harp: Interpretation of Rules of Customary International Law, Their Identification and Treaty Interpretation' in P Merkouris, J Kammerhofer, and N Arajärvi (eds), *The Theory, Practice, and Interpretation of Customary International Law* (Cambridge University Press 2022) 393; R Di Marco, 'Customary International Law: Identification versus Interpretation' in P Merkouris, J Kammerhofer, and N Arajärvi (eds), *The Theory, Practice, and Interpretation of Customary International Law* (Cambridge University Press 2022) 416.

[11] The typical example, found in a great number of CJEU rulings, is the Vienna Convention on the Law of Treaties (adopted 23 May 1969, entered into force 27 January 1980) 1155 UNTS 331. See also C-364/10 *Hungary v Slovakia* (n 1) (referring to '[customary rules] of multilateral agreements'). There are also cases where a multilateral treaty with EU participation qualifies as reflecting CIL norms, such as the UN Convention on the Law of the Sea (adopted 10 December 1982, entry into force 16 November 1994) 1883 UNTS 3, which is 'an expression of the current state of customary international maritime law' (General Court's judgment in Joined Cases T-344/19 and T-356/19 *Popular Front for the Liberation of Saguia el-Hamra and Rio de Oro (Front Polisario) v Council of the European Union* [2021] ECLI:EU:T:2021:640 [221]).

[12] See eg the views of AG Sharpston in *Opinion 2/15 (Free Trade Agreement between the European Union and the Republic of Singapore)* [2016] ECLI:EU:C:2016:992 (citing *Interhandel (Switzerland v United States of America)* (Preliminary Objections) [1959] ICJ Rep 6, 27, to find that it is a principle of customary international law that 'before a State gives diplomatic protection to its injured nationals, those nationals must first have exhausted local remedies' [539]); Opinion of AG Sharpston in Case C-158/14 *A and ors v Minister van Buitenlandse Zaken* [2016] ECLI:EU:C:2016:734 (citing *Military and Paramilitary Activities in and against Nicaragua (Nicaragua v USA)* (Merits) [1986] ICJ Rep 14, [218]–[219] and *Legality of the Threat of Use of Nuclear Weapons* (Advisory Opinion) [1996] ICJ Rep 226 [78]–[79], both used to identify customary principles of international humanitarian law); Opinion of AG Mengozzi in Case C-285/12 *Aboubacar Diakité v Commissaire général aux réfugiés et aux apatrides* [2013] ECLI:EU:C:2013:500 (referring to *Legality of the Threat or Use of Nuclear Weapons* (Advisory Opinion) [1996] ICJ Rep 226 [79], to assert the existence of 'intransgressible principles of international customary law'); the General Court's judgment in Case T-208/11 *LTTE v Council* [2014] ECLI:EU:T:2014:885 (referring to *Military and Paramilitary Activities in and against Nicaragua (Nicaragua v USA)* (Merits) [1986] ICJ Rep 14, to determine the existence of the customary principle of non-interference under international humanitarian law); Opinion of AG Wahl in Case C-179/13 *Raad van bestuur van de Sociale verzekeringsbank*

Court of International Justice (PCIJ),[13] using the ICJ/PCIJ rulings as a short route for establishing the existence of a CIL rule.[14] But is interpretation needed, then? Put differently, once a CIL norm has been identified, does its content become known? This is where the need for interpretation of such unwritten norms emerges. According to the CJEU, 'interpretation . . . clarifies and defines where necessary the meaning and scope of [a] rule as it must be or ought to have been understood and applied from the time of its coming into force'.[15] In interpretation generally, the CJEU has shown a preference for certain methods – namely, systemic, teleological, and dynamic interpretation – with a view to attaining the objectives of the European integration project as defined by the autonomous EU legal order. As part of EU law, CIL is, in principle, also subject to the same interpretive methods and practices.

This chapter aims to map and understand the ways in which the CJEU interprets CIL rules using its aforementioned toolbox and compares

v LF Evans [2014] ECLI:EU:C 2014:2015 (citing *United States Diplomatic and Consular Staff in Tehran (USA v Iran)* (Judgment) [1980] ICJ Rep 3 [45], to conclude that some provisions of the 1963 Vienna Convention on Consular Relations on consular privileges and immunities represent customary international law), which reference to the *Tehran Hostages* case was simply echoed in the CJEU's ruling as well (even going further than the ICJ by finding [36] that, at the time of the dispute, the 1963 Vienna Convention had the status of customary international law). For further examples, see J Odermatt, 'The International Court of Justice and the Court of Justice of the European Union: Between Fragmentation and Universality of International Law' in A Skordas (ed), *Research Handbook on the International Court of Justice* (Edward Elgar 2022) 696.

[13] eg the views of AG Sharpston in *Opinion 2/15 (Free Trade Agreement between the European Union and the Republic of Singapore)* (referring to *Mavrommatis Palestine Concessions (Greece v Britain)* (Objection to the Jurisdiction of the Court) [1924] PCIJ Series A No 2, 12, to underpin the CIL nature of certain modalities of exercising diplomatic protection by States [539] n 415); Opinion of AG Maduro in Case C-135/08 *Janko Rottman v Freistaat Bayern* [2010] ECLI:EU:C:2010:104 (citing *Nationality Decrees Issued in Tunis and Morocco* (Advisory Opinion) [1923] PCJ Series B No 4, 24, to identify the customary principle that 'questions of nationality are in principle within the reserved domain of States' [18]).

[14] R Higgins, *Problems and Process: International Law and How We Use It* (Oxford University Press 1994) 10; also quoted by Odermatt (n 12) 9. At times, even the decisions of other international courts or tribunals and the works of the UN International Law Commission are also referenced if the CJEU finds a *consensus generalis* as to the existence of CIL rule deducible from these international legal materials (for more, see F Pascual-Vives, 'The Identification of Customary International Law before the Court of Justice of the European Union: A Flexible Consensualism' in F Lusa Bordin, ATh Müller, and F Pascual-Vives (eds), *The European Union and Customary International Law* (Cambridge University Press 2022) 123.

[15] Case 61/79 *Amministrazione delle finanze dello Stato v Denkavit italiana Srl* [1980] ECR 1205 [16].

them to those that exist for the interpretation of treaties under the Vienna Convention on the Law of Treaties (VCLT). First, however, the CJEU's engagement with CIL in general (Section 2) and its general methods interpreting EU law (Section 3.1) will be briefly considered. Then, through a thorough review of relevant case law in Section 3.2, the core of this study, the chapter will seek to reveal what reasons lie behind the CJEU's particular approach, its interpretative choices, and its deviations from mainstream techniques, if any. The enquiry is guided by the following questions: does the CJEU's engagement with CIL interpretation display features that are unique to it? If so, what are they and to what extent is this the case? What factors influence the CJEU's preference for using diverse methods of interpretation of CIL? Is such uniqueness or lack of coherence likely to further fragment international law? And does it strengthen or weaken the authority of the EU Court as an influential judicial actor in this regard. Lastly, Section 4 will critically assess the specificities and challenges of CIL interpretation by the CJEU against the backdrop of the EU as a quasi self-contained regime and the *sui generis* nature of its legal order, its specific integration objectives, and the particularity of the judicial function the CJEU performs.

2 Assessing the Landscape: The CJEU's Engagement with CIL in General

At first sight, among the various sources of public international law codified in Article 38 of the ICJ Statute,[16] and even beyond that,[17] CIL seems to have limited importance from the perspective of EU law, particularly compared to written sources of international law, notably

[16] Statute of the International Court of Justice (adopted 26 June 1945, entered into force 24 October 1945) 33 UNTS 993.

[17] These include legally binding decisions of international organisations and unilateral acts of states (possibly also unilateral acts emanating from other subjects of international law, such as international organisations). These sources have been mostly identified by the ICJ; see *Legal Consequences for States of the Continued Presence of South Africa in Namibia (South West Africa) Notwithstanding Security Council Resolution 276 (1970)* (Advisory Opinion) [1971] ICJ Rep 16; *Nuclear Tests (Australia v France)* (Judgment) [1974] ICJ Rep 253, 267–68 [42]–[46]. Consider also ILC, 'Guiding Principles Applicable to Unilateral Declarations of States Capable of Creating Legal Obligations' (1 May–9 June and 3 July–11 August 2006) UN Doc A/61/10, 161. For a recent scholarly analysis of these 'extra-ICJ Statute' sources, see eg A Pellet, 'Article 38' in A Zimmermann and others (eds), *The Statute of the International Court of Justice: A Commentary* (Oxford University Press 2012) [87]–[110] (under Article 38); H Thirlway, *The Sources of International Law* (Oxford University Press 2014) 19–25.

treaties and decisions of international organisations. Yet, it is not ill-founded to argue that CIL rules play a more important role in the EU legal order than in the domestic legal systems of EU member states. The reason for this is that, unlike most states, the EU as a distinct international legal person could not or did not accede to a great number of international conventions that codify certain areas of (customary) international law.[18] As a consequence of therefore not being bound by codified treaty rules, the EU remains bound by parallel existing CIL norms,[19] which have to be applied by the CJEU when confronted with issues of international law in individual cases. Illustrative in this regard is the 1969 VCLT[20]: the CJEU regularly invokes its provisions and relies on its rules as written manifestations of identical CIL rules existing beyond the text itself.[21]

CIL is one of the classic sources of international law, and some of the key rules of the international legal order continue to exist in this unwritten, non-codified form.[22] There are too many to name here; suffice it to say that they can be found in ample numbers in the fields of diplomatic

[18] J Malenovský, 'Le juge et la coutume internationale: Perspectives de l'Union européenne et de la Cour de justice' (2013) 12 LPICT 225.

[19] ibid.

[20] As for its counterpart, the 1986 Vienna Convention on the Law of Treaties between States and International Organizations or between International Organizations (adopted 21 March 1986, not yet in force) UN Doc A/CONF.129/15, leaving aside the fact that it has not entered into force yet, the EU has decided not to become a party to it.

[21] See eg Case C-162/96 *Racke v Hauptzollamt Mainz* (n 1) [53] (as regards the customary rule of terminating/suspending a treaty by reason of a fundamental change of circumstances (*clausula rebus sic stantibus*), codified in art 62(1) VCLT); Case C-386/08 *Firma Brita GmbH v Hauptzollamt Hamburg-Hafen* [2010] ECLI:EU:C:2010:91 [44]–[45] (as concerns the relative effect of treaties (*pacta tertiis nec nocent nec prosunt*), expressed in art 34 VCLT); Case C-613/12 *Helm Düngemittel GmbH v Hauptzollamt Krefeld* [2014] ECLI:EU:C:2014:52 [37] (stating generally that 'rules contained in [the VCLT] apply to an agreement concluded between a State and an international organisation ... in so far as those rules are an expression of general international customary law.'); Case C–104/16 P *Council of the European Union v Front populaire pour la libération de la saguia-el-hamra et du rio de oro (Front Polisario)* [2016] ECLI:EU:C:2016:973 [86]–[87], [94], [97] (referring to the customary rule governing the territorial scope of treaties as codified in art 29 VCLT and the customary rules of treaty interpretation enshrined in art 31 VCLT).

[22] For an account of selected leading scholarly writings on CIL, see eg Merkouris, 'Interpreting the Customary Rules on Interpretation' (2017) (n 10) n 16 and the legal literature cited therein. See also PG Staubach, *The Rule of Unwritten International Law* (Routledge 2018); BD Lepard, *Customary International Law: A New Theory with Practical Applications* (Cambridge University Press 2010); BD Lepard (ed), *Reexamining Customary international Law* (Cambridge University Press 2017).

law, state responsibility, treaty law, international refugee law, international human rights law and international criminal law, for example.

CIL rules that have been recognised as part of the EU legal order in CJEU jurisprudence include the right of individuals to enter their own country;[23] the right to innocent passage and freedom of navigation under the law of the sea;[24] certain principles of the law of treaties (e.g. rules of treaty interpretation, the relative effect of treaties, their territorial scope);[25] the jurisdictional immunity of states;[26] the status and immunities of heads of state;[27] the right of self-determination and peoples' permanent sovereignty over their natural resources;[28] states' total and exclusive jurisdiction over their airspace; and the freedom to fly over the high seas[29] – and the list continues.[30]

The CJEU employs CIL first and foremost as an interpretative tool when dealing with the acts of EU institutions – for instance, when elucidating the meaning and content of such acts in preliminary ruling proceedings[31] in the light of international law binding upon the Union. Also, CIL has often been used by the CJEU to delimit the material scope and the boundaries of EU law, including the EU treaties.[32] This dynamic process of jointly – and, preferably, harmoniously – applying legal norms of different types and origins necessarily includes the interpretation of CIL rules, too. In theory, CIL can also serve as a ground on which to assess the legality of secondary EU law whose validity has been challenged. However, when private parties seek to invoke customary norms before the CJEU as a standard for reviewing of the legality of a given piece of EU legislation, it must be checked whether the CIL norm at hand is

23 Case 42/74 *Yvonne van Duyn v Home Office* [1974] ECR 1337.

24 Case C-286/90 *Anklagemyndigheden v Poulsen and Diva Navigation* (n 1).

25 Case C-386/08 *v Hauptzollamt Hamburg-Hafen* (n 21) [40]–[43] and the case law cited.

26 Case C-641/18 *LG v Rina SpA and Ente Registro Italiano Navale* [2020] ECLI:EU:C:2020:349.

27 Case C-364/10 *Hungary v Slovakia* (n 1).

28 Case C-104/16 P *Council v Front Polisario* (n 21); Case C-266/16 *Western Sahara Campaign UK v Commissioners for Her Majesty's Revenue and Customs and Secretary of State for Environment, Food and Rural Affairs* [2018] ECLI:EU:C:2018:118.

29 C-366/10 *ATAA* (n 1).

30 For a fairly comprehensive list, see eg D Kornobis-Romanowska, 'Effects of International Customary Law in the Legal Order of the European Union' (2018) 8 WRLAE 405, 415–17; see also Malenovský (n 18).

31 As provided in the Treaty on the Functioning of the European Union [2016] OJ C 202/47, art 267.

32 JF Delile, 'Les effets de la coutume internationale dans l'ordre juridique de l'Union européenne' (2017) 53 CDE 177–86, 190.

generally accepted; is capable of calling into question the competence of the EU to adopt secondary legislation; and can affect the rights that individuals derive from EU law or creates obligations under EU law in their regard.[33] Given that, in the words of the CJEU, 'a principle of customary international law does not have the same degree of precision as a provision of an international agreement',[34] CIL can thus generally be invoked as a ground to invalidate conflicting EU secondary legislation only in limited circumstances.[35] Given the less precise contours of customary norms, the CJEU has held that the judicial review of a piece of EU secondary legislation in the light of CIL must be limited to the question of whether, in adopting the legal act, the EU institutions made manifest errors of assessment concerning the conditions for applying such a CIL norm.[36]

3 The CJEU and the Interpretation of CIL: A Peculiar Path

Let us start with a baffling, but basic, preliminary question: why is interpretation – understood as attaching meaning to or elucidating meaning – needed in law? It has become a truism that legal notions have an 'open texture' (to use Hart's words[37]), manifesting themselves in some grey zone beyond the 'core of settled meaning' of a given norm.[38] Interpretation, which is inherent in any adjudicative exercise applying the law and implicit in the life-cycle of every rule,[39] is thus necessary to unpack, specify, and clarify the exact meaning of a particular legal norm and determine its content, irrespective of its source.[40] Not only are CIL

[33] C-366/10 *ATAA* (n 1) [107].

[34] Case C-162/96 *Racke v Hauptzollamt Mainz* (n 1) [52]; C-366/10 *ATAA* (n 1) [110].

[35] See Koutrakos (n 3) 311ff; A von Bogdandy and M Smrkolj, 'European Union Law and International Law' (2011) MPEPIL <https://opil.ouplaw.com/display/10.1093/law:epil/9780199231690/law-9780199231690-e620> [24].

[36] Case C-162/96 *Racke v Hauptzollamt Mainz* (n 1) [52]; C-366/10 *ATAA* (n 1) [110]. For a criticism of this test, see eg NAJ Croquet, 'The Import of International Customary International Law into the EU Legal Order: The Adequacy of a Direct Effect Analysis' (2013) 15 CYELS 47–81.

[37] HLA Hart, *The Concept of Law* (2nd edn, Oxford University Press 1994).

[38] HLA Hart, 'Positivism and the Separation of Law and Morals' (1958) 71 Harv L Rev 607; also cited by Merkouris, 'Interpreting the Customary Rules on Interpretation' (n 10) 134.

[39] Merkouris, 'Interpreting Customary International Law' (n 10) 347, 367.

[40] See also P Merkouris, *Article 31(3)(c) VCLT and the Principle of Systemic Integration: Normative Shadows in Plato's Cave* (Brill/Nijhoff 2015) 240–45; N Mileva and M Fortuna, 'Emerging Voices: The Case for CIL Interpretation – An Argument from Theory and an Argument from Practice' (*Opinio Juris*, 23 August 2019) <http://opiniojuris.org/2019/08/23/emerging-voices-the-case-for-cil-interpretation-an-argument-from-theory-and-an-

rules no exception; they are par excellence a case in point due to their unwritten character, and all the more so it there is no case law or precedent relating to the situation in which the CIL rule is to be applied.[41] This section will first outline the peculiarities of the interpretative practices and methods the CJEU employs (Section 3.1), and then identify and analyse the patterns revealed in relevant case law where the CJEU has engaged with CIL and its interpretation (Section 3.2).

3.1 *The CJEU and Interpretation of EU Law: The Basics, in Brief*

Unlike traditional international courts, whose authority to interpret international law is on an equal footing with that of national courts and which in principle do not have compulsory jurisdiction nor operate as part of a co-ordinated scheme, the CJEU is entrusted with the authentic interpretation of EU law and there is clear division of labour between it and the member states' national courts.[42] Also, the CJEU exercises exclusive and compulsory jurisdiction over matters falling under the EU treaties, having in this respect a role resembling to that of states' constitutional or supreme courts.

As a result, the CJEU has rapidly affirmed its interpretative practices and methods, which are somewhat different from those in international law. It applies methods that are similar to the interpretive techniques of a domestic constitutional court,[43] albeit with variations on a number of points. As early as the *Van Gend en Loos* case, the CJEU identified three

argument-from-practice/> accessed 25 June 2022; O Ammann, 'On the Interpretability of Customary International Law: A Response to Nina Mileva and Marina Fortuna' (*Opinio Juris*, 7 October 2019) <http://opiniojuris.org/2019/10/07/on-the-interpretability-of-customary-international-law-a-response-to-nina-mileva-and-marina-fortuna/> accessed 25 June 2022; Di Marco (n 10) 415. In a similar vein, the International Law Association established a study group on the content and evolution of rules of interpretation, whose final report also touched on the interpretation of CIL, albeit only in passing (see ILA, 'Study Groups: Content and Evolution of the Rules of Interpretation' (2022) <www.ila-hq.org/index.php/study-groups?study-groupsID=75> accessed 25 June 2022).

41 See also Di Marco (n 10) 419.

42 S Besson and ML Gächter-Alge, 'L'interprétation en droit européen: Quelques remarques introductives' in S Besson, N Levrat, and E Clerc (eds), *Interprétation en droit européen/Interpretation in European Law* (Schulthess 2011) 13–14.

43 See eg O Ammann, 'The Court of Justice of the European Union and the Interpretation of International Legal Norms. To Be or Not to Be a "Domestic" Court?' in S Besson and N Levrat (eds), *L'Union européenne et le droit international/The European Union and International Law* (Schulthess 2015) 153–78; J Odermatt, 'The Court of Justice of the European Union: International or Domestic Court?' (2014) 3 CJICL 696, 696–718.

key interpretative methods it employs – namely, giving consideration to 'the spirit, the general scheme and the wording of [the] provisions [of EU law]'[44] – which can be readily equated with, respectively, teleological, systemic, and grammatical interpretation of the law (generally applied in that order of priority in CJEU practice).

3.2 *The CJEU Interpreting CIL: Exploring and Understanding the Patterns*

The intellectual process consisting in interpreting the law must be distinguished from the identification of a CIL rule (i.e. determining the existence of such a norm). In accordance with Merkouris's fundamental distinction, interpretation is a deductive process after a given CIL rule has come into existence, whereas identifying a CIL rule is more of an inductive exercise.[45] Once a CIL norm has come into being (i.e. has implicitly been endorsed by the international community through state practice and *opinio juris*), its subsequent application in particular cases in the course of its lifespan will be subject to the deductive process of interpretation. What is mistakenly called 'interpretation' of state practice (or of both constitutive elements of a CIL norm) – an exercise that would be better termed the 'qualification', 'assessment', or 'evaluation' of the formative elements of CIL – should not be conflated with, and thus needs to be distinguished from, interpretation strictly speaking subsequent to the rule's emergence.[46] 'In this manner, interpretation focuses on how the rule is to be understood and applied *after the rule has come into existence*.'[47] However, some grey zones and overlaps persist. Let us take the example of exceptions under a given CIL rule. It might be debated whether delimiting the scope of particular exceptions is a purely deductive exercise, as such qualifying as *interpretation*; or whether recourse to the two-element test (assessment of state practice and *opinio juris*) is

[44] Case 26/62 *NV Algemene Transporten Expeditie Onderneming van Gend en Loos v Netherlands Inland Revenue Administration* [1963] ECR 3, 22.

[45] See Merkouris, 'Interpreting the Customary Rules on Interpretation' (n 10) 134–37. For a different, more permissive approach, employing the term 'interpretation' also for the phase of identifying and assessing the existence of state practice and its generally accepted nature, see Chasapis Tassinis (n 10).

[46] P Merkouris, *Interpretation of Customary International Law: Of Methods and Limits* (Brill Research Perspectives in International Legal Theory and Practice, Martinus Nijhoff/Brill 2022) 16–18.

[47] Merkouris, 'Interpreting the Customary Rules on Interpretation' (n 10) 136 (emphasis in original).

again necessary to determine whether such an exception exists as a self-standing rule, an exercise qualifying as *identification* of a CIL norm that is incidentally an exception to the main customary rule.[48] Another grey area is the dynamic relationship between a rule and its exceptions, which 'may well change and evolve over time or even on a case-by-case basis'.[49]

When the CJEU interprets CIL norms forming an integral part of the EU legal order, its interpretation – given that its rulings are binding *erga omnes* – also binds the member states, and consequently influences their practice and *opinio juris*. In other words, CJEU judgments engaging with CIL rules have a 'multiplying'[50] or 'snowball'[51] effect. Below we discuss four examples of CIL norms dealt with by the CJEU that well illustrate its approach to the interpretation of customary international law.

3.2.1 State Immunity from Jurisdiction

Let us first consider the scope and content of the CIL norm affirming the immunity of states from jurisdiction, which protects them from being sued in the courts of another sovereign state.[52] The ICJ has also engaged with the interpretation of this CIL norm, which demonstrates its importance in the international legal order.[53] The two leading CJEU judgments in this field – *Mahamdia* (C-154/11) and *Rina* (C-641/18) – are worth analysing together, given that the latter builds on and refers to the former. Both cases concerned the interpretation of the CIL rule of state immunity from jurisdiction as part of the EU legal order. In *Mahamdia*, the core legal issue was whether, in view of the jurisdictional immunity of states, it was possible for the dismissal of a worker who had been employed as a driver by a non-EU member state (Algeria) at its embassy in a member state (Germany) to be challenged in the courts of that member state. In *Rina*, the key issue was the application of

48 For more on exceptions under international law (including within the field of customary law), see L Bartels and F Paddeu (eds), *Exceptions in International Law* (Cambridge University Press 2020).

49 E Methymaki and A Tzanakopoulos, 'Freedom with Their Exception: Jurisdiction and Immunity as Rule and Exception' in L Bartels and F Paddeu (eds), *Exceptions in International Law* (Cambridge University Press 2020) 240.

50 Malenovský (n 18) 218 n 79.

51 Ammann (n 43) 170.

52 Issues pertaining to immunity from execution are not discussed here.

53 *Jurisdictional Immunities of the State (Germany/Italy; Greece intervening)* [2012] ICJ Rep 99 [55]. In its judgment no 238 of 2014 the Italian Constitutional Court took the view that the ICJ was wrong to interpret state immunity from civil jurisdiction as a customary norm.

the CIL rule of state immunity to private bodies to which a sovereign state (here Panama) has delegated the discharge of duties under international law (certification and classification of ships).

The outcome of the two cases was similar, confirming the relative nature of state immunity (as opposed to the classic understanding of it as absolute), but they touched on different aspects of this complex legal relationship. *Mahamdia* was limited to defining a state's immunity (that of Algeria) in a labour-related dispute: the CJEU found that employment-related court action concerning a member of an embassy's non-diplomatic staff brought in the country where the embassy was located did not fall within the scope of immunity from jurisdiction enjoyed by the embassy's home state before the courts of another country, for the chauffeur's dismissal by the embassy was an act performed *jure gestionis*.[54] The *Rina* ruling approached the question of immunity from another angle when stating that private actors do not enjoy automatic immunity from jurisdiction simply because states have delegated the performance of international obligations to them[55] – an interpretation that also avoids the risk of immunity destroying any legal action whatsoever.[56] In other words, the certification and classification of ships by private law bodies acting on behalf of third states (here Panama) do not qualify as acts performed *jure imperii*. In both of these cases the CJEU limited the *ratione materiae* scope of the CIL rule on immunity from jurisdiction by allowing for certain exceptions, such as disputes over contracts of employment and the activities of classification/certification of ships by private entities.

The CJEU's examination of the material scope of the customary norm of state immunity from jurisdiction was marked by a peculiar division of labour between the Advocates General and the bench of the court. After recognizing a lack of clarity and uncertainties around the customary rule of state immunity, the Advocates General carried out the substantive and in-depth, analysis of the meaning and (possible) material scope of state immunity and its exceptions. The outcome of this legal analysis (i.e. the contextual interpretation of the CIL norm) was in essence taken up by the CJEU in its rulings themselves, which simply refer to the key findings in

[54] On the current position regarding state immunity in employment-related cases under international law, see P Rossi, *International Law Immunities and Employment Claims* (Hart 2021).

[55] Case C-641/18 *LG v Rina* (n 26) [39].

[56] Case 154/11 *Ahmed Mahamdia v People's Democratic Republic of Algeria*, Opinion of AG Mengozzi (24 May 2012) ECLI:EU:C:2012:309 [22].

the opinions of the Advocates General, thereby merely asserting the CIL rule or the meaning the Advocates General accorded to it,[57] rather than citing or referring to any international legal materials supporting this conclusion.

In both cases, the interpretative engagement consisted in the difficult task of distinguishing between state acts performed *jure imperii* and those performed *jure gestionis*. The most intricate question lays in drawing a dividing line between these two types of acts and how to classify certain acts, including when a state acts as an employer and when a state's action is 'to some degree privatised'.[58] The interpretation of the customary principle of state immunity – and the aforementioned division of labour between the Advocates General and the CJEU in this exercise – is well illustrated by Advocate General Mengozzi's compelling comment in *Mahamdia* on the contemporary challenges faced in deciding whether certain acts of states are shielded from legal proceedings before foreign courts:

> The modern State has become a polymorphous actor in law and may act and enter into legal relations without, however, exercising its sovereignty or its public authority in doing so: I am thinking in particular of the State as a trader, but also, of course, the State as an employer. Because these different facets of the State's legal activity are not systematically accompanied by the exercise of powers as a public authority, they tend no longer to justify the automatic recognition of immunity from jurisdiction.[59]

The CJEU subsequently endorsed this interpretation in its judgment by summarily recalling the Advocate General's above observation about the exercise of public powers and its implications.[60]

Against this backdrop, the most intriguing question for present purposes is, what methods did the Advocates General and then the CJEU use to arrive at the conclusions reached? After recalling that state immunity is a corollary of the international law principle *par in parem non habet imperium* (a state cannot be subjected to the jurisdiction of another state),[61] the interpretative exercise focussed on delimiting the boundaries of possible exceptions to the main rule (state immunity), entailing that acts performed *jure gestionis* fall outside the exercise of public powers and

[57] For examples of this technique, see Case 154/11 *Ahmed Mahamdia v People's Democratic Republic of Algeria* [2012] ECLI:EU:C:2012:491 [55]; Case C-641/18 *LG v Rina* (n 26) [57].
[58] Case 154/11 *Mahamdia v Algeria*, Opinion of AG Mengozzi (n 56) [32].
[59] ibid [21].
[60] Case 154/11 *Mahamdia v Algeria* (n 57) [55].
[61] ibid [54]; Case C-641/18 *LG v Rina* (n 26) [56].

do not enjoy immunity. In essence, this exercise involved adducing evidence, of both state practice and *opinio juris*, that would substantiate the existence of such exceptions. In other words, the interpretation of the CIL norm (states enjoy immunity from jurisdiction) consisted not in applying systemic or teleological interpretative methods but rather in proving that certain exceptions exist as special, self-standing 'mini-rules' that still formed part of, and were derived from, the larger CIL principle. This approach can qualify as a sort of logical interpretation, carving out an exception and determining its content and limits within the boundaries of the 'mother' CIL norm, while also refining and chiselling it (states enjoy immunity from jurisdiction save for their *acta gestioni*). In this endeavour to delimit the scope of state immunity (or, conversely, that of permissible exceptions to it), the Advocate General opted for the concept of relative immunity and applied the two-elements method to prove its general acceptance as a custom:

> a rule of customary international law will only exist where a given practice actually exists that is supported by a firm legal view (*opinio juris*), that is to say, where a rule is accepted as law. It is in the light of that principle that it is necessary to determine whether, in accordance with the doctrine of relative immunity, the content of the principle of State jurisdictional immunity is such that the defendants may claim immunity.[62]

With a view to underpinning the concept of 'relative immunity' based on the fundamental distinction between acts performed *jure imperii* and those performed *jure gestionis*, the Advocate General turned to national legislation, domestic (German) case law, the jurisprudence of the ECtHR,[63] some (not widely ratified) conventions (heavily relying on their terms and regulatory logic)[64] and academic publications for evidence.[65] This technique of referring to a range of written instruments and case law which codify/recognize the above variant of the customary norm can be regarded as systemic interpretation.[66] Persuaded that the origins of state immunity lay in the sovereign equality of states, the CJEU

[62] Case C-641/18 *LG v Rina*, Opinion of AG Szpunar (n 4) [108].

[63] *Cudak v Lithuania* App no 15869/02 (ECtHR, 23 March 2010); *Sabel El Leil v France* App no 34869/05 (ECtHR, 29 June 2011).

[64] European Convention on State Immunity (adopted 16 May 1972, entered into force 11 June 1976) 1495 UNTS 181; United Nations Convention on Jurisdictional Immunities of States and Their Property (adopted 2 December 2004, not yet in force) UN Doc A/59/508.

[65] See Case C-641/18 *LG v Rina*, Opinion of AG Szpunar, nn 15, 21–23, 27, 31–32.

[66] Merkouris, 'Interpreting Customary International Law' (n 10) 299.

took the above-described assessment for granted and relied on this qualification in both judgments, opting for the relative nature of state immunity with the simple assertion that the doctrine of relative immunity replaced that of absolute immunity in our times.[67] Nonetheless, the CJEU added in *Rina*, as an extra argument corroborating this position, that a recital in a piece of EU secondary law[68] 'bears out the legislature's intention to give a limited scope to its interpretation of the customary international law principle of immunity from jurisdiction with regard to classification and certification of ships'.[69] This statement can also be considered as the expression of the emergence of a regional (European) CIL rule[70] on the matter – given that the EU exercises some of the public powers of its member states and the practice (here, law-making) of the organization may be equated with the practice of the member states.[71] In other words, the EU has functionally replaced the member states in a number of areas, including the one governed by the EU directive containing the recital quoted above, and were EU practice not taken into consideration in its own right as contributing to (regional) CIL norms, then 'Member States themselves would be deprived of or reduced in their ability to contribute to State practice.'[72]

3.2.2 Right of Self-Determination and States' Permanent Sovereignty over Their Natural Resources

The series of cases concerning the legality of extending the application of EU–Morocco trade and fisheries agreements to the territory of Western Sahara – *Front Polisario I*,[73] *Western Sahara Campaign UK*,[74] and *Front*

[67] As recalled in Case C-641/18 *LG v Rina*, Opinion of AG Szpunar [35].

[68] Directive 2009/15/EC of the European Parliament and of the Council of 23 April 2009 on common rules and standards for ship inspection and survey organisations and for the relevant activities of maritime administrations [2009] OJ L 131/47, recital 16.

[69] Case C-641/18 *LG v Rina* (n 26) [59].

[70] The ILC refers to 'particular customary international law' which applies only among a limited number of states, such as regional customary rules (ILC, 'Draft Conclusions' (n 9) Conclusion 16(1)). With respect to regional custom, the application of the two-element test is stricter. For case law references, see ibid, commentary to Conclusion 16.

[71] See similarly ILC, 'Draft Conclusions' (n 9) 117. On the EU's role and potential in general to contribute to the formation of CIL rules, see eg J Odermatt, *International Law and the European Union* (Cambridge University Press 2021) 44–58; J Vanhamme, 'Formation and Enforcement of Customary International Law: The European Union's Contribution' (2008) 39 NYIL 127–54.

[72] ILC, 'Third Report on Identification of Customary International Law by Michael Wood, Special Rapporteur' (4 May–5 June and 6 July–7 August 2015) UN Doc A/CN.4/682 [77].

[73] Case C-104/16 P *Council v Front Polisario* (n 21).

[74] Case C-266/16 *Western Sahara Campaign UK* (n 28).

Polisario II[75] – serves as another springboard for scrutinising the CJEU's engagement with the interpretation of CIL norms, notably the right of self-determination (of the people of Western Sahara in these particular cases) and states' permanent sovereignty over their natural resources as a corollary thereto.

Chronologically, it was in *Front Polisario I* that an Advocate General first engaged in an interpretation of the CIL principle[76] of states' permanent sovereignty over their natural resources and, to some extent, a people's right of self-determination. In his succinct analysis, the Advocate General did not make it clear whether the former is derived from the latter (which is the position generally accepted among international lawyers[77]); despite his silence on this matter, he nonetheless discussed permanent sovereignty over natural resources, which he considered as being somewhat anchored to the right of self-determination. When interpreting the meaning of the CIL principle of permanent sovereignty over natural resources and exposing its content and implications, the Advocate General relied[78] on the language and formulations of a series of UN General Assembly resolutions,[79]

[75] Case T-279/19 *Front populaire pour la libération de la Saguia el-Hamra et du Rio de oro (Front Polisario) v Council of the European Union* [2021] ECLI:EU:T:2021:639; Joined Cases T-344/19 and T-356/19 *Front populaire pour la libération de la Saguia el-Hamra et du Rio de oro (Front Polisario) v Council of the European Union* [2021] ECLI:EU:T:2021:640.

[76] To lift any ambiguity and avoid confusion, the term 'CIL principle' refers to customary norms being foundational in the edifice of the international legal order (as is the case with the norm under discussion here) and has nothing to do with the 'general principles of law' as per art 38(1)(c) of the ICJ Statute, another source of international law. In a similar vein, the CJEU also used the term 'the principle of permanent sovereignty over natural resources' in this case and, more generally, 'principles of customary international law' in a number of other cases (observed also by Delile (n 32) 162).

[77] See eg N J Schrijver, 'Fifty Years Permanent Sovereignty over Natural Resources: The 1962 UN Declaration as the *Opinio Iuris Communis*' in M Bungenberg and H Stephan (eds), *Permanent Sovereignty over Natural Resources* (Springer 2015) 15–28; R Pereira, 'Permanent Sovereignty over Natural Resources in the 21st Century: Natural Resource Governance and the Right to Self-Determination of Indigenous Peoples under International Law' (2013) 14 Melb JIL 8; M Saul, 'The Normative Status of Self-Determination in International Law: A Formula for Uncertainty in the Scope and Content of the Right?' (2011) 11 HRLR 628; C Drew, 'The East Timor Story: International Law on Trial' (2001) 12 EJIL 663.

[78] Case C-104/16 P *Council v Front Polisario*, Opinion of AG Wathelet (13 September 2016) ECLI:EU:C:2016:677 [292].

[79] UNGA Res 1803, 'Permanent Sovereignty over Natural Resources' (14 December 1962) UN Doc A/RES/1803/(XVII); UNGA Res 3201, 'Declaration on the Establishment of a New International Economic Order' (1 May 1974) UN Doc A/Res/3201(S.VI); UNGA Res 3281, 'Charter of Economic Rights and Duties of States' (12 December 1974) UN Doc

following the – criticised[80]– method applied by the ICJ in the *Democratic Republic of the Congo v Uganda* case.[81] Remarkably, however, and without explanation, he saw no *erga omnes* obligations implied in this CIL norm – unlike the two dissenting ICJ judges in the *East Timor* case,[82] the African Union[83] and several commentators,[84] all of whom have embraced the view that permanent sovereignty over natural resources is an essential principle of contemporary international law with *erga omnes* effect. As a consequence of this particular line of reasoning, the Advocate General concluded that permanent sovereignty over natural resources 'cannot establish the liability of the [EU] as the obligation not to recognise as legal a situation resulting from a serious infringement of an *erga omnes* obligation and not to render aid or assistance in maintaining that situation does not apply'[85] and, more broadly, the EU and its institutions cannot even infringe this obligation since they are not bound by it. Without going into a detailed critique of this statement, suffice it to say that this reasoning is hardly reconcilable with the CIL nature of this principle, which as such is an integral part of the EU legal order.

A/Res/3281/(XXIX); 'Activities of Foreign Economic and Other Interests Which Impede the Implementation of the Declaration on the Granting of Independence to Colonial Countries and Peoples in Territories under Colonial Domination', UNGA Res 46/64 (10 December 1992) UN Doc A/RES/48/46, UNGA Res 49/40 (9 December 1994) A/RES/49/40; UNGA Res 50/33, (6 December 1995) UN Doc A/RES/50/33.

80 See eg AM Weisburd, 'The International Court of Justice and the Concept of State Practice' (2009) 31 UPJIL 330.

81 *Case Concerning Armed Activities on the Territory of the Congo (Congo v Uganda)* (Merits) [2005] ICJ Rep 168 [244].

82 *East Timor (Portugal v Australia)* (Judgment) [1995] ICJ Rep 90, Dissenting Opinion of Judge Weeramantry 142, 197–99, 204 and Dissenting Opinion of Judge Skubiszewski 264, 270, 276.

83 Office of the Legal Counsel and Directorate for Legal Affairs of the African Union Commission, 'Legal Opinion on the Legality in the Context of International Law, Including the Relevant United Nations Resolutions and OAU/AU Decisions, of Actions Allegedly Taken by the Moroccan Authorities or Any Other State, Group of States, Foreign Companies or Any Other Entity in the Exploration and/or Exploitation of Renewable and Non-Renewable Natural Resources or Any Other Economic Activity in Western Sahara' (14 October 2015) [56].

84 FX Perrez, 'The Relationship between "Permanent Sovereignty" and the Obligation Not to Cause Transboundary Environmental Damage' (1996) 26 Evntl L 1187, 1192 (quoted by Pereira (n 77) n 61); P Gümplová, 'Restraining Permanent Sovereignty over Natural Resources' (2014) 53 EQdF 96; E Milano, 'The 2013 Fisheries Protocol between the EU and Morocco: Fishing 'too South' Continues . . . ' in M Balboni and G Laschi (eds), *The European Union Approach towards Western Sahara* (Peter Lang 2017) 151, 158–59.

85 Case C-104/16 P *Council v Front Polisario*, Opinion of AG Wathelet (n 78) [294].

There is in turn no mention of permanent sovereignty over natural resources in the CJEU's judgment, which instead focussed on the right of self-determination, without contemplating the possibility that its force field might extend to the CIL principle of permanent sovereignty over natural resources. Actually, the CJEU refrained from genuinely interpreting the right of self-determination. It essentially restated the basics concerning this right's addressees and beneficiaries (non-self-governing territories and peoples who have not yet achieved independence) and legal nature (a legally enforceable *erga omnes* right),[86] relying on the authority of an advisory opinion and a judgment handed down by the ICJ,[87] along with the 1970 UN General Assembly Resolution on Principles of International Law Concerning Friendly Relations and Co-operation among States.[88] The rest of its engagement with the principle is limited to the application of the norm in the specific context of Western Sahara as a non-self-governing territory, and is irrelevant to the subject under discussion here.

In *Western Sahara Campaign UK* – which was the second episode in this saga – the Advocate General started his analysis with the right of self-determination, which, following the textbook approach,[89] he characterised as a human right. This legal qualification better served the purposes of the EU legal order, as the concept of self-determination was thus squeezed into the category of fundamental rights as 'general principles of EU law'.[90] Through this move, the Advocate General could comfortably resort to the classic, judge-made interpretation techniques employed in unpacking the meaning and content of certain fundamental rights as general principles of EU law – namely, drawing inspiration from the guidelines supplied by international instruments for the protection of human rights 'on which the Member States have collaborated or to which

[86] Case C-104/16 P *Council v Front Poliario* (n 21) [88].

[87] ibid [91], referring to ICJ, *Western Sahara* (Advisory Opinion) [1975] ICJ Rep 12 [54], [56] and *East Timor (Portugal v Australia)* (Judgment) [1995] ICJ Rep 90 [29].

[88] Case C-104/16 P *Council v Front Polisario* (n 21) [90], referring UNGA Resolution 2625, 'Declaration on Principles of International Law Concerning Friendly Relations and Co-operation among States in Accordance with the Charter of the United Nations' (24 October 1970) UN Doc A/RES/2625(XXV). For more on this declaration, see eg JE Viñuales, *The UN Friendly Relations Declaration at 50: An Assessment of the Fundamental Principles of International Law* (Cambridge University Press 2020).

[89] For an opposing view, see eg Drew (n 77) 663 ('Despite its textbook characterization as part of human rights law, the law of self-determination has always been bound up with the notions of sovereignty and title to territory that what we traditionally consider to be 'human rights').

[90] Case C-266/16 *Western Sahara Campaign UK*, Opinion of AG Wathelet (10 January 2018) ECLI:EU:C:2018:1 [99]ff.

they are signatories'.[91] For this exercise, he relied on the International Covenant on Civil and Political Rights, the International Covenant on Economic, Social and Cultural Rights, the 1975 Helsinki Final Act, and 'several international authorities and instruments and . . . academic literature', as well as the jurisprudence of the ICJ.[92]

The Advocate General then went on to examine the right of self-determination as a (customary) principle of general international law with *erga omnes* effect. What is most interesting here is the way the Advocate General analysed whether this customary rule reflected a 'clear and precise obligation which is not subject, in its implementation or effects, to the adoption of any subsequent measure'.[93] Under EU law, these represent the criteria according to which a customary norm will have direct effect and hence can serve as a benchmark of legality for secondary EU legislation. To underpin this characterisation, the Advocate General first relied on the CJEU's ruling in *Front Polisario I* and the ICJ's advisory opinion in *Legal Consequences of the Construction of a Wall in the Occupied Palestinian Territory*,[94] followed by a number of international instruments affirming the right of self-determination where 'the content of that right is stated in detail'.[95] As a result of this interpretative analysis, he concluded that, from the viewpoint of its content, the customary law principle of self-determination is unconditional and sufficiently precise. It is thus sufficiently sharp-toothed to operate as a standard of conformity for assessing the validity of an allegedly contradictory piece of secondary EU law. Put differently, the outcome of this interpretative exercise boosted this principle's normativity and raised its judicial enforceability to a higher level.

Turning to the CIL principle of states' permanent sovereignty over their natural resources, the Advocate General rectified his position taken in *Front Polisario I* and held that this customary principle is binding on the EU – which can be seen as an implicit recognition of its *erga omnes* effect, contrary to *Front Polisario I*. In the subsequent analysis, the

[91] First stated in Case 4/73 *J Nold, Kohlen- und Baustoffgroßhandlung v Commission of the European Communities* [1974] ECR 491. Subsequent examples include Case 44/79 *Hauer v Land Rheinland Pfalz* [1979] ECR 3727; Case C-36/02 *Omega Spielhallen- und Automatenaufstellungs-GmbH v Oberbürgermeisterin der Bundesstadt Bonn* [2004] ECR I-9609 [35]; Joined Cases C-402/05 P and C-415/05 P *Kadi and Al Barakaat International Foundation v Council and Commission* (n 1) [283].

[92] Case C-266/16 *Western Sahara Campaign UK*, Opinion of AG Wathelet (n 90) [102].

[93] ibid [110] (formula taken from C-366/10 *ATAA* (n 1) [55]).

[94] ibid [110]–[112].

[95] ibid [115]–[122].

Advocate General found interpretative guidance in a new 'source of (soft) law' – a letter of 29 January 2002 from the UN Under-Secretary-General for Legal Affairs to the president of the UN Security Council, seeking to demonstrate that 'the exact legal scope and implications [of the principle of permanent sovereignty over natural resources] are still debatable',[96] including how to determine what constitutes exploitation of natural resources for the benefit of the people of a non-self-governing territory. The Advocate General went on to conclude that despite the uncertainties concerning the exact contours of this obligation inherent in this customary concept,[97] the principle of permanent sovereignty over natural resources is equally a sufficiently clear and precise norm, capable of forming the basis for a judicial review of acts of EU institutions,[98] including decisions concluding international agreements on behalf of the EU. These interpretative developments since the *Front Polisario I* case are noteworthy – although, here again, the Advocate General failed to discuss the ties between the right of self-determination and the principle of permanent sovereignty over natural resources, shedding no light on whether he considered the latter as logically flowing from the former.

Strange as it might seem, the CJEU did not engage with the right of self-determination or its corollary principle of states' permanent sovereignty over their natural resources in this case either. There is just a passing mention of self-determination as a rule of general international law, without any interpretive engagement with this CIL norm[99] – a mere assertion its customary nature based on ICJ case law and select UN General Assembly resolutions. The CJEU's tight-lipped approach to these two applicable CIL rules, which by contrast are discussed at length by the Advocate General, is even more restrained than in *Front Polisario I*. Its highly reserved stance might be explained by the fact that the EU Court had already set out the basic characteristics of the right of self-determination in its earlier ruling relating to the non-self-governing territory of Western Sahara and did not feel compelled to repeat those,

[96] UNSC, 'Letter Dated 29 January 2002 from the Under-Secretary-General for Legal Affairs, the Legal Counsel, Addressed to the President of the Security Council' (12 February 2002) UN Doc S/2002/161 [14].

[97] For more on these uncertainties and grey zones, see eg E Milano, 'Front Polisario and the Exploitation of Natural Resources by the Administrative Power' (2017) 2 EP 953, 960–66.

[98] Case C-266/16 *Western Sahara Campaign UK*, Opinion of AG Wathelet (n 90) [133]–[134].

[99] Case C-266/16 *Western Sahara Campaign UK* (n 28) [63].

and could simply refer to its findings in *Front Polisario I* by employing cross-references to this judgment *tout court*.

Most recently, the General Court reiterated the CJEU's statements on the customary character of the right of self-determination in *Front Polisario II*, referring to the same international legal authorities, including the ICJ and select UN General Assembly resolutions, as had been earlier relied upon by the Court of Justice.[100] However, no further interpretation followed: the General Court simply concluded that the people of Western Sahara enjoyed the right of self-determination[101] and then went on to focus on the more specific, technical (EU law) questions of the case without needing to delve further into the CIL character of the norm at hand.

The three cases outlined above show that neither the Advocate General nor the Court of Justice or the General Court have gone much beyond the mere identification of applicable rules of customary international law. There was very little interpretative engagement with the customary norms at issue; the discussion was instead rather technical, referring to international instruments of a general character (as CIL has been codified in quasi-universal conventions or enshrined in UN General Assembly resolutions) or to selected passages from leading ICJ judgments (or those of its predecessor). Consequently, the EU Court did not really engage in the exercise of complex interpretation of a CIL norm, but simply relied on other authoritative international legal materials, which it accepted as sufficiently illuminating on the meaning and (some aspects of) the content of a given CIL norm such as the right of self-determination and its derivative principle of permanent sovereignty over natural resources. With respect to the legal nature and possible legal effects of both CIL norms, greater novelty can be found in the opinions of the Advocates General, who recognised that, given their unconditional and sufficiently precise character, the norms could be invoked by private parties in court proceedings (direct effect).

It is noteworthy that the way the CJEU's apprehends the relationship between the right of self-determination and the permanent sovereignty over natural resources is somewhat similar to the ICJ's approach in deriving a norm from another CIL rule. The CJEU did not take a clear position on the relation between the latter CIL norm and the former, asserting its customary nature by simply invoking some supporting

[100] Joined Cases T-344/19 and T-356/19 *Front Polisario v Council* (n 75) [143].
[101] ibid [144].

international legal materials. There have been cases in which, similarly, the ICJ 'merely derived one legal standard from another without the exposition of specific state practice and *opinio juris*'.[102] Examples include *Questions Relating to the Seizure of Certain Documents*, where a state's right to communicate with its counsel and lawyers in a confidential matter was considered to stem from the principle of sovereign equality of states;[103] and the *Corfu Channel* case, where the specific obligation to give notification of the existence of a minefield in the Albanian territorial waters was held to derive from certain general and well-recognised principles, including every state's obligation not to knowingly allow its territory to be used for acts contrary to the rights of other states.[104] In these cases, the ICJ did not make it clear whether the derived, more specific obligations of a CIL nature were self-standing rules in their own right; hence, it did not carry out a full-fledged two-element assessment to determine the existence of these particular customary rules and 'thus freed itself from having to look for new evidence supporting' them.[105] This approach can be defended, though: it would not only be asking too much in every single case where an otherwise general customary concept is applied to individual circumstances, but also shows the power of interpretation of CIL. This argumentative technique finds support in the work of the ILC: the commentaries to the Draft Conclusions on the Identification of Customary International Law likewise acknowledge that:

> The two-element approach does not in fact preclude a measure of deduction as an aid, to be employed with caution, in the application of the two-element approach, in particular when considering possible rules of customary international law that operate against the backdrop of rules framed in more general terms that themselves derive from and reflect a general practice accepted as law.[106]

Against this backdrop, there is every reason to agree with the illuminating remarks of Chasapis Tassinis in this regard:

> By largely ignoring the concept of interpretation, our operating theories of custom may seem to reduce the complexity of that source by putting virtually all of the emphasis on gathering the appropriate evidence. ...

[102] Chasapis Tassinis (n 100) 264.

[103] *Questions Relating to the Seizure and Detention of Certain Documents and Data (Timor-Leste v Australia)* (Provisional Measures) [2014] ICJ Rep 147, 153 [27].

[104] *Corfu Channel (UK v Albania)* (Merits) [1949] ICJ Rep 4, 22.

[105] Chasapis Tassinis (n 10) 264.

[106] ILC, 'Draft Conclusions' (n 9)126, commentary to Conclusion 2, para. (5).

> Factoring interpretation into our analysis of customary international law may thus make identification seem less arbitrary while opening up more productive avenues in legal reasoning about this fundamental source of international law.[107]

3.2.3 Obligation Not to Defeat the Object and Purpose of a Signed Treaty prior to Its Entry into Force

A further situation in which the CJEU engages with the interpretation of CIL is when it acknowledges that a certain principle of EU law that it is developing has its origins in customary (general) international law or states that an existing general principle of EU law is actually a corollary of a very similar CIL norm. The outcome of this interpretative exercise is basically the 'mirroring' or 're-packaging' of the original CIL norm, for the purposes of the EU legal order, into a general principle of EU law, with all the legal implications that follow (e.g. the addressees of the norm are no longer merely states but also individuals and private operators; different legal effects kick in, including supremacy and direct effect, etc.). The case of *Opel Austria*, which concerns the interpretation of the CIL obligation not to defeat the object and purpose of a signed treaty pending its entry into force, is a famous example of that 're-packaging' or 'mirroring' technique.[108]

It is well known that many rules codified in the 1969 and 1986 VCLT reflect CIL. One key customary provision is the obligation laid down in their common Article 18, according to which:

> [a state/international organisation] is obliged to refrain from acts which would defeat the object and purpose of a treaty when:
>
> (a) it has signed the treaty or has exchanged instruments constituting the treaty subject to ratification, acceptance or approval, until it shall have made its intention clear not to become a party to the treaty; or
> (b) it has expressed its consent to be bound by the treaty, pending the entry into force of the treaty and provided that such entry into force is not unduly delayed.

The General Court referred to and applied this principle of a customary nature – which, in essence, is a concrete manifestation of the general

[107] Chasapis Tassinis (n 10) 266.

[108] J Odermatt, 'The European Union as a Global Actor and Its Impact on the International Legal Order' (PhD thesis, University of Leuven Department of Law 2016) 128–29; Odermatt (n 12) 24–25.

principle of good faith – in *Open Austria*,[109] although its reasoning and the operative part of the ruling was in the end not based on this international legal rule setting out a so-called interim obligation. The case concerned the validity of an EU regulation subjecting gearboxes produced by General Motors Austria to 5,9 per cent customs duty. Opel Austria challenged this additional customs levy imposed in response to alleged Austrian state aid, arguing that the contested regulation was in breach of the customary principle of good faith as codified in Article 18 of the 1969 VCLT. The contested regulation was adopted by the Council of the EU in December 1993, after the instruments of ratification of the Agreement on the European Economic Area (EEA) were exchanged[110] but before the EEA Agreement entered into force in January 1994. The EEA Agreement prohibited the imposition of any further customs duties between contracting parties. The General Court accepted the applicant's arguments that the then European Community was bound by this customary interim obligation as codified in Article 18 of the VCLT, which, it found, was the corollary of the EU law principle of the protection of legitimate expectations. Yet, as it was not convinced that private parties could rely directly on this customary principle of international law, it finally based its ruling quashing the contested regulation on the protection of legitimate expectations as a general principle of EU law,[111] which could be invoked by individuals and private operators. Subsequent cases have seen the CJEU clinging to the application of the principles of legitimate expectation and good faith as general principles of EU law, rather than relying on the customary interim obligation enshrined in Article 18 of the VCLT, even if the parties to the dispute based their arguments, at least in part, on this CIL principle.[112] This approach reveals the difficulties and uncertainties that not only contracting parties but also private entities risk encountering when, in a legal dispute, they directly invoke the CIL obligation not to defeat the object and purpose of a treaty.[113]

[109] Case T-115/94 *Opel Austria GmbH v Council of the European Union* [1997] ECR II-39 [93].

[110] Agreement on the European Economic Area (adopted 2 May 1992, entered into force 1 January 1994) 1801 UNTS 3.

[111] T-115/94 *Opel Austria* (n 109) [94]–[95].

[112] Case C-27/96 *Danisco Sugar AB v Allmänna ombudet* [1997] ECR I-6653; Case C-203/07 P *Hellenic Republic v Commission of the European Communities* [2008] ECR I-8161.

[113] J Klabbers, 'How to Defeat a Treaty's Object and Purpose Pending Entry into Force: Toward Manifest Intent' (2001) 34 VJTL 318.

The above reasoning allowed the CJEU to assert the autonomy of EU law, portraying it as an independent legal system that does not derive its authority from international law – and, in its own legal order, to apply general principles of EU law instead.

3.2.4 Territorial Scope of Treaties

The last example is also taken from the realm of the law of treaties. It is noteworthy that the CJEU almost always interprets customary law when resorting to VCLT rules, given that the EU is not bound by the VCLT itself but only by the equivalent customary rules and principles of treaty law that exist in parallel to the written instrument. Leaving aside the practice of the EU judiciary concerning the interpretation of the customary rules of treaty interpretation (as reduced to writing in Article 31 VCLT), an illustrative example from the realm of the law of treaties is where the CJEU (re-)interpreted the CIL rule on the territorial scope of treaties. The customary rule governing the territorial scope of treaties is codified in Article 29 VCLT, in a quite laconic manner, as follows: 'Unless a different intention appears from the treaty or is otherwise established, a treaty is binding upon each party in respect of its entire territory.'

At first sight, this provision looks straightforward and does not seem to call for further clarification. Yet, the complexities of the *Front Polisario I* and *Western Sahara Campaign UK* cases led the CJEU to engage with this rule and to attempt to deconstruct its components. In this process, the CJEU found support in international treaty-making practice[114] and pointed out that those treaties which apply beyond the territory of a state use the expressions 'under [the] jurisdiction of that State'[115] or 'any of the territories for whose international relations it is responsible'.[116] Given that 'territory of a state' is nowhere defined in international law, but rather thought to be self-explanatory, the CJEU then offered its own construction of 'territorial scope' as follows:

> a treaty is generally binding on a State in the ordinary meaning to be given to the term 'territory', combined with the possessive adjective 'its' preceding

[114] Case C-104/16 P *Council v Front Polisario* (n 21) [96].

[115] Convention against Torture and Other Cruel, Inhuman or Degrading Treatment or Punishment (adopted 10 December 1984, entered into force 26 June 1987) 85 UNTS 1465, art 2(1).

[116] European Convention for the Protection of Human Rights and Fundamental Freedoms (adopted 4 November 1950, entered into force 3 September 1953) 23 UNTS 2889, art 56(1).

> it, in respect of the geographical space over which that State exercises the fullness of the powers granted to sovereign entities by international law, to the exclusion of any other territory, such as a territory likely to be under the sole jurisdiction or the sole international responsibility of that State.[117]

As result of this interpretation, and coupled with the principles of good faith in performing treaties and the relative effect of treaties, the CJEU drew the conclusion that, as a non-self-governing territory, the Western Sahara was by no means under the territorial scope of the EU–Morocco bilateral fisheries agreement.

Some commentators,[118] citing the *travaux préparatoires* of the VCLT,[119] note that the customary rule enshrined in Article 29 VCLT was basically intended to set out a general rule concerning the territories of the state parties which applies as a fall-back clause in situations where a treaty does not define its territorial application. As Odermatt points out, '[t]he CJEU, however, gives much more significance to this provision, interpreting it to mean that a treaty only applies with respect to territory over which a state exercises full sovereign powers, unless there is an express provision providing for its application to other territory'. Does this mean then that the CJEU has re-interpreted a CIL norm, setting out stricter requirements for (EU member) states and the EU itself to follow when determining the territorial scope of their treaties? Kassoti answers affirmatively by insisting that as a result of this interpretation, whenever a treaty concluded by the EU is intended to produce extraterritorial effect its 'territorial scope' clause must be worded in such a way as to expressly provide for this effect.[120]

4 Lessons Learnt and Take-Aways

Any court that applies and interprets CIL rules does so in a specific legal and institutional context, and this goes for the CJEU, too. The way in which the CJEU interprets customary international law is largely influenced by the role customary international law plays in the cases brought

117 Case C-104/16 P *Council v Front Polisario* (n 21) [95]; also reiterated in Case C-266/16 *Western Sahara Campaign UK* (n 28) [68].

118 J Odermatt, 'Council of the European Union v Front Populaire pour la Libération de la Saguia-El-Hamra et Du Rio de Oro (Front Polisario)' (2017) 111 AJIL 736; E Kassoti, 'Between *Sollen* and *Sein*: The CJEU's Reliance on International Law in the Interpretation of Economic Agreements Covering Occupied Territories' (2020) 33 LJIL 381.

119 ILC, 'Draft Articles on the Law of Treaties with Commentaries' (4 May–19 July 1966) UN Doc A/CN.4/191, 213, commentary to Article 25 [5].

120 Kassoti (n 119) 380.

before it. As pointed out in Section 2, a CIL rule is traditionally applied before the CJEU for the purpose of interpreting and elucidating the meaning of provisions of secondary EU legislation.[121] Interpretation to ensure the consistency of EU law with CIL is a limited form of interpretive engagement by the CJEU with a particular CIL norm, for normally it is not the CIL rule that is at the centre of attention in the interpretative process but an EU law provision. As a result, the main task for the CJEU is not to interpret the CIL rule (which occupies a subsidiary position in this scenario) but, once it has found a relevant international legal rule and identified it as being of a customary nature, to use that rule as broader legal context, also binding on the Union, for the interpretation of the EU law provision at hand. A typical example of such use of a customary rule is when the CJEU is confronted with questions treaty law when dealing with an EU agreement and employs the VCLT 'rulebook' largely reflective of CIL. In other words, this is a sort of an interpretation of customary rules by proxy: the CJEU essentially interprets a VCLT provision not as a treaty rule – as the EU is not bound by the VCLT, it cannot legally engage with it as such – but as its customary law equivalent. The ruling in *Opel Austria* went even further by re-packaging the customary rule of not defeating the object and purpose of a signed treaty prior its ratification and, for the purposes of Union law, mirroring, as it were, its content in a general principle of EU law – namely, the protection of legitimate expectations. Likewise, when interpreting the CIL rule relating to the territorial scope of a treaty, the EU Court opted for a significant (restrictive) change to its meaning, reformulating the customary rule as crystallised in Article 29 of the VCLT and redefined it with more stringent requirements.

A specific form of employing CIL as an interpretive tool to clarify the meaning of EU law came up in the *Mahamdia* and *Rina* cases, where identifying the relevant CIL norm (the jurisdictional immunity of states) was not the most crucial task. The peculiar character of this CIL principle in procedural terms – i.e. denying the injured private party access to justice, which touches on a foundational value in the EU legal order: the right to an effective judicial remedy – required that the meaning, the boundaries, and the exceptions of state immunity be thoroughly examined before the CJEU could answer the questions

[121] See eg Case C-366/10 *ATAA*, Opinion of AG Kokott (6 October 2011) [109] ('customary international law has, up to now, been called upon only in relation to the interpretation of provisions and principles of EU law').

concerning the interpretation of certain provisions of the Brussels II Regulation on exercising jurisdiction in civil and commercial matters. Despite the key role of this CIL rule, it was the Advocate General alone who engaged in a proper interpretation of the norm, opting for its systemic and evolutive interpretation, the outcome of which was taken up by the CJEU as a pre-cooked finding.

In theory, the interpretation of a CIL norm could play a more central role before the CJEU when (private) parties rely on it as the review standard for challenging the validity of a legal act adopted by the EU institutions. This scenario, which occurred for the first time in the *ATAA* case, forces the CJEU to interpret the invoked CIL rule, and notably to run the two-pronged test developed in CJEU case law to determine the direct effect of the CIL rule – that is, whether the customary norm at hand is capable of calling into question the competence of the EU to adopt a given piece of secondary legislation and whether it may affect the rights that individuals derive from EU law.[122] The CJEU was faced with this question in the series of cases where Front Polisario relied on the customary right of self-determination and the permanent sovereignty over natural resources as grounds for invalidating the contested bilateral agreements between the EU and Morocco. Again, despite lengthy and illuminating legal analyses of the meaning and content of these CIL rules by the Advocates General, the CJEU opted for a different (and somewhat evasive) line of reasoning, resorting to the rules of treaty interpretation so as to avoid having to assess the legality of the contested EU acts against these customary norms of key significance.

What can one distil from the above observations? The selected rulings we have discussed demonstrate that the CJEU has been reluctant to undertake its own investigation into state practice and *opinio juris* in order to interpret a given norm of customary international law, most often stopping long before by simply asserting the existence of the CIL norm without conducting a deeper analysis. (It must be admitted that avoidance of the two-element test is not unusual in the case law of international and domestic courts.[123]) Instead, the CJEU preferred to refer to the case law of other international courts and tribunals,

[122] Case C-366/10 *ATAA* (n 1) [107]. See also Joined Cases 89/85, 104/85, 114/85, 116/85, 117/85 and 125/85 to 129/85 *Ahlström Osakeyhtiö and ors v Commission* (*Woodpulp*) [1993] ECLI:EU:C:1993:120 [14]–[18].

[123] S Choi and M Gularti, 'Customary International Law: How Do Courts Do It?' in CA Bradley (ed), *Custom's Future: International Law in a Changing World* (Cambridge University Press 2016) 117–47.

particularly the ICJ,[124] and occasionally select instruments of international law enshrining the customary rule in question (such external referencing can been regarded as a co-ordination technique to ensure consistency[125]). Other avoidance techniques on the part of the EU Court can also be observed. They include merely copying and pasting, in condensed form, the main findings of the interpretive analysis carried out by the Advocate General (*Mahamdia* and *Rina*); replacing the CIL norm in question with a corresponding general principle of EU law (*Opel Austria*); or simply looking for 'safer' avenues of legal reasoning, notably 'interpreting away' vital issues of CIL by using the toolbox of treaty interpretation and not touching on questions of interpretation of substantive customary rules of fundamental importance (such as the right of self-determination and the permanent sovereignty over natural resources) (*Front Polisario I-II* and *Western Sahara Campaign UK*).

Analysing the CJEU's judicial practice is an opportunity to explore the possible reasons and motivations behind the CJEU's guarded approach to the interpretation of CIL rules once they have been included in the set of legal norms applicable to a particular case. These reasons are manifold. First, the CJEU perceives its role as being more that of a domestic court than an international court, as a result of which it displays restraint when engaging with the interpretation of CIL that lies outside its comfort zone. Similar discomfort and hesitation can be seen in domestic courts,[126] where CIL norms raise difficulties in terms of ascertainment and legitimacy. Second, the EU Court's unease may be linked to a lack of resources and specialised knowledge in public international law,[127] which is compounded by the fact that in certain cases the CJEU has to prove the existence of state practice and *opinio juris* not only at the EU level but also in the international arena,[128] which is usually unchartered territory for the CJEU. A third explanatory factor is that, unlike the treaties to which the EU is a party, the EU has not given its explicit consent to CIL norms and may have had no role in their development. Customary international law is thus seen as something developed 'outside' the EU legal order and should therefore be 'mistrusted'.[129]

124 Odermatt (n 108) 119; Ammann (n 43) 171.

125 Pascual-Vives (n 14) 146.

126 Ammann (n 43) 172, 173, citing also PL Hoffmann, 'The 'Blank Stare Phenomenon': Proving Customary International Law in U.S. Courts' (1996) 25 GJICL 181, 181–90.

127 Malenovský (n 18) 233.

128 Ammann (n 43) 172.

129 Odermatt (n 108)125.

To sum up, the CJEU's engagement with the interpretation of CIL and its interpretation techniques – unlike the approach of the Advocates General in a number of instances – remain underdeveloped. There is thus room for improvement, including with a view to enhancing the CJEU's output legitimacy. This author agrees with those scholars who argue that the CJEU's application of CIL will be fully legitimate procedurally only if the accompanying interpretative reasoning is significantly improved.[130] Boldly asserting certain CIL rules without additional refinement and substantiation fails to convince other interpreters of international law. As most perceptively observed by Higgins, the CJEU's caution when it comes to CIL stands 'in marked contrast to the confidence shown as to its capabilities in international law shown by the Court in other cases'.[131] With the expansion of the EU's treaty-making activities[132] and its rising profile as a major (legal) actor on the global stage,[133] the number of cases before the CJEU pertaining to international law will continue to grow, which will make it all the more desirable for the EU Court to deal with these issues, including the interpretation of CIL, with greater confidence and authority.

This is the case in particular when several CIL rules are to be applied simultaneously and their relationship needs to be determined. A similar need arises, in a more dramatic fashion, where conflicting CIL norms apply in one and the same case before the CJEU. The time is ripe for a deeper and more convincing engagement with CIL on the part of the CJEU through reliance on a conceptually and methodologically sound framework for interpretation that will strengthen the unique judicial function it performs.

130 Ammann (n 43) 172–73, 178.

131 R Higgins, 'The ICJ, the ECJ and the Integrity of International Law' (2002) 52 ICLQ 9.

132 Consider, for instance, the European External Action Service database of international treaties to which the EU is a party: it covers more than 1,300 bilateral and multilateral agreements (with many references to international legal standards and principles). See Eur-Lex, 'Treaties Currently In Force' (2022) <http://ec.europa.eu/world/agreements/viewCollection.do> accessed 25 June 2022.

133 See eg D Kochenov and F Amtenbrink (eds), *The European Union's Shaping of the International Legal Order* (Cambridge University Press 2014); B van Vooren, S Blockmans, and J Wouters (eds), *The EU's Role in Global Governance: The Legal Dimension* (Oxford University Press 2013).

8

Judicial Effectiveness or Judicial Ambiguity

Is CIL Identification an Instrument for Judicial Activism in Excess?

LEONI AYOUB

1 Introduction

Effectiveness and efficiency in judicial decision-making are the most important objectives of any court. While this concerns primarily the final decisions that are rendered, this is also relevant to the judicial process and the legal reasoning that a court or tribunal carries out to reach its decision, in order to ensure continuity and coherence. Traditional understandings of the international judiciary have seen the judges' role as one where they discover and declare the law by applying it at face value to the legal issues that have arisen within the case, thereby achieving effectiveness through what is said to be direct and clear application of the law.[1] Indeed, '[international] judges have to apply the *law* and they have to apply the *law in force*'.[2] This would seemingly contrast with the picture of the judge as one who engages in developing the law in order to administer justice. This latter understanding sees the judges' role as involving an inherent form of creativity to meet the needs of the case

[1] Traditional views of domestic judges were influenced by positivists and formalists such as Francis Bacon and Montesquieu, who saw the function of the judge as a dependent 'mouthpiece of the law'. Grafted onto the international judiciary, this has resulted in an uneasy relationship between the international and domestic judiciaries as it has led to the expectation that the two have parallel roles. See S Besson, 'Legal Philosophical Issues of International Adjudication Getting Over the *Amour Impossible* between International Law and Adjudication' in CPR Romano, KJ Alter, and Y Shany (eds), *The Oxford Handbook of International Adjudication* (Oxford University Press 2013) 413 (emphasis added).

[2] H Lauterpacht, *The Development of International Law by the International Court* (Cambridge University Press 1982) 75.

before them,[3] while they may be accused of entering the field of law creation.

This dichotomy sits rather uneasily with the identification of customary international law (CIL), which is by its very nature unwritten and established by identifying evidence of state practice and *opinio juris.*[4] Accordingly, custom needs to be understood as 'the result of an *informal* process of rule-creation'.[5] This two-pronged approach to recognising CIL renders the degree of precision that is usually found in conventional law-making processes more difficult to achieve.[6] This is because of a paradoxical difficulty that exists between qualifying the rule as law while simultaneously seeking to apply and interpret it. This may lead to instances where courts are considered to assume the position of legislator by overstepping the powers granted to them, laying them more easily open to the reproach of engaging in judicial activism.

Although the concept of judicial activism has come to be frequently associated with the decisions of certain international courts,[7] it has particularly derogatory connotations, evoking the seemingly unorthodox judge who has taken the decision to derogate from established law and base their decision on a novel, or at least less common, interpretation of a legal principle. This raises the question of the possible role of activism in the determination of certain customary rules and the part it plays in their subsequent effectiveness or ambiguity.

[3] This approach is usually supported by what has been referred to as 'legal modernists' such as Oliver Wendell Holmes Jr, an analysis of which remains outside the scope of the present article. On judicial creativity regarding the judicial function, see generally M Kirby, *Judicial Activism: Authority, Principle and Policy in Judicial Method* (Sweet & Maxwell 2004); M Cappelletti, 'The Law-Making Power of the Judge and Its Limits: A Comparative Analysis' (1981) 8 Monash UL Rev 15.

[4] ILC, 'Draft Conclusions on Identification of Customary International Law, with Commentaries' (30 April–1 June and 2 July–10 August 2018) UN Doc A/73/10. The author recognises that this describes one methodology for recognising customary international law – namely, inductive reasoning. At the same time, there also exists a less popular method, called deductive reasoning, which is not commonly used. See M Bos *A Methodology of International Law* (Asser Institute 1984).

[5] ILA, Committee on Formation of Customary (General) International Law, Final Report, 'Statement of Principles Applicable to the Formation of General Customary International Law' (London 2000) 2 (emphasis in original).

[6] See in general ibid and ILC, 'Draft Conclusions' (n 4).

[7] On the International Court of Justice, see eg Lauterpacht (n 2); on the Court of Justice of the European Union (CJEU), see H Rasmussen, *On Law and Policy in the European Court of Justice: A Comparative Study in Judicial Policymaking* (Martinus Nijhoff 1986). See also H Rasmussen, 'Between Self-Restraint and Activism: A Judicial Policy for the European Court' (1988) 13 Eur L Rev 28.

The aim of this chapter is to examine instances of judicial activism in the decision-making of international courts and tribunals during the determination and application of CIL and how that allows for either judicial effectiveness or ambiguity. To do this, we will first set out the foundational parameters that need to be examined. We will describe the process by which custom is created and set out the customary rule on which our analysis will focus – namely, the indispensable parties principle.[8] We will then turn to judicial effectiveness, its definition and consequence for the judicial function, and in particular how it can be identified. We will then provide a definition of, and guidelines for identifying, judicial activism in international courts. With these elements in mind, the discussion will then return to an analysis of relevant case law regarding the indispensable parties principle and the use, or not, of judicial activism in such cases. Lastly, we will evaluate whether custom has been used as an instrument for judicial activism and, if yes, enquire into how the judicial function itself has enabled this.

2 CIL and the Judicial Process

Typically unwritten, CIL is determined through state practice and acceptance as law (*opinio juris*). Nevertheless, the recognition of customary international rules remains a difficult task,[9] as it requires a particular process through which the interpreter (the judge) can arrive at a conclusion of the existence of a law or rule under custom. [10] Further, the question arises as to what extent the courts engage in the identification and determination of CIL proper or fall victim to what has been termed 'pulling a rabbit out of [their] hat' by simply asserting what they think the law is.[11]

[8] Modern international law refers primarily to the change in the perception of public international law since the end of the Second World War. The international legal system shifted from one in which states had existed alongside each other in 'cohabitation' to one characterized by cooperation between them through the creation of common structures at the end of the Second World War. See W Friedmann, *The Changing Structure of International Law* (Stevens & Sons 1964). This change also saw the creation of a new world court, the International Court of Justice (ICJ), in accordance with the Charter of the United Nations (UN Charter) and the Statute of the International Court of Justice (ICJ Statute) (adopted 26 June 1945, entered into force 24 October 1945) 892 UNTS 119, following the dissolution of the Permanent Court of International Justice (PCIJ).

[9] See Bos (n 4); ILC (n 4) 126.

[10] M Bos, 'The Identification of Custom in International Law' (1982) 25 GYIL 9.

[11] S Talmon, 'Determining Customary International Law: The ICJ's Methodology between Induction, Deduction and Assertion' (2015) 26 EJIL 417.

The determination of custom has a direct relationship with the judicial function and the judicial process. As Maarten Bos has argued, proof of custom is a 'process of thought' leading to a judicial pronouncement, which thereafter forms undeniable proof of a legal relationship and indicates the existence of a legal norm or law.[12] Thus, the very identification of the customary rule can indicate the judge's state of mind and, by extension, the possible use of activism or restraint. Furthermore, this process of reasoning to identify a customary rule reflects the progress and evolution of the judicial process.[13] This is because the element of identifying custom is so intrinsically linked to the judicial process – it being a process itself – that it may shed light as to the judicial function assumed.[14]

In a similar vein, the present author considers that the interpretation of custom also reflects the state of the judge's mind and the 'process of thought' followed to arrive at its possible application.[15] Indeed, while methodology in interpretation rests beyond the confines of this analysis, interpretation is more than just deciphering what the language of a rule means; it goes further and asks: 'What law does this [rule] make? How does it fit into the rest of the *corpus juris*?'[16] By extension, if interpretation of custom comes in the form of interpretation of previous evidence of state practice and *opinio juris*, we can identify the ever-evolving judicial function and its role in the creation of the law.

As we will see in the following analysis, the method of identification and interpretation of custom grows to become a vital element in the very creation of the judicial function. By contrast, if this method is lacking, the court has fallen into the trap of 'pulling a rabbit out of its hat', contributing to inconsistency and incoherence, where the court simply 'asserts the law as it sees fit'.[17]

[12] Bos (n 4).
[13] ibid.
[14] Talmon (n 11).
[15] The author notes that Bos (n 10) had argued that there exists no interpretation of custom. However, as this paragraph will show, interpretation is, by its very nature, the act of the judge carrying out their reasoning.
[16] Play on words found in W Baude and SE Sachs, 'The Law of Interpretation' (2017) 130 Harv L Rev 1079, 1083 that refer to the interpretation of legal texts ('What law did this instrument make? How does it fit into the rest of the *corpus juris*?).
[17] Talmon (n 11).

2.1 *The Indispensable Parties Principle and CIL*

As custom forms a broad corpus of law, the present analysis will be confined to the principle of indispensable parties, as articulated by the International Court of Justice (ICJ) in the *Monetary Gold Removed from Rome* case.[18] Aware of the difficulties surrounding the history and legal origins of this principle[19] and the objections that exist as to its nature as a rule or principle of customary international law[20] the present author nevertheless argues that it is precisely this confusion that makes it worth examining, as the role played by the international judiciary in its evolution offers ample scope for discussion. This, in turn, provides the opportunity to scrutinise the work and analysis carried out and to open a discussion on the role of activism and restraint in relation to custom in general.[21]

Recognised in international law as a governing principle and a piece of conventional wisdom,[22] this principle essentially affirms that a court or tribunal will not decide a case if the decision will affect the legal rights of a third state which is indispensable to the resolution of the dispute before it. This principle is most often framed as an absolute,[23] yet without any particular source attributed to it.[24] Considering that different principles may be derived from 'different sources of international law at different times and even the same principle may be simultaneously shaped by

[18] *Case of the Monetary Gold Removed from Rome in 1943* (Preliminary Question) [1954] ICJ Rep 19. It is recognised that this was not the first international case to have made reference to such a right. The recognition of a third state's rights was made in the 1899 *Boundary between British Guiana and Venezuela* case where the arbitral tribunal delivered its award while noting that it would be 'subject and without prejudice to any questions now existing, or which may arise, to be determined between the government of her Britannic Majesty and the Republic of Brazil, or between the latter Republic and the United States of Venezuela' (cited in M Paparinskis, 'Revisiting the Indispensable Third Party Principle' (2020) 1 RDI 49, 56).

[19] ibid 66.

[20] See eg O Pomson, 'Does the *Monetary Gold* Principle Apply to International Courts and Tribunals Generally?' (2019) 10 JIDS 88; see also D Akande, 'Introduction to the Symposium on Zachary Mollengarden & Noam Zamir "The *Monetary Gold* Principle: Back to Basics"' (2021) 115 AJIL Unbound 140; P d'Argent, 'The *Monetary Gold* Principle: A Matter of Submissions' (2021) 115 AJIL Unbound 149; J McIntyre, 'Rules Are Rules: Reconceiving *Monetary Gold* as a Rule of Procedure' (2021) 115 AJIL Unbound 144.

[21] Words inspired by Pomson (n 20) 117.

[22] T Sparks, 'Reassessing State Consent to Jurisdiction: The Indispensable Third Party Principle before the ICJ' (2022) 91 NJIL 216, 217.

[23] ibid 217.

[24] Paparinskis (n 18) 66.

various elements of the legal order',[25] we can see how the principle can be the result of a variety of sources, one of which could arguably be CIL.[26]

As this analysis sets out to demonstrate, the indispensable parties principle has by now not only acquired general acceptance within the international legal system but is also called upon quite frequently in practice.[27] The principle affords an opportunity to analyse both its identification and its subsequent application as a customary rule: while *Monetary Gold* may or may not reflect a rule of custom that existed at the time of the ruling, subsequent international courts have allowed us to understand it as such today. Furthermore, as the principle has a procedural character,[28] this enables a direct link between judicial effectiveness and judicial activism, because the very need for effective procedures is directly linked to the effective administration of justice.[29]

3 The Judicial Function and Its effectiveness

Judicial effectiveness in international law is a controversial concept.[30] This is but a natural corollary to the diverging opinions of what the judicial function precisely entails and what the role of a judge is. Indeed, various definitions and models of effectiveness have been introduced in an attempt to define the concept of judicial effectiveness.[31] One common definition is what has been described as the goal-based rationale[32] according to which 'an action is effective if it accomplishes its specific objective aim'.[33] In other words, the court or tribunal must be fulfilling the judicial function which it was tasked to fulfil.[34] To do this, one must identify what that judicial function consists of and the desired outcomes

25 ibid.

26 Pomson (n 20) 117. Paparinskis also considers this possibility but rejects it: Paparinskis (n 18) 69–70.

27 Pomson (n 20).

28 See in general Paparinskis (n 18) 67 and McIntyre (n 20).

29 P Gaeta 'Inherent Powers of International Courts and Tribunals' in LC Vohrah (ed), *Man's Inhumanity to Man: Essays on International Law in Honour of Antonio Cassese* (Kluwer Law International 2003) 353.

30 See generally Y Shany, *Assessing the Effectiveness of International Courts* (Oxford University Press 2014) ch 1.

31 ibid 13–14.

32 ibid.

33 ibid.

34 Y Shany, 'Assessing the Effectiveness of International Courts: A Goal-Based Approach' (2012) 106 AJIL 225.

it ought to generate:[35] international courts and tribunals are created to settle the disputes referred to them, 'to do justice' between the litigant states and render a binding judgment.[36] By contrast, judicial ambiguity reflects the judge who does not render effective decisions, one who is not able to fulfil the full spectrum of the judicial function, so that the judgment, while possibly resolving the case, also raises ancillary questions as to its effectiveness and coherence. This, of course, can only be measured by defining what that judicial function is. To be able to so define, or measure, the judicial function, three components are proposed that will allow the examination of the decision-making of the courts and tribunals at the international level.[37]

The first component is the idea that decisions serve a public, in addition to a private, function.[38] On the one hand, there exists the commonly accepted task consisting in resolving the dispute between the two parties to the case the so-called private function.[39] On the other hand, there exists the public function of an international court, which goes beyond the settlement of that dispute and extends into the realm of positively creating norms that can generate obedience among the members of the community regulated by that system of norms.[40] This latter function is linked to the proper administration of international justice by helping to create a body of coherent rules and laws and ensuring overall efficiency in judicial decision-making.[41]

This is closely related to our second component: the emergence of a 'new posture of international courts and tribunals [that] is the "spirit of systemic harmonisation"'.[42] Although the international legal system has

[35] Shany (n 30).

[36] C Brown, 'Inherent Powers in International Adjudication' in CPR Romano, KJ Alter and Y Shany (eds), *The Oxford Handbook of International Adjudication* (Oxford University Press 2013) 828.

[37] For greater detail, see L Ayoub, *Judicial Activism and Restraint in the Creation of the International Judicial Function: How Have Activism and Restraint Shaped the International Courts?* (Ridderprint 2021) ch 1.

[38] Brown, 'Inherent Powers in International Adjudication' (n 36); C Brown, 'The Inherent Powers of International Courts and Tribunals' (2006) 76 BYIL 195.

[39] Brown, 'Inherent Powers in International Adjudication' (n 36); Brown, 'The Inherent Powers of International Courts and Tribunals' (n 38).

[40] Brown, 'Inherent Powers in International Adjudication' (n 36); Brown, 'The Inherent Powers of International Courts and Tribunals' (n 38).

[41] Brown, 'Inherent Powers in International Adjudication' (n 36); Brown, 'The Inherent Powers of International Courts and Tribunals' (n 38).

[42] A Peters, 'The Refinement of International Law: From Fragmentation to Regime Interaction and Politicization' (2017) 15 IJCL 671, 671, quoting *Al-Dulimi and Montana Management Inc. v Switzerland*, App no 5809/08 (ECtHR, 26 November 2013).

been described as fragmented, giving the impression of isolated regimes, there is a growing rapprochement[43] and the creation of common standards, as exemplified through court decisions that allow for a more unified system than that which initially meets the eye.[44] This describes the web that is gradually being woven in the international legal system through progressive collectivisation, with many components of international law being endorsed through mutual recognition and respect between states.[45] Customary international law forms part of this collectivised web.

Thirdly, while the notion of judicial law-making may be difficult to reconcile with the traditional understanding of the role of the international judiciary, it has come to be accepted that a judge's role also comprises an element of law creation through its identification, interpretation and application.[46] This is not to contradict the idea that judges must identify and apply the law at hand, but to argue that, in identifying and applying that law, they are, through the very nature of the judicial process, also creating it. In other words, through the act of judicial reasoning and interpretation, judicial law-making *ipso facto* exists, in some shape or other, under the guise of judicial interpretation.[47]

For present purposes, effectiveness reflects a combination of these three components. It should be noted that while precedent and any attention given to previous court decisions is largely denied at the international level,[48] the international judicial function nevertheless aims to create coherence and consistency through its decision-making. The ICJ ascribes considerable authority to previous decisions, over and above the habitual practice of citation.[49] In fact, it has been said that it 'commonly formulates new rules under the cover of interpretation'[50] and, further, that the 'Court's interpretation ... contributes to the creation of what it finds'.[51]

[43] ibid.
[44] ibid.
[45] ibid.
[46] See the discussion in CG Weeramantry, 'The Function of the International Court of Justice in the Development of International Law' (1997) 10 LJIL 309.
[47] ibid.
[48] Sparks (n 22) 219.
[49] ibid 219–20.
[50] ibid 220, quoting A Pellet and D Müller, 'Article 38' in A Zimmermann and others (eds), *The Statute of the International Court of Justice: A Commentary* (3rd edn, Oxford University Press 2019) 956, who characterise this as 'de facto legislative power'.
[51] ibid, quoting GI Hernandez, *The International Court of Justice and the Judicial Function* (Oxford University Press 2014) 90.

Ambiguity, here, refers not only to judgments that are ineffective or textually unclear, but reflect a judge who deviates from this triad, rendering decisions that neither contribute to norm creation nor form a part of the collectivised web of international law but instead leave the resolution of the dispute unclear and do not necessarily fit within the overall systemised collective. Where the coherence and consistency of a decision are in question, we find ambiguity.

4 Judicial Activism and Judicial Restraint

4.1 A Definition

Before commencing the analysis, it is important that the terms 'judicial activism' and 'judicial restraint' be defined. As former CJEU judge Pescatore noted '[w]hat is described by one as activism is seen by another as a just and necessary safeguard'.[52] Therefore, the determination of a judicially activist or restraint decision will always be a matter of degree.[53] Despite its relatively widespread usage, the term 'judicial activism' has no unified meaning. Although judicial activism is commonly attributed to the law-creating nature of the role of judges, and restraint to rejection of that law-creating role, these attributions provide little as to the nature or content of these principles. Indeed, it has even been asserted that 'judicial activism is simply the label used for decisions one does not like'.[54]

International legal scholars have nevertheless attempted various definitions of judicial activism, which offer some indication as to how it might be discerned. Hugh Thirlway identified two types of activism: activism in the 'formal sense', which arises when the judge 'deals with an issue the decision on which is not essential to the resolution of the dispute before him . . . [but wishes] to "enrich and develop" the law';[55] and 'substantive activism', which arises when the judge is 'dissatisfied with existing law . . .

[52] Cited in G Conway, *The Limits of Legal Reasoning and the European Court of Justice* (Cambridge University Press 2012) 17–18.

[53] EW Thomas, *The Judicial Process: Realism, Pragmatism, Practical Reasoning and Principles* (Cambridge University Press 2008) 93; also L Reid, 'The Judge as a Lawmaker' (1972) 12 J Soc Public Teachers of Law 22.

[54] Lindquist, 'Identifying Judicial Activism' in SA Lindquist and FB Cross (eds.), *Measuring Judicial Activism* (Oxford University Press 2009) 30, quoting E Chemerinsky, 'The Rhetoric of Constitutional Law' (2002) 100 Mich L Rev 2000, 2019.

[55] H Thirlway 'Judicial Activism and the International Court of Justice' in N Ando, E McWhinney and R Wolfrum (eds), *Liber Amicorum Judge Shigeru Oda* (Kluwer Law International 2002) 75.

[and] . . . will be ready to indulge in something close to open law-creation in order to base his decision'.[56] Former ICJ judge Kooijmans objected to both activism and restraint before the ICJ, steering away from the 'destructive trap' of activism and the ineffectiveness of restraint, 'which closes windows',[57] and introducing instead the concept of 'proactive judicial policy'.[58] To him, the judicial role is 'to utilise those aspects of the case which have a wider interest or connotation in order to enrich and develop the law'.[59] Lara Pair considered the 'ultimate criterion for judicial activism'[60] to be the focus on 'avoidance of an unjust result' and 'creative reasoning rather than strict application of the law'.[61]

Judicial restraint has been even more illusory, yet some helpful definitions can also be found. Lauterpacht described a court that exercises restraint as one which 'refrains from explaining rules in detail'[62] as it 'may create . . . the impression the court was laying down new rules of law'.[63] Judge Kooijmans similarly qualified restraint as the court that 'wilfully abstain[s] from using the opportunity . . . to provide clarification on a matter which [. . .] is highly controversial'.[64]

Former ECtHR judge Mahoney defined the two concepts in parallel. He did not approach activism and restraint as two 'conflicting theories as to how judges should go about decision-making'.[65] Instead, he referred to 'making interpretation choices', with judicial activism being 'neutralised' by the exercise of judicial self-restraint.[66] Therefore, activism involves '[modifying] the law from what it previously was or was stated to be in the existing legal sources',[67] while restraint is a technique necessary in order to move 'proceedings forward by incremental steps in specific contexts rather than by dramatic leaps in the dark'.[68] These two forces ultimately

[56] ibid.
[57] P Kooijmans, 'The ICJ in the 21st Century: Judicial Restraint, Judicial Activism, or Proactive Judicial Policy' (2007) 56 ICLQ 741, 746.
[58] ibid.
[59] ibid.
[60] L Pair, 'Judicial Activism in the ICJ Charter Interpretation' (2001–02) 8 ILSA J Intl Comp L 181.
[61] ibid.
[62] Lauterpacht (n 2) 89.
[63] ibid.
[64] Kooijmans (n 57) 746.
[65] See generally P Mahoney, 'Judicial Activism and Judicial Self-Restraint in the European Court of Human Rights: Two Sides of the Same Coin' (1990) 11 HRLJ 57.
[66] ibid.
[67] ibid.
[68] ibid.

work together within judicial decision-making in a 'coherent path of continuity'.[69] Activism and restraint are 'two sides of the same coin',[70] both aimed at giving the law a coherent structure.

Judge Mahoney's description seems to be the one best suited to the nature of the international judicial function and the legal system within which it acts. Viewing the two notions in terms of their complementarity is an effective way of understanding activism and restraint, transcending traditional black-and-white definitions to better reflect the true nature of the judicial process. After all, 'rules are not picked from trees':[71] even if the legal principles are clear and the law is clearly enunciated, 'someone' will have had to develop them – a competent law-determining agency, a court.[72]

4.2 *Identifying Activism and Restraint within the Overall Context of International Law*

With the above in mind, identifying activism and restraint remains a difficult exercise, as observed through the lack of any such theoretical framework within the literature on international law.[73] Further, identifying activism and restraint must be placed within the overall context of the international legal system, whose characteristics are inseparably linked to how and why certain decisions may or may not be considered instances of judicial activism.

One must first recall that the international legal system is considered to be a system of states:[74] the settlement of disputes remains largely dependent on the consent of the states involved,[75] and the exercise of jurisdiction by international courts and tribunals is not integrated into an institutionalised and mandatory legal system as at the domestic level.[76] It must also be recalled that states have the upper hand by choosing whether to create a court in the first place, by deciding on the nature of the

[69] ibid.

[70] ibid.

[71] Weeramantry (n 46) 312; BN Cardozo, *The Nature of the Judicial Process* (Yale UP 1939) 103.

[72] See generally Weeramantry (n 46).

[73] Only two exceptions (an insufficient number) can be found: F Zarbiyev 'Judicial Activism in International Law: A Conceptual Framework for Analysis' (2012) 3 JIDS 247 and Pair (n 60).

[74] A Cassese, *International Law* (2nd edn, Oxford University Press 2004) 3.

[75] ibid 4.

[76] Gaeta (n 29).

agreement that will institute a court or tribunal[77] and the substantive law which will apply[78] and, in most instances and particularly important here, by choosing to be a party to a case.

As a result, the first indisputable factor pointing to judicial activism would be a ruling that explicitly goes against the will of the parties and the principle of state consent. Ruling against the accepted law in force would be an example of this, but so too would be deciding against what states have previously explicitly accepted as the law, be it in treaties and conventions, statements, public opinions or judicial proceedings.[79] Next, and flowing from this first factor, judicial activism involves modifying the law from what it was previously accepted to be. The focus here would be on the legal rules or principles themselves and their amendment, as opposed to the will or the consent of the state. It could involve departing from previous interpretations of a principle that were already accepted as law in such a way as to create incoherence or uncertainty. These are all indications of a judge who is 'making sense'[80] of new law, possibly due to dissatisfaction with existing law, the law which was, by and large, already recognised and accepted by that system of states. A third indication of activism, which is somewhat related to the former two, would consist in changing a judicial process or procedure in flagrant opposition to accepted customary practice.

Another characteristic of the international legal system, which leads to our next criterion, is the material incompleteness of international law.[81] This is the presumption that international law, by its very nature, has not evolved or become detailed enough to be seen as a complete system of laws, rules or norms,[82] thus leaving huge gaps in legal regulation. Despite this, legal certainty through judicial decisions is required. The act of deriving legal reasoning from abstract ideas or principles without any necessary legal certainty as to their true definition could reflect judicial activism but also restraint, as it might lead the judge to refrain from deciding.[83] However far-fetched they may be, judicial decisions are

77 Cassese (n 74) 170.
78 ibid.
79 ILC, 'Draft Conclusions (n 4) 10.
80 Mahoney (n 65).
81 This plays on the words of Lauterpacht, who in H Lauterpacht, *The Function of Law in the International Community* (Oxford University Press 2011) ch 5, referred to 'the formal and material completeness of international law'.
82 This is in fact an idea put forward in HLA Hart *The Concept of Law* (2nd end, Clarendon 1994).
83 Talmon (n 11) 434.

expected to ensure certainty, and coherent reasoning is needed to support the ultimate decision rendered. Equally, a clearly result-oriented decision, either lacking in judicial interpretation or pulling a rabbit out of its hat, can be a characteristic of both activism and restraint, since the result sought could indicate the mental state of the court in taking the decision and its intention to either expand or retract the law. Finally, refusing to interpret or expand upon a legal point raised by the parties or to even carry out any interpretation would be an indication of judicial restraint, as Lauterpacht and Kooijmans noted.

5 Recognition of the Indispensable Parties Principle

Although the indispensable parties principle has come to be accepted as a governing principle or conventional wisdom in international law, its true origins remain controversial.[84] The introduction of the principle in its current state occurred in the case of *Monetary Gold*, where the ICJ held that it 'will not exercise its jurisdiction where the legal interests of a third State "would not only be affected by a decision, but would form the very subject-matter of the decision"'.[85] In its reasoning, the ICJ turned to the principle of consent to explain its rationale, holding that 'to adjudicate . . . would run counter to a well-established principle of international law *embodied* in the Court's statute, namely, that the Court can only exercise jurisdiction over a State with its consent'[86] In other words, the ICJ found that even in a duly constituted bilateral contentious case it would not have jurisdiction if it appeared that the principal issue to be decided affected a third state which was not a party to the proceedings.[87] Even though that third state would not be bound by the court's decision,[88] it nevertheless considered that state's interests with such regard that it was precluded from exercising jurisdiction.[89] Arguably, in its attempt to protect the interests of unaware third states, the ICJ assumed a function that sought to protect the interests of the general international community.

84 Paparinskis (n 18) 217.

85 *Monetary Gold* (n 18) 17.

86 ibid (emphasis added).

87 S Rosenne, *The Law and Practice of the International Court, 1920–2005* (Brill 2006) ch 9.

88 ICJ Statute (n 88) art 59 states: 'The decision of the Court has no binding force except between the parties and in respect of that particular case.'

89 Pomson (n 20) 88.

A closer look at the language used by the ICJ is required. This is because while the ICJ alluded to an interpretation of the ICJ Statute, a reading of both the text of the Statute and the decision do not evidence such a link. In fact, even the use of the word 'embodied' seems problematic. Firstly, the term is technically unclear[90] and lacks any legal meaning. Further, the fact that the ICJ Statute is silent with regard to third parties[91] and their consent leaves it unclear as to where the court identified this principle so 'embodied'. Notably, Article 36 of the ICJ Statute that deals with consent focuses on the consent of the 'parties that refer the case to it', not that of third states.[92] Furthermore, a survey of other decisions from the same era fails to provide any indication as to the meaning of the word, even though the ICJ had proven itself capable of expanding upon legally unclear terms at the time.[93] Additionally, if the court meant to derive the *Monetary Gold* principle from the overarching principle of consent alone, it could have done so without the reference to the ICJ Statute and certainly without using the word 'embodied'. Worthy to note, at this stage, is also the previous ICJ decision in the *Corfu Channel* case, where neither the court nor the parties seemed to have had any issue with addressing the dispute in the absence of a third state, Yugoslavia.[94]

This ICJ's ambiguous language, presented with little explanation and confined to one paragraph in a nineteen-page decision, provides little understanding as to the true source of the indispensable parties principle.[95] While the court used the words 'principle of international law', it certainly does not appear to be interpreting the issue of *audi alteram partem*, a general principle of law,[96] as it did not mention the case law of the Permanent Court of International Justice or other tribunals to support its reasoning.[97] In truth, the lack of justification by the court can

[90] Paparinskis (n 18) 63.

[91] With the exception of the right to intervene under ICJ Statute (n 8) art 62.

[92] See generally Z Mollengarden and N Zamir, 'The *Monetary Gold* Principle: Back to Basics' (2021) 115 AJIL 41, 57.

[93] Paparinskis (n 18) 68, such an example being *Nottebohm (Liechtenstein v Guatemala)* (Preliminary Objection) [1953] ICJ Rep 111.

[94] *The Corfu Channel Case (United Kingdom v Albania)* (Merits) [1949] ICJ Rep 4. See discussion of the case in Paparinskis (n 18) 82 and Pomson (n 20) 93.

[95] Paparinskis (n 18) 66.

[96] Pomson (n 20) 96.

[97] For example, it could have mentioned the advisory opinion of the PCIJ in *Status of Eastern Carelia*, holding that: 'It is well established in international law that no State can, without its consent, be compelled to submit its disputes with other States either to mediation or to arbitration, or to any other kind of pacific settlement.' *Status of Eastern Carelia* (Advisory Opinion) [1923] PCIJ Rep 6.

only be interpreted as pure assertion, as pulling a rabbit out of its hat. In applying our judicial activism or judicial restraint criteria to this case, the situation gets even more complex. As already noted, a lack of justification is usually an indication of judicial restraint – something supported by Hersch Lauterpacht, who noted the 'degree of caution' with which the court decided this case.[98]

The approach taken by the Court is also result-orientated, which supports a clear activist judgment. It introduced a new abstract principle, which it claimed it found in the Statute, but did so without legal certainty since the Statute itself is silent. It ultimately transformed the issues before it into a question of third-party legal interests and introduced the 'essential parties' concept, yet unclear as to where it applied it from, which could imply a change in judicial process of the court. On the one hand, the court created a principle of protection for states not parties to a dispute; on the other, it did so by ignoring the dispute before it, rendering an ineffective judgment.

The first case of interest to have followed *Monetary Gold* was *Nicaragua,*[99] where the indispensable parties principle was pleaded by one of the parties to the dispute as one of numerous grounds for objecting to the court's jurisdiction.[100] In this instance, the court rejected the plea; dedicating a paragraph to the matter, it remarked that the 'circumstances of the *Monetary Gold* case probably represent the limit of the power of the Court to refuse to exercise its jurisdiction',[101] making it necessary for the third party to be 'truly indispensable to the pursuance of the proceedings'.[102] One may wonder whether the wording 'the limit of the power' constitutes a reaffirmation of the principle of *Monetary Gold*[103] or rather reflects the discontent of the court, at the time, with the usefulness of this principle. Due to the lack of any reasoning, as an attempt to clarify the principle in substance, a restraint approach can be detected. However, considering the numerous other matters decided upon in the *Nicaragua* decision, the issue of the non-application of the *Monetary Gold* principle would seem inconsequential.

98 Lauterpacht (n 2).

99 *Military and Paramilitary Activities in and against Nicaragua* (*Nicaragua v United States of America*) (Jurisdiction and Admissibility) [1984] ICJ Rep 392.

100 ibid 8–9.

101 ibid [88].

102 ibid.

103 Pomson (n 20) 100.

The principle was examined again in the case of *Certain Phosphate Lands in Nauru.*[104] Here, the ICJ held that while a decision in the case might have implications for a third party, 'no finding in respect of that legal situation will be needed as a basis of the Court's decision'.[105] This was in contrast to *Monetary Gold*, where determination of the legal interests of the third party would have been a prerequisite to decide upon the dispute.[106] In order to create a distinction, the court seems to have treated the issue in the *Nauru* case as one of *degree* of the possible implications for the third State,[107] expanding the principle of indispensable parties through an interpretation alone and without even having applied it, and despite the claim in *Nicaragua* that those were the limits of its application. This idea was clarified in the separate opinion of Judge Shahabuddeen, who noted that 'the test is not merely one of sameness of subject-matter, but also one of whether . . . the Court is making a judicial determination of the responsibility of a non-party State'.[108] Here, there seems to be an allusion to the principle of consent, rather than an interpretation of the Statute as was alluded to in *Monetary Gold*, yet the court makes no such direct reference. In any event, a comparison of the facts of the two cases, *Nauru* and *Monetary Gold*, and their inherent similarities make it difficult to understand the resulting decision in each case.[109]

The question that preoccupied the court seems to have been the *intensity* of the effect of the judgment on the legal interests of an absent state.[110] This shows a court attempting to translate *Nicaragua*'s allusions to 'appropriate circumstances' and 'limits' into a more judicially administrable test,[111] as suggested by Judge Shahabuddeen's explanation. Accordingly, it would seem that the court borrowed its reasoning from

[104] *Certain Phosphate Lands in Nauru* (*Nauru v Australia*) (Preliminary Objections) [1992] ICJ Rep 240.

[105] ibid.

[106] *Nicaragua* (n 99) [88]; N Zamir, 'The Applicability of the *Monetary Gold* Principle in International Arbitration' (2017) 33 Arb Int'l 523, 527 n 14, quoting Bola Ajibola; Pomson (n 20) 100.

[107] H Thirlway, *The Law and Procedure of the International Court of Justice* (Oxford University Press 2013) ch 1; Mollengarden and Zamir (n 92) 52, quoting, in particular, Judge Schwebel.

[108] *Certain Phosphate Lands in Nauru* (n 104) Separate Opinion of Judge Shahabudeen 270, 296.

[109] Mollengarden and Zamir (n 92) 52.

[110] ibid 52; *Certain Phosphate Lands in Nauru* (n 104) Separate Opinion of Judge Schwebel 329, 335.

[111] Mollengarden and Zamir (n 92) 52.

domestic law,[112] possibly through normative deduction,[113] by introducing a form of joint and several responsibility into the reasoning of international law: while the breach was committed jointly by different states, it does not preclude the admissibility of the claim against one of those responsible actors.[114] This is arguably to protect the public function the court wishes to fulfil. The court's judgment is an analysis, not of the ICJ Statute but instead of the practice of the court's previous decision, an indication that it was interpreting its very own practice to reach a conclusion in the present case.

In considering the activism or restraint criteria, we can see this as a clearly result-oriented decision through borrowing principles from other legal systems, which indicates a proactive tendency on the part of the court. Arguably, in 'clarifying' the principle, the court seems to have caused, nevertheless, further confusion as to when the indispensable parties principle is applied, opening the door to future inconsistency, which can possibly imply a modification of the law or the procedure in question. This is furthered through the four dissenting opinions to the judgment, including both the president and the vice-president of the ICJ at the time,[115] one of whom noted that 'the protection afforded the absent States by Article 59 in the quite exceptional situation of this case would be notional rather than real'.[116]

Despite its activism, the *Nauru* case failed to establish an 'administrable test' for the principle,[117] as became evident in the case of *East Timor*,[118] where the ICJ attempted to build on its *Monetary Gold* analysis by changing the narrative yet again. In contrast to the treatment of the matter as one of degree seen in the *Nauru* case, the case of *East Timor* considered a temporal precondition instead[119] – namely, by holding that it would first have to decide on that third state's actions (or inactions), it could 'not make such a determination in the absence of the consent of [the third party]'.[120] In determining that the treaty-making capacity of

[112] See the discussion on joint and several jurisdiction in Paparinskis (n 18) 83.
[113] Description of normative deduction can be found in Bos (n 4) and Talmon (n 11).
[114] Paparinskis (n 18) 83.
[115] Dissenting Opinions by President Jennings, Vice-President Oda, Judge Ago and Judge Schwebel.
[116] *Certain Phosphate Lands in Nauru* (n 104) Separate Opinion of Judge Schwebel 329, 342.
[117] Mollengarden and Zamir (n 92).
[118] *East Timor* (*Portugal v Australia*) [1995] ICJ Rep 90.
[119] Mollengarden and Zamir (n 92) 54.
[120] *East Timor* (n 118) [28].

the third, absent, state would form an integral part of its decision, it effectively put a stop to the trend of rejecting the *Monetary Gold* principle. It ultimately delivered a narrow interpretation of the *Monetary Gold* principle, without any reasoning as to why it considered the issue in temporal terms rather than as a matter of degree.[121]

This is clearly a result-oriented approach, whereby the decision itself can be regarded as a decision not to decide, turning the reasoning back to one of assertion. Although the court did engage in some analysis of the submissions of the parties, it rejected them without providing an explanation. It based its rejection on consent rather than on the ICJ Statute, which indicates an interpretation of an unwritten principle (though without any clear indications from the court, this remains speculation on the part of the present author). This case drew reactions from within the court in the form of two dissenting opinions,[122] which brought up the unresolved issue of the *erga omnes* nature of the subject matter.[123] By again modifying the process whereby the indispensable parties principle is identified, the ICJ went around its *Nauru* decision and returned to *Monetary Gold*, which resulted in greater lack of coherence regarding the principle.[124] The refusal of the court to decide on *erga omnes* rights, which involve a public concern, leaves questions as to the role of the court in this matter.[125] The principle was used to limit the possible public function the ICJ could have assumed as the principal judicial organ of the UN,[126] considering its widespread jurisdictional powers.[127] The court furthermore elaborated the principle abstractly and without any legal certainty, which was a further indication of the restraint with which it acted. The lack of interpretation and any indication as to the source of the temporal element increased the already existing ambiguity over when the *Monetary Gold* principle applies or does not apply. Finally, this refusal to rule on a highly controversial matter shows judicial restraint par excellence.

121 Zamir (n 106) 527.
122 *East Timor* (n 118) Dissenting Opinion of Judge Weeramantry 139, 224.
123 ibid; Kooijmans (n 57).
124 See discussion of case generally in Mollengarden and Zamir (n 92).
125 It is beyond the purpose of this paper to speculate as to why it wished to leave these questions unanswered.
126 ICJ Statute (n 8) art 1; UN Charter art 92.
127 ICJ Statute (n 8) art 36(1): 'The jurisdiction of the Court comprises all cases which the parties refer to it and all matters specially provided for in the Charter of the United Nations or in treaties and conventions in force.'

6 Indispensable Parties and Other International Tribunals

6.1 The Principle Applied

As we have seen, one measure of judicial effectiveness is to consider whether the decisions of international courts are harmonised at a systemic level, meaning that principles of law accepted and endorsed by some courts become accepted as applying to other judicial institutions across the international stage. Telling, in this regard, are the decisions concerning the indispensable parties principle before other tribunals and courts.

Notable is the case of *Larsen* v. *Hawaiian Kingdom,*[128] which is the only case in which the principle was applied in such a manner as to prevent an international tribunal from exercising its jurisdiction.[129] The arbitral tribunal, constituted under the auspices of the Permanent Court of Arbitration (PCA), ultimately dismissed the case for lack of authority to 'exercise jurisdiction over a State unless that State has given its consent to that jurisdiction'.[130] It upheld this test because the tribunal 'operates within the general confines of public international law',[131] thus extending the application of the principle beyond the ICJ's mandate and beyond what the ICJ had pronounced on the principle. The tribunal can be said to have added to the definition of the *Monetary Gold* case, going beyond what the ICJ had previously considered to be a matter of the ICJ Statute, in a hint of judicial activism. Another possible consideration to take into account here is the fact that the parties' real motive may have not been to resolve the dispute between them but rather to raise publicity for the cause of the Hawaiian nationalist movement by having the tribunal render an opinion on the legal status of Hawaii.[132] The tribunal's choice to uphold the principle may have been heavily influenced by the need to reject the case in any way possible.

The indispensable parties principle was also raised in the *South China Sea Arbitration (Philippines/China),*[133] where an intervening third state, Malaysia, asked the tribunal to reject jurisdiction on the basis that it might affect its rights and obligations as an absent third state. Without

[128] *Lance Paul Larsen v The Hawaiian Kingdom* (Final Award) (2001) PCA.
[129] Pomson (n 20) 104.
[130] *Larsen* (n 128) [11.17].
[131] ibid.
[132] Pomson (n 20) 104.
[133] *The South China Sea Arbitration* (*The Republic of Philippines v The People's Republic of China*) (Final Award) (2016) PCA.

providing any explanation beyond the decision of the ICJ in *Nicaragua*, the tribunal took the view that Malaysia 'overstated' the *Monetary Gold* principle, as the 'more expansive reading would impermissibly constrain the practical ability of courts and tribunals to carry out their function'.[134] Remarkably, in contrast to the narrow interpretation the ICJ applied in *East Timor*, this tribunal saw an expansive reading as *limiting* the judicial function. Clarifying that the relevant issues in the case concerned 'areas to which Malaysia makes no claim',[135] it held the latter's interests were not affected. Interestingly, the difference in reasoning between the ICJ's shaping of the rule as we know it today and the tribunal's approach to is suggestive of activism, leading to dis-harmonisation and, by consequence, ambiguity.

Mention must also be made of the *M/V Norstar* case before the International Tribunal for the Law of the Sea (ITLOS),[136] where the tribunal 'acknowledge[d] that the notion of indispensable party is a well-established procedural rule in international judicial proceedings'.[137] It nevertheless refrained from applying the principle in that specific case,[138] leaving an unexplained reference to the principle, insufficient for deeper examination.

6.2 *Lack of Relevance of the Principle*

Although the indispensable parties principle has, by and large, been accepted as well established, the role of the ICJ in creating a new rule of law remains questionable, as its role as a rather reluctant lawmaker arises. This is particularly pertinent when one considers that certain other international courts have rejected the relevance of the principle. In this vein, we can see the complete rejection of the principle in the opinion of Advocate General Wathelet in the *Western Sahara Campaign* v. *United Kingdom*[139]case before the Court of Justice of the European Union (CJEU), who rejected its application as it would allegedly automatically preclude the possible examination or review of international agreements

[134] ibid [640].
[135] ibid.
[136] *M/V 'Norstar' (Panama v Italy)* (Preliminary Objections, Order of 15 March 2016) ITLOS Rep 2016, 44.
[137] ibid [172].
[138] ibid [173].
[139] C-266/16 *Western Sahara Campaign UK* Opinion of Advocate General Wathelet [2018] ECLI:EU:C:2018:1.

between the EU and third states.[140] The Advocate General's lack of analysis suggests that he was exercising judicial restraint. Prior to that, a World Trade Organization (WTO) panel also held that there is no concept of 'essential parties' in WTO law,[141] despite examining the case law of the ICJ and using it as evidence to elaborate on the content of the principle.[142] Most recently, in 2021, the International Criminal Court refused to apply the principle when requested, on the grounds that its jurisdiction did not concern inter-state disputes but dealt instead with natural persons.[143] Without a doubt, these decisions indicate the failure of the *Monetary Gold* principle to achieve support within the international judicial community both in terms of fostering harmonisation and as a new rule of international law.

The European Court of Human Rights (the ECtHR) has also taken a differentiated approach to this principle. In the case of *Bankovic*[144] the ECtHR ruled out any need to decide on an objection raised that was based explicitly on the *Monetary Gold* principle[145] as it declined jurisdiction over other issues in the case that apparently took precedence over any rights deriving from the absent third state principle. Similarly and maybe particularly tellingly is the fact that the same court has had no difficulty providing detailed consideration of the conduct of states not parties to its proceedings or sometimes not even members of the Council of Europe.[146] This, for instance, occurred when the facts of the case pointed to a possible violation of the Convention, as most famously occurred in *Soering*,[147] where the court decided against the extradition of the applicant to a third state because it was quite possible that that absent third state would violate the Convention. Interestingly, the question of the essential third party was not even raised, despite the court having explicitly taken decisions in that regard. It is thus evident that this

[140] ibid [57].

[141] WTO, *Turkey: Restriction on Imports of Textiles and Clothing Products – Report of the Panel* (31 May 1999) WT/DS34/R [9.10].

[142] ibid [9.8]–[9.11].

[143] *Situation in the State of Palestine*, Decision on the 'Prosecution request pursuant to article 19(3) for a ruling on the Court's territorial jurisdiction in Palestine' (5 February 2021) ICC-01/18 [58]–[60].

[144] *Banković and ors v Belgium and ors*, App no 52207/99 (Admissibility) (ECtHR, 12 December 2001).

[145] ibid [83].

[146] Paparinskis (n 18) 77.

[147] *Soering v United Kingdom* App no 14038/88 (ECtHR, 7 July 1989).

was a result-oriented decision made with the intention of solidifying the law and as such is indicative of judicial activism.

7 Effectiveness or Ambiguity?

7.1 Consolidation of the Indispensable Parties Principle

As seen in the Introduction, the interaction between the use of certain principles of customary international law and judicial activism can yield an uncomfortable relationship. This is one where the inherent tension between custom's recognition of unwritten law through the identification of state practice and *opinio juris* and judicial activism's 'creative reasoning rather than strict application of the law' seek to co-exist.[148] An analysis of whether the indispensable parties principle as identified in *Monetary Gold* qualifies as custom lies outside the confines of the present discussion. However, it is interesting to note the overlap between custom and activism in the judicial process that enables the principle to be characterised as one of customary law. Although the principle had appeared in international decisions prior to *Monetary Gold*, the ICJ seems to have pulled a rabbit out of its hat when applying it in that case. The existence of prior references to the rule, of which the court made no mention, makes its approach a form of continuity in the judicial interpretation of this principle rather than a new apparition altogether. However, its vague terminology left the source of the rule open[149] and gave way to its subsequent evolution – a clear lack of coherence and consistency in the decision.

Additionally, it cannot be denied that, despite not having been applied by tribunals, the rule has been relied on repeatedly by states, which indicates its acceptance as law and in practice.[150] Indeed, it has also been argued that the lack of objections to a string of judicial decisions

148 Pair (n 60).

149 On the possible sources of the principle, see Paparinskis (n 18); Pomson (n 20).

150 See Special Tribunal for Lebanon, *In the Matter of El Sayed*, Decision on Appeal of Pre-Trial Judge's Order Regarding Jurisdiction and Standing, Appeals Chamber (10 November 2010) CHIAC/2010102 [47], where the tribunal examined how a lack of objection could be deemed acceptance as law and existence of practice. Further examples of ICJ cases referring to the indispensable parties principle include *Maritime Delimitation and Territorial Questions between Qatar and Bahrain (Qatar v Bahrain)* (Verbatim Record CR 2000/12) [25]; *Obligations Concerning Negotiations Relating to Cessation of the Nuclear Arms Race and to Nuclear Disarmament (Marshall Islands v Pakistan)* (Jurisdiction and Admissibility) (Counter-Memorial of Pakistan, 1 December 2015).

may signify support for a positive customary rule.[151] What this analysis has shown is a judicial process of thought which, through activism and restraint, has been able to create what can best be described as a principle of customary *procedural* law.

7.2 The Judicial Function and the Indispensable Parties Principle

Returning to the effectiveness or ambiguity of international courts in the application of the indispensable parties principle, and since its re-introduction in international legal discourse through the *Monetary Gold* case, there are several observations that can be made.

There is a very important distinction that need to be drawn between, on one hand, the cases where the principle was applied, and, on the other, the cases where the principle was recognised but not applied. In *Monetary Gold* we saw that the ICJ sought to uphold an indisputable public function, which was to protect the interests of third states not parties to the proceedings. It did so, even if this meant rejecting the entire case and despite the parties having consented to its jurisdiction. We must also consider the utility of leaving dispute unaddressed. A case in point is *East Timor*, where questions of *erga omnes* and self-determination arose. As former ICJ judge Kooijmans established, restraint is reflected in instances where the court refuses to decide on a matter which is highly controversial, as happened in this case. The ICJ did not even attempt to provide an answer to these long-standing questions, which would have benefitted the international legal scene – something it was perfectly qualified to do, given its wide jurisdictional powers. Even though reference was made to Article 59 of the ICJ Statute, according to which the decision would be binding only upon the states parties to the proceedings, the ICJ was nonetheless unwilling to decide upon the legal interests of any third state. The refusal to decide was clearly a policy decision, as it was also for the PCA tribunal in *Larsen*, where a decision would have promoted the wrong political gains.

By contrast, and quite interestingly, we can also see a public function in deciding on the dispute, as was apparent in *Nicaragua* and *Certain Phosphates of Nauru*, so much so that in this latter case the court considered that even though other states could also be held liable, it was sufficient that liability arose for that one state party alone. This was an interesting reasoning, outside the bounds of what had been previously

[151] See Paparinskis (n 18) 220.

accepted. Notable also are the approaches taken in other courts. Advocate General Wathelet's comment in *Western Sahara* was indicative of the very bounds of the principle, yet also demonstrates the restraint implicit in a refusal to decide. What if a dispute arising out of a convention with a third party only affects the legal interests of a member state of the EU? Similarly, the rejection of the principle in the *South China Sea* arbitration and by the ECtHR in *Bankovic* show a public function quite different from the one assumed by the ICJ in those two cases in accepting the indispensable party principle. In truth, we can see how the reasoning of the tribunals alluded to greater public benefit in deciding rather than not deciding the cases.

As already observed, judicial effectiveness also calls for systemic harmonisation at the international level – something the indispensable party principle also fails to meet. If there is any consistency in the decisions examined, it ironically lies in their disharmony, for the manner in which the principle is applied, whether within a single court or across several courts. This is evidenced, for example, in the lack of coherent or continuous reasoning across the decisions of the ICJ. At the same time the principle was openly accepted by most international courts and tribunals as an established rule of international law, despite not being applied. If we come back to the utility of the principle and its effectiveness at the international level, the lack of its use could be indicatory of its lack of any effectiveness. If the idea is to create a form of 'transnational public order'[152] whereby all the courts and tribunals share a set of principles, even at the procedural level, creating predictability and coherence at the international level, then the indispensable party rule certainly does not meet this standard.

Turning finally to the judge's role as reluctant lawmaker, the question arises as to whether, in adjudicating *Monetary Gold,* or even *East Timor*, the ICJ has made law. The wording of the *Monetary Gold* judgment alludes to a principle already accepted in international law – something that could be reflected in previous decisions of international courts and tribunals, as seen above, despite the fact that the court did not mention any. Conceivably, the principle may have existed as one of custom, without further substance as to its content. Going beyond the acceptance of the principle, whatever its source might be, subsequent ICJ cases attempted to create a methodology through which this principle would be applicable. However, this methodology, or 'law', has been rejected

[152] Peters (n 42) 696, referring to *'ordre public transnational'*.

repeatedly by other international courts and on most occasions by the ICJ itself. This is where the question of methodology in custom becomes even more important: does the occasional recognition, but not application, of a rule, make law?

8 Conclusion

Coming back to the use activism and restraint to drive customary international law forward to yield effectiveness, there are numerous questions posed within this analysis in that regard. Going back to the elements of the judicial function, the preceding paragraph has indicated the very inability of the *Monetary Gold* principle to create judicial effectiveness.[153] Instead, what can be seen is ambiguity, lack of coherence and a clear rejection of the principle by several courts.

The lack of certainty over both the source and true application of the indispensable third party principle leaves much to be desired. The ICJ's assertion that the principle exists as embodied in the ICJ Statute and the subsequent recognition and evolution of its methodology raise questions about the relationship between customary norms and the use of activism to identify them. The lack of judicial reasoning points to the principle being used to avoid larger questions of law raised by the facts of a particular case. Such reticence is by and large an ingredient of judicial ambiguity and ineffectiveness. Although effectiveness may arguably have made an appearance in the original *Monetary Gold* case, depending on one's perspective it appears to have been short-lived.

In conclusion, while a clear answer certainly cannot be provided through the examination of just one principle, the use of mere assertion, often under the guise of CIL, certainly alludes to the use of custom as a tool by which judicial activism manifests itself in excess.

[153] This would be in line with what Mollengarden and Zamir (n 92) argue, in particular when they support the idea that 'that the Monetary Gold principle is irreconcilable with the ICJ Statute's jurisdictional architecture'.

9

Judicial Dialogue between International Courts in the Interpretation of Customary International Human Rights Law

SILVIANA COCAN

1 Introduction

The identification and interpretation of customary international law (CIL) by both domestic and international courts and tribunals has been thoroughly studied in legal scholarship. However, little is known about the engagement in judicial dialogue by, in particular, international human rights courts and the impact that it has on the interpretation of custom in this particular field. In the international legal order, international bodies protecting human rights were conceived to be formally independent, in contrast with domestic tribunals governed by a hierarchical principle of organisation. Indeed, except for the International Court of Justice (ICJ), which has general jurisdiction in matters related to international law, international courts exercise limited jurisdiction, usually determined by a constitutive treaty. Many judicial and quasi-judicial bodies co-exist independently of each other across the many legal systems that protect human rights, be it globally or at regional level. Despite the horizontality of this ordering, judicial dialogue has emerged as a spontaneous practice in the case law of international courts, part of a larger judicial globalization phenomenon. Judicial globalization involves interacting judicially 'across, above and below borders, exchanging ideas and cooperating in cases involving national as much international law'.[1] Although judicial globalization is becoming more common, binding precedent still does not exist in the international

[1] A Slaughter, 'Judicial Globalization' (2000) 40 VJIL 1104.

legal order,[2] rather, judicial dialogue has arisen within the context of the jurisdictionalisation of international human rights law at both domestic and international levels.

There is no universal agreement on the meaning of judicial dialogue. Judicial dialogue can be defined as merely the spontaneous reference to the case law of other courts and tribunals by a particular judicial body, whether domestic or international. It can be described also as a comparative and interpretative approach to cross-cutting issues faced by multiple legal systems – this is the case with the protection of human rights. Indeed, judicial dialogue can be understood as a practice engaged in spontaneously by courts, either in a sporadic fashion through occasional references to the case law of other courts or as part of a more systematic approach in which references to foreign case law are used repeatedly and consistently over time in the process of interpretation. For the purpose of this contribution, the notion of judicial dialogue encompasses the notion of cross-referencing,[3] These terms are used interchangeably to describe the reference to case law or international instruments that are outside the international court's own judicial system and that are used for interpretation purposes.[4]

References to international instruments and to other courts' case law are often intertwined, as the interpreter tends first to contextualise the legal norms within the broader system of analogous rules that are part of other systems, then afterwards refers to or quotes extensively the relevant case law which interprets the analogous rules. Therefore, the practice of

[2] G Guillaume, 'The Use of Precedent by International Judges and Arbitrators' (2011) 2 JIDS 5.

[3] A Jones, 'Judicial Cross-Referencing and the Identity of the International Criminal Court' (2018) 43 NCJIL 72; E Maculan, 'Judicial Definition of Torture as a Paradigm of Cross-Fertilisation: Combining Harmonisation and Expansion' (2015) 84(3) NJIL 456.

[4] S Cocan, *Le dialogue entre juridictions et quasi-juridictions internationales de protection des droits de la personne: L'exemple de la prohibition de la torture et autres peines ou traitements cruels, inhumains ou dégradants* (LGDJ 2020); EF Mac-Gregor, 'What Do We Mean When We Talk about Judicial Dialogue? Reflections of a Judge of the Inter-American Court of Human Rights' (2017) 30 HHRJ 89; C Burchard, 'Judicial Dialogue in Light of Comparative Criminal Law and Justice' in P Lobba and T Mariniello (eds), *Judicial Dialogue on Human Rights: The Practice of International Criminal Tribunals* (Brill 2015) 56; J Allard and L Van Eynde, 'Le dialogue des jurisprudences comme source du droit: Arguments entre idéalisation et scepticisme' in I Hachez (ed), *Les sources du droit revisitées*, vol 3: *Normativités concurrentes* (Anthemis 2013); C Romano 'Deciphering the Grammar of the International Jurisprudential Dialogue' (2009) 41(4) NYUJILP 755; B Frydman, 'Conclusion: Le dialogue des juges et la perspective idéale d'une justice universelle' in *Le dialogue des juges: Actes du colloque organisé le 28 avril 2006 à l'Université Libre de Bruxelles* (Bruylant 2007).

judicial dialogue leads to a contextualization of rules within the international legal order as a whole and the taking account of judicial practice and the interpretation given by other courts to analogous rules in the field of international human rights law. Firstly, it sets out the basis for a normative contextualisation, interpreting legal rules protecting human rights within the broader context of international instruments such as treaties, customs, soft law documents and general principles of international law. Secondly, it facilitates systemic contextualisation in the process of interpreting human rights obligations through the overall logic and perspective of the universal and regional systems while taking into account their common coherence and scope based on the universality of human rights in spite of each legal system's independence. On the one hand, judicial dialogue is a tool for normative contextualisation of rules protecting human rights, whether written or unwritten, according to the interpretation of their scope and content given by other international bodies in comparable legal matters. On the other hand, the practice of judicial dialogue reflects the search for a systemic contextualisation that would anchor the interpretation process in the light of other analogous systems – as all the systems protecting human rights in the international legal order have a common purpose based on an overarching principle that is the limitation of state power through the promotion and the protection of rights inherent to all human beings, without discrimination.

When the interpreter sets out the basis for normative and systemic contextualisation by taking into account external references when engaging in the interpretation process, the approach follows the following steps: (1) the interpreter compares two analogous rules and realises that other judicial bodies have interpreted the same rules in other legal disputes; (2) this comparative approach leads the interpreter to take into account in the interpretation process the general coherence of the foreign system protecting human rights; (3) the interpreter evaluates if references to the rules and the case law established in this analogous system outside the interpreter's own judicial system could be relevant – according to principles, rules and methods commonly admitted in that particular system; and finally (4) the interpreter possibly decides to incorporate external elements such as judicial decisions of other systems if they meet the objective of the interpreter's legal reasoning, which is subject to constraints imposed by the interpreter's own system. Given all this, the belief that fragmentation negatively affects international law is perhaps exaggerated, at least insofar as international human rights law is concerned. Indeed, the aim of universality and the interdependent character of the rights affirmed in the Universal Declaration of Human Rights in 1948,[5] leads one to think that the universal and regional systems protecting human rights are more likely to have practices in common and intersections, making combinative and overarching interpretations not only possible but inevitable.[6]

Section 2 discusses the role of judicial dialogue in the identification and the interpretation of customary international human rights law. It highlights how customary rules of human rights law arise through the practice of international courts as they interpret written provisions codified in universal or regional instruments while taking into account other courts' case law. Section 3 addresses the issue of judicial dialogue as an interpretation approach that ensures judicial objectivity and judicial dialogue's impact on customary international human rights law. In conclusion, Section 4 provides a forward-looking analysis of how judicial dialogue may play a role in ensuring a higher degree of normative convergence on cross-cutting issues in the protection of human rights.

2 The Use of Judicial Dialogue in the Identification and the Interpretation of Customary International Human Rights Law

In the field of international human rights law, the identification and interpretation of customary rules are often interlinked. International courts interpret international instruments, state practice and *opinio juris* in order to ascertain whether there exists a general rule belonging to customary international law alongside the written rule codified in a treaty. For instance, judicial dialogue has been used as a tool in the identification and interpretation of *jus cogens* norms protecting human rights, such as the prohibition of torture, which is also part of CIL. By engaging in judicial dialogue, judges have taken into account the case law of other courts to identify customary rules crystallised through the practice of international bodies. This process allowed the judges to conclude that the binding nature of provisional measures has become a common practice across many systems of human rights protection.

5 UNGA Res 217A(III) (10 December 1948) UN Doc A/RES/3/217 A, 71.

6 L Burgorgue-Larsen, '"Decompartmentalization": The Key Technique for Interpreting Regional Human Rights Treaties' (2018) 16(1) IJCL 187.

2.1 *Blurred Lines between the Identification and the Interpretation of Customary International Human Rights Law*

2.1.1 General Considerations on the Identification and the Interpretation of Customary Rules

A distinction is not always clearly drawn in human rights case law between the recognition of a written norm as customary and its judicial interpretation. If the rule is codified in a treaty that is the source of the judicial body's jurisdiction, the existence of the rule is not in question, and yet the rule needs to be interpreted before it is applied to a specific factual situation. If we are in the presence of an unwritten norm that might be considered customary international human rights law, the judicial body establishes, at a precise moment, that a rule has become customary because of widespread ratification of relevant international instruments, state practice and *opinio juris* while also taking into account other relevant materials such as case law, soft law instruments, resolutions, reports of international institutions and legal doctrine. Through this process, the rule is identified as being part of customary law and binding on states without prior or explicit consent. Within this framework, international courts not only evaluate state practice and *opinio juris* in identifying a customary rule, but very often include references to fundamental values, considerations of humanity and the case law of other courts, whether domestic or international, so as to clarify the content and the scope of international obligations.

The International Law Commission (ILC) highlighted in its 2018 report on the identification of customary international law[7] that it is necessary to ascertain the presence of two elements: state practice and *opinio juris*. The report includes an assessment of evidence indicative of each element.[8] The ILC examined state conduct and state practice in order to determine the existence of a customary rule[9]. It has also stated that '[d]ecisions of international courts and tribunals, in particular of the International Court of Justice, concerning the existence and content of rules of customary international law are a subsidiary means for the

[7] ILC, 'Fifth Report on Identification of Customary International Law' (30 April–1 June 2018 and 2 July–10 August 2018) UN Doc A/CN.4/717 paras 96–100.

[8] ibid, Annex: 'Draft conclusions adopted on first reading, with the Special Rapporteur's suggested changes', Conclusions 1–3.

[9] ibid, Annex, Conclusion 5: 'State practice consists of conduct of the State, whether in the exercise of its executive, legislative, judicial or other functions.'

determination of such rules'.[10] The ILC pointed out that the process of determining the existence and content of customary rules could also take into account decisions of national courts, but that they would have a less important role, depending on the context.[11]

This acknowledgement on the identification of customary rules has specific implications in the field of human rights. Indeed, the practice of international tribunals and the emergence of customary international human rights law mark a reversal of the logic informing the process of identifying customary rules. In contrast to other fields of international law, in which customary law appeared first and was codified afterwards in binding treaties, 'in international human rights law, custom did not precede treaty, it followed it'.[12] Consequently, normative convergence in the practice of human rights bodies may lead to cross-cutting rules that are common to all the systems, whether at universal or regional level, and which could also be part of positive law in domestic legal orders. It can reveal the substantive interdependence of international obligations laid down in the case law of international courts to protect human rights. The way in which the courts' case law and interpretative statements have contributed to the process of identifying customary rules can be illustrated by considering the scope and content of peremptory norms.

2.1.2 The Intersection between the Identification and the Interpretation of Human Rights and *Jus Cogens* Norms

Although Article 53 of the Vienna Convention on the Law of Treaties[13] (VCLT) clarified what is meant by *jus cogens* norms in international law, no concrete examples were given of these norms, leaving it up to international bodies to define what these norms are. For instance, in 1994, in its General Comment 24, the Human Rights Committee observed: 'Reservations that offend peremptory norms would not be compatible with the object and purpose of the Covenant. Although treaties that are mere exchanges of obligations between States allow them to reserve *inter*

[10] ibid, para 99 ('it seems difficult to deny that greater caution is called for when seeking to rely on decisions of national courts, which may reflect a particular national perspective and may not have international law expertise available to them').

[11] ibid.

[12] WA Schabas, *The Customary International Law of Human Rights* (Oxford University Press 2021) 2.

[13] Vienna Convention on the Law of Treaties (adopted 23 May 1969, entered into force 27 January 1980) 1155 UNTS 331.

se application of rules of general international law, it is otherwise in human rights treaties, which are for the benefit of persons within their jurisdiction.'[14] In the Committee's view, 'provisions in the Covenant that represent customary international law (and *a fortiori* when they have the character of peremptory norms) may not be the subject of reservations.'[15] The Human Rights Committee lists the customary rules found in the Covenant as follows:

> Accordingly, a State may not reserve the right to engage in slavery, to torture, to subject persons to cruel, inhuman or degrading treatment or punishment, to arbitrarily deprive persons of their lives, to arbitrarily arrest and detain persons, to deny freedom of thought, conscience and religion, to presume a person guilty unless he proves his innocence, to execute pregnant women or children, to permit the advocacy of national, racial or religious hatred, to deny to persons of marriageable age the right to marry, or to deny to minorities the right to enjoy their own culture, profess their own religion, or use their own language. And while reservations to particular clauses of Article 14 may be acceptable, a general reservation to the right to a fair trial would not be.[16]

However, in its subsequent general comments, the Human Rights Committee did not restate this conclusion nor renew this affirmation concerning customary rules that cannot be subject to any reservations. Furthermore, no other human rights body has made a similar statement declaring all these human rights to be *jus cogens*. Therefore, it is difficult to identify with certainty the customary rules of human rights that are both part of positive law, alongside conventional provisions, and have a peremptory character.

In this context, identification and interpretation of customary rules can be seen as 'interconnected judicial operations'[17] that are explicitly differentiated throughout the process of legal reasoning. As international courts refer to customary rules in their case law, there is indeed a 'distinction between customary norms and State practice

[14] HRC, 'General comment on issues relating to reservations made upon ratification or accession to the Covenant or the Optional Protocols thereto, or in relation to declarations under article 41 of the Covenant' CCPR/C/21/Rev.1/Add.6 (1994) para 8.

[15] ibid.

[16] ibid.

[17] M Fortuna, 'Different Strings of the Same Harp: Interpretation of Customary International Rules, Their Identification and Treaty Interpretation' (2020, revised 2021) University of Groningen Faculty of Law Research Paper 48/2020, 1 <https://papers.ssrn.com/sol3/papers.cfm?abstract_id=3798476> accessed 6 March 2022.

with *opinio juris*'.[18] In scholarship it has been pointed out that, when applied to treaty law, 'interpretation and identification are two separate processes'; whereas 'with regard to customary rules, since they are unwritten, it is difficult to distinguish their identification from their interpretation'.[19] Moreover, the existence of customary international law 'is determined inductively through an examination of two elements, state practice and *opinio juris*'.[20] In other words, a state practice must implicitly be interpreted as being general and repeated throughout time and this general practice must be accepted as law in accordance with Article 38(1)(d) of the Statute of the International Court of Justice.[21] Once customary rules have been identified, they can, like treaties, also be subjected to interpretation, their unwritten nature allowing a more flexible interpretation where their content is uncertain or vague. As pointed out by Judge Tanaka

> Customary law, being vague and containing gaps compared with written law, requires precision and completion about its content. This task, in its nature being interpretative, would be incumbent upon the Court. The method of logical and teleological interpretation can be applied in the case of customary law as in the case of written law.[22]

This statement allows us to reach the conclusion that not only are unwritten customary rules open to interpretation so as to become fully applicable to a particular matter, but also that the process of interpretation can follow a teleological approach informed by the object and purpose of the rule. When the customary rule's object and purpose is to protect human dignity and integrity by constraining states in their behaviour, an extensive interpretation would be one that leads to a broadening of the content of state obligations in order to enhance the protection of the individual. On the other hand, a restrictive interpretation would tend to limit the scope of application of legal rules by giving much weight to State practice and explicit consent.

[18] ibid 6–7.

[19] R Di Marco, 'Customary International Law: A Foreword to Identification v. Interpretation' (2019) TRICI-Law Research Paper 009/2019, 14 <www.academia.edu/43325436/Customary_International_Law_a_Foreword_to_Identification_v._Interpretation> accessed 6 March 2022.

[20] P Merkouris, 'Interpreting the Customary Rules on Interpretation' (2017) 19 ICLR 129.

[21] Statute of the International Court of Justice (adopted 26 June 1945, entered into force 24 October 1945) 892 UNTS 119.

[22] *North Sea Continental Shelf Cases (Germany v Denmark; Germany v Netherlands)* (Merits) [1969] ICJ Rep 3, 181 (Dissenting Opinion of Judge Tanaka).

2.2 *Judicial Dialogue as a Tool in the Identification and Interpretation of* Jus Cogens *Norms Protecting Human Rights*

The ILC's special rapporteur Dire Tladi recalled that if 'a State has objected to a rule of customary international law while that rule was in the process of formation, the rule is not opposable to the State concerned for so long as it maintains its objection'.[23] However, the ILC emphasised that 'the persistent objector rule does not apply to peremptory norms of general international law (*jus cogens*)'.[24] This conclusion 'flows from both the universal application and hierarchical superiority of [these norms] . . . that apply to all States'.[25] In its 2019 report on the peremptory norms of general international law, the ILC affirmed that '[c]ustomary international law is the most common basis for peremptory norms of general international law (*jus cogens*)'.[26] adding that '[t]reaty provisions and general principles of law may also serve as bases for peremptory norms of general international law (*jus cogens*)'.[27] It also observed that '[d]ecisions of international courts and tribunals, in particular of the International Court of Justice, are a subsidiary means for determining the peremptory character of norms of general international law',[28] as is the case with the determination of CIL. In the ILC's 2022 report Dire Tladi provided the most recent list of norms considered to be part of *jus cogens* and which reflect fundamental values for the international community as a whole. They include the prohibition of aggression; the prohibition of genocide; the prohibition of crimes against humanity; the basic rules of international humanitarian law; the prohibition of racial discrimination and apartheid; the prohibition of slavery; the prohibition of torture; and the right of self-determination.[29] It is interesting to note that this list partially overlaps with customary rules identified as

[23] ILC, 'Draft Conclusions on Identification of Customary International Law' (adopted by the ILC at its seventieth session, in 2018) Conclusion 15, para 1 <https://legal.un.org/ilc/texts/instruments/english/draft_articles/1_13_2018.pdf> accessed 26 May 2024.

[24] ILC, 'Report of the International Law Commission: Seventy-First Session (29 April–7 June and 8 July–9 August 2019)' (2019) UN Doc A/74/10, 145, Conclusion 14, para 3.

[25] ILC, 'Draft Conclusions on Identification and Legal Consequences of Peremptory Norms of General International Law (*jus cogens*), with Commentaries' (adopted by the ILC at its seventy-third session, in 2022) 58 <https://legal.un.org/ilc/texts/instruments/english/commentaries/1_14_2022.pdf> accessed 26 May 2024.

[26] ILC, 'Report of the International Law Commission' (n 24) 143, Conclusion 5, para 1.

[27] ibid, Conclusion 5, para 2.

[28] ibid, Conclusion 9, para 1.

[29] ILC, 'Fifth Report on Peremptory Norms of General International Law (*jus cogens*)' (2022) UN Doc A/CN.4/747, 76.

such in legal scholarship, examples of which are 'the prohibition of genocide and torture, the prohibition of slavery and piracy, the rules on State responsibility, the principle of non-refoulement and the no-harm rule'.[30]

In Conclusion 14, the special rapporteur pointed out that '[a] rule of customary international law not of a peremptory character ceases to exist if and to the extent that it conflicts with a new peremptory norm of general international law (*jus cogens*)'.[31] This statement could be relevant in future cases dealing with the relationship between legal norms that are not at an equivalent hierarchical level. It could determine the effect of a *jus cogens* norm when there is a conflict with a customary rule, such as the normative interaction between the prohibition of torture and the rule on state immunity before foreign jurisdictions. An extensive interpretation of Conclusion 14 would lead to neutralisation of the CIL immunity rule's precedence over the peremptory norm when the application of the first rule renders ineffective in its scope the customary rule that has *jus cogens* status. However, for that to be the case, one must first consider that there is an existing conflict between, on the one hand, international customary law on immunities and, on the other, *erga omnes* obligations and *jus cogens* norms. The main uncertainty lies in the relationship between customary rules related to state immunities and the hierarchical character of *jus cogens* norms that should entail effective legal consequences. The ILC's special rapporteur stated:

> The hierarchical superiority of peremptory norms of general international law (*jus cogens*) over customary international law was ... recognized in *Al-Adsani v. the United Kingdom*,[32] in which the European Court of Human Rights (ECtHR) determined, having considered *Prosecutor v. Furundžija*,[33] that peremptory norms of general international law (*jus cogens*) are those norms that enjoy 'a higher rank in the international hierarchy than treaty law and even "ordinary" customary rules'.[34]

The ECtHR affirmed that 'the right under Article 3 not to be subjected to torture or to inhuman or degrading treatment or punishment enshrines

[30] Merkouris (n 20).

[31] ILC, 'Report of the International Law Commission' (n 24) 145 Conclusion 14, para 2. See also ibid 183–84.

[32] *Al-Adsani v United Kingdom*, App no 35763/97 (ECtHR, 21 November 2001) [60].

[33] *Prosecutor v Furundžija*, ICTY-95-17/I-T (10 December 1998) [144]–[147], [151]–[154]. See also *Prosecutor v Delalic and ors*, ICTY-96-21-T (16 November 1998) [454]; *Prosecutor v Kunarac*, ICTY-96-23-T and ICTY-96-23/1 (22 February 2001) [466].

[34] ILC, 'Report of the International Law Commission' (n 24) 182.

one of the fundamental values of democratic society' and that '[i]t is an absolute right, permitting of no exception in any circumstances'.[35] If the special rapporteur was indeed recalling the well-established case law of the European Court, it could have been criticised for its contradictions and limited legal consequences in terms of state accountability.

This precedent established by the ECtHR has led to a legal loophole in the case of grave human rights violations that occur extraterritorially and implicate a foreign state. Even in such exceptional circumstances, the customary law on immunities exercises a constraining effect on the legal consequences in terms of state responsibility, as individuals will have no access to justice. Indeed, as affirmed by the ECtHR itself:

> Notwithstanding the special character of the prohibition of torture in international law, the Court is] unable to discern in the international instruments, judicial authorities or other materials before it any firm basis for concluding that, as a matter of international law, a State no longer enjoys immunity from civil suit in the courts of another State where acts of torture are alleged.[36]

The dissent of Judges Rozakis and Caflisch from the *Al-Adsani* v. *the United Kingdom* solution, which was adopted by only nine votes in favour and eight against, showed the division among the judges at the time. The following words in the dissenting opinion show that the adoption of a radically different interpretation could have been possible:

> By accepting that the rule on prohibition of torture is a rule of *jus cogens*, the majority recognise that it is hierarchically higher than any other rule of international law ... For the basic characteristic of a *jus cogens* rule is that ... it overrides any other rule which does not have the same status. In the event of a conflict between a *jus cogens* rule and any other rule of international law, the former prevails.[37]

On the one hand, the ICJ followed the ECtHR's precedent and ruled in its *Jurisdictional Immunities of the State* case[38] that there was no conflict between the rule on state immunities in civil proceedings and *jus cogens* norms, as the former is of a procedural nature while the latter are of a substantive nature. This case dealt with both a debate around the

[35] *Al-Adsani v United Kingdom* (n 32) [59].

[36] ibid [61].

[37] *Al-Adsani v United Kingdom* (n 32) Joint Dissenting Opinion of Judges Rozakis and Caflisch (joined by Judges Wildhaber, Costa, Cabral Barreto and Vajić).

[38] *Jurisdictional Immunities of the State (Germany v Italy; Greece intervening)* (Judgment) [2012] ICJ Rep 99 [92]–[93].

identification of an exception to state immunities where there are violations of *jus cogens* norms, as affirmed by the Italian Supreme Court in its *Ferrini* case,[39] and the resolution of a possible conflict of norms between the customary rule on immunities and the absolute prohibition of torture. An analysis of domestic and international case law led the ICJ to reject any exception to the regime of state immunity from foreign jurisdiction, even in the case of violations of peremptory norms. As a result of this restrictive interpretation, the prohibition on torture becomes devoid of substance in an extraterritorial context: its peremptory nature is illusory and impracticable, its legal effects and effective sanctions existing only in a theoretical imaginary, given that state immunity prevails as a *sine qua non* prior to any judicial proceedings.

On the other hand, with regard to peremptory norms, the case law of other international courts and tribunals has also been used to identify the emergence of customary international legal rules determined by other courts that are binding on all states and not limited in their application. In the *Furundžija* case, the Trial Chamber of the International Criminal Tribunal for the Former Yugoslavia (ICTY) found that the prohibition of torture had not only become part of customary international law but had also reached the status of a *jus cogens* norm.[40] The ICTY has also stated that the prohibition of rape within the context of an armed conflict had become a rule of customary international law despite the lack of a universal definition of rape in international law,[41] the tribunal using the principle of the protection of human dignity to define the act of rape after analysing contradictory national legislations.[42] The tribunal also defined the criteria of torture in armed conflict after recalling that '[t]he broad convergence of ... international instruments and international jurisprudence demonstrates that there is now general acceptance of the main elements contained in the definition set out in article 1 of the Torture Convention',[43] applicable in times of both peace and armed conflict.

It is also interesting to note that when the case law of international tribunals refers to the prohibition of torture as a customary norm that is part of *jus cogens*, the formula used is usually 'prohibition of torture' and

39 P De Sena and F De Vittor, 'State Immunity and Human Rights: The Italian Supreme Court Decision on the *Ferrini* Case' (2005) 16 (1) EJIL 89.

40 *Prosecutor v Furundžija* (n 33) [154].

41 ibid [168].

42 Fortuna (n 17).

43 *Prosecutor v Furundžija* (n 33) [161].

not the universal treaty's broader wording, which reads 'the prohibition of torture and other cruel, inhuman or degrading treatment or punishment'.[44] Therefore, it is not clearly stated whether the proscription of inhuman or degrading treatment characterised by a minor gravity as compared with torture also fall under customary international law and could be qualified as a peremptory norm. For instance, in *Questions Relating to the Obligation to Prosecute or Extradite* case the ICJ stated that:

> the prohibition of torture is part of customary international law and it has become a peremptory norm (*jus cogens*).
>
> That prohibition is grounded in a widespread international practice and on the *opinio juris* of States. It appears in numerous international instruments of universal application (in particular the Universal Declaration of Human Rights of 1948, the 1949 Geneva Conventions for the protection of war victims; the International Covenant on Civil and Political Rights of 1966 ; General Assembly resolution 3452/30 of 9 December 1975 on the Protection of All Persons from Being Subjected to Torture and Other Cruel, Inhuman or Degrading Treatment or Punishment), and it has been introduced into the domestic law of almost all States; finally, acts of torture are regularly denounced within national and international fora.[45]

The court recalled that although Article 4 of the Convention against Torture requires states parties to criminalise such acts, 'the obligation to prosecute the alleged perpetrators of acts of torture under the Convention applies only to facts having occurred after its entry into force for the State concerned'.[46] Nevertheless, it is not clear whether only the prohibition of torture is part of customary international law as a *jus cogens* norm or whether this prohibition necessarily also entails procedural obligations strongly linked to the effectiveness of the prohibition as a customary norm. Furthermore, as regards the Convention against Torture, the definition of acts of torture is strongly linked to states obligations as it requires involvement of a public official, whereas this is not the case with torture defined as a crime against humanity involving the liability of individuals.[47]

[44] Convention against Torture and Other Cruel, Inhuman or Degrading Treatment or Punishment (adopted 10 December 1984, entered into force 26 June 1987) 1465 UNTS 85.

[45] *Questions Relating to the Obligation to Prosecute or Extradite (Belgium v Senegal)* (Judgment) [2012] ICJ Rep 422 [99].

[46] ibid [100].

[47] Y Tan, 'The Identification of Customary Rules in International Criminal Law' (2018) 34 (2) UJIEL 109. See Rome Statute of the International Criminal Court (adopted 17 July 1998, entered into force 1 July 2002) 2187 UNTS 3, arts 7(f) and 8(2)(a)(ii).

Finally, in the *Prosecutor* v. *Furundžija* case, the ICTY analysed treaty provisions of international humanitarian law and human rights law,[48] recognised the numerous states parties to those treaties and, acknowledging that 'torture in time of armed conflict is prohibited by a general rule of international law', observed that '[i]n armed conflicts this rule may be applied both as part of international customary law and – if the requisite conditions are met – qua treaty law, the content of the prohibition being the same'.[49] With respect to the content of the prohibition of torture under conventional and customary international law, the tribunal remarked that states had the obligation not only to prohibit and punish torture but also to prevent any potential breaches of the prohibition of torture as well as any inhuman or degrading treatment, as had been 'authoritatively held by the European Court of Human Rights'[50] in the *Soering* case.[51] The ICTY concluded that 'international rules prohibit not only torture but also (i) the failure to adopt the national measures necessary for implementing the prohibition and (ii) the maintenance in force or passage of laws which are contrary to the prohibition'.[52] This conclusion is reinforced by the *jus cogens* nature of the prohibition of torture and the fact that it imposes *erga omnes* obligations designed to produce a 'deterrent effect'.[53] For the tribunal, the peremptory character of the prohibition of torture has effects at the inter-state level, such as de-legitimising any legislative, administrative or judicial act authorising torture,[54] and at the individual level, enabling every state 'to investigate, prosecute and punish or extradite individuals accused of torture, who are present in a territory under its jurisdiction'.[55]

Analyses of the international case law related to the prohibition of torture have shown that its customary nature and content flow from the coherence of general principles of international law and treaty provisions applicable in international humanitarian and human rights law, analysed in the light of the international courts' case law. It also appears that the customary prohibition of torture has distinct content and scope, binding all states as a peremptory norm of international law and giving rise to *erga omnes* obligations.

48 *Prosecutor v Furundžija* (n 33) [137]–[138].
49 ibid [139].
50 ibid [148].
51 *Soering v United Kingdom*, App no 14038/88 (ECtHR, 7 July 1989).
52 *Prosecutor v Furundžija* (n 33) [148].
53 ibid [154].
54 ibid [155].
55 ibid [156].

2.3 *Cross-References and the Crystallisation of a New Customary Rule: The Example of the Binding Nature of Provisional Measures*

Consideration of other international instruments and the associated case law resulting from their interpretation by other courts can also lead to the identification of new customary rules, as exemplified by the binding nature of provisional measures. In the case of *Mamatkoulov and Askarov* v. *Turkey* before the ECtHR, the applicants alleged that their extradition to Uzbekistan by the Turkish authorities exposed them to a real risk of ill-treatment proscribed by Article 3 of the European Convention on Human Rights (ECHR). The court had indicated an interim measure in application of Rule 39 of its Rules of Court. The provisional measure requested a suspension of the extradition proceedings for the purpose of establishing whether the risk of ill-treatment existed. Turkey's failure to comply with the measure indicated by the Court raised the issue of the mandatory nature of interim measures and whether there was a breach of the effective exercise of the right of individual application guaranteed by Article 34 of the ECHR.

The *LaGrand* case[56] before the ICJ dealt with a dispute related to alleged violations of the Vienna Convention on Consular Relations of 24 April 1963 on the grounds that the applicants had been tried and sentenced to death without having been informed of their rights, as required under Article 36(1)(b) of the Vienna Convention. The ICJ indicated provisional measures, calling upon the United States to suspend the execution of the death penalty, but the respondent state failed to comply with the court's order made under Article 41 of the ICJ Statute. The court had therefore to determine whether the provisional measures had a binding effect. It reached the following conclusion:

> It follows from the object and purpose of the Statute, as well as from the terms of Article 41 when read in their context, that the power to indicate provisional measures entails that such measures should be binding, inasmuch as the power in question is based on the necessity, when the circumstances call for it, to safeguard, and to avoid prejudice to, the rights of the parties as determined by the final judgment of the Court.[57]

[56] *LaGrand (Germany v United States of America)* (Judgment) [2001] ICJ Rep 466.

[57] ibid [102]. The ICJ confirmed this interpretation in *Avena and Other Mexican Nationals (Mexico v United States of America)* (Judgment) [2004] ICJ Rep 12.

The ECtHR has referred extensively to the *LaGrand* case decided by the ICJ,[58] in which the mandatory nature of provisional measures was established after decades of doctrinal debates.[59] It should be noted that in its *Cruz Varas* case[60] the ECtHR took a different position as it considered that its procedural rules were not equal to a conventional instrument approved and adopted by states, making it impossible to affirm the binding nature of interim measures in comparison with other systems. Nevertheless, in the *Mamatkoulov* case the ECtHR emphasised that 'in the light of the general principles of international law, the law of treaties and international case-law, the interpretation of the scope of interim measures cannot be dissociated from the proceedings to which they relate or the decision on the merits they seek to protect'.[61] The ECtHR stressed the specificity of interim measures within the inter-American system, where the power of the Inter-American Court of Human Rights (IACtHR) to order such measures has an explicit conventional basis.[62] The ECtHR also recalled, however, that the ICJ in its *LaGrand* case, the IACtHR, the Human Rights Committee and the Committee against Torture

> have confirmed in their reasoning in recent decisions that the preservation of the asserted rights of the parties in the face of the risk of irreparable damage represents an essential objective of interim measures in international law. Indeed, it can be said that, whatever the legal system in question, the proper administration of justice requires that no irreparable action be taken while proceedings are pending.[63]

Although there was no change to the ECtHR's procedural rules over the years, nor any amendment to the ECHR, cross-references to the case law of other international bodies allowed the ECtHR to establish the mandatory nature of its provisional measures and to conclude that 'a failure by a respondent State to comply with interim measures will undermine the effectiveness of the right of individual application

[58] *Mamatkulov and Askarov v Turkey*, App no 46827/99 and 46951/99 (ECtHR, 4 February 2005) [48].

[59] JM Pasqualucci, 'Interim Measures in International Human Rights: Evolution and Harmonization' (2005) 38 VJTL 1; J Kammerhofer, 'The Binding Nature of Provisional Measures of the International Court of Justice: The "Settlement" of the Issue in the *LaGrand* Case' (2003) 16 LJIL 67.

[60] *Cruz Varas and ors v Sweden*, App no 46/1990/237/307 (ECtHR, 20 March 1991).

[61] *Mamatkulov and Askarov v Turkey* (n 58) [123].

[62] ibid [49]–[53].

[63] ibid [124].

guaranteed by Article 34 and the State's formal undertaking in Article 1 to protect the rights and freedoms set forth in the Convention'.[64]

In their joint partly dissenting opinion, Judges Caflisch, Türmen and Kolver criticised the court's reasoning. They noted that the ICJ, for instance, was interpreting Article 41 of the ICJ Statute, a provision of a constitutive treaty, whereas the ECtHR was interpreting its procedural rules, to which states have not given their consent.[65] They stressed that by relying on international instruments and precedents from other international bodies, the ECtHR departed from its own case law and exercised 'a legislative function, for the Convention as it stands nowhere prescribes that the States Parties to it must recognise the binding force of interim measures indicated'.[66] As regards crystallisation of the binding nature of provisional measures on the basis of normative convergence in the international legal order, the dissenting judges finally concluded:

> There must, however, be a *customary rule* allowing international courts and tribunals, even in the absence of a treaty provision, to enact Rules of Procedure, a rule which may include the power to *formulate* interim measures. But that rule cannot be taken to include the power to *prescribe* such measures.[67]

It is interesting to note that the ECtHR departed from its own precedent, set previously in the *Cruz Varas* case. It founded its legal reasoning, notably, not on state practice or *opinio juris* but on the general principles of international law, the law of treaties and international case law,[68] and on the fact 'the right of individual application is no longer dependent on a declaration by the Contracting States'.[69] Even though not affirmed explicitly, the court acknowledged this as a departure from its previous case law, the practice of international courts and tribunals having revealed the binding nature of interim measures to be now part of general international law.

In this example from the ECtHR, cross-references to the case law of other courts were used as a tool to counteract the negative consequences arising from so-called absolute state sovereignty and to bypass normative constraints. The co-ordination and harmonisation of international case law minimises divergent interpretations of a common legal rule such as

[64] ibid [125].
[65] ibid [148].
[66] ibid [151].
[67] ibid [162] (emphasis in original).
[68] ibid [123].
[69] ibid.

the binding nature of provisional measures. Interim measures ordered by judicial bodies are aimed at preventing irreversible damage to the rights of parties during executive, legislative and political decision-making processes. As a matter of fact, the binding nature of provisional measures is linked to their function, as the purpose of judicial proceedings is to ensure effective protection of human rights by state authorities required to act in accordance with the rule of law.

Therefore, the growth of multidimensional dialogue between international bodies protecting human rights, between national judges and between international bodies and national judges contributes to the emergence of a network within the international judiciary.[70] Although operating against the backdrop of distinct and independent legal systems in the international legal order, the international judiciary shares common judicial practices that help to define norms of reference and minimum standards of protection. Nevertheless, these norms and standards need to be incorporated into national legal orders for full applicability and effectiveness, since the primary responsibility to ensure the respect of human rights is devolved to national authorities. Even in the absence of an explicit written rule, international bodies, by applying and interpreting human rights obligations and by sanctioning violations implicating the international responsibility of states, aim to place limits on the exercise of power by framing executive, legislative and political process within the rule of law.

3 Judicial Dialogue as an Approach to Interpretation Leading to Jurisprudential Objectivism and Its Impact on Customary International Human Rights Law

If the will and consent of sovereign states remain at the very foundation of international law and legal systems protecting human rights, the examples previously mentioned and the practice of judicial dialogue show the emergence of jurisprudential objectivism – this arises from a judicial body's independence and impartiality regarding its nature and functions. Furthermore, jurisprudential objectivism is closely connected to increasing jurisdictionalisation in international law, as demonstrated by the multiplication of international courts and tribunals in

[70] G Ulfstein, 'Towards an International Human Rights Judiciary?' in J Ebbesson and Others (eds), *International Law and Changing Perceptions of Security: Liber Amicorum Said Mahmoudi* (Brill 2014).

diverse fields, especially human rights. Their protection was internationalised with the adoption of the Universal Declaration of Human Rights in 1948, which was the starting point for the internationalisation of human rights protection and has served as a source of inspiration for legally binding treaties. Thus, jurisprudential objectivism embodies a form of autonomy arising from judicial practice that does not depend on states' interests nor on political or diplomatic views. Moreover, jurisprudential objectivism asserts itself in the face of the will of states when an international court refers spontaneously to decisions or international instruments that are outside its own judicial system, and therefore not included in its constitutive treaty that has been ratified by states parties. The notion of jurisprudential objectivism reflects both the jurisdictionalisation of international obligations and the margin of appreciation exercised by international courts in the interpretation processes. The principles of limited jurisdiction and the required consent to jurisdiction are cornerstones of the very existence of international judicial bodies. The scope of the will and consent of states will be constrained by judicial practice, as the interpretation processes used in case law can lead to objective conclusions, binding on states and detached from the principle of voluntarism.

Jurisprudential dialogue can also be used to identify the emergence of CIL rules determined by other courts, binding on all states, not limited in their application and that do not need express consent – and a fortiori for *jus cogens* norms that entail *erga omnes* obligations. In contrast to conventional rules, which can be subject to reservations, 'this cannot be so in the case of general or customary law rules and obligations which, by their very nature, must have equal force for all members of the international community, and cannot therefore be the subject of any right of unilateral exclusion exercisable at will by any one of them in its own favour'.[71]

It is important to emphasise the persuasive authority of the international judiciary and its capacity to build normative convergence through the use of external sources that show an interpretive convergence in the first place. Not only does the practice of judicial dialogue create checks and balances in the international legal order through the comparison of multiple points of view in regard to the interpretation of a specific legal rule; it also enhances the quality of the judgments and their reasoning. When external sources are incorporated in the interpreter's decision, this improves the legal ruling not only with respect to the

[71] *North Sea Continental Shelf* (n 22) [63].

requirements of the interpreter's own system but also in light of the legal requirements that apply in other foreign systems. Consequently, the solution adopted in the court's decision will be strengthened by a more coherent legal argument, as it has relied on other judicial decisions that reached the same solution when faced with common legal issues.

A stronger legal argument can also enhance the persuasive authority recognised in supranational judgments and decisions that lack the power of enforcement attached to national tribunals and authorities. The legal reasoning and the arguments used in judicial decisions allow the addressees to better understand the extent of their obligations arising from conventional and customary international human rights law. In other words, the practice of referring to multiple sources of law when justifying a legal ruling, whether these sources are judicial decisions or international instruments that show a converging normative content, will enhance the authority of external sources where legal reasoning and justification demonstrate the existence of cross-cutting obligations that do not apply to only one specific legal system but are common to several of them or are part of general CIL.

Indeed, the notion of public international order can be linked to the development of case law of international bodies protecting human rights.[72] These bodies serve as a last resort to judge human rights violations when the action of national jurisdictions has been insufficient. At the national level, safeguarding public order and security can be used to justify legal restrictions and derogations from the general law in exceptional circumstances. At the international level, the notion of public international order embodies shared values and common principles arising from the necessity to protect human integrity and dignity as cornerstones of the universality of human rights. Public international order also implies the respect of minimum standards and norms of reference, notably through *jus cogens* norms and *erga omnes* obligations that are common to legal systems and of interest to the international community as a whole. It is also strongly linked to normative convergence and to jurisprudential objectivism. Normative convergence derived from case law leads to the emergence and the consolidation of jurisprudential objectivism, restraining voluntarism. International obligations that protect core human rights are not based on the will of states but are instead derived from the universality

[72] EJ Solares, 'Las normas internacionales convencionales de derechos humanos y su contribución al orden público internacional' (2014) 14 RDUNED 325; A Orakhelashvili, 'State Immunity and International Public Order' (2002) 45 GYIL 226.

attached to these rights and the protection of the rule of law[73] through the respect of minimum standards and norms of reference in light of which human rights violations have to be assessed.[74] Jurisprudential objectivism results from the practice of international human rights tribunals that leads to strengthening spontaneous international law, beyond binding written agreements, through the identification of cross-cutting customary rules. As judges' impartiality and independence are central to the scope and function of judicial power, even though political distrust or states' unwillingness to comply with international obligations may limit their margin of appreciation and lead to negotiated judicial decisions, the binding nature of international customary rules is not altered but rather its effects are being neutralised. Jurisprudential objectivism can also be illustrated by the role played by international courts and tribunals in the determination of customary rules, *erga omnes* obligations and *jus cogens* norms that are directly applicable in domestic legal orders, without requiring any legislative implementation or state consent, as they are not defined in conventional instruments but implicitly ensue from them.

Finally, judicial dialogue can be seen as a way to co-ordinate and harmonise the interpretation of key principles of international law, whether written or unwritten, and to acknowledge the international judiciary as a set of mutual interactions and influences between legal systems that strengthen governance in the realm of justice. International bodies, whether judicial or quasi-judicial, and national judges, whether ordinary or constitutional, should engage constantly and on a long-term basis in judicial dialogue, especially when common legal problems are at stake, as is often the case with human rights issues. This implies cooperation and solidarity among those courts and other stakeholders, counteracting the perception that there is a supranational government of judges emerging in the international legal order, in competition with national tribunals and undermining the sovereignty of states.

Nevertheless, there remains the challenge of disseminating the jurisprudential achievements and case law of international bodies in national legal orders, which is the primary responsibility of state authorities. Formal or informal meetings, exchanges and any other kinds of regular

[73] EU Petersmann, '"Constitutional Justice" Requires Judicial Cooperation and "Comity" in the Protection of "Rule of Law"' in F Fontanelli, G Martinico and P Carrozza (eds), *Shaping Rule of Law through Dialogue* (Europa Law 2010).

[74] S Gardbaum, 'Human Rights as International Constitutional Rights' (2008) 19 (4) EJIL 749; H Keller and AS Sweet (eds), *A Europe of Rights: The Impact of the ECtHR on National Legal Systems* (Oxford University Press 2008).

interactions and relations that can be developed both between international and national judges could constitute an essential lever to the implementation of a multi-dimensional network spreading information about improvements, challenges and difficulties faced in human rights case law. Undoubtedly, judicial dialogue is a catalyst for strengthening the international judiciary in a globalised world marked by an ever-growing receptivity to external sources. Indeed, just as international bodies refer to one another, they also tend to incorporate references to national tribunals whose case law is relevant to a particular legal matter. National tribunals themselves tend to incorporate domestic norms, international treaties binding on their state, decisions and judgments from national or international jurisdictions and other non-judicial bodies in their interpretation processes. In parallel, many constitutional courts have taken to normative borrowings as a common practice in the process of applying and interpreting national constitutions.[75] This acknowledgement of their relevance shows an intensification of judicial dialogue at a multi-dimensional level, both horizontal and vertical, but always spontaneous, without any notion of hierarchy, the initiative of engaging in such dialogue and the implications to be drawn being at the discretion of the interpreters participating in such extraterritorial governance.

It is also important to note the role of national judges in defining, applying and taking into account customary international human rights law in domestic court decisions. The protection of human rights is left primarily to national state authorities and judges, with international tribunals intervening only after domestic remedies have been exhausted. Even in states where there is a dualist system of incorporating international law, it has been highlighted that customary international law is immediately applicable without any need of further proceedings or measures,[76] while ratified treaties require a specific law of implementation to enter into force in the national legal system.[77] Moreover, customary human rights rules are not only customary but also generally belong to *jus cogens* and give rise to *erga omnes* obligations.[78]

[75] T Groppi and MC Ponthoreau, *The Use of Foreign Precedents by Constitutional Judges* (Hart 2013).

[76] PH Verdier and M Versteeg, 'International Law in National Legal Systems: An Empirical Investigation' (2015) 109 AJIL 528.

[77] *Nevsun Resources Ltd v Araya*, Supreme Court of Canada, 2020 SCC 5 [82]–[90]. See also *R. v Hape*, Supreme Court of Canada, 2007 SCC 26 [39].

[78] *Barcelona Traction, Light and Power Company Limited (New Application: 1962) (Belgium v Spain)* [1970] ICJ Rep 3 [33]–[34].

4 Concluding Remarks

The practice of judicial dialogue through references to external instruments and the case law of other courts reflects the existence of common standards that transcend the differences and independence between legal systems and emerge as a determining factor in the interpretation and application of rules shared by multiple treaties protecting human rights. Therefore, the eventuality of common standards and norms of references that could be identified in decisions or legal instruments coming under the jurisdiction of other international bodies results in a de facto expansion of possibilities offered to the power of interpretation. Consequently, judicial power attributed to a particular body is strengthened in its relations and interactions with other judicial powers in a mutual process of self-regulation embodied in the practice of judicial dialogue. Indeed, reference to the practice and achievements of other legal systems not only extends the margin of appreciation of the interpreter but also narrows it. Spontaneously, the interpreter will refer to other decisions and instruments that could limit their interpretive possibilities by showing a different state of law, a lack of consensus, or the existence of a strong alternative common interpretation regarding the legal matter at issue. The practice of judicial dialogue belongs within the multiplication of international tribunals and courts linked to the jurisdictionalisation of international human rights law. Far from resulting in a government of judges, it improves extraterritorial governance by a slow but constant movement towards harmonisation through openness to external sources when engaging in interpretation. This practice acquires legitimacy through the sovereign will of states that initially chose to create judicial bodies in the international legal order and to accept their jurisdiction and the margin of appreciation inherent in it.

If mutual inspiration and normative borrowings between international bodies protecting human rights do not always lead to more protective interpretations of human rights, legal precedents could be used as a bulwark against fragmentation by contributing to the realisation of a 'global community of courts'[79] through cross-referencing of legal norms and decisions. Indeed, the international legal system can be seen

[79] AM Slaughter, 'A Global Community of Courts' (2003) 44 HILJ 191; AM Slaughter, 'Building Global Democracy' (2000) 1 CJIL 223; AM Slaughter, 'Judicial Globalization' (2000) 40 VJIL 1103; AM Slaughter, 'A Typology of Transjudicial Communication' (1994) 29(1) URLR 99.

'as a collection of communities of practice',[80] each area of international law being embodied in a 'community of practice' sharing its own conventions, leading principles and rules concerning argumentation and authority. In the field of the protection of human rights, the universal system and the regional systems each represent one 'community of practice', co-existing but exercising different jurisdiction and having various functions, while still having a common object and purpose – namely, the protection of human dignity and integrity in accordance with the principle of universality. Indeed, as stated in the ICJ's famous obiter dictum in the *Barcelona Traction* case:[81]

> [A]n essential distinction should be drawn between the obligations of a State towards the international community as a whole, and those arising vis-à-vis another State in the field of diplomatic protection. By their very nature the former are the concern of all States. In view of the importance of the rights involved, all States can be held to have a legal interest in their protection; they are obligations *erga omnes*.
>
> Such obligations derive, for example, in contemporary international law, from the outlawing of acts of aggression, and of genocide, as also from the principles and rules concerning the basic rights of the human person, including protection from slavery and racial discrimination. Some of the corresponding rights of protection have entered into the body of general international law (*Reservations to the Convention on the Prevention and Punishment of the Crime of Genocide*, Advisory Opinion, ICJ Reports 1951, p. 23); others are conferred by international instruments of a universal or quasi-universal character.[82]

Any judicial body interpreting human rights related to its jurisdiction, stands to gain from the global perspective of international law by integrating external sources in its margin of appreciation. Risks and issues arising from the fragmentation of international law were highlighted by Judge Gilbert Guillaume in his address to the General Assembly of the United Nations on 26 October 2000, in which he emphasised that establishing '[a] dialogue among judicial bodies is crucial'.[83] Fragmentation was also discussed thoroughly in the final report of the

[80] HG Cohen, 'International Precedent and the Practice of International Law' in MA Helfand (ed), *Negotiating State and Non-State Law: The Challenge of Global and Local Legal Pluralism* (Cambridge University Press 2015) 185–86.

[81] *Barcelona Traction, Light and Power Company Limited* (n 78).

[82] ibid [33]–[34].

[83] 'Address by H.E. Judge Gilbert Guillaume, President of the International Court of Justice, to the United Nations General Assembly, 26 October 2000, 5 <www.icj-cij.org/public/files/press-releases/9/2999.pdf> accessed 11 May 2024.

study group of the ILC, adopted on 13 April 2006.[84] Discussions and conclusions emphasised the multiplication of international jurisdictions and positive legal rules in this decentralised order, seen as a threat to the unity and coherence of international law. During recent years, however, the development of judicial dialogue between international bodies protecting human rights has shown that in spite of their independence and the absence of a hierarchical principle of organisation, the power of interpretation that might lead to divergent jurisprudential achievements tends to self-regulate. Even though external references are not included systematically in all decisions and judgments of international courts and tribunals, they tend to be mentioned in important judgments and decisions, notably when common legal issues of great importance are at stake or when cross-cutting rules appear to be part of CIL. Spontaneous normative borrowings seem to extend the margin of appreciation and interpretative authority of any international court, for, in referring to instruments and decisions that are not initially part of its system, it goes beyond the limits set by the instrument defining its jurisdiction, functions and powers. However, the taking account of similar case law when ruling on analogous legal issues in human rights matters opens the way to common solutions reflecting normative convergence. This all contributes to the process of harmonisation in the application and interpretation of human rights instruments and identification of rules that have become part of customary international law. Moreover, because judicial dialogue is not a binding obligation, a particular body's openness to external sources illustrates a search for and willingness to embrace the implicit perspective of universal justice in reflection of the universality characterising fundamental human rights notwithstanding differences of culture, tradition and legal practice.[85]

[84] ILC, 'Fragmentation of International Law: Difficulties Arising from the Diversification and Expansion of International Law, Report of the Study Group of the International Law Commission' (13 April 2006) UN Doc A/CN.4/L.682.

[85] Frydman (n 4) 157.

PART III

CIL and Its Interpretation in the Normative Universe

Drifting towards Coherence?

10

General Principles of Law and the Interpretation of CIL

CRAIG EGGETT

1 Introduction

The interpretation of unwritten norms is fraught with difficulty. Without the settled text of a treaty, interpreters of unwritten norms are without a basic linguistic framework within which they may conduct their search for meaning. In such situations, the boundaries between the existence of a norm and the determination of its content can become blurred. Interpreters may return to the evidence of the norm's existence (such as state practice) in order to determine its content or it may be that interpretation itself is part of the constitutive process of unwritten norms. This confusion is exacerbated by a lack of established methods and procedures for the interpretation of unwritten international law. Customary rules are, of course, a type of unwritten international law. Yet, custom is not alone in this category. There are other, even more nebulous, unwritten norms: general principles of law. While it is commonplace to speak of custom and general principles under the umbrella of 'general international law',[1] it is unclear whether questions of interpretation are to be approached in the same manner for both categories of norms or whether custom and general principles may assist in the interpretation of one another.

My central objective in this chapter is to examine the interactions between these two categories of norms in the context of interpretation.

[1] M Wood, 'Customary International Law and the General Principles of Law Recognized by Civilized Nations' (2019) 21 ICLR 307, 310–11. For a range of views on the meaning of 'general international law', see G Tunkin, 'Is General International Law Customary International Law Only?' (1993) 4 EJIL 534; C Tomuschat, 'General International Law: A New Source of International Law?' in R Pisillo Mazzeschi and P De Sena, *Global Justice, Human Rights and the Modernization of International Law* (Springer 2018) 185.

More specifically, I consider whether (and if so to what extent) general principles of law may play a role in the interpretation of customary rules. In approaching this task, I have structured the chapter in three main sections. First, it is necessary to make explicit some assumptions and presumptions about the nature of the norms under examination and the potential relationships between them. To this end, in Section 2 I clarify how I understand general principles of law – that is, as a separate kind of rules distinct from both custom and principles in the true sense of the term. In essence, I view general principles as a distinct category of (mainly secondary) *rules* that come into existence as a result of a dynamic process of assertion and confirmation involving a range of actors, with a particularly prominent role played by courts and tribunals. Further, I briefly sketch how, on the basis of this understanding, I view the potential relationships between general principles of law and customary law. Building on this foundation, I then turn to examine two possible roles for general principles of law in the interpretation of customary rules. In Section 3 I consider whether, as a distinct category of rules, general principles of law may form part of the legal framework relied upon when interpreting international law generally, and custom in particular. Finally, in Section 4 I examine whether it is within the scope of general principles of law to play a part in the systemic interpretation of customary rules, both as the source of the rule on systemic interpretation and as other 'relevant rules' of international law. The core of the argument presented in this chapter is that general principles of law could be the source of many of international law's general rules on interpretation, including those applicable to custom, and that an enhanced reliance on general principles could facilitate further coherence in the interpretation of customary rules.

2 A Theory of General Principles in International Law

Until rather recently, 'general principles of law' had received considerably less academic attention than treaties and custom. The inclusion of general principles of law in the programme of work of the International Law Commission (ILC) has, in no small part, contributed to a significantly heightened interest in the subject.[2] Despite this substantial

[2] For an overview of the ILC's work, see ILC, 'Analytical Guide to the Work of the International Law Commission: General Principles of Law' <https://legal.un.org/ilc/guide/1_15.shtml> accessed 15 March 2022. For an overview of recent literature on general principles, see C Eggett, 'General Principles as Systemic Elements of International Law' (PhD thesis, Maastricht University 2021) ch 1.

rise in scholarly debate on the topic, it would still be accurate to describe general principles as 'the most enigmatic [of the] sources of international law'.[3] Simply put, there is more disagreement about more aspects of general principles than the other sources. The very nature of these norms, their functions, their creation, and their importance remain unsettled questions. It is, of course, likely that the ILC's work and the body of literature that has followed and to come will help to solidify the foundations of general principles. Yet, at this stage, it remains necessary to explicitly articulate how I understand general principles and their place in international law. This is particularly pressing as my theory of general principles has aspects that contrast with the mainstream (if there is such a thing in this field), including some departures from the positions adopted in the work of the ILC.

In short, I view general principles of law as concrete *rules* of law, distinct from broader, value-laden principles in the strict sense of the term. General principles, in my view, are developed not (solely) from the practice of states or through transposition from domestic law. Instead, they develop (usually incrementally) as the result of a dynamic process of assertion and contestation by a range of international actors: certain 'systemic officials'. Courts and tribunals play a particularly prominent role in the development of general principles, and recourse to this category of rules is typically made where there is the need for a secondary rule not found in the other sources. In the sections that follow, I expand on the idea that general principles are rules, before explaining the processes through which they may be ascertained. In both parts, I endeavour to clarify the key points of distinction and interaction between general principles, on the one hand, and principles *stricto sensu* and customary law, on the other.

2.1 'General Principles of Law' as a Category of Rules

The term 'general principles' is sometimes used in a rhetorical sense to convey the perceived importance or broad and general character of the norm(s) in question. A set of general rules that form the basis of an area

[3] R Kwiecień, 'General Principles of Law: The Gentle Guardians of Systemic Integration of International Law' (2017) 37 PYIL 235, 235. See also M Paparinskis, 'Conclusions: General Principles and the Other Sources of International Law' in M Andenas and others (eds), *General Principles and the Coherence of International Law* (Brill/Nijhoff 2019) 117, 117 (claiming that general principles constitute 'the most peculiar source').

of law may be described as general principles – a nod to their foundational character. Beyond this rhetorical use, the label may be used to capture a range of types of norms and their functions in the international legal system. For some, general principles are fundamental norms underlying the system as a whole;[4] for others, they are considered of little importance, a class of subsidiary norms[5] or 'inchoate custom'.[6] Further, general principles are occasionally conflated with other notions such equity[7] or *jus cogens* norms.[8] Against this backdrop, it is important to clarify that when I use the term 'general principles of law' I am referring to a distinct category of norms – namely, those referred to in the Article 38(1)(c) of the Statute of the International Court of Justice.[9] These norms are, in my view, a separate type of unwritten *rules*, clearly distinct from both customary law and principles in the true sense of the term. This position is consonant with the both the history of the drafting of Article 38 and the invocation and application of general principles before international courts and tribunals.[10] I take this position on the basis of my understanding of the foundations of the international legal system as a whole and, while it would be impractical to explain this fully here,[11] central to this understanding is the distinction of kind between rules and principles.

Reference to general principles within the meaning of Article 38(1)(c) of the ICJ Statute is distinct from reference to principles in the strict sense of the term. Principles *stricto sensu* are value-based optimisation commands that influence the development and interpretation of rules[12] and can frequently be expressed as 'should' statements. As such, they are

[4] G Boas, *Public International Law: Contemporary Principles and Perspectives* (Edward Elgar 2012) 107 (referring to 'foundational principles').

[5] M Bogdan, 'General Principles of Law and the Problem of Lacunae in the Law of Nations' (1977) 46 NJIL 37, 39.

[6] Kwiecień (n 3) 242.

[7] E Milano, 'General Principles *Infra, Praeter, Contra Legem*? The Role of Equity in Determining Reparation' in M Andenas and others (eds), *General Principles and the Coherence of International Law* (Brill/Nijhoff 2019) 65.

[8] R Kolb, 'General Principles of Law, *Jus Cogens* and the Unity of the International Legal Order' in M Andenas and others(eds), *General Principles and the Coherence of International Law* (Brill/Nijhoff 2019) 60.

[9] Statute of the International Court of Justice (adopted 26 June 1945, entered into force 24 October 1945) 33 UNTS 993.

[10] See generally Eggett (n 2) ch 3, pt 4.

[11] For elaboration, see Eggett (n 2) ch 1.

[12] R Alexy, 'On the Structure of Legal Principles' (2000) 13 Ratio Juris 294, 295; R Dworkin, *Taking Rights Seriously* (Harvard University Press 1977) 27.

wholly separate from rules, which issue definitive commands following the fulfilment of one or more conditions.[13] Of course, that general principles and principles *stricto sensu* are distinct does not mean that they operate in isolation. There are meaningful interactions between all categories of norms in the international legal system, with rules (including general principles of law) giving concrete legal expression to principles *stricto sensu.* In turn, principles perform a guiding role in international law, influencing the interpretation and development of the system and the application of its rules. The extent of this interaction between principles and rules may differ depending on the context and norms in question. It may even be that there is a closer relationship between principles and general principles then there is between principles and other categories of rules. It may also be that it is (only) through a general principle of law that a principle *stricto sensu* is granted protection in international law through the imposition of a specific obligation. Nevertheless, such a close relationship would not detract from the existence of the distinction between the two.

If this distinction between general principles and principles *stricto sensu* is accepted, questions arise as to the distinction between general principles and customary law. Both of these are unwritten norms of (predominantly) general application. Yet, once again, it should be made clear that custom in the sense of Article 38(1)(b) of the ICJ Statute refers specifically to a category of unwritten *rules.* So, references to 'customary principles' or 'principles of customary law' are,[14] in my view, references to *principles* in the strict sense of the term and distinct from the customary *rules* that generate specific legal rights and obligations following from the existence of the required state practice and *opinio juris.*[15] While, as with any of the sources of international law,[16] there is scope for overlap, custom and general principles tend to perform distinct functions.

[13] R Dworkin, 'The Model of Rules' (1967) 35 UCLR 14, 25. I elaborate on this understanding of the rules vs principles distinction elsewhere. See Eggett (n 2) ch 3, pt 2. See also, C Eggett, 'The Role of Principles and General Principles in the "Constitutional Processes" of International Law' (2019) 66 NILR 197.

[14] For an example, see *Legality of the Threat or Use of Nuclear Weapons (Advisory Opinion)* [1996] ICJ Rep 226 [79].

[15] *North Sea Continental Shelf Cases (Germany v Denmark; Germany v Netherlands)* (Merits) [1969] ICJ Rep 3 [60]–[76].

[16] See generally T Broude and Y Shany (eds), *Multi-Sourced Equivalent Norms in International Law* (Hart 2011). The ICJ explicitly acknowledged the parallel application of treaty-based and customary rules in *Military and Paramilitary Activities in and against Nicaragua (Nicaragua v United States of America)* (Merits) [1986] ICJ Rep 14 [178].

Customary rules tend to be primary rules;[17] they impose obligations and grant rights, generally to states, on the basis of their general practice and acceptance that such practice is legally expected. General principles, conversely, are generally secondary rules[18] that arise in the context of dispute settlement and in the absence of an applicable treaty or customary rule.[19] This distinction in function between general principles and custom is linked to the distinctions between the respective means through which these kinds of rules are ascertained. This is further explained in Section 2.2.

2.2 Ascertainment by 'Systemic Officials': The Centrality of Courts and Tribunals

Like all rules, general principles must be ascertained on the basis of certain criteria. It is clear that Article 38(1)(c)'s reference to 'civilized nations' is problematic and cannot be maintained. Already in the *North Sea Continental Shelf* case, Judge Ammoun noted that this term is inconsistent with the UN Charter and was introduced as a form of power politics by European colonial powers.[20] Judge Ammoun advocated for a more inclusive approach when referring to domestic systems of law, calling for the term 'civilized' to be dropped and referring to (the far more inclusive) 'universal' support for general principles by 'all … nations'.[21] While not expecting *universal* support, the recent work of the ILC seems consonant with Judge Ammoun's basic position, with the current version of Draft Conclusion 2 stating: 'For a general principle of law to exist, it must be generally recognized by [the community of

[17] Primary rules are understood as those that impose obligations, grant rights, or assign a legal status.

[18] Secondary rules are understood as those that regulate the creation, modification, interpretation, and application of other rules.

[19] See generally the norms identified in works such as C Kotuby Jr and L Sobota, *General Principles of Law and International Due Process: Principles and Norms Applicable in Transnational Disputes* (Oxford University Press 2017) and B Cheng, *General Principles of Law as Applied by International Courts and Tribunals* (Cambridge University Press 1953).

[20] *North Sea Continental Shelf* (n 15) Separate Opinion of Judge Ammoun 133–35. That this term is inappropriate and useless has also been noted in scholarly works. See eg A Pellet, 'Article 38' in A Zimmermann and CJ Tams (eds), *The Statute of the International Court of Justice: A Commentary* (2nd edn, Oxford University Press 2012) para 261 (noting that this phrase is 'devoid of any particular meaning').

[21] *North Sea Continental Shelf* (n 15) Separate Opinion of Judge Ammoun 135.

nations].'[22] The ascertainment of general principles is the focus of the ILC's Second Report,[23] and eight of its fourteen Draft Conclusions are concerned with this topic.[24] In short, and from the starting point of general recognition by the community of nations, the ILC's position on ascertainment is predicated on a distinction between general principles that are derived from domestic systems and those that are formed within the international legal system.[25] From this foundation, the ILC proceeds to elaborate on the processes through which each kind of general principle is formed. For general principles of domestic origin, the ILC adopts a two-step approach requiring '(a) the existence of a principle common to the principal legal systems of the world; and (b) its transposition to the international legal system'.[26] Here, it is clear that the ILC follows the trend of reliance on a comparative approach to domestic systems,[27] with Draft Conclusion 5 explaining that:

> 1. To determine the existence of a principle common to the principal legal systems of the world, a comparative analysis of national legal systems is required.
> 2. The comparative analysis must be wide and representative, including different legal families and regions of the world.
> 3. The comparative analysis includes an assessment of national legislations and decisions of national courts.[28]

On the issue of transposition, the ILC makes reference to the need for a general principle to be compatible with 'fundamental principles of international law' and notes that it must be the case that 'the conditions exist for its adequate application in the international legal system'.[29] In relation to the latter requirement, the ILC explained that this concerns

[22] ILC, 'Second Report on General Principles of Law' (27 April–5 June and 6 July–7 August 2020) UN Doc A/CN.4/741, 58 para 13. In his discussion of this term, the special rapporteur explains its appeal as being due to its consonance with Article 15(2) of the International Covenant on Civil and Political Rights (adopted 16 December 1966, entered into force 23 March 1976) 999 UNTS 171.

[23] ILC, 'Second Report on General Principles of Law' (n 22).

[24] ILC, 'Third Report on General Principles of Law' (18 April–3 June and 4 July–5 August 2022) UN Doc A/CN.4/753, 52–53.

[25] ILC, 'Second Report on General Principles' (n 22) 58 (Draft Conclusion 3).

[26] ibid 58 (Draft Conclusion 4).

[27] See eg J Ellis, 'General Principles and Comparative Law' (2011) 22 EJIL 949; N Jain 'Comparative International Law at the ICTY: The General Principles Experiment' (2015) 109 AJIL 486.

[28] ILC, 'Second Report on General Principles' (n 22) 58 (Draft Conclusion 5).

[29] ibid 58 (Draft Conclusion 6).

the suitability or appropriateness of a prospective general principle to be applicable in inter-state relations.[30]

When it comes to general principles that are formed within the international legal system, the ILC notes three factors for their ascertainment in Draft Conclusion 7 – namely, that:

> (a) a principle is widely recognized in treaties and other international instruments;
> (b) a principle underlies general rules of conventional or customary international law; or
> (c) a principle is inherent in the basic features and fundamental requirements of the international legal system.[31]

While these appear to be alternative, the special rapporteur notes that these forms of recognition are not mutually exclusive and that they may co-exist as evidence of wide and representative recognition of a general principle by states.[32]

The ILC's account of the ascertainment of general principles is, of course, extremely helpful in exploring this foundational issue. I would, however, question the persistence of the distinction between general principles of domestic law origin and those that develop purely on the international plane.[33] In my view, following from the requirement of general recognition, the focus should be on whether there is sufficient international support for the identification of an international norm.[34] While prevalence in domestic systems may be an important factor in the ascertainment of general principles, the drawing of a distinction between general principles of a domestic origin and international general principles is an oversimplification. All general principles must find the required level of support in international law. The idea of transposition from domestic to international law, while going some way in acknowledging this need, is inadequate. This is for two related reasons. First, the notion that a common core of a norm can be extrapolated from domestic systems to the international legal system is rather artificial. Reference to domestic systems may support the idea that a prospective norm is linked with notions of legal logic, but the act

[30] ibid para 96.

[31] ibid 58 (Draft Conclusion 7).

[32] ibid para 121.

[33] This is frequently asserted in the literature; see eg C Redgwell, 'General Principles of International Law' in S Vogenauer and S Weatherill, *General Principles of Law: European and Comparative Perspectives* (Hart 2017) 9; P Dailler, M Forteau, and A Pellet, *Droit international public* (8th edn, LGDJ 2009) 380.

[34] I explore this in more detail elsewhere; see Eggett (n 2) ch 4.

of transposition is, in essence, the same as establishing recognition in and consonance with international law. Second, it does not reflect the reality that a norm applicable only in a handful of domestic systems may nevertheless become a general principle if it finds support from other actors, instruments, or norms. In asserting the existence of a prospective general principle, actors can (and do) refer to both domestic and international sources in support of their claim. Put differently, there is a certain overlap between the factors referred to in Draft Conclusions 5 and 7.

As noted by the ILC in its Second Report, there is potential overlap between the evidence used in the ascertainment of general principles and that used for the identification of custom, particularly when it comes to domestic legislation and judicial decisions.[35] In the view of the ILC, the distinction between the methodology used to identify each source is preserved by the need for *opinio juris* for custom and transposition in the case of general principles.[36] In my view, while there is indeed some overlap between these sources, the distinction in ascertainment methodologies boils down to the fact that the centre of gravity for custom is the practice and views of states, while with general principles of law this lies with a broader range of actors, particularly courts and tribunals. States are indeed relevant for general principles, and it may be that a general principle may not form contrary to the will of states, but there is no need to identify a link to the subjective and objective position taken by a majority of states, as is the case with customary law. I acknowledge here that this position is predicated on what may be considered a narrow understanding of the constitutive elements of custom. If it is assumed that there is a more significant role for non-state actors in the creation of custom, then the distinction between the two categories of unwritten rules becomes blurred and it may be more sensible to label all unwritten rules as custom and to equate general principles with principles in the true sense. However, this position is not consonant with the drafting of the PCIJ Statute, the practice of courts and tribunals,[37] or the position of the ILC. It is with this understanding of general principles in mind that the discussion in subsequent sections is developed.

[35] ILC, 'Second Report on General Principles' (n 22) paras 107–12.

[36] ibid paras 110–11.

[37] For an excellent recent overview of the drafting of Article 38(1)(c) and international decisions involving general principles, see I Saunders, *General Principles as a Source of International Law: Article 38(1)(c) of the Statute of the International Court of Justice* (Hart 2021) chs 2–6.

3 General Principles as Part of the Interpretative Architecture of International Law

It has been argued that international law on interpretation has a 'treaty focus',[38] meaning that 'international legal interpretative doctrine remains firmly rooted in the law of treaties, even as scholars push for a wider lens'.[39] Explaining this position, Duncan Hollis refers to the challenges present in the ascertainment of unwritten sources, which results in the central position of treaties, specifically the rules contained in Articles 31 and 32 of the Vienna Convention on the Law of Treaties (VCLT) of 1969,[40] in the body of norms that guide the interpretation of international law.[41] Indeed, it is clear that the VCLT rules are core elements in the interpretative architecture of international law, with both judicial decisions[42] and academics[43] asserting that they form part of customary international law. On the basis of the aforementioned understanding of general principles and customary law, it is arguable that such assertions are not commonly supported by reference to the required state practice and *opinio juris*. That being said, this is largely a question of semantics, as I would not question that these rules are part of general international law. Yet, from this starting point, two issues arise in relation to the interpretation of customary international law. First, whether the general international law equivalents of the VCLT rules apply to unwritten rules (in the same way as they do to treaties) and, second, whether there are other norms at play in the interpretation of international law.

Precisely mapping this interpretative infrastructure is a challenging task, particularly in the case of unwritten rules, where the lines between law ascertainment and content determination (interpretation) may appear

[38] DB Hollis, 'Sources in Interpretation Theories: An Interdependent Relationship' in S Besson and J d'Aspremont, *The Oxford Handbook on the Sources of International Law* (Oxford University Press 2017) 429.

[39] ibid 430.

[40] Vienna Convention on the Law of Treaties (adopted 23 May 1969, entered into force 27 January 1980) 1155 UNTS 331.

[41] Hollis (n 38) 432.

[42] See eg *Application of the Convention on the Prevention and Punishment of the Crime of Genocide (Bosnia and Herzegovina v Serbia and Montenegro)* (Merits) [2007] ICJ Rep 43 [109]–[110]; *Restrictions on Imports of Tuna- United States*, GATT Dispute Settlement Panel Report (1994) 33 ILM 839, 892; *Arbitral Award of 31 July 1989 (Guinea-Bissau v Senegal)* [1991] ICJ Rep 53 [70].

[43] See eg G Hernández, *International Law* (2nd edn, Oxford University Press 2022) 196; J Crawford, *Brownlie's Principles of Public International Law* (9th edn, Cambridge University Press 2019) 366.

difficult to draw.[44] Nevertheless, as a preliminary matter, it should be made clear that interpretation of customary rules is not only possible, but necessary.[45] While there are key differences between the interpretation of written and unwritten rules, the content of all rules will be expressed in written form of one kind or another. Naturally, the processes of ascertainment of unwritten rules may themselves involve interpretation of some kind, but this does not change the fact that the content of the rules will be subject to interpretation once they have been ascertained.[46] Put differently, the criteria for the existence of a customary rules are distinct from the rules as such.[47] The interpretation of custom should thus be viewed as 'the act of determining/construing the content of customary rules the existence of which is unchallenged'.[48]

My central argument in this section is that general principles of law could play a key role when considering these questions in the context of interpreting customary rules. If, as asserted, general principles are a distinct category of (predominantly) secondary rules, they could serve as a basis for international law's general rules of interpretation, in particular in the case of interpreting unwritten rules such as those of customary international law. Before expanding on this claim further, it is necessary to consider the normative composition of the interpretative architecture of international law. In seeking to describe this legal framework, authors and judges have deployed a range of terms to denote differences in the nature, function, and origin of norms that aid the process of interpretation.

3.1 Maxims, Methods, Principles, and Rules of Interpretation

The body of international law concerned with interpretation is normatively heterogenous. In other words, the task of interpreting an

44 P Merkouris, 'Interpreting Customary International Law: You'll Never Walk Alone' in P Merkouris, D Peat, and N Arajärvi (eds), *The Theory, Practice, and Interpretation of Customary International Law* (Cambridge University Press 2022) 348.

45 For a contrary view, see eg A Gourgourinis, 'The Distinction between Interpretation and Application of Norms in International Adjudication' (2011) 2 JIDS 31, 36.

46 See generally P Merkouris, 'Interpreting the Customary Rules on Interpretation' (2017) 19 ICLR 126.

47 This argument is elaborated upon in M Fortuna, 'Different Strings of the Same Harp: Interpretation of Customary International Rules, Their Identification and Treaty Interpretation' in P Merkouris, D Peat, and N Arajärvi (eds), *The Theory, Practice, and Interpretation of Customary International Law* (Cambridge University Press 2022) 399–401. See also O Chasapis Tassinis, 'Customary International Law: Interpretation from Beginning to End' (2020) 31 EJIL 235, 245–46.

48 Fortuna (n 47) 404.

international legal rule is not regulated by rules alone;[49] the process of interpretation is 'highly context-specific'.[50] It may even be argued that there is such a high degree of discretion for interpreters that there is but a marginal role for norms that guide this process.[51] The reality of this discretion does not, it is argued, remove the relevance of norms of interpretation. There are norms that regulate the approach taken by interpreters, but it can be very difficult to determine the existence and content of these norms. This difficulty is reflected in the terms used to explain approaches to and limits of interpretation in international law. For example, reference has been made to 'rules',[52] 'principles',[53] 'methods',[54] and 'maxims'[55] of interpretation. The intended content of such labels may differ depending on the user, but an essential distinction for present purposes is that between concrete (definitive) *rules* of interpretation and other norms and notions that may provide (non-definitive) guidance for those engaging in the task of interpretation. Specific rules on interpretation may regulate the basic steps that must be taken by, or impose certain obligations on, the interpreter in specific situations. For example, it may be a rule that the first port of call must always be the text itself or that certain methods can be used only if others fail.[56] Other norms – certain maxims or principles of interpretation – may simply provide general guidance or relevant factors for the process of

[49] P Merkouris and D Peat, 'Final Report on the Interpretative Practice of the PCIJ/ICJ' (International Law Association, 79th Biennial Conference, Kyoto, 2020) 1 (making the same point in relation to the practice of the PCIJ/ICJ).

[50] D Peat, *Comparative Reasoning in International Courts and Tribunals* (Cambridge University Press 2019) 18.

[51] ibid 19 (referring to, inter alia, H Lauterpacht, 'Restrictive Interpretation and the Principle of Effectiveness in the Interpretation of Treaties' (1949) 26 BYBIL 48.

[52] A Bianchi, D Peat, and M Windsor (eds), *Interpretation in International Law* (Oxford University Press 2015) pt IV (referring also to 'strategies' in pt V); A Orakhelashvili, *The Interpretation of Acts and Rules in Public International Law* (Oxford University Press 2008) pt IV (referring also to 'methods' as part of the 'regime' of interpretation). See also the language used in VCLT (n 40) art 39.

[53] C McLachlan, 'The Principle of Systemic Integration and Article 31(3)(c) of the Vienna Convention' (2005) 54 ICLQ 279; J Klingler, Y Parkhomenko, and C Salonidis (eds), *Between the Lines of the Vienna Convention? Canons and Other Principles of Interpretation in Public International Law* (Kluwer Law International 2019).

[54] O Ammann, *Domestic Courts and the Interpretation of International Law: Methods and Reasoning Based on the Swiss Example* (Brill 2020); N Arajärvi, *The Changing Nature of Customary International Law: Methods of Interpreting the Concept of Custom in International Criminal Tribunals* (Routledge 2014).

[55] Merkouris and Peat (n 49) 7–15; F Macagno, D Walton, and G Sartor, 'Pragmatic Maxims and Presumptions in Legal Interpretation' (2017) 37 Law Philos 69.

[56] Such is the case with the rules contained in VCLT (n 40) arts 31 and 32.

interpretation while not mandating a specific course of action for the interpreter. A potential example of such a norm is the notion of *per analogiam* interpretation.[57] While the relevance and scope of this notion in international law are unsettled,[58] it would seem that this would merely be a tool to be used at the discretion of the interpreter to aid in their task.

The precise scope of a prospective norm of interpretation is not always clear and there may be overlap between different notions. Yet, as explained, the initial task when mapping this legal framework should be a distinction between rules of interpretation and other, non-definitive, norms. Indeed, in my view, the legal framework for the interpretation of international law consists of a collection of rules and principles. It seems, however, that this framework is not clearly and comprehensively defined. There are a number of prospective or candidate norms that may – or may not (yet) – be part of international law. These candidate norms are commonly linked to basic notions of legal logic and their existence in a range of domestic law systems, and may be expressed in the form of certain Latin maxims.[59] The connections with notions of legal logic and domestic law suggest a role for general principles of law in the development of this interpretative framework. As explained above, general principles in the sense of Article 38(1)(c) of the ICJ Statute are frequently explained with reference to basic ideas of legal law and a comparative examination of domestic systems. Yet, the exact role of general principles will, once again, depend on the position taken on the nature of this category of norms. According to my understanding of general principles as a distinct category of *rules*, only accepted norms that impose concrete obligations on the interpreter can be considered as general principles of law in the sense of Article 38(1)(c) of the ICJ Statute. Other general, non-definitive, norms that may be found in domestic systems do not fall within this category. However, it may be that they are accepted principles *stricto sensu* providing first-order and non-definitive reasons to reach a particular result without specifically requiring this. To reiterate, the position taken here is not aimed at minimising the potential impact of such principles, which may effectively facilitate a pragmatic approach to interpretation in international law.

57 Interpretation by analogy: the notion that recourse may be had to the interpretation of rules in other contexts as inspiration for the case at hand.

58 Merkouris and Peat (n 49) 14 (explaining that, while the ICJ has used methodology that resembles *per analogiam*, it has not elaborated on this notion).

59 For a good overview of the appearance of such maxims in the decisions of the PCIJ and ICJ, see Merkouris and Peat (n 49) 7–15.

3.2 *General Principles as Rules of Interpretation (of Custom)*

It is clear that there are such things as *rules* of interpretation in international law. This much is evident from the VCLT of 1969. Typically seen as embodying the 'general rule' on interpretation,[60] Article 31 of the VCLT of 1969 imposes obligations on interpreters to take into account certain factors and circumstances surrounding the language, background, and broader context of the rule in question. These rules impose obligations of conduct on interpreters, yet there is certainly room to place the emphasis on different factors and circumstances. Within the general rule of Article 31(1) of the VCLT of 1969, for example, it is generally considered that there is no hierarchy of elements and that the different aspects listed – good faith, ordinary meaning, context, and object and purpose – should be considered as part of a single process.[61] The rules in the VCLT are, of course, treaty rules. If there are more generally applicable rules of interpretation, they will have to be based on another source of international law: either custom or general principles of law. Indeed, the mainstream position is that any general rules on the interpretation of international law are grounded in custom. This is true for the general international law equivalents of the VCLT rules, which have been held as part of customary law.[62] In Sections 3.2.1 and 3.2.2 it is argued that general principles of law will frequently be a more appropriate basis for such generally applicable rules of interpretation.

3.2.1 The Case for General Principles as a Source of Rules of Interpretation

As a preliminary point, it should be noted that rules of international law may be based on multiple sources of law. That is to say, similar or identical rules emanating from different sources – treaties, custom, or general principles – may exist and apply in parallel.[63] Therefore, rules of interpretation that are present in one source – say, a treaty such as the

[60] M Villiger, *Commentary on the 1969 Vienna Convention on the Law of Treaties* (Brill/ Nijhoff 2009) 423, 435.

[61] ibid 435–36.

[62] See eg *Maritime Dispute (Peru v Chile)* (Judgment) [2014] ICJ Rep 3 [57]; *Territorial Dispute (Libyan Arab Jamahiriya v Chad)* (Judgment) [1994] ICJ Rep 6 [41]; *Oil Platforms (Islamic Republic of Iran v United States of America)* (Preliminary Objections) [1996] ICJ Rep 182 [23]. For a detailed examination of this, see M Fitzmaurice and P Merkouris, *Treaties in Motion: The Evolution of Treaties from Formation to Termination* (Cambridge University Press 2020) 147–58.

[63] See generally T Broude and Y Shany (eds), *Multi-Sourced Equivalent Norms in International Law* (Hart 2011). The ICJ explicitly acknowledged the parallel application

VCLT of 1969 – may also exist as custom and/or general principle of law. In many instances, then, the presence of a norm of general international law (custom or general principle) may be irrelevant where there is a treaty rule applicable to the party in question.

It is clear that there are rules of interpretation beyond the specific context of the VCLT of 1969, even if it is merely the case that the VCLT rules have general international law equivalents. Indeed, the rules reflected in the VCLT have been deemed to apply both to treaties that pre-date their codification in the Vienna Convention[64] and to other sources of law,[65] thereby necessitating their existence in general international law. A rule found in the VCLT of 1969 has a different scope of application from an identical customary rule or general principle. Not only could such a rule apply to all treaties; it could also apply to rules emanating from the other sources of law, in particular customary rules.[66] There is, therefore, a need to determine whether such unwritten rules exist. As mentioned, it is most commonly asserted that the application of these rules beyond the context of the VCLT is due to the parallel existence of these rules as custom. This position is consonant with the broader trend to equate all unwritten rules of international law as customary. Given that customary international law is a clearer concept (or at least, less unclear) than general principles, this is unsurprising. Indeed, this claim may, in many circumstances, have merit; customary law has clearly been instrumental in the development of the international legal system. Yet, such arguments should be examined more closely, as there are significant implications for automatic (over-)reliance on custom as a vehicle for such rules. While there may be general rules of international law that fulfil the requirements of customary law, it should not be assumed, as is frequently the case, that all general international law rules are grounded in custom. As Sir Robert Jennings observed, 'most of

of treaty-based and customary rules in *Military and Paramilitary Activities in and against Nicaragua (Nicaragua v United States of America)* (Merits) [1986] ICJ Rep 14 [178].

64 See eg *Legality of Use of Force (Serbia and Montenegro v Belgium)* (Preliminary Objections) (2004) ICJ Rep 279 [100]; *Kasikili/Sedudu Island (Botswana v Namibia)* (Judgment) [1999] ICJ Rep 1045 [18]; *Dispute Regarding Navigation and Related Rights (Costa Rica v Nicaragua)* (Judgment) [2000] ICJ Rep 237 [47].

65 This aspect is less settled but seems perfectly logical. Most prominently, the rule on systemic interpretation as contained in Article 31(3)(c) of the VCLT is argued to be applicable to customary rules. See eg P Merkouris, *Article 31(3)(c) VCLT and the Principle of Systemic Integration: Normative Shadows in Plato's Cave* (Brill/Nijhoff 2015) ch 4; Fortuna (n 47) 411.

66 In the case of a general customary rule of interpretation, this would of course be subject to any modification to its scope of application as a result of persistent objection. See *Anglo-Norwegian Fisheries (United Kingdom v Norway)* (Judgment) [1951] ICJ Rep 116, 131.

what we perversely persist in calling customary international law is not only *not* customary law; it does not even faintly resemble customary law'.[67]

The process for the determination of custom has traditionally centred on the fulfilment of two elements: widespread and consistent state practice and the accompanying belief by states that such conduct is legally required (*opinio juris*).[68] The formation of custom has received renewed attention in the recent work of the International Law Commission (ILC), which sought to provide further guidance on the identification of customary rules.[69] While acknowledging the broader context in which these two elements must be assessed,[70] the ILC reaffirmed the focus on the two elements of custom and the centrality of states to the formation of customary rules.[71] While the ILC specified the need for 'systematic and rigorous analysis' of state practice and *opinio juris* in assessing the formation of a customary rule, it has been widely noted that this is seldom the case in reality, with courts simply asserting the existence of a customary rule with little or no evidence.[72] This is, of course, unsatisfactory. The existence of all international legal rules is premised on the fulfilment of conditions of validity and the fulfilment of these conditions must be supported by evidence. For customary rules, this evidence is found in the actions and views of states. This evidence may be assessed by courts and tribunals, but the focus is on what states are doing and claiming. Yet, many rules of interpretation – like many other secondary rules – have developed in international law through the decisions of international courts and tribunals, as it is predominantly these actors that are faced with the task of interpretation. In many instances, it would not be accurate to say that these rules have fulfilled the requirements of

[67] See eg R Jennings, 'The Identification of International Law' in B Cheng (ed), *International Law: Teaching and Practice* (Stevens & Sons 1982) 5.

[68] *North Sea Continental Shelf Cases (Germany v Denmark; Germany v Netherlands)* (Judgment) [1969] ICJ Rep 3 [60]–[76].

[69] ILC, 'Draft Conclusions on Identification of Customary International Law, with Commentaries' (30 April–1 June and 2 July–10 August 2018) UN Doc A/73/10.

[70] See eg ibid, Draft Conclusion 3 and the accompanying commentary, 126–27 (referring to the 'context' and 'underlying principles' of a rule).

[71] See eg ibid, Draft Conclusion 4 and the accompanying commentary, 130–32 (explaining that 'States play a pre-eminent role in the formation of customary international law, and it is principally their practice that has to be examined in identifying it'; noting also a limited role played by the practice of international organisations in certain circumstances).

[72] S Talmon, 'Determining Customary International Law: The ICJ's Methodology between Induction, Deduction and Assertion' (2015) 26(2) EJIL 417, 434–40; C Ryngaert and D Hora Siccama, 'Ascertaining Customary International Law: An Inquiry into the Methods Used by Domestic Courts' (2018) 65 NILR 1, 1–2.

custom. The rules have developed out of necessity, with reference to domestic law and the broader context and features of the international legal system. It may be argued that the assertion of such norms by states before international courts and tribunals is sufficient to demonstrate their customary status. At best, the assertions of states may be seen as evidence of *opinio juris*, but it is rarely the case that the practice of states supports the existence of such norms. The actor relevant in the act of interpretation is, typically, a judicial body. Questions of interpretation come before international courts and tribunals, which, in the absence of established norms, search for and confirm the existence of rules governing the process of international adjudication. In determining the existence and content of such rules of interpretation, as with many other secondary rules in international law, courts and tribunals have not limited themselves to an assessment of the elements of customary law but have had recourse to a broader range of factors, including domestic law and principles *stricto sensu*.[73]

3.2.2 Candidates for General Principles of Interpretation

As mentioned, some of the general rules of interpretation of international law – whether based in custom or general principles – will also be treaty rules contained in the VCLT. In the context of the law of treaties and on the basis of the jurisprudence of the ICJ, Sir Gerald Fitzmaurice compiled a list of six principles of interpretation.[74] These were:[75] (1) the principle of actuality (textuality); (2) the principle of natural and ordinary meaning; (3) the principle of integration;[76] (4) the principle of effectiveness; (5) the principle of subsequent practice; and (6) the principle of contemporaneity. These principles set out a general process for the interpretation of international rules, which was later taken up in the drafting of the VCLT of 1969. Indeed, many of the notions identified by Fitzmaurice and later included in the VCLT have a long history in the decisions of international courts and tribunals,[77] as well as established pedigree as basic elements of

[73] See generally Kotuby and Sobota (n 19).

[74] ILC, 'Fifth Report on the Law of Treaties' (1966) UN Doc A/CN.4/183 and Add.1–4, 220.

[75] For a discussion, see M Fitzmaurice, 'The Practical Working of the Law of Treaties' in M Evans, *International Law* (5th edn, Oxford University Press 2018) 138, 152–53 (explaining that the three final principles 'take effect subject to' the first three principles).

[76] That treaties are to be interpreted as a whole and as part of their overall context. This is not to be confused with 'systemic integration' (interpretation) in the sense discussed in Section 4.

[77] H Thirlway, *The Law and Procedure of the International Court of Justice: Fifty Years of Jurisprudence Volume II* (Oxford University Press 2013) pt 2, ch 2.

legal logic in domestic systems. Some of these principles may be more difficult to apply in the context of the interpretation of customary rules. For example, it may be more difficult to apply the principle of integration to a rule not based in a specific and authoritative text. Further, there are inherent difficulties that arise in assessing subsequent practice in the context of customary rules, as questions may arise as to whether such practice is part of the formation of new rules or the interpretation of existing rules. Nevertheless, on the basis of the historical background to these principles and their subsequent acceptance in the VCLT and judicial decisions, it seems convincing that they form part of general international law and so could be used as an approach to the interpretation of customary rules. Yet, as described above, it should not merely be assumed that these general rules are customary, as their acceptance has not been a clear result of the actions and views of states but of judicial bodies striving for a framework of secondary rules to aid in the task of interpretation in the absence of an applicable treaty rule.

In addition to, or perhaps as part of, the basic rules reflected in the VCLT of 1969, it may be possible to argue for the existence of other rules of interpretation grounded in general principles. A clear candidate includes the uncontroversial proposition that an interpretation of a rule cannot contradict a *jus cogens* norm.[78] Indeed, this interpretation rule is logical given the nature and role of *jus cogens* norms and the consequences of their violation. This was advanced by the Islamic Republic of Iran in the *Oil Platforms* case, where it was argued that:

> Under Article 53 of the Vienna Convention ... a provision of a treaty which conflicts with a norm of *jus cogens* is void ... That is to say, the treaty as a whole is void. These rigorous provisions must in turn generate a stringent principle of interpretation, so that any provision of a treaty is to be interpreted, if at all possible, so as not to conflict with such a rule.[79]

While not specifically endorsing the rule of interpretation as formulated by Iran, the ICJ explained that it was required to interpret the treaty rule

[78] *Application of the Convention on the Prevention and Punishment of the Crime of Genocide (Bosnia and Herzegovina v Serbia and Montenegro)* (Judgment) [2007] ICJ Rep 43, Joint Declaration of Judges Shi and Koroma [2]; *Gabčíkovo-Nagymaros Project (Hungary v Slovakia)* (Judgment) [1997] ICJ Rep 7, Separate Opinion of Judge Bedjaoui [6].

[79] *Oil Platforms (Islamic Republic of Iran v United States of America)* Reply and Defence to Counter-Claim, Islamic Republic of Iran, vol I (10 March 1999) 164–65 <www.icj-cij.org/sites/default/files/case-related/90/8630.pdf> accessed 1 April 2022.

in question (Article XX of the Treaty of Amity[80]) in conformity with the rules on the use of force.[81] The existence of such a rule has been recently confirmed by the ILC in the context of its work on *jus cogens*.[82]

There are other candidates for rules of interpretation that should be classified as general principles of law. Whether these prospective norms are to be considered as general principles of law or principles *stricto sensu* will depend on their precise scope and content. Take, for example, the collection of 'maxims'/'cannons' of interpretation in the practice of the PCIJ and ICJ, as identified by Merkouris and Peat.[83] The scope for notions such as *in dubio mitius*,[84] *effet utile*,[85] and *per analogiam*[86] to constitute general principles of law will very much depend on their precise context in the international legal system. It is beyond the scope of this chapter to consider these notions/norms in detail, but what is critical is whether courts and tribunals elucidate clear conditions for their application and whether this involves the imposition of obligations on the interpreter. There is considerable practice in support of such norms, and so it seems that there is potential for the development of rules in the form of general principles here. That being said, depending on the precise content of the norm, it may be that these norms amount to principles *stricto sensu*. For example, the 'principle of effectiveness' is clearly viewed as part of international law and as being of relevance to the interpretation of international rules.[87] Its

80 Treaty of Amity, Economic Relations and Consular Rights between the United States and Iran (adopted 15 August 1955, entered into force 16 June 1957) 284 UNTS 93.

81 *Oil Platforms (Islamic Republic of Iran v United States of America)* (Judgment) [2003] ICJ Rep 161 [40]–[41]. The rule prohibiting the use of force is mentioned by the ILC in its illustrative list of *jus cogens* norms: ILC, 'Fourth Report on Peremptory Norms of General International Law (*jus cogens*) by Dire Tladi, Special Rapporteur' (2019) UN Doc A/CN.4/727 para 60.

82 ILC, 'Fifth Report on Peremptory Norms of General International Law (*jus cogens*)' (2022) UN Doc A/CN.4/747, Conclusion 20.

83 Merkouris and Peat (n 49) 7–15.

84 Essentially, the idea of restrictive interpretation. See eg *Free Zones of Upper Savoy and District of Gex (France v Switzerland)* (Merits) [1932] PCIJ Ser A/B No 46, 12 (declaring that 'in case of doubt, a limitation of sovereignty must be construed restrictively').

85 The interpretation adopted should be the one that gives effect to a rule, as opposed to an interpretation that renders the rule meaningless and ineffective, or, put differently, the idea that a rule should be given its 'proper effects'. See *Whaling in the Antarctic (Australia v Japan; New Zealand intervening)* (Judgment) [2014] ICJ Rep 226, Separate Opinion of Judge Cançado Trindade [54].

86 Interpretation by analogy. The notion that recourse may be had to the interpretation of rules in other contexts as inspiration for the case at hand.

87 See eg GI Hernández, 'Effectiveness' in J d'Aspremont and S Singh, *Concepts for International Law: Contributions to Disciplinary Thought* (Edward Elgar 2019) 237; O Hathaway,

precise content, however, is less clear. It may, for example, not require an interpreter to strive to assign the greatest possible effectiveness to a rule, but instead merely to seek to avoid an interpretation that avoids depriving a rule of any effects altogether.[88] In this sense, it may be seen to underlie the general rules of interpretation set out in Article 31 of the VCLT of 1969.[89] Whether such norms are considered general principles of law will depend on courts and tribunals continuing to deliberate on them.

4 General Principles, Custom, and Systemic Interpretation[90]

A particularly prominent tool in the interpretation of unwritten rules is the notion of systemic integration. More precisely, against the background of broader principles of coherence and consistency in the international legal system,[91] there is a specific *rule* of systemic interpretation. This rule requires that interpreters take into account 'any relevant rules of international law applicable in the relations between the parties'.[92] The central objective of this rule of interpretation is coherence and consistency in the international legal system. The development of general principles of law, too, has links to such notions. This final section explores the interaction between this rule of systemic interpretation and general principles in international law. Once general principles are understood to be rules, two issues arise with regard to systemic interpretation: first, whether this rule on systemic interpretation can itself be considered a general principle and, second, whether and how the interpretation of customary rules occurs in light of general principles as 'relevant rules of international law'.

4.1 *Systemic Interpretation as a General Principle of Law*

The idea that international rules should be interpreted coherently and consistently with the normative environment in which they exist is inherently attractive. Such coherence is linked to the idea of international

L Johnson, and F Ní Aoláin, 'An Introduction: Effectiveness in International Law' (2014) 108 ASIL Proc 1 and the other contributions to this annual meeting.

[88] Merkouris and Peat (n 49) 10, referring to G Fitzmaurice, '*Vae victis* or Woe to the Negotiators: Your Treaty or Our "Interpretation" of It?' (1971) 65 AJIL 358.

[89] *Whaling in the Antarctic*, Separate Opinion of Judge Cançado Trindade (n 85) [54].

[90] For the purposes of this chapter, the terms 'systemic interpretation' and 'systemic integration' are used interchangeably.

[91] Merkouris, *Article 31(3)(c) VCLT* (n 65) 2; McLachlan (n 53) 279.

[92] Reflected in VCLT art 31(3)(c).

law as a legal system, and the imposition of an obligation on interpreters to respect and facilitate this systemic coherence is a logical foundation of the international legal order.[93] McLachlan has claimed that systemic integration has the status of a 'constitutional norm' in international law.[94] It is clear that the obligation to systemically interpret international rules has a strong pedigree in the international legal system, perhaps as an 'unconscious part of the interpretation process'.[95] While undoubtedly part of international law beyond the VCLT of 1969, it may be questioned whether the rule on systemic interpretation is customary, as is the standard claim, or whether it is better conceived of as a general principle of law. It is clear that this norm is a *rule* of international law, more specifically one that imposes an obligation of conduct on interpreters to 'take into account' certain factors. Further, it should be noted that this rule has a long history in the decisions of courts and tribunals,[96] including by the ICJ in *Oil Platforms*.[97] The prominence of courts and tribunals in the development of this international rule, together with its close relationship with principles *stricto sensu* (such as coherence[98]), suggest its characterisation as a general principle as opposed to a customary rule.

4.2 General Principles as 'Relevant Rules of International Law'

Already in the *Georges Pinson* case reference was made to the need to interpret rules in accordance with 'general principles of international law'.[99] If general principles of law are rules, they are rules of general

93 For an overview of the systemic nature of international law, see Eggett (n 2). ch 2. See also R Higgins, *Problems and Processes: International law and How We Use It* (Clarendon Press 1995) 1, 8 (arguing that international law is more accurately understood as a normative system and process rather than a set of rules.

94 McLachlan (n 53) 280. While this view illustrates the perceived importance of this norm, reference to 'constitutional' elements in international law should be treated with caution. On constitutional analogies in international law generally, see L Helfer, 'Constitutional Analogies in the International Legal System' (2003) 37 LLALR 193.

95 ILC, 'Fragmentation of International Law: Difficulties Arising from the Diversification and Expansion of International Law; Report of the Study Group of the International Law Commission' (13 April 2006) UN Doc A/CN.4/L.682 para 414.

96 Oft-cited early examples of decisions in which systemic interpretation was used by arbitral tribunals include *Georges Pinson Case (France/United Mexican States)* Award of 13 April 1928, UNRIAA, vol V, 422; *Différend concernant l'accord Tardieu-Jaspar (Belgium/France)* Award of 1 March 1937, UNRIAA, vol III, 1713.

97 *Oil Platforms* (n 81) [40].

98 See generally the contributions in M Andenas and others (eds), *General Principles and the Coherence of International Law* (Brill/Nijhoff 2019).

99 *Georges Pinson Case* (n 96) 422.

application.[100] It therefore seems they could frequently play a role as 'relevant rules of international law applicable in relations between the parties'. However, two clarifications should be made here. Firstly, frequent recourse to something labelled as a '(general) principle' may not be reference to a general principle in the sense of Article 38(1)(c) of the ICJ Statute. Instead, this may be a reference to principles *stricto sensu*.[101] For example, reference may be made to 'general principles' such as 'sovereignty'[102] or 'humanity'[103] when approaching the interpretation of rules. These, of course, play a key role in interpretation as they help determine the meaning of rules to which they are related, but this practice is not part of the obligation to consider other applicable *rules*.[104] Second, it should be emphasised that there is a need to identify *relevant* rules for the purposes of systemic interpretation. This would cover rules that exist in parallel in multiple sources, but it may also cover rules that deal with similar subject matter or adopt similar wording.[105] It will be recalled that general principles, partly due to the process of their ascertainment, tend to be secondary rules that emerge in the absence of any treaty or customary rules. As such, the scope for parallel or overlapping rules may be more limited than in the case of interpretation in the light of treaties or custom, which tend to concern primary rules.

There are examples in which courts and tribunals seem to have interpreted rules against the backdrop of general principles. For example, in *Golder* v. *United Kingdom*, the European Court of Human Rights referred explicitly to Article 38(1)(c) of the ICJ Statute, concluding that there was a general principle of law regarding access to civil courts when interpreting Article 6 of the European Convention on Human Rights.[106] Similarly, in *Furundžija* the Trial Chamber of the International Criminal Tribunal for the Former Yugoslavia was tasked with determining the

[100] Eggett (n 2) 158–63.

[101] Indeed, it has been argued that, as relevant principles *stricto sensu* (as understood in this chapter), Article 38(1)(c) of the ICJ Statute could be part of the process of interpretation. See eg I Saunders *General Principles as a Source of International Law: Article 38(1)(c) of the Statute of the International Court of Justice* (Hart 2021) 212–13.

[102] *Immunities and Criminal Proceedings (Equatorial Guinea v France)* (Preliminary Objections) [2018] ICJ Rep 1 [57].

[103] For an overview in the context of the law of armed conflict, see MN Schmitt, 'Military Necessity and Humanity in International Humanitarian Law: Preserving the Delicate Balance' (2010) 50(4) VJIL 795.

[104] Villiger (n 60) 433.

[105] See eg *Maritime Delimitation in the Indian Ocean (Somalia v Kenya)* (Preliminary Objections) [2017] ICJ Rep 3 [91].

[106] *Golder v United Kingdom*, App no 4451/70 (ECtHR, 21 February 1975) 213.

scope of the offence of rape in its statute. The chamber conducted a review of domestic approaches to this question and made reference to the principle (*stricto sensu*) of human dignity.[107] It should be noted that in such cases there may be a need to identify a prospective general principle before it can be used in the systemic interpretation of a treaty or customary rule. As mentioned at the outset, general principles of law have received comparatively little attention in international law. There is, therefore, significant unrealised potential for their use as a tool for the development of new rules. In some fields, this potential may also include scope for the development of new *primary* rules of international law.[108] For example, there are several unwritten primary rules in international environmental law that seemed to originate not in the practice of states but in the reasoning of courts and tribunals. These include the obligation to prevent transboundary harm[109] and the obligation to notify other states in the event of such harm.[110] It may be expected that the renewed interest in general principles in scholarship and by the ILC may lead to a greater role played by these norms in the development of new international rules. If this is the case, the scope for general principles to influence the systemic interpretation of customary rules would be further enhanced.

5 Concluding Remarks

This chapter has explored the interface between two developing fields at the very foundations of international law: the nature of general principles of law and the interpretation of customary rules. Central to the ongoing discussion on the nature, function, and place of general principles in the international legal system is the question of the interaction between general principles and other international legal norms. Questions of interpretation are a prominent area of such interaction, and, assuming general principles to be secondary rules of international law, there is significant potential for the development of general principles of interpretation. For the most part, the discussions sketched in this chapter may appear to amount to an exercise in (inconsequential) labelling. Yet, when approaching a task as challenging as that of mapping the interpretative

107 *Prosecutor v Furundžija* (Judgment) ICTY-95-17/1 (10 December 1998) [182]–[184].

108 Eggett (n 2) 163–68.

109 *Trail Smelter Arbitration (United States v Canada)* [1941] 3 UNRIAA 1905, 1965; *Corfu Channel (United Kingdom v Albania)* (Judgment) [1949] ICJ Rep 4, 22.

110 *Blockade of Portendic (Great Britain v France)* [1843] 42 BFSP 1377.

architecture of custom, the labels used matter. As important as customary rules are, it is inaccurate to use 'customary international law' as shorthand for any and all norms beyond treaties. There are clear distinctions to be drawn between the different categories of rules and principles that constitute 'general international law'. This exploration of the role of general principles in the interpretation of custom illustrates the normative heterogeneity of general international law, providing a foundation for further examination of the precise contours of the structures that govern the interpretation of unwritten rules and other systemic questions of international law.

11

Interpretation of Customary Rules by Reference to Treaties and General Principles of Law

MARINA FORTUNA

1 Introduction

In its case law, the International Court of Justice (ICJ) has repeatedly suggested the idea that rules of customary international law (CIL) do not operate in a vacuum but, instead, are to be understood against the background of other rules of the international legal system.[1] This observation, although somewhat unsurprising, shows that the sources of international law exist in close interconnection – something that is also visible if one looks at the rules of interpretation contained in Article 31 of the Vienna Convention on the Law of Treaties (VCLT). Accordingly, 'any relevant rules of international law applicable in the relations between the parties' must be taken into account, together with the context, when interpreting treaty provisions.[2] The question addressed in this chapter is whether or not the same can be said of the interpretation of *customary* rules. In other words, if we look at the practice of international courts and tribunals, is it possible to reach the conclusion that CIL rules, too, must be interpreted with the cognizance of any relevant rules of international law applicable between the parties?

To answer this question, I have enquired into the practice of international courts and, in particular, into the ways in which, if at all, they use

This chapter is a slightly modified version of chapter 4 of my PhD thesis 'Interpretation of Customary International Law in International Courts', published by Ridderprint in October 2023. The chapter is based on research conducted in the context of the project 'The Rules of Interpretation of Customary International Law' ('TRICI-Law'). This project received funding from the European Research Council (ERC) under the European Union's Horizon 2020 Research and Innovation Programme (Grant Agreement No. 759728).

[1] See n 12.

[2] Vienna Convention on the Law of Treaties (adopted 23 May 1969, entered into force 27 January 1980) 1155 UNTS 331, Article 31.

treaties and general principles of law – the other two sources of international law contained in Article 38 of the ICJ Statute – to interpret the content of customary rules. Here, following my previous writings on the subject of CIL interpretation, I understand interpretation as an act of discerning the content and scope of the customary *rule*, rather than interpreting the elements of custom – state practice and *opinio juris*. While in this chapter I engage in a critical reading of the judgments, I leave aside as being outside the scope of this chapter my musings on the interpretability of CIL.[3]

According to the ILC's draft conclusions on the identification of CIL, other rules, such as those contained in treaties, can aid determination of a customary rule's existence.[4] Our focus, then, will be on studying the judgments of international courts with a view to demonstrating how they use treaties and general principles to establish the content of customary rules whose existence is not disputed by the parties.[5]

To facilitate the analysis of the case law and the accompanying argumentation, the chapter has been structured in three sections. Section 2 unpacks the various meanings of systemic interpretation that can be found both in legal scholarship and in practice and which will be used as an analytical framework for the subsequent analysis. Sections 3 and 4 analyse the case decisions in which international courts and quasi-judicial bodies have used treaties and general principles of law in construing the content of customary rules. Section 5 examines case law in which the interpretation of a CIL rule is carried out by reference to the body of rules of which it is part.

[3] For my previous writings, see M Fortuna, 'Different Strings of the Same Harp: Interpretation of Rules of Customary International Law, Their Identification and Treaty Interpretation' in P Merkouris, J Kammerhofer and N Arajarvi (eds), *The Theory, Practice, and Interpretation of Customary International Law* (Cambridge University Press 2022); M Fortuna, 'Interpretation of Customary International Law in International Courts' (PhD thesis, University of Groningen 2023) <https://research.rug.nl/en/publications/interpretation-of-customary-international-law-in-international-co> accessed 26 May 2024.

[4] ILC, 'Draft Conclusions on Identification of Customary International Law, with Commentaries' (30 April–1 June and 2 July–10 August 2018) UN Doc A/73/10, 142.

[5] On systemic interpretation of CIL rules, see also A Bleckmann, 'Zur Feststellung und Auslegung von Völkergewohnheitsrecht' (1977) 37 ZaöRV 505, 526–27; P Merkouris, *Article 31 (3) VCLT and the Principle of Systemic Integration: Normative Shadows in Plato's Cave* (Brill 2015) 266.

2 The Multiple Meanings of Systemic Interpretation as an Analytical Framework

It is common practice among international courts and tribunals to use customary rules to interpret treaties. One frequently cited example is the *Jan Mayen* case, where the ICJ stated that Article 6 of the 1958 Convention on the Continental Shelf must be interpreted and applied by reference to customary law.[6] Pronouncements similar to those made in the *Jan Mayen* case usually fall within the ambit of Article 31(3)(c) of the VCLT, according to which 'any relevant rules of international law applicable in the relations between the parties'[7] must be taken into account, together with context, in interpreting treaty provisions. This rule is usually referred to in case law and literature as the principle/rule of systemic interpretation[8] or systemic integration.[9] Confusingly, however, both of these terms have been used to convey not one but four different meanings.

Firstly, a textual analysis of Article 31(3)(c) shows this paragraph to be part and parcel of the core rule according to which treaty provisions must be interpreted in accordance with the ordinary meaning the words are to be given in their context and in the light of their object and purpose. In addition to context, Article 31(3)(c) states that any relevant rules of international law applicable in the relations between the parties must be taken into account *in the determination of the ordinary meaning of the terms.* As aptly noted by Tzekvelos, 'Article 31(3)(c) expands the semantic field of the provisions of a convention'.[10] One example of this is when interpreters look at the use of the same term in another treaty that is in

6 *Maritime Delimitation in the Area between Greenland and Jan Mayen (Denmark v Norway)* (Merits) [1993] ICJ Rep 38 [46].

7 Vienna Convention on the Law of Treaties (n 2) art 31.

8 An example in this sense is *Certain Iranian Assets (Islamic Republic of Iran v United States of America)* (Preliminary Objections) [2019] ICJ Rep 7, 72 (Separate Opinion of Judge Brower).

9 ILC, 'Report of the Study Group, Fragmentation of International Law: Difficulties Arising from the Diversification and Expansion of International Law: Conclusions' UN Doc A/CN. 4/L. 702 (18 July 2006) 84 para 413. For a more comprehensive enumeration of the different ways in which this rule is referred to, see P Merkouris, 'Principle of Systemic Integration' para 2 (2020) MPEiPro, <https://opil.ouplaw.com/view/10.1093/law-mpeipro/e2866.013.2866/law-mpeipro-e2866> accessed 13 May 2024.

10 V Tzekvelos, 'The Use of Article 31(3)(c) of the VCLT in the Case Law of the ECtHR: An Effective Anti-Fragmentation Tool or a Selective Loophole for the Reinforcement of Human Rights Teleology? Between Evolution and Systemic Integration' (2010) 31 MJIL 621, 651.

force between the parties and use it to further a particular understanding of the term. This is the first meaning of systemic interpretation.

The second meaning that has been ascribed to systemic interpretation is that of an interpretation of a rule against the background of the system of law as a whole. At the Institut de Droit International, this position was expressed by Verdross, who stated that 'a treaty must be interpreted in light of general law and general principles of law'.[11] According to the ICJ, 'a rule of international law, whether customary or conventional, does not operate in a vacuum; it operates in relation to facts and *in the context of a wider framework of legal rules of which it forms only a part*'.[12] Depending on how it is applied, this meaning of systemic interpretation may either converge with the first meaning – if the ordinary meaning is determined by reference to these other principles or rules – or go beyond it and result in what Alexy and Adler describe as the use of systemic arguments in interpretation.[13]

This second meaning is markedly different from what Article 31(3)(c) prescribes,[14] which is to use any relevant rules for the determination of ordinary meaning in the light of context and of object and purpose. It is important to note that Article 31(3)(c) mentions the use of any relevant rules applicable between the parties and not any relevant rules generally. Only reference to all relevant rules would in fact suggest that the rules as a whole should be taken into account for interpretative purposes. According to this second understanding, systemic interpretation is essentially a use of systemic arguments that involves placing the rule in the system of international law as a wider form of context.[15]

Another meaning of systemic interpretation is reflected in Verzijl's dictum in the *Georges Pinson Case*, where he noted that every treaty must

[11] Comments by Verdross, Institut de Droit International, Annuaire vol 43/I (Bath Session September 1950) 438, 456.

[12] *Interpretation of the Agreement of 25 March 1951 between the WHO and Egypt* (Advisory Opinion) [1980] ICJ Rep 73 [10] (emphasis added); *Legal Consequences for States of the Continued Presence of South Africa in Namibia (South West Africa) Notwithstanding Security Council Resolution 276 (1970)* (Advisory Opinion) [1971] ICJ Rep 16 [53]; *Jadhav (India v Pakistan)* [2019] ICJ Rep 418, 516 (Declaration of Judge Robinson).

[13] R Alexy and R Adler, *A Theory of Legal Argumentation* (Oxford University Press 2011) 240.

[14] *A contrario*, the ILC Study Group on Fragmentation established that the rule 'points to a need to take into account the normative environment more widely'. See ILC, 'Report of the Study Group' (n 9) para 415.

[15] ibid para 414. See also LM Bentivoglio, *Interpretazione del Diritto e Diritto Internazionale* (Pavia 1953) 209; PG Staubach, *The Rule of Unwritten International Law: Customary Law, General Principles and World Order* (Routledge 2018) 156.

be considered to refer tacitly to general principles of international law for all those matters that it does not clarify in express terms.[16] This is different from systemic interpretation as meaning that other relevant rules must be used to determine the sense to be given to the words used in the treaty. Instead, it is a form of gap-filling, a technique to avoid a pronouncement of *non liquet*. And while Verzijl's statement conditions recourse to general principles of law on the lack of an express resolution of the issue in conventional rules, systemic interpretation/integration has also been argued to support what essentially is an incorporation of extraneous rules and their application to the case, even when there is no clause providing for such reference.[17] The issue here is that the use of what is termed systemic interpretation would in this case be in violation of the obligation of good faith in interpretation.[18] Moreover, as Moreno-Lax rightfully points out, 'Article 31(3)(c) VCLT should indeed be taken as a rule of interpretation, rather than a source of directly applicable law'.[19]

Finally, systemic interpretation or integration has also been interpreted in a way that equates it with an interpretation that allows for co-ordination of norms in the case of indirect or, what de Wet and Widmar call, broad normative conflict.[20] The case law of the ECtHR, which refers to it as harmonization, is a good example of this approach,[21] although, strictly speaking and interpreting the Article 31(3) holistically, it goes

[16] *Georges Pinson Case (France/United Mexican States)* Award of 13 April 1928, UNRIAA, vol V, 422 [50] ('Toute convention internationale doit être réputée s'en référer tacitement au droit international commun, pour toutes les questions qu'elle ne résout pas elle-même en termes exprès et d'une façon différente.').

[17] See also C McLachlan, 'The Principle of Systemic Integration and Article 31(3)(C) of the Vienna Convention' (2005) 54 ICLQ 279; A Gourgourinis, 'The Distinction between Interpretation and Application of Norms in International Adjudication' (2011) 2(1) JIDS 31, 51.

[18] V Moreno-Lax, 'Systematising Systemic Integration' (2014) 12 JICJ 907, 922.

[19] ibid.

[20] E De Wet and J Vidmar, 'Conflicts between International Paradigms: Hierarchy versus Systemic Integration' (2013) 2 GlobCon 196, 208.

[21] See eg *Loizidou v Turkey*, App no 15318/89 (18 December 1996) [43]; *Fogarty v United Kingdom*, App no 37112/97 (21 November 2001) [35]; *McElhinney v Ireland*, App no 31253/96 (21 November 2001) [36]; *Banković and ors v Belgium*, App no 52207/99 (12 December 2001) [57]; *Cudak v Lithuania*, App no 15869/02 (23 March 2010) [56]; *Sabeh El Leil v France*, App no 34869/05 (29 June 2011) [48]; *Oleynikov v Russia*, App no 36703/04 (14 March 2013) [56]; *Hassan v United Kingdom*, App no 29750/09 (16 September 2014) [102]; *Radunović and ors v Montenegro*, App no 45197/13, 53000/13 and 73404/13 (25 October 2016) [63]; *Rinau v Lithuania*, App no 10926/09 (14 January 2020) [185].

beyond what Article 31(3)prescribes. In the words of Tzevelekos, the European Convention on Human Rights 'benefits from the latter [international law] through absorption of normative elements which, although absent from its "imperfect" text, are both complementary and necessary for the effective promotion of its special scopes'.[22]

To sum up, this means that other rules may essentially fulfil four different functions, all under the label of systemic integration: (1) other rules may serve as an aid to determine the ordinary meaning of the terms; (2) other rules may be used as a tool for systemic arguments; (3) other rules may be used as tools for gap-filling; or (4) other rules may be used as a tool for the resolution of a normative conflict. The latter two go beyond our understanding of interpretation. I will use this framework as a reference point for my analysis, in the following three sections, of case law where customary rules have been interpreted.

3 Interpretation of Customary Rules by Reference to Treaties

While, according to Article 38 of the ICJ Statute, international custom is a separate source of law, it exists in close interconnection with the other sources of international law. This is clear from the ILC's draft conclusions, according to which '[v]arious materials other than primary evidence of alleged instances of practice accepted as law (accompanied by *opinio juris*) may be consulted in the process of determining the existence and content of rules of customary international law'.[23] Such materials include 'treaties, resolutions of international organizations and intergovernmental conferences, judicial decisions (of both national and international courts), and scholarly works'.[24] The ILC then adds that 'such texts may assist in collecting, synthesizing or interpreting practice relevant to the identification of customary international law, and may offer precise formulations to frame and guide an inquiry into its constituent elements'.[25]

According to an empirical study conducted by Choi and Gulati, treaties are the most frequently used materials for the identification of

[22] Tzevelkos (n 10) 650.
[23] ILC 'Draft Conclusions' (n 4) 142.
[24] ibid.
[25] ibid. An example in this sense is *Responsibilities and Obligations of States with Respect to the Activities in the Area (Request for Advisory Opinion Submitted to the Seabed Dispute Chambers)* (Advisory Opinion) ITLOS Reports 2011, 10 [169].

customary rules.[26] Treaties can codify, crystallize and even generate customary rules.[27] Treaties that codify pre-existent custom are known as declaratory, and whether a treaty is declaratory of CIL is determined by analysing the preamble of the treaty or by looking at the *travaux préparatoires* for confirmation that this was the intention of the parties.[28] Most treaties, however, fall into the category of *partly* declaratory treaties,[29] meaning that some provisions are codifications, whereas others are not.

At the same time, because treaties and custom originate from two different processes of law creation,[30] treaties do not absorb CIL even when they codify it. This means that custom does not cease to exist upon being codified; it runs its course parallel to the treaty.[31] This is what the ICJ conveyed through the following statement in the *Nicaragua* case:

> even if a treaty norm and a customary norm relevant to the present dispute were to have exactly the same content, this would not be a reason for the Court to take the view that the operation of the treaty process must necessarily deprive the customary norm of its separate applicability.[32]

Moreover, as the ICJ argued, custom continues to apply even between the states that are parties to the treaty.[33] This means that while different in nature and form, custom and treaty often overlap in substance. But treaties can also crystallize emergent customs,[34] where crystallization means that the custom was *in statu nascendi* when the treaty was drafted

[26] SM Choi and M Gulati, 'Customary International Law: How Do Courts Do It?' in C Bradley (ed), *Custom's Future: International Law in a Changing World* (Cambridge University Press 2016) 117.

[27] *North Sea Continental Shelf Cases (Federal Republic of Germany/Denmark; Federal Republic of Germany/Netherlands)* [1969] ICJ Rep 3 [37]; *Case Concerning Military and Paramilitary Activities in and against Nicaragua (Nicaragua v United States of America)* [1986] ICJ Rep 14 [177]. See also RB Bilder and others, 'Disentangling Treaty and Customary International Law: Remarks' (1987) 81 ASIL Proc 157, 159; BB Jia, 'The Relations between Treaties and Custom' (2010) 9(1) Chinese JIL 81, esp. 92; ILC 'Draft Conclusions' (n 4) 143.

[28] Y Dinstein, 'The Interaction between Customary International Law and Treaties' (2007) 322 RdC 243, 360–63.

[29] ibid 355.

[30] Jia (n 27) 97.

[31] Dinstein (n 28) 386–87.

[32] *Military and Paramilitary Activities in and against Nicaragua* (n 27) [175].

[33] Dinstein (n 28) 396.

[34] ibid 352.

but became a customary rule subsequently.[35] They can also generate custom, where a provision created in the process of the drafting of a treaty becomes customary because it is widely followed even by non-parties.[36]

According to the ILC, all three types of treaties – those that codify custom, those that crystallize custom and those that generate custom – can be used in the process of CIL identification. Yet, as the ILC itself points out, a distinction needs to be drawn between the use of conduct in relation to treaties as state practice, where behaviour such as voting patterns is used as evidence for one of the elements of CIL, and the use of treaties as a reflection of CIL,[37] where actual treaty provisions are used as the container of a customary rule, because they have codified, crystallized or generated a customary rule.

The use of treaties for what is, or what in some cases the courts frame as, interpretation of customary rules in international courts and quasi-judicial bodies tends to fall into two categories: (1) the use of treaty provisions to interpret CIL; or (2) the use of elements from treaty interpretation to interpret CIL.

In none other than the *Nicaragua* case, where the ICJ established the relationship between treaties and custom, it also noted that 'while the Court has no jurisdiction to consider that instrument [the Charter of the Organization of the American States] as applicable to the dispute, it may examine it to ascertain *what light it throws* on the *content* of customary international law'.[38] This statement was made in connection with the question of whether the lawful use by a third state of collective self-defence depended on a request from the attacked state.[39] After examining the provisions of the OAS Charter and the Inter-American Treaty of Reciprocal Assistance, the ICJ concluded that there was no rule allowing for the exercise of collective self-defence without a prior request made by the attacked state.[40] In this case, the court frames its reasoning as a form of interpretation. Yet, it ends up applying the requirement contained in the OAS Charter and the 1947 Rio Treaty, according to

35 ibid 358.

36 ibid. For a comprehensive analysis of the relationship between CIL and treaties, see also M Villiger, *Customary International Law and Treaties: A Manual on the Theory and Practice of the Interrelation of Sources* (2nd ed, Brill 1997).

37 ILC 'Draft Conclusions' (n 4) 143.

38 *Military and Paramilitary Activities in and against Nicaragua* (n 27) [196] (emphasis added).

39 ibid [196].

40 ibid [199].

which the measures of collective self-defence must be taken at the request of the attacked state. This led to the following conclusion:

> [T]he Court finds that in customary international law, whether of a general kind or that particular to the inter-American legal system, there is not rule permitting the exercise of collective self-defence in the absence of a request by the State which regards itself as the victim of the attack.[41]

In other words, the ICJ engaged in a form systemic integration as a gap-filling exercise bordering on law-making.

The second case under analysis is the *Nuclear Weapons Advisory Opinion*,[42] which concerned the permissibility of the use and threat of use of nuclear weapons. The issue was controversial because international humanitarian law, including customary rules, lacked specific rules that would govern the use or threat of use of nuclear weapons in particular. One of the members of the bench, Judge Guillaume, appended a separate opinion, in which he stated that the rules of the *jus ad bellum* – in this particular case Article 51 of the UN Charter – could provide a *clarification* of the rules of the *jus in bello*.[43] To answer the question on the extent to which the use or threat of use of nuclear weapons was permitted in international law, Judge Guillaume, largely following the ideas set out in the main advisory opinion, emphasized that given the content of Article 51, according to which nothing shall impair a state's right of self-defence, the use of nuclear weapons is allowed.[44]

Judge Guillaume further opined that customary rules of humanitarian law must also be 'completed by reference to the rules concerning the collateral damage which attacks on legitimate military objectives can cause to civilian populations',[45] as contained in the Additional Protocol to the Geneva Conventions. Therefore, the only prohibition in customary humanitarian law was on the use of weapons that could not distinguish between civilian and military targets, which, according to the judge, was not necessarily the case with nuclear weapons.[46]

[41] ibid.

[42] *Legality of the Threat or Use of Nuclear Weapons* (Advisory Opinion) (1996) ICJ Rep 226, Separate Opinion of Judge Guillaume [8].

[43] ibid.

[44] ibid.

[45] ibid [5].

[46] ibid.

In both cases there was a legal gap, which was resolved by what was framed as an interpretative exercise and which, if accepted as such, would fall under the third meaning of systemic interpretation outlined in Section 2. Whereas in the first case the customary rules on self-defence were completed with the requirement of a request on the basis of a reference to the OAS conventions, in the second case treaty rules were used to make the argument that rules of customary international law do not prohibit the use or threat of use of nuclear weapons. In both cases, the answer was sought outside CIL or its constituent elements – there was no mention of either state practice or *opinio juris* – instead, the reasoning was framed as an attempt at clarification or explanation, both of which are more akin to interpretation rather than orthodox ascertainment of customary rules. While in its draft conclusions the ILC established that treaties may 'assist in collecting, synthesizing or interpreting practice relevant to the identification of customary international law, and may offer precise formulations to frame and guide an inquiry into its two constituent elements',[47] it is clear that the function of treaties in these cases goes beyond this and extends to interpretation *lato sensu* of the content of CIL in a way that completes it.

Two other cases, both from the practice of international and internationalized criminal courts, show a different facet of systemic interpretation. In *The Prosecutor* v. *Kunarac* the Trial Chamber of the International Criminal Tribunal for the Former Yugoslavia (ICTY) sought to establish the definition of torture under customary international law.[48] After noting that the definition given in the Convention against Torture[49] could be taken as representing customary international law, the Trial Chamber stated that Article 1 of the Convention against Torture could nevertheless be used as an interpretational aid.[50] In a similar vein, in *The Prosecutor v. Chea* the Pre-Trial Chamber of the Extraordinary Chambers in the Courts of Cambodia (ECCC) found that the expression 'other inhumane acts' in connection with crimes against humanity was likely a CIL rule and then stated that:

> in determining what constitutes 'inhumane' conduct reference could be made to: 1) serious breaches of international law regulating armed conflict

[47] ILC 'Draft Conclusions' (n 4) 142.

[48] *The Prosecutor v Kunarac and ors* (Judgment) ICTY-96-23-T and ICTY-96-23/1 (22 February 2001) [194]–[195].

[49] Convention against Torture and Other Cruel, Inhuman and Degrading Treatment or Punishment (adopted 10 December 1984, entered into force 26 June 1987)1465 UNTS 85.

[50] ibid 482.

> from 1975–1979, *including the grave breaches provisions of the 1949 Geneva Conventions* or 2) serious violations of the fundamental human rights norms protected under international law at the relevant time.[51]

In these cases, other treaty provisions seem to have been used for construing the meaning of the customary rule, which comes closest to the first meaning of systemic interpretation described in Section 2.

Another pair of cases – or two individual opinions, to be more precise – illustrate how elements of treaty interpretation have been used in an interpretative argument on customary rules. The first example is the dissenting opinion of Judge Sørensen in the *North Sea Continental Shelf* case,[52] where he noted that:

> If the provisions of a given convention are recognized as generally accepted rules of law, this is likely to have an important bearing upon any problem of *interpretation* which may arise. *In the absence of a convention* of this nature, any question as to the exact *scope* and *implications of a customary rule* must be answered on the basis of a detailed analysis of the State practice out of which the customary rule has emerged. If, on the other hand, the provisions of the convention serve as evidence of generally accepted rules of law, it is legitimate, or even necessary, to have recourse to *ordinary principles of treaty interpretation*, including, if the circumstances so require, an examination of *travaux préparatoires*.[53]

Unlike in the previous pair of cases, where treaties themselves were used to construe and complete the content of customary rules, in this case Judge Sørensen, while not actually making an interpretation on the basis of elements of treaty interpretation, clearly advocated in its favour, but only in cases where the treaty codifies, crystallizes or generates rules of CIL. In such a case, the argument goes, judges may resort to considering even the preparatory work of the treaty.

The second example is Judge Shahabudeen's dissent from the Decision on Interlocutory Appeal from the ICTY in *Hadžihasanović*. In this case the tribunal was called upon to determine whether a superior could be punished under the principle of command responsibility for acts

[51] *Prosecutor v Chea*, Case no 002 (ECCC Pre-Trial Chamber Decision on Appeals by Nuon Chea and Ieng Thirith against the Closing Order, 15 February 2011) [164] (emphasis added).

[52] *North Sea Continental Shelf Cases* (n 27).

[53] ibid, Dissenting Opinion of Judge Sørensen 244 (emphasis added).

committed by subordinates prior to the assumption of command.[54] When determining the scope of action of the customary principle of command responsibility, Judge Shahabudeen argued that 'any interpretation [of the customary rule] can be made *by reference to the object and purpose of the provisions laying down the doctrine*'[55] – Articles 86 and 87 of Protocol I Additional to the Geneva Conventions.

A final example that illustrates this approach is the judgment of the Appeals Chamber of the ICTY in *The Prosecutor* v. *Aleksovski*.[56] In examining the standard of control for the purposes of establishing the international character of an armed conflict, the Appeals Chamber opined that:

> To the extent that it provides for greater protection of civilian victims of armed conflicts, this [the overall control test] different and less rigorous standard is wholly consistent with the fundamental purpose of Geneva Convention IV, which is to ensure 'protection of civilians to the maximum extent possible'[57]

In other words, the Appeals Chamber favoured the overall control test applied in *The Prosecutor* v. *Tadić* over the effective control test applied in *Nicaragua* and used the purpose of Geneva Convention IV as an argument to buttress its position.[58] This statement evokes, to some extent, Article 32 of the VCLT, according to which supplementary means of interpretation may be used to confirm the meaning arrived at through the general rule. However, it is not so much a supplementary means of interpretation, as foreseen in Article 32, but rather the consistency of the chosen standard with the *purpose of a treaty* that is being used here to confirm the choice in favour of the overall control standard. At the same time, the argument relies on the need to ensure normative harmony or consistency between the chosen standard and the convention in relation to which it applies. All in all, in terms of qualification, here it seems that the courts are engaged in an operation akin to that of systemic interpretation in its second meaning – as a tool for crafting systemic arguments.

[54] *The Prosecutor v Hadžihasanović and ors* (Interlocutory Appeal) ICTY-01-47-AR72 (16 July 2003).

[55] ibid, Dissenting Opinion of Judge Shahabudeen [11] (emphasis added).

[56] *The Prosecutor v Aleksovski* (Appeals Chamber Judgment) ICTY-95-14/1-A (24 March 2000).

[57] ibid [146].

[58] *The Prosecutor v Tadić* (Appeals Chamber Judgment) ICTY-94-1-A (15 July 1999) [194].

4 Interpretation of Customary Rules by Reference to General Principles

While it seems that general principles have no role to play in the identification of CIL, in the practice of courts, especially criminal courts, it can be seen how the two can be embedded in judicial reasoning, often to the point of confusion. A few words, then, must first be said about the conceptual embeddedness and difference between general principles and custom.[59]

References to principles in the case law of international courts frequently cause confusion because it is unclear whether they are referring to fundamental principles of international law or those belonging to a branch of international law or to general principles of law recognized by civilized nations.[60] The latter, in turn, may be variously defined as domestic law principles that are common to all/most States, such as estoppel;[61] as natural law principles, such as equity or considerations of humanity;[62] as principles that originate from international relations;[63] or as 'general propositions underlying the various rules of law which express the essential qualities of juridical truth itself'.[64] Because of this lack of agreement or clear-cut definition of (general) principles, their analysis is often embedded with that of custom.[65] This is seen especially where ad

[59] See *Case Concerning Pulp Mills on the River Uruguay (Argentina v Uruguay)* (Judgment) [2010] ICJ Rep 14, Separate Opinion of Judge Trindade [17].

[60] See eg *Military and Paramilitary Activities in and against Nicaragua* (n 27) [220]. It has also been argued that '[t]he constituent elements of custom and general principles are notoriously vague'. See J Pauwelyn, RA Wessel and J Wouters, 'Informal International Lawmaking: An Assessment and Template to Keep It Both Effective and Accountable' in J Pauwelyn, RA Wessel and J Wouters (eds), *Informal International Lawmaking* (Oxford University Press 2012) 508.

[61] GI Tunkin, *Theory of International Law* (Harvard University Press 1974) 202.

[62] A Verdross, 'Les principes généraux du droit dans la jurisprudence internationale, 1935' (1935) 52 RdC 193, 228.

[63] AC Arend, 'Toward Understanding of International Legal Rules' in RJ Beck, AC Arend and RD Vander Lugt, *International Rules: Approaches from International Law and International Relations* (Oxford University Press 1996) 289, 297–98; T Klenlein, 'Customary International Law and General Principles: Rethinking Their Relationship' in B Lepard (ed), *Reexamining Customary International Law* (Cambridge University Press 2016) 133, 133-139; G Gaja, 'General Principles of Law' para 19 (2020) MPEPIL <https://opil.ouplaw.com/display/10.1093/law:epil/9780199231690/law-9780199231690-e1410> accessed 14 May 2024.

[64] B Cheng, *General Principles of Law as Applied by International Courts and Tribunals* (Cambridge University Press 2006) 24.

[65] M Dordeska, *General Principles of Law Recognized by Civilized Nations (1922–2018): The Evolution of the Third Source of International Law through the Jurisprudence of the*

hoc courts and tribunals declare their aim to be the establishment of customary international law at a particular point in time, whereas in actual fact they are surveying the domestic legislation of states, not as state practice but for the purpose of finding a common denominator in the definition of specific crimes.[66]

The embeddedness between general principles and custom can be seen not only in case law but also in those writings of legal scholars that propound a broad understanding of the concept of customary international law.[67] The confusion is due to, or at least so it seems, the early practice of the Permanent Court of International Justice (PCIJ). For instance, in the *Lotus* case the PCIJ observed that 'rules of law binding upon States therefore emanate from their own free will as expressed in conventions or by *usages generally accepted as expressing principles of law*'.[68] What adds to the confusion is that in its more recent practice, the ICJ seems to have requalified as CIL norms that it previously considered to be general principles.[69]

The absence of a clear-cut distinction can even be found in the conclusions of the ILC. The ILC's stance is that the '"rules" of customary international law . . . may be referred to as "principles" because of their more general and more fundamental character'.[70] In other words, it is admitted that general principles can be of a customary origin (also given that CIL is part and parcel of general international law) and are distinguished from regular customary rules by possessing a higher degree of abstractness.[71] The practice of international courts and tribunals seems to support this view, at least to a certain degree.[72] If, however, a neat distinction is maintained between general principles and CIL, then, given the former's high degree of generality, general principles constitute

Permanent Court of International Justice and the International Court of Justice (Brill 2020) 54.

66 See eg *Prosecutor v Chea and Samphan*, Case no 002/02 (ECCC Judgment, 16 November 2018) [392], esp [396], [409]–[410].

67 Cheng (n 64) 23.

68 *The Case of S.S. Lotus* (Judgment) [1927] PCIJ Series A No 10, 18 (emphasis added).

69 Dordeska (n 65) 153–56. See also K Wolfke, *Custom in Present International Law* (2nd revised edn, Martinus Nijhoff 1993) 105–08.

70 ILC, 'Draft Conclusions' (n 4) 124.

71 Tunkin (n 61) 124; H Lauterpacht, 'Some Observations on the Prohibition of "Non Liquet" and the Completeness of the Law' in *Symbolae Verzijl* (Martinus Nijhoff 1958) 196; K Wolfke, 'Some Persistent Controversies Concerning Customary International Law' (1993) 24 NILR 1, 12.

72 *Pulp Mills* (n 59) [101].

a residual category, acting as a filler when the other two sources – treaties and CIL – are unable to resolve the dispute.[73]

According to Judge Trindade of the ICJ, general principles of law 'orient the interpretation and application of the norms and rules of this legal order, be they *customary* or conventional'.[74] The ICTY seems to share this view. In *The Prosecutor* v. *Kupreškić*,[75] the Trial Chamber, by taking into account *other principles*, expressed its clear support for a systemic approach when examining the prohibition of attacks on civilian populations. The Trial Chamber argued that to establish 'the scope and purport'[76] of the customary rules on the requirement of proportionality between collateral damage and direct military advantage and the prohibition of the use of indiscriminate means or methods of warfare, it was necessary to interpret them by reference to elementary considerations of humanity, which the Trial Chamber framed as being 'illustrative of a general principle of international law'.[77]

In *The Prosecutor* v. *Furundžija*, the Trial Chamber had to decide on the definition of rape and the forms of behaviour that fell under this offence and, in particular, whether oral penetration could qualify as rape.[78] The Trial Chamber firstly stated that the prohibition of rape in armed conflict had evolved into a norm of customary international law,[79] yet found that international law (whether treaty or custom) contained no definition of rape.[80] Subsequently, it scrutinised national legislation and, as a result, established that while national laws generally converged around the definition of rape as 'the forcible sexual penetration of the human body by the penis or the forcible insertion of any other object into either the vagina or the anus',[81] there were discrepancies concerning whether oral penetration qualified as rape or a different type of sexual assault.[82] The question of whether the definition of rape included or excluded oral penetration was decided by reliance on the principle of

[73] See X Shao, 'What We Talk about When We Talk about General Principles of Law' (2021) 20/2 Chinese JIL 219.
[74] *Pulp Mills* (n 59) Separate Opinion of Judge Trindade [216] (emphasis added).
[75] *The Prosecutor v Kupreškić* (Judgment) ICTY-95-16-T (14 January 2000).
[76] ibid [526].
[77] ibid [525].
[78] *The Prosecutor v Furundžija* (Judgment) ICTY-95-17/1-T (10 December 1998).
[79] ibid [168].
[80] ibid [174].
[81] ibid [181].
[82] ibid [178]–[182].

respect for human dignity as 'the essence of the whole corpus of international humanitarian law as well as human rights law'.[83] The inclusion of oral penetration in the definition of rape, both as a treaty and a customary prohibition, was preferred because this solution appeared to be 'consonant with this principle'.[84] Judging from these two cases, it appears that general principles of law are used mainly for making systemic arguments that would determine the scope of the customary rule, thus falling under the second meaning of systemic interpretation.

An example of how the language of systemic interpretation can be misused is found in *Case 002*, where the ECCC Trial Chamber stated that 'as recognised by the Pre-Trial Chamber, having regard to *general principles of law* can *assist* when *defining the elements of an international crime*, where that crime has otherwise been recognised in *customary international law*'.[85] After surveying the legislation of different countries, the Trial Chamber concluded that the *mens rea* of murder as a crime against humanity included *dolus eventualis*.[86] While announcing what appears a systemic approach towards the interpretation of the elements of the crimes found in CIL, the Pre-Trial Chamber ended up surveying the legislation of states and, given that the majority included *dolus eventualis* as the mental element for this crime, established that this had been the *mens rea* for murder prior to 1975.

5 Interpretation of Customary Rules by Reference to the System of Rules as a Whole

To complement the case law analysed in the previous sections, where other rules were used to construe custom, mention should lastly be made of a case where judges relied on a system of rules in its entirety to interpret the customary rule on attribution. In *The Prosecutor v. Tadić*, when arguing against the use of the *Nicaragua* effective control test in this case, the Appeals Chamber made the overarching argument that 'a first ground on which the *Nicaragua* test as such may be held to be unconvincing is based on the very *logic* of the entire *system* of international law on State responsibility'.[87] It subsequently added that:

[83] ibid [183].
[84] ibid.
[85] *Prosecutor v Chea and Samphan* (n 66) [638] (emphasis added).
[86] ibid [650].
[87] *The Prosecutor v Tadić* (n 58) [116] (emphasis added).

> the whole body of international law on State responsibility is based on a realistic concept of accountability, which disregards legal formalities and aims at ensuring that States entrusting some functions to individuals or groups of individuals must answer for their actions, even when they act contrary to their directives.[88]

In addition, it stated that the same logic had to apply to the questions on the appropriate control test.[89] Overall, when looking at the argument advanced by the Appeals Chamber, it appears to conflate teleological considerations with systemic ones in order to show why the effective control test is at odds with the whole system of state responsibility. In subsequent paragraphs, the Appeals Chamber examined state practice and *opinio juris* to show how the effective control was not rooted in practice.[90] However, this was done only subsequently and as an additional argument to the first teleological-systemic argument advanced, which means that it supports the argument being made here that ascertainment of state practice and *opinio juris* cannot be considered the only methods of determining the content of CIL rules in the case law of international courts and tribunals. This is an instance of a classic systemic argument in interpretation combined with teleological considerations, which shows that systemic arguments in the wider sense are not alien to the interpretation of customary rules.

6 Conclusion

Systemic treaty interpretation is ever-present in the practice of international courts and tribunals. While the term does not at first glance appear equivocal, it has in fact been used to refer to four different operations. Firstly, it may denote the act of using other rules as an aid to determine the meaning of treaty terms. Secondly, it can mean the use of systemic interpretative arguments. Thirdly, it has been used to refer to the act of gap-filling and, lastly, to the act of resolving conflicts between norms.

As this chapter has shown, systemic interpretation is also not foreign to CIL rules and, as with treaties, different variants of systemic interpretation have emerged in the practice of international courts. The most common is the use of systemic interpretative arguments, where other

88 ibid [121].
89 ibid [122].
90 ibid [124]ff.

rules or the rules of the system taken as a whole are used to construe the content of a customary rule.

That systemic interpretation is equally capable of applying to customary rules not only advances our understanding of CIL interpretation but is further proof of the enduring interconnection between CIL and the two other sources of international law – treaties and general principles of law.

12

Reconciling Conflicting Norms of CIL

Towards a Method of Practical Concordance at the ICJ

RAPHAEL OIDTMANN

1 Introduction

The risk of possibly conflicting norms of customary international law (CIL) has received increased attention in recent international legal scholarship and practice.[1] In the absence of commonly accepted or authoritative rules of conflict that may mitigate the ramifications which stem from a possible clash of opposing obligations under CIL, legal scholars and practitioners alike almost instinctively turn towards competent (judicial) authorities, thereby seeking advice on how to strike a balance between conflicting norms in conformity with applicable legal frameworks and regimes. The emergence of this 'legal dilemma' hence calls for, and even heralds, an established and accepted modus operandi to which international judges and adjudicators – as competent authorities – can resort in relevant situations. This basic constellation of juxtaposing norms pointing in different directions is of significant relevance, most importantly with regard to the operations of the International Court of Justice (ICJ), designated as 'the principal judicial organ of the United Nations'[2] and competent to adjudicate on 'any question of international law'.[3]

[1] One possible conceptualization of this clash was proposed by Jeutner, who framed it as a 'legal dilemma' arising from situations in which 'an actor confronts an irresolvable and unavoidable conflict between at least two legal norms so that obeying or applying one norm necessarily entails the undue impairment of the other'. See V Jeutner, *Irresolvable Norm Conflicts in International Law: The Concept of a Legal Dilemma* (Oxford University Press 2017) 20. The contingency of opposing international legal norms has previously been expounded by Pauwelyn, who distinguished between 'genuine' and 'apparent' conflict(s); see J Pauwelyn, *Conflict of Norms in Public International Law: How WTO Law Relates to Other Rules of International Law* (Cambridge University Press 2003) 237–74.

[2] Charter of the United Nations (adopted 26 June 1945, entered into force 24 October 1945) 892 UNTS 119, art 92.

[3] Statute of the International Court of Justice (adopted 26 June 1945, entered into force 24 October 1945) 892 UNTS 119, art 36(2)(b).

The tension inherent in the coincidence of contrary, yet equally valid and established, norms of CIL has hence become an increasingly real issue in recent years. For example, it arises in relation to the scope and application of *ratione personae* immunity from prosecution and adjudication enjoyed by heads of state, heads of government, and ministers of foreign affairs for international (core) crimes. The underlying conflict has become especially manifest in the *Al Bashir*[4] case at the International Criminal Court (ICC). The case concerns acts committed by the former Sudanese president Omar Al Bashir, who has been charged with genocide, crimes against humanity, and war crimes in the context of the situation in Darfur – referred to the International Criminal Court by the United Nations (UN) Security Council under its Chapter VII powers[5] – and is the subject of two arrest warrants issued in recent years.[6] Beyond the question of Al Bashir's imputed individual criminal responsibility for these international crimes, this case subsequently triggered a series of interrelated legal and legislative developments in a number of states parties to the Rome Statute[7]. Most importantly, they concerned constitutional issues flowing from the fact that Al Bashir had sojourned on the territory of states parties to the Rome Statute notwithstanding the pending arrest warrants and related legal obligations under the Statute.[8] Accordingly, the case of Al Bashir has offered an enduring illustration of some of the inherent tensions that might arise between two possibly conflicting, yet imperative, norms of CIL:[9] on the one hand, the established principle of *ratione personae* immunity applicable to heads of state,

[4] *The Prosecutor v Omar Hassan Ahmad Al Bashir*, ICC-02/05-01/09 (6 June 2005).

[5] UNSC Res 1593 (31 March 2005), UN Doc S/S/RES/1593, para 1.

[6] *The Prosecutor v Omar Hassan Ahmad Al Bashir*, ICC-02/05-01/09-1 (4 March 2009); *The Prosecutor v Omar Hassan Ahmad Al Bashir*, ICC-02/05-01/09-94 (12 July 2010).

[7] Rome Statute of the International Criminal Court (opened for signature 17 July 1998, entered into force 1 July 2002) 2187 UNTS 90.

[8] The notion of legal obligations incumbent on state parties under the Rome Statute's regime of co-operation for purposes of arrest was expeditiously addressed by the Appeals Chamber of the International Criminal Court in connection with a visit Al Bashir had made to Jordan in March 2017. See *Judgment in the Jordan Referral re Al Bashir Appeal*, Appeals Chamber, Decision, ICC-02/05-01/09-397-Corr (6 May 2021).

[9] The issue on a CIL norm (i.e. immunity *ratione personae*) and corresponding treaty obligations for state parties under Articles 27 and 98 of the Rome Statute. It is submitted that for the purposes of this chapter – leaving aside the question of legal obligations stemming directly from the Rome Statute regime – the Al Bashir case suits as a blueprint for illustrating a clash of conflicting CIL norms of necessitating the application of practical concordance *in situ*.

heads of government, and ministers of foreign affairs;[10] and, on the other, the imperative to end impunity for international (core) crimes by facilitating individual criminal responsibility under international law.

This cursory sketch of two CIL norms in possible conflict with one another points, however, to a more structural tension – namely the question of applying and reconciling (seemingly) opposing legal principles in concrete circumstances. Thus far, international courts and tribunals, including the ICJ, have regularly refrained from outlining, conceiving, and imposing coherent analytical and prescriptive means of establishing an equilibrium between (partially) opposing norms of CIL *in situ*. Yet, devising such means – i.e. the creating transparent and selective rules of collision – could arguably assist international judges in striking a reasonable and credible balance in reconciling conflicting norms of CIL in concrete cases. In this chapter it is submitted that in such circumstances international adjudicative bodies could contemplate resorting to the German constitutional law principle of practical concordance (*praktische Konkordanz*) and thereby draw on a legal methodology that has become well established and is regularly applied by the German Federal Constitutional Court when ruling on fundamental rights.[11] The principle is applied in cases where there is a conflict between fundamental norms of equal (constitutional) rank, neither of which can be fully or partially overridden.[12] A core objective of practical concordance is thus the careful balancing of the two legal norms so as to allow each to be as fully effective as possible. Given that any legal arrangement needs to be assessed in context, practical concordance denotes essentially both a relationship of qualified precedence and a method of resolving

[10] See eg ILC, 'Immunity of State Officials from Foreign Jurisdiction: Texts and Titles of the Draft Articles adopted by the Drafting Committee on First Reading' (31 May 2022) UN Doc A/CN.4/L.969, Draft Article 3.

[11] For a cursory overview of the German Federal Constitutional Court's legal-theoretical reasoning and approach, including the notion of practical concordance, see M Heilbronner and S Martini, 'The German Federal Constitutional Court' in A Jakab, A Dyevre, and G Itzcovich (eds), *Comparative Constitutional Reasoning* (Cambridge University Press 2017) 356–93.

[12] This notion prima facie resembles an approach commonly referred to as 'harmonization through interpretation', as found in the case law of the European Court of Human Rights (ECtHR). See eg *Al-Adsani v The United Kingdom* App no 35763/97 (ECtHR21 November 2001), in which the ECtHR had to reconcile rules of state immunity with an individual's right of access to a court. While conceptually related, given that practical concordance applies to rules of equal rank, it is argued that 'harmonization through interpretation' and practical concordance operate on different conceptual planes.

conflicting legal standards – that is, establishing a specific rule of conflict *in situ*.

This chapter's objective is threefold. Firstly, it discusses an example of a dichotomous conflict of CIL norms – namely, between the rule on immunity *ratione personae* and the rule on individual criminal responsibility. Secondly, the notion of practical concordance is introduced and then (re-)conceptualized as a form of an adjudicative reasoning that international courts and tribunals, including the ICJ, can apply to (better) address situations in which there is a potential conflict between CIL norms. Thirdly, the chapter will offer some tentative thoughts on how to address possible ramifications arising for international judges called upon to adjudicate in cases where such conflicts occur and thereby outline how practical concordance might assist in addressing underlying legal dilemmas.

2 The Interplay between Personal Immunity and Individual Criminal Responsibility

There has been much scholarly debate around the controversial question of immunity *ratione personae*, or personal immunity from criminal jurisdiction. It appears to be a well-established principle of CIL that heads of state, heads of government, and foreign ministers are considered to enjoy extensive immunity as individuals during their time in office, such immunity covering both private and official conduct.[13] It implies that since these officeholders represent and even incarnate the state throughout their tenure, any affront to their dignity and inviolability should, by extension, amount to an affront to the state they represent.[14]

This understanding of immunity *ratione personae* was confirmed the International Court of Justice in the *Armed Activities* case, affirming that 'it is a well-established rule of international law that the Head of State, the Head of Government and the Minister for Foreign Affairs are deemed to represent the State merely by virtue of exercising their functions,

[13] For a comprehensive introduction, see D Akande and S Shah, 'Immunities of State Officials, International Crimes, and Foreign Domestic Courts' (2010) 21 EJIL 815.

[14] This understanding is echoed the International Law Commission's work on the immunity of State officials from foreign criminal jurisdiction See ILC (n 10) Draft Articles 3 ('[H]eads of State, Heads of Government, and Ministers for Foreign Affairs enjoy immunities *ratione personae* from the exercise of foreign criminal jurisdiction') and 7 (personal immunities 'shall not apply in respect of . . . crimes under international law', listing the crime of genocide, crimes against humanity, war crimes, the crime of apartheid, torture, and enforced disappearance).

including for the performance, on behalf of the said State, of unilateral acts having the force of international commitments'.[15] Further substantiation of immunity *ratione personae* for heads of state as CIL can be found in the Vienna Convention on the Law of Treaties.[16] Codifying pre-existing CIL,[17] the Convention states: 'In virtue of their function and without having to produce full powers, the following are considered as representing their State: (a) Heads of State, Heads of Government and Foreign Ministers, for the purpose of performing all acts relating to the conclusion of a treaty.'[18]

The notion of immunity *ratione personae* under CIL becomes particularly relevant in matters concerning international criminal justice and related questions of jurisdiction. In the *Arrest Warrant* case, the ICJ examined whether individuals entitled to personal immunity might be charged and subsequently prosecuted in domestic courts for having allegedly committed international crimes. It clarified that 'in international law it is firmly established that ... certain holders of high-ranking office in a State, such as the Head of State, Head of Government and Minister for Foreign Affairs, enjoy immunities from jurisdiction in other States, both civil and criminal'.[19] As far as criminal proceedings before foreign courts were concerned, however, the court underlined that foreign affairs ministers would enjoy full and unlimited *ratione personae* immunity, elaborating that:

> throughout the duration of his or her office, he or she when abroad enjoys full immunity from criminal jurisdiction and inviolability ...
>
> In this respect, no distinction can be drawn between acts performed by a Minister of Foreign Affairs in an 'official' capacity, and those claimed to have been performed in a 'private capacity', or, for that matter, between acts performed before the person concerned assumed office as Minister for Foreign Affairs and acts committed during the period in office.[20]

[15] *Case Concerning Armed Activities on the Territory of Congo (Democratic Republic of Congo v Rwanda)* (Jurisdiction and Admissibility) [2006] ICJ Rep 6 [46].

[16] Vienna Convention on the Law of Treaties (opened for signature 23 May 1969, entered into force 27 January 1980) 1155 UNTS 331 (VCLT).

[17] On codification of CIL, see H Thirlway, *International Customary Law and Codification: An Examination of the Continuing Role of Custom in the Present Period of Codification of International Law* (Brill 1972). See also *Legal Consequences for State of the Continued Presence of South Africa in Namibia* (Advisory Opinion) [1971] ICJ Rep 3 [94].

[18] VCLT (n 16) art 7(2).

[19] *Case Concerning the Arrest Warrant of 11 April 2000 (Democratic Republic of Congo v Belgium)* [2002] ICJ Rep 3 [51].

[20] ibid [54]–[55].

Confirming and further substantiating the applicability of immunity *ratione personae* in proceedings before domestic courts, the ICJ acknowledged and, moreover, clarified in what circumstances the personal immunity enjoyed by an officeholder would not preclude criminal prosecution. This would be the case if the proceedings took place in their home country, or if the home state decided to waive their immunity. Beyond that, once an individual ceased to hold office, they would no longer enjoy the privileges and immunities accorded by international law in third states. Thus, provided it had jurisdiction under international law, a foreign court could try a former foreign affairs minister of another state for acts allegedly committed prior to or after their term in office, as well as for acts alleged to have been committed in a private capacity during the minister's term in office.[21]

In an obiter dictum, the court pointed out that both incumbent and former foreign affairs ministers could be pursued in criminal proceedings before 'certain international criminal courts, where they have jurisdiction'.[22] In particular, this would apply to the International Criminal Tribunal for the Former Yugoslavia, the International Criminal Tribunal for Rwanda,[23] and – though still in the process of being created at the time the judgment was rendered – the International Criminal Court. It was also noted that the latter's founding legal document, the Rome Statute, expressly provided that: 'Immunities or special procedural rules which may attach to the official capacity of a person, whether under national or international law, shall not bar the Court from exercising its jurisdiction over such a person.'[24] Although this differentiation in the application of *ratione personae* immunity between the international and domestic spheres expressed in an obiter dictum was not unequivocally endorsed by the entire bench,[25] the judgment pointed to

[21] ibid [61].

[22] ibid.

[23] In both instances the authority to adjudicate individuals accorded *ratione personae* immunity stemmed from the tribunal's creation and mandate under Chapter VII of the United Nations Charter. See UNSC Res 827 (25 May 1993) UN Doc S/RES/827, as amended by UNSC Res 1877 (7 July 2009) UN Doc S/RES/1877 (Statute of the International Criminal Tribunal for the Former Yugoslavia); UNSC Res 955 (8 November 1994) UN Doc S/RES/955 (Statute of the International Criminal Tribunal for Rwanda).

[24] Rome Statute (n 7) art 27(2).

[25] See *Arrest Warrant Case* (n 19), Joint Separate Opinion of Judges Higgins, Kooijmans, and Buergenthal [51] – 'The international consensus that the perpetrators of international crimes should not go unpunished is being advanced by a flexible strategy, in which newly established international criminal tribunals, treaty obligations, and national courts all

a tacit consensus *in statu nascendi*, according to which certain and future international criminal courts and tribunals with the necessary jurisdiction over international core crimes might indict and prosecute both incumbent and former holders of the highest offices of state. Accordingly, the *ratione personae* immunity to which such individuals would otherwise be entitled in connection with such offences would no longer apply.

As a relatively new development, this re-configuration of the legal and conceptual understanding of the role and functions of *ratione personae* immunity under (customary) international law has become the object of increasingly close scholarly scrutiny in recent years, particularly in relation to heads of state. Historically, heads of state have been seen as enjoying considerably broad, if not absolute, immunity from foreign jurisdiction – in part, reflecting and reinforcing the prevailing belief in states' sovereign immunity. However, a tangible decline in the deference paid to incumbents of highest state offices and the concomitant replacement of the former absolute immunity by a more qualified and conditional approach towards immunity, as well as an increasing emphasis on functional rather than personal status as the referential frame for according immunity, have, in sum, led to the above-described legal and conceptual re-alignment. As a result, *ratione personae* immunity for heads of states is now scrutinized in a far more critical manner. That said, the degree and extent of this change, and thus of the re-conceptualization of the scope of *ratione personae* immunity in respect of both substance and application have remained rather unclear.[26] This may in part be due to the fact that the legal construct of *ratione personae* immunity resembles a *sui generis* phenomenon: accordingly, analogies with the legal categorization of other state offices – such as, most importantly, diplomatic

have their part to play. We reject the suggestion that the battle against impunity is "made over" to international treaties and tribunals, with national courts having no competence in such matters.'). In emphasizing both a future role for domestic judicial systems and increased importance for international adjudicative strategies, the joint separate opinion takes an unequivocal stance (albeit not explicitly) in favour of positive complementarity, which has become something of a leitmotif in contemporary international criminal justice. See eg C Stahn, *A Critical Introduction to International Criminal Law* (Cambridge University Press 2019) 223.

[26] As can be seen from a motion moved by African UN member states provisionally tabled for the seventy-third session of the General Assembly, requesting an advisory opinion on the matter from the ICJ. See UNGA, 'Request for an Advisory Opinion of the International Court of Justice on the Consequences of Legal Obligations of States under Different Sources of International Law with Respect to Immunities to Heads of State and Government and other Senior Officials' (18 July 2018) UN Doc A/73/144.

agents – are far from ideal, as they do not fully account for the specificities of personal immunity. Given that only a few international courts have thus far addressed the jurisdictional implications of *ratione personae* immunity in a comprehensive and authoritative manner, its legal status – both internationally and in domestic contexts – is still being dealt with primarily as a matter of CIL.[27] Thus, while neighbouring foundational principles of international law, such as the sovereign equality of states or sovereign immunity, are clearly helpful in delineating the scope and nature of immunities *ratione personae*, those principles are insufficient to arrive at a comprehensive and contemporary determination of the formers' status under CIL.

The last twenty-five years have thus seen growing unease in international legal scholarship over unconditionally according almost unlimited personal immunity, given the emergence of an array of international crimes and the growing number of capable international adjudicative bodies having jurisdiction to rule on them.[28] The concern to guarantee human rights protection has led to increasing deliberation on the possibility of legally challenging the conduct of heads of state, heads of government, and ministers of foreign affairs, including, in a limited number of cases, also in the courts of foreign states and, in particular, in a growing number of international criminal courts and tribunals, with a view to possibly overriding the previously accepted conceptualization of personal immunity conferred on those selected individuals under CIL.

Assuming that immunity for heads of state, heads of government, and ministers of foreign affairs is still – notwithstanding the aforementioned efforts, most notably on the part of the International Law Commission,[29] to codify it – primarily based on CIL, no clear indication has been given as to how this principle may be properly reconciled with other, potentially conflicting customary norms that have the same legal rank. This is most importantly the case when the principle of *ratione personae* immunity comes up against that of individual criminal responsibility, aimed at ending impunity for international core crimes. This latter

[27] Recognizing this fact, the ILC included the topic of immunity of state officials from foreign criminal jurisdiction in its long-term working agenda in December 2007 and has since published (preliminary) results of its progress in periodic reports. See also UNGA Res 62/66 (8 January 2008) UN Doc A/RES/62/66 ('Report of the International Law Commission on the Works of its Fifty-Ninth Session') operative para 7.

[28] See eg KJ Alter, 'The Multiplication of International Courts and Tribunals after the End of the Cold War' in CPR Romano, KJ Alter, and Y Shany (eds), *The Oxford Handbook of International Adjudication* (Oxford University Press 2014).

[29] See n 27.

principle has two fundamental dimensions: firstly, it confirms that individuals can be held accountable directly under international law for certain criminal offences, thereby becoming subjects of international law and bypassing the state as an intermediary. Secondly, it implies that individuals may incur personal culpability for these specific offences and can therefore be held accountable for their conduct within the international arena.

Outside the laws of war – in which context individual combatants, are to be held liable, albeit to a limited degree, in the case of violations of international humanitarian law in their home jurisdictions – individual criminal responsibility has been recognized under CIL for offences such as piracy, crimes against peace, and crimes against humanity, and has subsequently been affirmed for other kinds of crimes in various international treaties that address the protection of human rights, both in times of war and peace.[30] Conversely, certain international crimes that have been codified in international treaties are considered to have (subsequently) entered the corpus of CIL – for example, the crime of genocide.[31]

Individual criminal responsibility as a norm of CIL has its foundations in the so-called Nuremberg Principles, espoused in the wake of World War II. On 11 December 1946, the United Nations General Assembly unanimously adopted Resolution 95(I),[32] in which it '[a]ffirms the principles of international law recognized by the Charter of the Nuremberg Tribunal and the judgment of the Tribunal'.[33] Simultaneously, the General Assembly instructed the body that later became known as the International Law Commission to draft guiding principles essentially reflecting the Nuremberg and Tokyo Charters' foundational provisions

[30] See D Guilfoyle, *International Criminal Law* (Oxford University Press 2016) 185.

[31] See Convention on the Prevention and Punishment of the Crime of Genocide (opened for signature 9 December 1948, entered into force 12 January 1951) 78 UNTS 277. The inherent *dédoublement fonctionnel* of (individual) criminal responsibility and the responsibility of states parties to give effect to its fundamental purposes, inter alia through prosecutorial activities, has subsequently been endorsed in a number of international treaties; see A Cassese, 'Remarks on Scelle's Theory of "Role Splitting" (*dédoublement fonctionnel*) in International Law' (1990) 1 EJIL 210.

[32] This provides further substantiation of the norm's CIL status, given that unanimous acceptance of a UNGA resolution could be interpreted as an authentic interpretation of the UN Charter, thus expressing the international community's belief in the creation of a new CIL norm. See BD Lepard, *Customary International Law: A New Theory with Practical Applications* (Cambridge University Press 2010) 208–17.

[33] UNGA Res 95(I) (11 December 1946) UN Doc A/RES/95 ('Affirmation of the Principles of International Law Recognized by the Charter of the Nuremberg Tribunal').

and the jurisdictional mandates of their respective tribunals. During the ILC's deliberations, the question of the need to determine whether the rules applied by both adjudicative bodies already constituted applicable principles of international law arose. Given that this was the interpretation of the UN General Assembly in its Resolution 95(I), the legal nature of the principles was considered sufficiently established. During the following years, a growing number of domestic criminal courts of different kinds referred to the Nuremberg Principles, thereby endorsing and accepting their nature and scope as general principles of (international) criminal law. For example, in the *Eichmann* case, the District Court of Jerusalem emphasised that Resolution 95(I) showed the Nuremberg Principles to be part of CIL.[34] Following similar reasoning, the International Criminal Tribunal for the Former Yugoslavia confirmed the overall customary law status of individual criminal responsibility in *Tadić*.[35]

The notion of individual criminal responsibility therefore lies at the very core of the international criminal justice system. However, it increasingly depends upon interactions with cognate legal concepts and other sub-realms of international law. Therefore, how individual criminal responsibility develops in the future will be a function of related legal principles such as an (international) duty to prosecute for defined criminal offences; international legal rules on immunities and amnesties; and the likelihood of co-operation between international criminal courts and tribunals, domestic justice systems, and states more broadly. The actual extent to which individual criminal responsibility might thus (still) be evaded through the application of particular legal principles – such as *ratione personae* immunity – has therefore remained a controversial and steadily evolving phenomenon, featuring in an ever-increasing number of cases before international criminal courts and tribunals – for example, *Taylor*[36] and *Kallon and Kamara*[37] before the Special Court for Sierra Leone and *Karadzic*[38] before the International Criminal Tribunal for the Former Yugoslavia.

[34] *Attorney General v Adolf Eichmann*, District Court of Jerusalem, Judgment, Criminal Case no 40/61, 11 December 1961.

[35] *The Prosecutor v Dusko Tadić* (Interlocutory Appeal) ICTY-94-1-A (2 October 1995).

[36] *Prosecutor v Charles Ghankay Taylor* (Judgment) SCSL-03-01-T (18 May 2012).

[37] *Prosecutor v Morris Kallon and Brima Buzzy Kamara* (Decision on Challenge to Jurisdiction) SCSL-2004-15-AR72(E) (13 March 2004) (in relation to issues of amnesty).

[38] *Prosecutor v Radovan Karadzic* (Judgment) ICTY-95-5/18-T (24 March 2016) (in relation to the issue of a promise not to prosecute).

It is this complex legal entanglement that is at the root of the somewhat uneasy interplay and interdependence between *ratione personae* immunity and individual criminal responsibility as potentially conflicting CIL norms. As explained in Section 1, this predicament has been notably highlighted by the case of (former) Sudanese president Al Bashir and the charges brought against him before the International Criminal Court for his alleged role in the Darfur conflict.

3 Introduction of Practical Concordance into International Adjudication

The notion of practical concordance has its origin in German constitutional law; it can be thought of as a guiding (legal) principle and is particularly characteristic of human rights jurisprudence. Deriving from the Latin *concodare* (to agree), the principle of practical concordance is regularly applied as a means of arriving at a legal equilibrium in human rights cases in which there is a risk of conflict between constitutional norms of equal rank, neither of which should take precedence over the other and both of which call for protection. In relation to possibly conflicting constitutional principles, the intention is to strike a deliberate balance that allows both legal principles to produce their effects as harmoniously and fully as possible. Typically applied to concrete constitutional scenarios, in which possibly conflicting fundamental norms need to be reconciled, practical concordance is informed by case-specific logic, in which legal interests and preferences need to be interpreted in the light of other constitutional principles and purposes. It therefore represents a conditional and, possibly, temporary prioritisation between norms of equal constitutional rank. As a distinct method of reconciling conflicting constitutional norms by balancing them against one another and scrutinising them vis-à-vis other legal considerations, practical concordance can thus be conceived as a specific rule on collision. This is not to say, however, that practical concordance is to be applied unconditionally; it is not applicable in cases in which the legal norm in question might collide with higher-ranking or more specific norms, or in which the norm might contradict general legal norms and principles – the colliding norm would in such cases lie outside practical concordance's scope of application.[39]

[39] An elaborate exploration of the factual limitations of practical concordance (in German) can be found in M Schladebach, 'Praktische Konkordanz als Verfassungsrechtliches Kollisionsprinzip: Eine Verteidigung' (2014) 53 Der Staat 263.

The notion of practical concordance owes its place in the German constitutional law debate above all to the German academic Konrad Hesse, who defined the principle as a method according to which '[c]onstitutionally protected legal interests must be co-ordinated with each other in the solution in such a way that each of them becomes reality. ... [L]imits must thus be set for both legal interests so that each may attain optimal effectiveness.[40] According to the definition provided by Hesse, the realization of one legal interest shall not be at the expense of the other, which also excludes an over-hasty weighing or accommodation of conflicting legal positions. In that sense, practical concordance is geared towards an overall imperative of constitutional unity and thus of both coherence and impartiality, the ultimate aim being to establish a lasting balance while at the same time furthering both legal interests at issue. In this respect, practical concordance could be considered an emanation of the principle of proportionality. Expressed differently, practical concordance realizes two seemingly different, yet inherently interlinked, objectives – namely, to reconcile conflicting norms through a harmonized interpretation and to facilitate an equilibrium among norms.

This explains the widespread attention and approval given to practical concordance in domestic constitutional debates in several (mostly German-speaking) countries. The principle is today generally recognized as a constitutionally grounded balancing mechanism between potentially conflicting legal norms, the aim of which is to achieve an equilibrium between those norms and thereby generate a state of practical concordance. The concrete scope and character of practical concordance has been delineated first and foremost by the German Federal Constitutional Court in its fundamental rights jurisprudence.[41] In general, the principle serves in cases of collision between fundamental rights that are guaranteed without qualification and is thus applicable to a broad range of fundamental rights collisions and interrelated conflicting constitutional principles. It has been questioned, however, whether the factual

[40] K Hesse, *Grundzüge des Verfassungsrechts der Bundesrepublik Deutschland* (20th edn, CF Müller 1999) 74 ('Verfassungsrechtlich geschützte Rechtsgüter müssen in der Problemlösung einander so zugeordnet werden, dass jedes von ihnen Wirklichkeit gewinnt. [. . .] [B]eiden Gütern müssen Grenzen gesetzt werden, damit beide zu optimaler Wirksamkeit gelangen können.' English translation by this chapter's author.)

[41] See eg Bundesverfassungsgericht, Order of First Senate (17 December 1975) 1 BvR 63/68; Bundesverfassungsgericht, Order of First Senate (3 November 1987) 1 BvR 1257/84; Bundesverfassungsgericht, Order of First Senate (7 March 1990) 1 BvR 1215/87.

application of practical concordance in the sense of a systemic method of interpretation can place limits (possibly unintended) on the protective scope normally inherent in an unconditionally guaranteed fundamental right. If the conflicting constitutional provision amounts to a limitation in itself, this may justify the imposition of limits, provided the norm collision concerned is addressed and balanced in the spirit of practical concordance. On this particular issue, constitutional jurisprudence has remained rather patchy.

The foundational idea on which practical concordance is grounded also constitutes the basis for what other constitutional scholars, such as Peter Lerche, have identified as the components of an appropriate balancing of conflicting, yet constitutionally protected and relevant, interests as a way of legitimizing contingent restrictions on fundamental rights.[42] This approach lends itself to situations in which the absence of an explicit authorization to restrict fundamental rights may need to be compensated by imparting constitutional legitimation. The rationale implicitly underlying practical concordance has subsequently been adopted by constitutional orders outside Germany – for example, in France[43] and Switzerland,[44] where the notion has been taken up, sometimes unchanged, in both constitutional law scholarship and fundamental rights jurisprudence.

Although international law recognizes the existence of conflicting norms and provisions and has long-developed rules of conflict at its disposal, including general principles of law such as *lex specialis derogat legi generali*,[45] – the tension between conflicting CIL norms may lead to profound legal dilemmas when adjudicative bodies, including the ICJ, are confronted with such conflicts. As the corpus of international law expands and becomes more fragmented, this legal-theoretical problem is likely to have ramifications and repercussions in both scholarly discourse and judicial practice. In the absence of authoritative rules of conflict that address this enduring tension, practical concordance can be used by international judges, alongside existing methods of

[42] P Lerche, *Übermaß und Verfassungsrecht: Zur Bindung des Gesetzgebers an die Grundsätze der Verhältnismäßigkeit und der Erforderlichkeit* (Heymann 1961).

[43] Conseil constitutionnel (18 January 1995) Decision no 94-352.

[44] Federal Supreme Court of Switzerland (12 October 2012) BGE 139 I 16.

[45] For a comprehensive account, see S Borelli, 'The (Mis-)Use of General Principles of Law: *Lex Specialis* and the Relationship between International Human Rights Law and the Laws of Armed Conflict' in Laura Pineschi (ed), *General Principles of Law: The Role of the Judiciary* (Springer 2015) 265.

interpretation such as the principle of effectiveness, systemic integration, or the principle of harmonization,[46] as a distinct analytical lens through which they can balance conflicting legal norms instead of preferring one norm to another one.

Section 4, sketches a possible way of introducing practical concordance into the legal toolkit employed by judges of international courts, including the ICJ. This transposition exercise seeks not to delineate yet another legal-methodological concept that can be regularly applied in a formal manner but rather to draw intellectual inspiration from the principle of practical concordance. The aim is to provide a tangible dimension and a name to the dilemma of reconciling conflicting CIL norms. The exercise aspires to raise awareness of this distinctive quandary among adjudicators, with a view to contributing to their reasoning and encouraging reflection on possible ways of establishing an equilibrium of legal interests in the concrete cases they handle.

4 'What a Judge Gotta Do': Thoughts on Reconciling Conflicting CIL Norms at the ICJ

So, how can the judges of international adjudicative bodies make use of practical concordance in their daily work on the bench, and in particular at the ICJ? This section will propose various adjudicative 'lenses' whereby practical concordance might possibly contribute towards a more comprehensive assessment.

In recent years, international judges have increasingly become an object of research in themselves for international legal scholars.[47] Matters such as (legal) socialization[48] or international judges' role in constituting court authority[49] have featured extensively in recent academic writings. These studies have shown that international judges carry with them an individualized legal fingerprint and trajectory, which

[46] See eg A Peters, 'The Refinement of International Law: From Fragmentation to Regime Interaction and Politicization' (2017) 15 IJCL 671.

[47] See eg D Terris, CPR Romano, and L Swigart, *The International Judge: An Introduction to the Men and Women Who Decide the World's Cases* (Brandeis University Press 2007); R Mackenzie and others, *Selecting International Judges: Principle, Process, and Politics* (Oxford University Press 2010). For a view more focused on international criminal law, see J Powderly, *Judges and the Making of International Criminal Law* (Brill 2020).

[48] MR Madsen, 'Who Rules the World? The Educational Capital of the International Judiciary' (2018) 3 UC Irvine J Intl Transl Comp L 97.

[49] KJ Alter, LR Helfer, and MR Madsen (eds), *International Court Authority* (Oxford University Press 2018).

determines the (legal) reasoning they pursue in any given case before them. Recalling that the principle of practical concordance has its origins in German constitutional law – and has thus far been mostly restricted thereto – it is no surprise that the concept has not (yet) expanded more broadly across international legal scholarship and penetrated the everyday practice of international judges.[50] Mindful of this caveat, the following thoughts are but a tentative and initial attempt to introduce the notion of practical concordance into contemporary international legal thinking.

In brief, practical concordance may fulfil a threefold function for international judges called upon to reconcile conflicting CIL norms. Firstly, it may serve as a methodological-analytical prism through which the customary norm(s) in question may be viewed, scrutinized, and de-constructed while being mindful of the need to achieve an equilibrium of norms. This implies that the substantive scope of each norm will necessarily be circumscribed. It could be said that this readiness to engage in a balancing process requires a mindset similar to that displayed when judges rule *ex aequo et bono*.

Secondly, although the above-mentioned equilibrium of norms is to be sought *in situ* – that is, pursued by international judges in the concrete cases before them – applying practical concordance at the same time requires the broader picture to be taken into consideration – that is, international judges must ponder the results of weighing different norms against one another and take account of the legal effects that might result across various (sub-)branches of international law. This applies particularly to the ICJ, which, as the 'principal judicial organ of the United Nations'[51] is of fundamental significance in the future development and practice of international law. With each decision they render, the ICJ judges address not only the legal interests at issue in the case before them but also the repercussions this may have for the domain of international law more broadly. Practical concordance could be regarded as a further aid in performing this role, accommodating international judges' dual role as, on the one hand, authoritative arbitrators and legal interpreters in any given case before them and, on the other hand, international legal

[50] For an insightful (and external) perspective on international legal scholarship in Germany, see E Benvenisti, 'The Future of International Law Scholarship in Germany: The Tension between Interpretation and Change' (2007) 67 Heidelberg J Intl L 585. On the conceptual difference between harmonization of conflicting legal norms and practical concordance, see also n 12.

[51] UN Charter (n 2) art 92.

norm entrepreneurs, entrusted with developing international law in accordance with a constantly changing legal-political environment.

Thirdly, the application of practical concordance both enables and obliges international judges to take a 'think outside the box' approach when addressing legal dilemmas arising from the concurrence of possibly conflicting CIL norms and thereby to engage in judicial creativity. When applied in a given case, practical concordance requires established norms of (customary) international law to be balanced against one another in order to find an equitable solution to a previously disregarded legal dilemma. For this, interdisciplinary thinking and unorthodox legal approaches are needed. It also offers a way of upholding past precedence while striving for *de lege ferenda*.

Practical concordance should not therefore be regarded as a sophisticated and novel concept in legal theory. Rather, it denotes a distinct methodological lens through which cases that deal with conflicting CIL norms may be viewed, analysed, and resolved – hence putting a strong emphasis on considerations of balancing and compensation. Whether, to what extent, and in what way practical concordance may make inroads into the practices of international courts, especially the ICJ, remains to be seen. The compensatory character of practical concordance, which seeks an accommodation between prima facie contradictory CIL norms could emerge as a potential game-changer particularly whenever the ICJ is called upon to provide advisory opinions. It could, for example, help in answering the question of how to reconcile the *ratione personae* immunity enjoyed by heads of state, heads of government, and ministers of foreign affairs under international law with the pursuit of individual criminal accountability for international core crimes.

How, to what extent, and with what results might practical concordance be used by ICJ judges? While it might seem a somewhat vain exercise to ponder potential decisions *in abstracto*, and without wishing to interfere with judicial autonomy, a brief thought experiment will help to show how practical concordance could be applied to resolve conflicting CIL norms.

For this thought experiment, let us suppose that the ICJ is to render an advisory opinion at the request of the United Nations General Assembly[52] on whether, how, and under what conditions two prima facie conflicting CIL norms–*ratione personae* immunity and individual criminal responsibility – may be reconciled. Our illustration will involve

[52] See n 26.

the (fictious) case of a sitting head of state accused of being responsible for an international crime falling within the jurisdiction of an international criminal tribunal legally empowered to adjudicate on such a situation. Faced with this (simplified) scenario, an international judge will need to take two initial steps. The first will be to analyse each (customary) norm and define its scope of application and the legal interests it protects, so as to distil the legal dilemma posed by the concurrence of the legal interests each norm seeks to protect. The second step will consist in delineating each norm's legal nucleus – that is, the normative core to be preserved and without which the norm in question would become meaningless. This exercise will necessarily need to be placed within the context of the concrete case at hand and thus take account of the notional and circumstantial specifics of the case.

Taking this line of thinking a step further and applying it to the norms of *ratione personae* immunity and individual criminal responsibility, the establishment of an equilibrium between the norms would mean that neither norm is applied unrestrictedly, yet their overall applicability is upheld. As regards *ratione personae* immunity, this balancing could lead to confirmation that, for example, heads of state continue to enjoy extensive privileges, in particular before domestic courts, and that their previously unconditional immunity could be curtailed only where the individual is charged with a core crime of concern to the international community as a whole and this charge is made before a competent international criminal court or tribunal with the necessary jurisdiction. This qualified understanding of *ratione personae* immunity is the direct result of its being confronted with the other norm in question – namely, individual criminal responsibility. Although a bedrock principle in individualizing international justice, allowing the actual perpetrators of atrocious crimes (humans as opposed to states) to be held accountable, this principle would have to comport with the importance accorded to individuals who enjoy *ratione personae* immunity on account of their unique role as state representatives. For its part, therefore, the principle of individual criminal responsibility will have to be curtailed so that this limited circle of officeholders are prosecuted only before a competent international criminal court or tribunal with the necessary jurisdiction and only for a crime of concern to the international community as whole.

This (hypothetical) act of balancing can truly be considered an instance of practical concordance as the international judge will have engaged in a deliberate process of weighing both norms against one another and safeguarding each by ensuring that it remains intact and is not compromised or conceptually subordinated to the other. It should be pointed out that the balancing process could also lead to a different result, depending on the circumstances of the case. In our illustration, it can be claimed that both norms conserve their overall legitimacy and efficiency in protecting the fundamental legal interest(s) to which they relate and thus the substantive validity of those norms. *In concreto*, it would mean that a competent international criminal tribunal is required to prosecute a sitting head of state who enjoys *ratione personae* immunity save where that head of state is charged with crimes of concern to the international community as a whole. Although in this case the pendulum could be said to have swung more towards one of the two norms, the other norm's overall applicability and validity in similar or different constellations is not undermined.

5 Conclusion

The present contribution has sought to introduce the notion of practical concordance into international adjudication and, in particular, into the everyday practice of international judges, thereby making the principle applicable in situations where possibly conflicting norms of CIL must be reconciled *in situ*. Far from a full-fledged legal-theoretical concept, practical concordance as presented here is rather a state of mind conducive to establishing an equilibrium between legal norms of equal rank and a distinct methodological approach in addressing legal dilemmas. It is hoped this contribution will spur further reflection on how to confront cases in which norms of CIL may conflict with one another, and thus point to the greater leverage offered by a more nuanced weighing of contradictory legal norms and principles.

13

Indicators of Coherence and the Interpretation of CIL

CHARALAMPOS GIANNAKOPOULOS

1 Introduction

Interpretation is ubiquitous in everyday life. We constantly interpret a variety of objects, including texts, signs, gestures, works of art, intentions, and human practices and interactions. Interpretation is central to the practice of international law, too. Arguing about international law's content is the everyday business of international lawyers, and this often includes arguing about the existence and content of norms of customary international law (CIL). Although a number of scholars recognise that CIL can be interpreted,[1] disagreements remain as to the precise methods, modalities, and extent of CIL interpretation. Such disagreements are born of a common concern to secure competently made, coherent, and accurate interpretations of CIL, given the latter's non-textual nature.

My aim in this chapter is to explore in a preliminary manner two related questions regarding CIL interpretation: (1) is it necessary, or even possible, to strive towards coherence in the interpretation of CIL? And (2) are there any possible indicators of (in-)coherence in that respect? Providing answers to these questions depends on how one understands

[1] eg P Merkouris, J Kammerhofer, and N Arajärvi (eds), *The Theory, Practice, and Interpretation of Customary International Law* (Cambridge University Press 2022); O Chasapis Tassinis, 'Customary International Law: Interpretation from Beginning to End' (2020) 31 EJIL 235; P Merkouris, 'Interpreting the Customary Rules on Interpretation' (2017) 19 ICLR 126; D Alland, 'L'interprétation du droit international public' (2013) 362 RdC 41, 82–88; A Orakhelashvili, *The Interpretation of Acts and Rules in Public International Law* (Oxford University Press 2008) ch 15; R Kolb, *Interprétation et création du droit international: Esquisse d'une herméneutique juridique moderne pour le droit international public* (Bruylant 2006) 219ff; C de Visscher, *Théories et réalités en droit international public* (4th edn, Pedone 1970) 171–72.

coherence in the first place, including its relation to legal reasoning. A substantial part of the chapter will therefore deal with that as well.

Coherence is here envisaged as a state of axiological compatibility existing among a set of independent beliefs, statements, reasons for action, and so on, which are expressed at any level of abstraction. The degree of compatibility of the set is a function of the existence of internal structures of mutual, reciprocal support among the elements of the set, so that some of the elements are supported by other elements and vice versa.[2]

Based on this understanding, I make three broad claims. First, coherence is related to, yet still independent of, concepts like consistency, correctness, and comprehensiveness (and its corollary, predictability); and, moreover, it has two dimensions (one substantive, the other methodological) which are both relevant in law (Section 2). Second, this makes coherence particularly relevant to legal reasoning, where its dual dimension translates into a similar dual role that is also at once substantive and methodological (Section 3). Given this, coherence in law is more than a simple goal or a results-oriented ideal. It is also a method of constructing one's reasoning and of deliberating about one's interpretative choices. It is therefore both possible and, indeed, necessary to strive for coherence in the interpretation of CIL if one wishes to claim authority for, and persuade others of, one's interpretation. Third, striving for coherence in the interpretation of CIL means being cognisant of three kinds of processes – namely, framing, contextualising, and iteration/reflexivity (Section 4). These can serve as indicators of (in-)coherent interpretations; however, they themselves are interpretative in nature and therefore can be subject to debate and reasonable disagreement.

2 The Independent Concept of Coherence

We tend to place value on coherence because it implies that something, or someone, makes sense and is intelligible. Being incoherent, by contrast, causes frustration and confusion. Coherence is thought to be a desirable attribute to have in virtually every aspect of one's life. The legal field is no exception, where there exists a vast literature on

[2] To note, the requisite strength of the mutually supporting relations cannot be determined in the abstract but rather depends on the standards of rationality prevalent in the domain of human endeavour in which one finds oneself. The standards of rationality in ethics or morality, for example, are not necessarily the same as those found in scientific rationality and empirical proof.

coherence in law in general and a large consensus that coherence suits law and legal reasoning particularly well.[3] However, coherence remains a largely under-theorised concept in the field of international law. One can, for example, find passing references to coherence in the ILC's work on the fragmentation of international law. Therein, the ILC indicates that there exists a link between coherence and the principle of systemic integration under Article 31(3)(c) of the Vienna Convention on the Law of Treaties (VCLT).[4] Beyond that, however, coherence seems to be generally regarded by the ILC as co-terminous with mere legal security and predictability, which is to say it is seen as a formal principle devoid of its own independent content.[5] One sees a similar picture in other areas of international law, notably international investment law, where concerns of incoherence in arbitral awards have been raised for years alongside concerns about a perceived lack of judicial consistency, correctness, and predictability.[6] Here, too, coherence is regarded as valuable, yet the content given to it is often interchangeable with that of legal certainty, predictability, and legal authority.[7]

[3] For a non-exhaustive list, see A Amaya, *The Tapestry of Reason: An Inquiry into the Nature of Coherence and Its Role in Legal Argument* (Hart 2015); N MacCormick, *Rhetoric and the Rule of Law* (Oxford University Press 2005); J Hage, 'Law and Coherence' (2004) 17 Ratio Juris 87; J Raz, 'The Relevance of Coherence' (1992) 72 BULR 273; R Alexy and A Peczenik, 'The Concept of Coherence and Its Significance for Discursive Rationality' (1990) 3 Ratio Juris 130; R Dworkin, *Law's Empire* (Harvard University Press 1986); BB Levenbook, 'The Role of Coherence in Legal Reasoning' (1984) 3 Law Philos 355. See generally Y Radi, 'Coherence' in J d'Aspremont and S Singh (eds), *Concepts for International Law: Contributions to Disciplinary Thought* (Edward Elgar 2019) 105 (and additional references therein).

[4] ILC, 'Fragmentation of International Law: Difficulties Arising from the Diversification and Expansion of International Law, Report of the Study Group of the International Law Commission' (13 April 2006) UN Doc A/CN.4/L.682, 211 para 419.

[5] eg ibid 248 para 491 ('Coherence is, however, a formal and abstract virtue. For a legal system that is regarded in some respects as unjust or unworkable, no added value is brought by the fact of its being coherently so.').

[6] UNCITRAL, 'Report of Working Group III (Investor-State Dispute Settlement Reform) on the Work of Its 36th Session (Vienna, 29 October–2 November 2018)' (6 November 2018) UN Doc A/CN.9/964, 6–11 paras 25–63.

[7] eg C Schreuer, 'Coherence and Consistency in International Investment Law' in R Echandi and P Sauvé (eds), *Prospects in International Investment Law and Policy* (Cambridge University Press 2013) 391 ('Coherence and consistency are desirable qualities in any legal system. A legal system is coherent if its elements are logically related to each other and if it shows no contradictions. A legal system is consistent if it treats identical or similar situations in the same way and if it gives equal treatment to the participants in the system.'). Similarly, C Schreuer, 'Diversity and Harmonization of Treaty Interpretation in Investment Arbitration' in M Fitzmaurice, O Elias, and P Merkouris (eds), *Treaty Interpretation and the Vienna Convention on the Law of Treaties: 30 Years On* (Martinus Nijhoff 2010) 139 ('The need for a coherent case law is evident. It strengthens the predictability of decisions and enhances their authority.').

Therefore, before we can ponder the role of coherence in interpreting CIL, one key question must be answered: what is coherence and what is its role in legal reasoning more generally? This section seeks to answer the first half of that question (what is coherence?) by demarcating coherence's scope from other, related concepts like legal consistency, correctness, and comprehensiveness (and its corollary predictability).[8] The goal is not simply to reduce confusion by disentangling the meaning of concepts but also to set proper expectations of the concept of coherence in the process. The second half of the question (the role of coherence in legal reasoning) is dealt with in Section 3.

2.1 Coherence and Consistency in Law

Consistency means absence of contradiction.[9] Propositions are consistent if each can without contradiction be asserted in conjunction with every other proposition in the same set, and with their conjunction.[10] Consistency is thus an absolute and logical property: any two propositions either are or are not consistent. By contrast, the conditions of satisfaction of coherence are less precise. The quality of being coherent is often conveyed through mental images and metaphors.[11] It is often said, for instance, that something is coherent if it hangs together well, if its parts fit and are mutually supportive, if it is intelligible, if it flows from or expresses a unified viewpoint; whereas the same thing would be incoherent if it is unintelligible, fragmented, or disjointed.[12] More generally, an attribute of coherence is that the object of enquiry 'makes sense', whereas an attribute of incoherence is that it does not.[13]

[8] To note, this chapter does not intend to offer a full account of the concept of coherence or an exhaustive analysis of its different facets. For an effort in that direction, see Amaya (n 3).

[9] LA Kornhauser and LG Sager, 'Unpacking the Court' (1986) 96 Yale LJ 82, 103.

[10] MacCormick (n 3) 190.

[11] eg JM Pérez Bermejo, 'Coherence: An Outline in Six Metaphors and Four Rules' in M Araszkiewicz and J Šavelka (eds), *Coherence: Insights from Philosophy, Jurisprudence and Artificial Intelligence* (Springer 2013) 93; L Moral Soriano, 'A Modest Notion of Coherence in Legal Reasoning: A Model for the European Court of Justice' (2003) 16 Ratio Juris 296.

[12] K Kress, 'Coherence' in D Patterson (ed), *A Companion to Philosophy of Law and Legal Theory* (2nd edn, Wiley-Blackwell 2010) 521; S Bertea, 'The Arguments from Coherence: Analysis and Evaluation' (2005) 25 OJLS 369, 371–72 (and additional references therein); Raz (n 3) 276.

[13] MacCormick (n 3) 189–93.

Neil MacCormick once used the following humorous example to make the distinction between consistency and coherence stand out more clearly. MacCormick asks us to imagine a house where the cleaning rules are as follows: leave everything as untidy as possible on Mondays, Wednesdays, and Fridays, but tidy everything up to the highest perfection on Tuesdays, Thursdays, and Saturdays (Sundays are reserved for resting). These rules can be easily observed, in the sense that none infringes upon the other, but they surely give rise to an unreasonable, indeed absurd, way of living, since they do not seem to serve any immediately discernible end – in short, they make no sense. The image of coherence painted by this example, and the general descriptions above, is that of a network – an interdependent web – between propositions and their justification standing or falling together.[14]

Transposed to law, it is therefore possible to restate the quality of being coherent – that is, a function of the ability to 'make sense' – as the degree to which a set of propositions are rationally related to each other and to the ordering values or principles that are thought to justify them – which MacCormick usefully summarised in the pithy phrase 'axiological compatibility among two or more rules, all being justifiable by reference to some common principle or value'.[15]

Aiming for axiological compatibility involves a conscious effort to bring two or more propositions into accord with each other. As such, coherence is not an absolute property but rather a matter of degree and interpretation. Whereas consistency 'is or is not', coherence can be 'more or less'. In the same vein, unlike coherence, consistency as a logical property remains agnostic towards the merits of the positions that are made consistent.[16] Thus, ironically, greater consistency may actually perpetuate injustice. It follows that between consistency and coherence,

[14] Pérez Bermejo (n 11) 97 ('This image [of the net] describes the structure and organization of the coherentist systems . . . [as] highly interconnected cells or neurons, sustained through the mutual support of all [their] elements and permanently open to learning by reacting to any external input.'); Raz (n 3) 287 ('[W]e attribute beliefs, goals, and actions to people, not singly but in interdependent clumps. This interdependence means nothing other than a presumption of coherence.'). Similarly, but in a different disciplinary context (text linguistics), see RA de Beaugrande and WU Dressler, *Introduction to Text Linguistics* (Longman 1981) ch V para 23 ('Coherence will be envisioned as the outcome of combining concepts and relations into a network composed of knowledge spaces centred around main topics.').

[15] See the analysis in MacCormick (n 3) 189–93, 230–31.

[16] T Schultz, 'Against Consistency in Investment Arbitration' in Z Douglas, J Pauwelyn, and JE Viñuales (eds), *The Foundations of International Investment Law: Bringing Theory into Practice* (Oxford University Press 2014) 297.

consistency is the subordinate and dependent concept. For example, a perceived inconsistency between two judicial decisions may be interpreted away if one goes higher in the level of abstraction and considers the more general norms, principles, or values that have justified them. By the same token, two legal positions that appear consistent because they yield the same outcome may still not cohere if one looks at the norms, principles, or values that have justified them.

2.2 Coherence and Correctness in Law

Unlike coherence and consistency, coherence and correctness in law are generally not conflated with each other at a conceptual level or treated as interchangeable. However, because coherence is not agnostic towards the merits of the propositions that are made coherent, it is sometimes proposed that a requirement associated with coherence is the ability to arrive at right answers. That is to say, it is sometimes proposed that a coherent whole should be able to determine the single correct outcome in particular cases.[17] However, this is not precisely the case, and the statement thus requires more nuance so as to avoid introducing distorting expectations of coherence. While there exists correlation between coherence and correctness, it is doubtful that this extends to causation. To see why, we must further distinguish between determinate and demonstrable correctness.

Something is *determinately* correct when the reasons offered in its support compel it, which is to say when they carry the greatest weight out of all other competing, plausible reasons supporting it.[18] Determinate correctness is an instance of so-called *ontological* objectivity, which seeks to describe the way things are – their nature and existence – in this case by making particular reference to their ability to produce accurate answers.[19] By contrast, something is *demonstrably* correct when its

[17] Kress (n 12) 528–29. Kress calls this the 'completeness' requirement of coherence.

[18] On compelling reasons, see W Lucy, 'Adjudication' in JL Coleman, KE Himma, and SJ Shapiro (eds), *The Oxford Handbook of Jurisprudence and Philosophy of Law* (Oxford University Press 2004) 230–31.

[19] MH Kramer, *Objectivity and the Rule of Law* (Cambridge University Press 2007) ch 1. Conversely, something is indeterminate when the reasons that can be offered for or against it are all of equal strength and weight, so that no decision or choice is ultimately better than any other. To note, being ontological states, determinacy and indeterminacy are positive claims that must be argued for rather than merely assumed as default positions (on this, see R Dworkin, 'Objectivity and Truth: You'd Better Believe It' (1996) 25 Philos Public Aff 87, 129–31).

determinate, or at least plausible, correctness can be demonstrated to the satisfaction of everyone, or virtually everyone. Demonstrable correctness is thus an instance of so-called *epistemic* objectivity, which refers to the state of rational agents having formed a justified belief regarding the correctness of the object in question.[20] Determinate and demonstrable correctness are not absolute properties, but matters of degree. The stronger the reasons offered in support of an outcome, the more they would determine that outcome and, by extension, the more likely it would be that others are persuaded of the outcome's correctness.

The above applies to the legal field as well. Law has an arguable character, meaning that statements about its content are in reality arguments supported by reasons whose relative strength and manner of deployment can vary.[21] Evaluating the force of competing legal arguments is bound to be a matter of degree and calls for the exercise of judgement.[22] Correctness in law, therefore, cannot be simply reduced to a mere pronouncement (e.g. 'the law demands *x*', or 'party A must bear liability') but is rather a combination of the content of the pronouncement and the content and structure of the reasons offered in supporting it.[23] The quality of correctness in law is always determined and demonstrated relatively to a set of strung-together premises and assumptions acting as reasons favouring some outcomes or courses of action over others.

[20] Kramer (n 19) 17.

[21] On law as a 'culture of argument and interpretation', see JB White, 'Law as Language: Reading Law and Reading Literature' (1982) 60 Tex L Rev 415, 436.

[22] MacCormick (n 3) 14–15.

[23] eg compare the majority decision in *Oil Platforms (Iran v USA)* (Judgment) [2003] ICJ Rep 161 [31]–[78]; with *Oil Platforms*, Separate Opinion of Judge Higgins [40] – [54] and Separate Opinion of Judge Kooijmans [41]–[63]. In *Oil Platforms*, the court's majority concluded that the destruction by the United States of two Iranian oil platforms, under suspicion of involvement in the attack on two US vessels, was not a legitimate exercise of self-defence under the CIL on the use of force. In their separate opinions, Judges Higgins and Kooijmans concurred with the final outcome (that is, the United States could not rely on the law on the use of force to justify its actions), yet took issue with what they saw as several systemic flaws in the decision – namely (i) that the majority had implicitly changed the framing of the dispute, from that of a commercial dispute brought under a commercial treaty between Iran and the United States, to one about the unlawful use of force; (ii) that the majority had used Article 31(3)(c) of the VCLT inappropriately to incorporate by reference the totality of the CIL on the use of force as applicable law; and (iii) that, in so doing, the majority had violated its jurisdictional mandate. Put differently, and despite their ultimate agreement with the decision's *dispositif*, for Judges Higgins and Kooijmans, the *Oil Platforms* decision was on the whole incorrect given the process of reasoning and justification followed by the majority.

Because coherence is axiological compatibility with guiding norms, values, or principles, coherence is thus linked to legal correctness in the following manner. One person's 'correct' interpretation or decision may still be thought to cohere better than another's, given the justification offered for each interpretation or decision, and given the method used to arrive at them. In other words, the existence of a coherent process of reasoning would mean that its outcome has a claim to correctness, but also that such a claim would not be absolute since another person's process of reasoning may have been performed better, thus making the latter person's proposed outcome arguably more coherent and with a stronger claim to correctness.

It follows, then, that coherence and correctness in law are not necessarily equivalent properties. An otherwise coherent process of justification may still result in an outcome which we may regard as legally incorrect for being in tension with collective attitudes and beliefs. One may use an appropriate method and link together the various aspects of the legal system in a competent manner (e.g. by properly identifying the relevant materials, legal norms, or past practices) but may nonetheless make a substantive, value-laden interpretation of them, with which at least some participants in the legal system may not agree. By the same token, determining that an outcome is coherent cannot be exclusively a function of the extent to which the decision is considered to be correct in its substance. One may reach a correct decision in substance, which everyone would agree that the law ought to provide, but do so through contradictory reasoning or through a not well-justified process, where the various elements of the legal system have not been linked together adequately or accurately. In such a case, we would be inclined to conclude that coherence is lacking, despite the moral appeal that the outcome itself may have.

2.3 *Coherence and Comprehensiveness in Law*

Yet a third requirement often associated with coherence is that of comprehensiveness, meaning the absence of gaps or uncertainties and the corresponding ability to readily supply an answer to each and every question that may be raised.[24] In the legal field, comprehensiveness can be linked to the value of predictability – that is, the ability of the law's addressees to determine in advance the legal consequences of their

24 Kress (n 12) 528.

actions. Comprehensiveness and predictability are properties that obtain in degrees. Enhancing comprehensiveness, in the sense of expanding the range of readily available answers to distinct questions of law, can result in greater predictability for the legal system's addressees.

It may be a reasonable assumption to make that if a legal system is sufficiently comprehensive and thus exhibits a high degree of predictability, then it would also be coherent. However, it can be doubted whether such a connection would necessarily exist. Comprehensiveness does seem to improve the chances of overall coherence but probably cannot guarantee it, and, conversely, coherence does seem to improve the chances of eventually experiencing comprehensiveness over time (and hence predictability) but probably cannot guarantee that either.[25] As was the case with correctness previously, correlation does not equal causation.

The above conclusions follow logically from the previous examination of the links between coherence, consistency, and correctness. Because coherence is characterised by axiological compatibility, as opposed to mere non-contradiction, the predictability that would normally result from a nominally consistent line of interpretations or applications of the law does not mean that these would necessarily exhibit coherence also. Furthermore, one need not be fully comprehensive in scope, or perfectly predictable at the outset, to be coherent. This again applies especially in law, considering the well-recognised need for change and progressive development following the occurrence of novel situations not covered in existing legal instruments or following a change in collective attitudes and beliefs. By the same token, the inverse also holds true. Coherence does not preclude the need at times to strike a different path from what past consistent practice may indicate. Nor does coherence preclude the existence of gaps in the law.

2.4 Summing-up

How do consistency, correctness, and comprehensiveness fare as determinants of coherence? In the abstract, one may be inclined to say that the occurrence of all three is necessary to describe an object of study as coherent in ideal theory. Thus, the perfect co-existence of all three elements will necessarily render the object of study perfectly coherent in an ideal situation. Conversely, the absence of all three elements would render the object incoherent. However, based on the preceding analysis,

[25] ibid.

the same conclusion does not seem to follow in practical, non-ideal situations. Indeed, three general points can be made in this respect.

First, although certainly desirable for coherence to exist, consistency is not a necessary or sufficient requirement of it. The presence or absence of consistency does not necessarily mean that coherence obtains or that coherence is forfeit. In fact, consistency seems to be the dependent concept when seen against coherence. Often, it is a sense of coherence that makes us either disregard contradictions as being only apparent (and thus capable of being interpreted away) or, indeed, call them out as being true.[26]

Second, correctness is likewise not a necessary determinant of coherence. Although there exists a correlation between legal correctness (both determinate and demonstrable) and coherence, this does not extend to causation, given the law's arguable character and the scope within it for debate and reasonable disagreement. Legal pronouncements may not always be determinately correct, yet they could still exhibit congruence with some of the system's principles or values and be supported by a competently drafted statement of reasons. Incoherence resulting from a complete disregard of a system's norms, practices, and principles, or from a complete disregard of the ways of structuring and presenting legal arguments, are likely to be rare.

Third, the same considerations apply also with respect to comprehensiveness as a determinant of coherence. Some unpredictability resulting from an absence of comprehensiveness is not necessarily a sign of incoherence. The law is always a work-in-progress and unpredictable outcomes may be caused by legal actors using novel doctrines, arguments, or theories that are not yet settled or widely accepted in the current state of the discipline.

The above leads to the conclusion that coherence is an independent concept having its own content. Were it not, we could only perceive it to the extent, if any, that it entails or is entailed by consistency, correctness, and comprehensiveness. That is to say, the conclusion 'coherent or incoherent' would necessarily follow from any statement about the law, so long as we considered that statement to be consistent, correct, or comprehensive (predictable). However, this does not appear to be the case in practice. To the contrary, we are ultimately not precluded from

[26] MacCormick (n 3) 190 ('A story can be coherent on the whole and as a whole, though it contains some internal inconsistencies – and in this case, the sense of the overall coherence of the story may be decisive for us in deciding which among pairs of inconsistent propositions to disregard as anomalies in an overall coherent account or opinion.' (footnote omitted)).

perceiving coherence in practice or from debating about coherence meaningfully, even when some of the above-identified elements are satisfied to a lesser extent or even entirely missing.

In the same vein, striving for coherence in the determination and interpretation of CIL should not mean that consistency, correctness, or predictability will be necessary outcomes, although they may be probable and, indeed, highly hoped-for outcomes. Does this then make coherence practically irrelevant when engaging in CIL interpretation or, for that matter, in any form of legal reasoning? Section 3 argues that it does not.

3 Practical Legal Reasoning and the Dual Role of Coherence

Legal reasoning is the principal means through which lawyers argue about the existence and content of law. This makes it natural to enquire about the role that coherence may have to play therein. Yet, answering this question presupposes answering a more fundamental question first: what kind of reasoning is legal reasoning? There are two candidate-types to consider in this respect: the theoretical and the practical. A fundamental difference between the two relates to their respective conditions of validity and the outcomes that each type of reasoning seeks to achieve.

Starting from the proposition that, much like other kinds of normative reasoning, legal reasoning is practical rather than merely theoretical, this section argues that seeing legal reasoning as practical leads to the conclusion that coherence has a dual role to play therein, a role that is at once substantive and methodological. The section concludes by hinting at three interpretative processes acting as possible indicators of (in-)coherence in legal reasoning, termed 'framing', 'contextualisation', and 'iteration'/'reflexivity'. Their importance for the interpretation of CIL is subsequently examined in Section 4.

3.1 Theoretical versus Practical Reasoning

In theoretical argumentation, one adduces reasons for or against forming a belief about what is or is not the case in reality.[27] Theoretical reasoning is thus reasoning principally about questions of fact, explanation, and prediction.[28] As such, it has a backward-looking and a forward-looking

[27] N MacCormick, 'Argumentation and Interpretation in Law' (1993) 6 Ratio Juris 16, 16. MacCormick uses the term 'speculative' to refer to theoretical reasoning.

[28] RJ Wallace, 'Practical Reason', *The Stanford Encyclopedia of Philosophy* (Spring edn, 2020) <https://plato.stanford.edu/entries/practical-reason/> accessed 12 June 2024.

dimension. It is backward-looking when it looks at events that have occurred and asks why or how they have occurred. It is forward-looking when it uses past observations and the rules of logic to attempt a true determination about what is going to happen in the future. Given its format and reliance on the rules of logic, theoretical reasoning can be challenged in two ways: first, *substantively*, when the premises used are not accurate, thus leading to a necessarily inaccurate outcome (inaccurate assessment or collection of data); or, second, *formally*, when the syllogism itself violates the rules of logical consequence or entailment (impermissible moves between otherwise accurate premises).

Practical reasoning is different. Practical reasoning is reasoning about what to do when faced with a problematic situation. As such, it does not stop at formulating an opinion or belief about what the case may be, as theoretical reasoning does, but continues until one commits to a course of action. Put differently, practical reasoning attaches to a project an actor has (be it a problem requiring solution or a goal to be achieved) and seeks to identify the course of action that would lead to the satisfactory completion of that project.[29] From this fundamental point, a number of key differences between theoretical and practical reasoning emerge.

First, whereas the ends in a theoretical inference are clearly defined and certain (i.e. ascertaining the truth of a proposition or accepting it as a matter of belief), this is not always the case in a practical inference. Indeed, when we contemplate possible courses of action in practice, we often come across phenomena like complexity, uncertainty, instability, uniqueness, or value-conflict.[30] In these situations the ends cannot always be taken as given – which is to say, without some prior attempt at ascertaining their desirability or appropriateness as ends to be achieved in the first place.[31] Therefore, in resolving a practical problem, an actor must also deliberate in order to prioritise or reconcile competing ends, including also the requirements underpinning the available courses of action to meet these ends.[32] Reconciling and prioritising may lead the actor to choose a different course of action and to even amend their original goal. Practical deliberation thus requires the actor to

[29] V Descombes, *Le Raisonnement de l'ours: Et autres essais de philosophie pratique* (Seuil 2007) 21.

[30] DA Schön, *The Reflective Practitioner: How Professionals Think in Action* (Basic Books 1983) 39.

[31] ibid 41.

[32] Descombes (n 29) 23–24.

simultaneously determine *how* to do what seems like a good idea of doing as well as *whether* it really is a good idea to do it in the first place.[33]

Second, because ends in practical contexts are not beyond challenge or amendment, rationality in practical reasoning is not based only on logical entailment (as in theoretical reasoning) but also on plausibility. This means that although the outcome of a properly conducted theoretical inference will be the same for everyone, this is not a guarantee in a practical inference.[34] Two actors may both reason correctly from a logical point of view but still arrive at different courses of action, since there may be multiple suitable ways to achieve the same intended goal. Accordingly, rationality in a practical inference is a function of the degree to which a desirable end x is achieved by a course of action y, subject to any competing or countervailing reasons for not doing y given the possible existence of an additional, also desirable, end z. By enlarging the scope of the debate in this manner, the rationality of a practical inference may be affirmed or challenged.[35]

Third, because of the above characteristics, practical inferences can be challenged in three ways: first, *substantively*, when the premises used are not accurate; second, *formally*, when the inference itself violates the rules of logical consequence or entailment; or third, *defeasibly*, through the introduction of additional contexts to the enquiry that do not necessarily make existing premises inaccurate yet, on balance, render them inappropriate and replaceable by better premises.[36]

[33] ibid 26; Schön (n 30) 39–40 expresses the same idea by pointing out that the principal preoccupation in theoretical contexts (which Schön calls the 'model of technical rationality') is problem-solving, whereas the principal preoccupation in practical contexts is both problem-solving and problem-setting.

[34] Descombes (n 29) 23.

[35] ibid 27. Consider a simple example. My desire to keep myself cool during a warm day makes my decision to turn on the air-conditioning logical and rational. However, upon reflection I may decide that my desire to keep cool will have to be reconciled with my equally strong desire to maintain a low carbon footprint in my daily activities. I may even decide that maintaining a low carbon footprint must take priority because of climate change. In this case, turning on the air-conditioning is incompatible with my amended goal, thus making it a less desirable course of action than simply opening the window and letting a cool breeze into the room. I may therefore conclude that what I *ought* to do in this case – what I am compelled to do, given my amended objectives – is to open the window.

[36] For an argument in favour of reason-based logic as a framework for practical reasoning in international law, see Chapter 2.

3.2 Legal Reasoning as Practical Reasoning

Traditional depictions of legal reasoning in international legal academia have closely tracked the theoretical model of reasoning just described.[37] Legal reasoning is thus often depicted as a chain of logical deduction consisting of a syllogism of the form 'if *p* then *q*', where *p* stands for a proposition of law and *q* stands for the consequence that follows from it.[38] The reasoner's role is to input the set of facts that match the applicable proposition of law in order to get the legally prescribed solution. The more difficult the case, the more complex the chain of reasoning. Although this picture of legal reasoning can be challenged for being outdated and overly formalistic, it remains the prevailing narrative when it comes to CIL. That is, in relation to CIL, the above picture is often reversed by saying that the reasoner's task is to identify the rule of CIL that is hidden in the raw facts of state practice in a process of logical induction.[39] Thus, the fundamentally syllogistic 'if *p* then *q*' format of reasoning is retained.

However, although often presented outwardly as a chain of demonstrable theoretical reasoning, legal reasoning better fits the format of practical reasoning.[40] Indeed, legal reasoning exhibits the three main characteristics of practical reasoning identified previously.

In the first place, legal reasoning intends to lead to action and not simply to the formation of a belief about the way things are in the current

[37] eg G Abi-Saab, 'Cours général de droit international public' (1987) 207 RdC 9, 214.

[38] cf N MacCormick, *Legal Reasoning and Legal Theory* (Oxford University Press 1978) 23.

[39] eg Merkouris (n 1) 134–37; Y Dinstein, 'The Interaction between Customary International Law and Treaties' (2006) 322 RdC 243, 265; AE Roberts, 'Traditional and Modern Approaches to Customary International Law: A Reconciliation' (2001) 95 AJIL 757, 758; MH Mendelson, 'The Formation of Customary International Law' (1998) 272 RdC 155, 181; Abi-Saab (n 37) 176–77 (distinguishing the inductive process of 'traditional custom' from the deductive process of 'new custom'); C de Visscher, *Problèmes d'interprétation judiciaire en droit international public* (Pedone 1963) 16; also ILC, 'Draft Conclusions on Identification of Customary International Law, with Commentaries' (30 April–1 June and 2 July–10 August 2018) UN Doc A/73/10, 126 para 5; *Delimitation of the Maritime Boundary in the Gulf of Maine Area (Canada/USA)* (Judgment) [1984] ICJ Rep 246 [111].

[40] In fact, the outward depiction of legal reasoning as a syllogism of a logical deduction or induction is likely the performative aspect of the whole process, insofar as one has already worked out the way to a conclusion and is now putting things in form to demonstrate the validity and accuracy of the conclusion to others. By the same token, the syllogistic format may also be an exercise in authority – for instance, by a court that wishes to project the image that the law actually demands, and indeed, has always demanded, the outcome this court has pronounced.

state of the law. States typically invoke law and make arguments about the law to justify taking a course of action in the future, to justify having taken a course of action in the past, and to block other states' justifications for following one course of action rather than another. Similarly, when seised of a case, international adjudicators do not simply declare the law in the abstract; they commit themselves to a course of action by handing down a decision in favour of a disputing party, which is tailored to the particular circumstances of the case presented before them.

In the second place, legal reasoning is a purposive activity. And yet, as the ILC has also affirmed, the law's ends are not always clearly defined, indisputably certain, or entirely uniform.[41] Take international investment law. The preambles of international investment agreements indicate that states enter into them for a variety of reasons, including, for instance, to protect their investors abroad, to stimulate investment flows in their territory, or to contribute to their economic development. The choice to give foreign investors access to investor-state dispute settlement has also been justified on multiple grounds, including as an additional incentive to invest in another country[42] or as a way to depoliticise investment disputes by removing them from the domain of diplomatic protection.[43]

The same considerations apply, arguably with greater force, in the case of CIL. As Gorobets points out, customary norms are community norms.[44] Therefore, even when it is a small group of states or, indeed, a single state that originally sparked the creation of a CIL norm (one can

[41] ILC, 'Fragmentation of International Law' (n 4) 23 para 34 ('[Legal reasoning] cannot be understood as reaffirming something that already "exists" before the systemic effort itself. There is no single legislative will behind international law. Treaties and custom come about as a result of conflicting motives and objectives – they are "bargains" and "package-deals" and often result from spontaneous reactions to events in the environment. But if legal reasoning is understood as a *purposive* activity, then it follows that it should be seen not merely as a mechanic application of apparently random rules, decisions or behavioural patterns but as the operation of a whole that is directed toward some human objective. Again, lawyers may disagree about what the objective of a rule or a behaviour is. But it does not follow that no such objective at all can be envisaged. Much legal interpretation is geared to linking an unclear rule to a purpose and thus, by showing its position within some system, to providing a justification for applying it in one way rather than in another.' (emphasis in original)).

[42] A Broches, 'The Convention on the Settlement of Investment Disputes between States and Nationals of Other States' (1972) 136 RdC 331, 348.

[43] *Corn Products International, Inc v United Mexican States* (Award) ICSID Case No ARB (AF)/04/1 (18 August 2009) Separate Opinion of Andreas F Lowenfeld [1].

[44] K Gorobets, 'Practical Reasoning and Interpretation of Customary International Law' in P Merkouris, J Kammerhofer, and N Arajärvi (eds), *The Theory, Practice and*

think of the 1945 Truman proclamation on the continental shelf here), these states may not be regarded as the norm's authors in exactly the same way as the contracting parties to a treaty are that treaty's authors.[45] The juridical goals of the original 'creators' of a CIL norm are not immune from re-appraisal and re-interpretation by all subsequent actors who may seek to invoke and apply that norm in practice.

The conclusion would not be different even if one were to focus on purely doctrinal goals associated with the law – such as ensuring legal certainty, justice, or the rule of law – and sought to determine how these should be promoted through legal reasoning. We would still need to perform an act of interpretation of these abstract goals case by case, in light of the institutional role of the international actor who advances the legal argument in each instance. In short, interpretability of ends appears to be a ubiquitous feature of legal reasoning.

In the third place, legal reasoning is defeasible. Some legal questions can be genuinely difficult to answer. People who are competent and well informed about the law can still reasonably disagree about its content, despite starting from similar premises and advancing formally valid syllogisms. When lawyers disagree, they do so not only by challenging the accuracy of each other's chosen premises or the logical consequence of their syllogism, but also by pointing out missing premises or missing contexts in a competing argument, which may render that argument less plausible or convincing.[46]

3.3 *A Dual Role for Coherence*

To recap, legal reasoning is practical in the sense that it seeks to motivate a situated actor, who has certain goals, into committing to a particular

Interpretation of Customary International Law (Cambridge University Press 2022) 374–75.

45 ibid.

46 eg Z Douglas, 'Other Specific Regimes of Responsibility: Investment Treaty Arbitration and ICSID' in J Crawford, A Pellet and S Olleson (eds), *The Law of International Responsibility* (Oxford University Press 2010) 824. Therein Douglas criticises the decision in *Hussein Nuaman Soufraki v The United Arab Emirates* (Award) ICSID Case No ARB/02/7 (7 July 2004), not by challenging the accuracy of any of the tribunal's chosen premises or the logical consequence of its syllogism, but by pointing out two things: first, that the tribunal's decision in fact implies that the nationality requirements of the ICSID Convention track the doctrine of nationality of claims under diplomatic protection (implied, missing premise in the decision); and second, that this disregards the intentions of the ICSID Convention drafters, who did not see an equivalency between the Convention and diplomatic protection (introducing as countervailing reason the relevance of the parties' intentions in the course of treaty interpretation).

course of action. In practical reasoning, an interactive and iterative relationship exists between the actor's goals, the course of action chosen, and the mental steps taken in between – all these are, moreover, open to deliberation and modification in the course of reasoning. Thus understood, legal reasoning exhibits important coherence-related features. Because it is practical, legal reasoning spans out in a web of clustering reasons for action, rather than extending linearly as a chain. Moreover, by having interpretable goals, legal reasoning relies on axiological compatibility between these goals, the reasons that justify pursuing them, and the appropriateness of the steps taken to achieve them in practice. In other words, like practical reasoning, legal reasoning is meant to lead one to a conclusion about what ought to be done (or not done) given one's evaluation of a problematic situation to be resolved or a goal to be achieved. The strength of a legal argument thus comes principally from the force of the connection – the degree of mutual supportiveness – between these various clusters of reasons.[47] The latter, in turn, is a function not only of the desirability of the reasons used but also of the way in which these reasons have been structured and made to interact in pursuit of the chosen goal.

What role, then, does coherence play in legal reasoning? I believe it plays a dual role, which is at once substantive and methodological. On the one hand, when faced with a legal problem, one must frame the legal question at issue; identify the normative context, including the governing values, principles, and other norms of conduct, that will guide the decision-making process; and, in so doing, also reflect on one's institutional role and aims (including on their limits) in the legal system. Coherence here implies an overall congruence with the body of knowledge and value prevalent in the legal system in question,[48] and thus operates in a clearly normative way as a substantive principle. It assists in formulating, even if in the abstract, the end, purpose, or state of affairs to be achieved and the reasons supporting it in principle.

On the other hand, having come up with the end, purpose, or state of affairs to be achieved, one must then proceed by following an iterative process whereby one identifies concrete courses of action to fit the chosen end, purpose, or state of affairs; considers the impact on the identified actions of any countervailing ends, purposes, or states of affairs; in the

[47] Pérez Bermejo (n 11) 97–98; Soriano (n 11) 311ff.

[48] A Aarnio, *The Rational as Reasonable: A Treatise on Legal Justification* (D Reidel Publishing 1987) 189–90.

process potentially reassesses the desirability of the end, purpose, or state of affairs originally chosen; and, if so, reformulates amended courses of action, as appropriate, to fit the reassessed end, purpose, or state of affairs to be achieved. The idea of coherence here takes on a methodological hue. It describes a reflexive process of internal deliberation and a manner of structuring all relevant elements into a justifying narrative that seems at least plausible, if not compelling, to the community at large.

Singled out from the above are three mental processes associated with coherence in law as potential indicators: (1) acts of framing, (2) acts of contextualising, and (3) acts of iteration/reflexivity. Section 4 offers some preliminary thoughts on how these three processes may fit within the interpretation of CIL.

4 Indicators of (In-)Coherence and the Interpretation of CIL

There exists a link between coherence's dual role in legal reasoning and the interpretation of CIL. In particular, the three interpretative processes of framing, contextualising, and reflecting can act as indicators of the coherence or incoherence of one's proposed interpretation of a CIL norm. The word 'indicators' is key, however, as it points to something less than a determinative test. Indeed, it is argued here that acts of framing, contextualising, and reflecting are themselves interpretative in nature and their successful deployment can therefore be the subject of debate and reasonable disagreement. Moreover, my listing of the three processes in the above manner does not mean to indicate a strict separation between them or their strictly sequential application in practice. Rather, I see these processes as three interdependent facets of the same interpretative operation.

An additional clarification must also be offered before proceeding. Perhaps unsurprisingly, the very term 'interpretation' can itself be subject to interpretation and to different understandings in different fields. In a broad sense, any act of apprehension of meaning and any 'reading' of a situation, no matter how commonplace, intuitive, or unmediated, can be said to involve interpretation.[49] This is not the common understanding of interpretation in international law. Interpretation in the latter is

[49] MacCormick (n 27) 19–20. More generally, see A Bianchi, 'Textual Interpretation and (International) Law Reading: The Myth of (In)determinacy and the Genealogy of Meaning' in PHF Bekker, R Dolzer, and M Waibel (eds), *Making Transnational Law Work in the Global Economy: Essays in Honour of Detlev Vagts* (Cambridge University Press 2010) 34.

often understood in a narrower sense predicated on the existence of doubt about the meaning or the proper application of a pre-existing rule.[50] In this narrower sense, CIL interpretation can be seen as taking place only after a CIL rule has been identified;[51] whereas the broader sense would see interpretation as permeating the entire lifecycle of CIL, from its formation and identification to the apprehension of its meaning now and in the future. The latter approach thus leaves open the interesting, but still somewhat controversial, possibility of state practice being a subject of interpretation also.[52]

In what follows, I have in mind the broader sense of interpretation just identified. I understand interpretation as elucidating the content of legal norms, but also as a reasoned 'reading' of a situation populating it with meaning. I recognise that my use of the term has implications about the way one understands the concept of law itself. However, I will not offer any arguments on that here, nor, more generally, on the plausibility of shifting to an interpretative conception of international law.[53]

4.1 Framing

Practice is the foundation of CIL's existence and content: it is practice that becomes law if it is accepted as such by states.[54] Yet, identifying the elements of practice to figure into one's ascertainment or interpretation of a CIL norm does not proceed on a blank slate. Rather, it presupposes a prior framing of a legal question in need of an answer, or of a problematic situation in need of resolution, forming the contours of a 'project' that the interpreter intends to complete as their legal goal.[55] The 'project', appropriately framed, helps to kick-start and guide the enquiry methodologically as well as substantively.[56] Thus understood, acts of framing are interpretative in at least three ways.

[50] eg RK Gardiner, *International Law* (Pearson Longman 2003) 79; MacCormick (n 27) 19–20.

[51] eg Merkouris (n 1) 135–36; Orakhelashvili (n 1) 496–97.

[52] eg Gorobets (n 44) 375; Chasapis Tassinis (n 1) 241–47.

[53] However, for an argument moving in that direction, see C Giannakopoulos, *Manifestations of Coherence and Investor-State Arbitration* (Cambridge University Press 2022) chs 2–3.

[54] ILC, 'Draft Conclusions' (n 39) Draft Conclusion 2.

[55] For a more detailed exploration of this thesis, see also Chapter 1.

[56] Also R Kolb, 'Selected Problems in the Theory of Customary International Law' (2003) 50 NILR 119, 130 ('[T]here is no induction without a prior element of axiomatic or deductive

In the first place, framing helps to formulate legally acceptable goals to be achieved through the ascertainment of the content of a CIL norm. As Hakimi points out, international actors do not approach CIL as detached observers, but rather as 'advocates advancing their own preferences'.[57] An understanding of the interpreter's institutional role is therefore important. Different international actors have different institutional roles, affecting the kind of questions that can be asked, the legal problems that need resolving, or the arguments that can be made. For instance, states enjoy greater freedom in devising policy goals to be pursued through legal means. States can thus generate arguments about possible new CIL norms, or about new meanings to be assigned to existing CIL norms, simply by acting and by justifying such action against existing practice or against their reasoned views about the action's appropriateness or desirability in the legal system.[58] By contrast, the institutional role of international adjudicators is more constrained. When determining the content of a CIL norm, adjudicators can proceed acceptably only by attempting to reconstruct the intentions of those states that have engaged in relevant practice and substantive argumentation in relation to a putative CIL norm.[59]

In the second place, framing helps to impose order and priority in the virtual infiniteness of state practice. One cannot hope to isolate those elements of state practice that would be relevant for examination, or to assess their legal relevance, unless one has already framed with some degree of specificity a legal problem to resolve or a legal goal to achieve. If, for instance, one wishes to advocate for a new, less strict content of the CIL minimum standard of treatment of aliens in the context of foreign investment protection, one should look for evidence of such content, among others, in the development of investment treaty provisions over

reasoning. It is impossible to induce anything if the framework within which the induction shall take place is not defined.').

[57] M Hakimi, 'Making Sense of Customary International Law' (2020) 118 Mich L Rev 1487, 1507. Stated more provocatively, Kolb (n 56) 133 ('[C]ustom is not an objective reality emerging from a bundled set of facts, but a subjective projection of beliefs grounded in values to the extent these are not contradicted by practice.').

[58] eg 'Proclamation 2667: Policy of the United States with Respect to the National Resources of the Subsoil and Sea Bed of the Continental Shelf' (28 September 1945) 10 Fed Reg 12305, recitals 1 (policy rationale), 3 (policy rationale), and 4 (normative basis).

[59] Staying with the continental shelf example, see *North Sea Continental Shelf Cases (Germany/Netherlands; Germany/Denmark)* (Judgment) [1969] ICJ Rep 3 [63] (recognising the CIL status of the continental shelf, among other reasons, because Articles 1–3 of the 1958 Convention on the Continental Shelf were at that time regarded by states as reflecting at least emerging rules of CIL).

time, interventions made by states before international forums such as UNCITRAL or UNCTAD, positions taken by states in arbitration or in non-disputing state party submissions made in the context of investment disputes, relevant diplomatic exchanges, or even judgments by domestic courts addressing grievances of foreign investors.[60]

At the same time, the weight, authority, or priority of different sources of evidence of practice are all relative, meaning that some materials of practice may only be relevant prima facie and that an assessment must be made case by case.[61] Thus, in the third place, framing the legal issue appropriately also helps the interpreter to determine the kind of practice they should establish or look for.[62] For example, in *Nicaragua* v. *Honduras*, the ICJ considered in obiter that in certain circumstances the application of the CIL principle of *uti possidetis* could be extended to the delimitation of maritime boundaries (as opposed to being confined to the determination of territorial boundaries), in particular when this is in connection with historic bays and territorial seas.[63] No new evidence of state practice or *opinio juris* was offered for this statement, yet arguably none was needed given the framing of the issue. That is, extending the application of *uti possidetis* from the determination of territorial boundaries to the delimitation of some maritime boundaries may be said to have been a continuation, by analogy, of the ICJ's prior conclusion, in *Frontier Dispute*, that *uti possidetis* is a 'principle of a general kind which is logically connected with ... decolonization wherever it occurs'.[64] Put differently, from the point of view of the juridical aim of securing respect for existing boundaries at the moment of independence,[65] determining a maritime boundary between two newly independent states following decolonisation is not unlike determining a territorial boundary between them.[66]

60 On the various forms of admissible practice, see ILC, 'Draft Conclusions' (n 39) Draft Conclusion 6.

61 ibid Draft Conclusions 11–14.

62 On the importance of framing in this respect, see also KA Johnston, 'The Nature and Context of Rules and the Identification of Customary International Law' (2021) 32 EJIL 1167, 1172–74.

63 *Territorial and Maritime Dispute between Nicaragua and Honduras in the Caribbean Sea (Nicaragua v Honduras)* (Judgment) [2007] ICJ Rep 659 [232]–[234].

64 *Frontier Dispute (Burkina Faso/Republic of Mali)* (Judgment) [1986] ICJ Rep 554 [23].

65 ibid.

66 More generally on the prevalence of analogical reasoning in the determination of CIL, see Kolb (n 56) 131; but for a view against, see Orakhelashvili (n 1) 496. On the various interpretative techniques used in determining CIL, see generally Orakhelashvili (n 1) 497ff; P Merkouris, 'Interpreting Customary International Law: You'll Never Walk

In short, framing kick-starts the interpretative enterprise by singling out what is, prima facie, legally relevant in determining the content of a CIL norm. In doing so, one necessarily 'bakes in' certain assumptions, notably about the existing state of the law, about acceptable ends to be pursued, and about one's institutional role and capacities in the international legal system.[67] Framing thus goes hand in hand with an often-implied process of normative contextualisation.

4.2 *Contextualising*

Implied in framing is contextualising. The latter involves seeing one's object of enquiry against an accepted system of background knowledge so as to infer normative content out of it. In the case of CIL, contextualisation takes place when seeking to determine the existence of a CIL norm by carving out an area of relevant practice, and also when seeking to determine the meaning or scope of an already established CIL norm by re-assessing practice that has already been identified in the past. In that sense, like framing, contextualisation in CIL interpretation is indispensable, since mere regularity of conduct cannot lead to a normative conclusion on its own and in the absence of some background context.[68] That is, a collection or a pattern of state conduct cannot by itself be transformed into a reason to act in any particular way absent a rule, goal, or principle acting as the normative context that creates the necessary connections between the observable instances of conduct.[69]

Contextualising practice is an interpretative act, in that it can in principle take place at various levels of abstraction. A pattern of conduct

Alone' in P Merkouris, J Kammerhofer, and N Arajärvi (eds), *The Theory, Practice, and Interpretation of Customary International Law* (Cambridge University Press 2022); as well as Chapter 5.

67 Echoing Westerman (Chapter 1), one might then indeed say that *opinio juris* counts double in the determination of CIL. For a similar view, see Johnston (n 62) 1181–83.

68 GJ Postema, 'Custom in International Law: A Normative Practice Account' in A Perreau-Saussine and JB Murphy (eds), *The Nature of Customary Law: Legal, Historical and Philosophical Perspectives* (Cambridge University Press 2007) 285 ('Thus, mere regularities of behaviour taken alone – the *usus* or "state practice" of international law discourse – not only fail to constitute customs of international *law*, they fail to constitute customs of *any sort*, including those of "comity", because they fail to constitute *norms*.' (emphasis in original)). Generally, on the context-dependent nature of meaning-making, see JR Searle, 'The Background of Meaning' in JR Searle, F Kiefer, and M Bierwisch (eds), *Speech Act Theory and Pragmatics* (D Reidel Publishing 1980).

69 JC Hage, *Reasoning with Rules: An Essay on Legal Reasoning and Its Underlying Logic* (Springer 1997) 75–77; also Kolb (n 56) 130.

may be identified as relevant state practice when seen against broad areas of international law that already include a network of rules, goals, or principles (e.g. use of force, treatment of aliens abroad) as well as against specific international legal rules or doctrines (e.g. *uti possidetis*, minimum standard of treatment of aliens). Fixing the level of abstraction thus becomes a choice of critical normative importance. The chosen level of abstraction determines not only whether one has identified enough evidence of practice to formulate a CIL norm, but also whether the identified evidence is of the right sort or whether altogether different evidence must be looked for instead.

Take the ICC appeals chamber decision in *Al Bashir*, which held that there was no CIL rule of head-of-state immunity before international courts (as opposed to before domestic courts) that is applicable in the horizontal relationship between states in situations where the ICC has issued an arrest warrant against a head of state.[70] Put differently, for the appeals chamber, head-of-state immunity would not apply even if the ICC had requested the surrender of a head of state who hailed from a non-state party to the ICC. The ICC appeals chamber concluded so after pointing to the fact that no evidence of practice or *opinio juris* could be adduced for the existence of a CIL rule of head-of-state immunity in these situations.

For present purposes, one can point out the following vis-à-vis the content-determinative nature of contextualisation. The ICC seems to have initially framed the pertinent legal question adequately (i.e. does head-of-state immunity apply between state parties and non-state parties to an international court when that court has issued an arrest warrant against a head of state?), yet seems to have contextualised its assessment of observable practice narrowly compared to the question (i.e. is there evidence to suggest a rule that states recognise immunity for each other's heads of state when an *international* court has issued an arrest warrant?).[71] Having done so and having observed no such evidence, the

[70] *The Prosecutor v Omar Hassan Ahmad Al Bashir* (Judgment in the Jordan Referral re Al-Bashir Appeal) ICC-02/05-01/09-397-Corr (6 May 2019) [1]–[2], [113]–[117].

[71] Narrowly contextualising practice may be regarded as a symptom of what Hakimi calls the 'rulebook conception' of CIL, which, according to her, dominates CIL orthodoxy. For Hakimi (n 57) 1497, the 'rulebook conception' presupposes that CIL manifests entirely as a body of rules, meaning that 'a proposition can be CIL only if it applies more or less in the same way in all cases of a given type, rather than vacillates without discernible criteria from one situation to the next'.

ICC appeals chamber came to the inescapable conclusion that no rule of CIL exists mandating immunity in these situations.

The outcome could have been markedly different had the contextualisation taken place at a higher level of abstraction, for instance by considering the underpinnings of the doctrine of head-of-state immunity. If one takes the view that the doctrine derives from the principle of sovereign equality, then the fact that the immunity may be raised before an international rather than a domestic court becomes immaterial. Instead, what would be critical is whether the head of state whose immunity is waived is a national of a state party to the international court in question. If they are not, the CIL rule on immunity would still apply, since waiving it would violate the principle of sovereign equality.[72] Moreover, making the latter argument does not require one to search for additional evidence of state practice or *opinio juris*. In fact, it makes the kind of evidence that the appeals chamber was searching for in this instance beside the point.

Crucially, despite the critical interpretative importance of contextualisation, there appear to exist no determining criteria, and no defined metarules, for what the appropriate level of abstraction is in each case a CIL interpreter contextualises practice.[73] The case rather seems to be that the CIL interpreter, much like other practitioners grappling with doubt or ambiguity in law and elsewhere, must make such determinations on the spot, in the act of interpreting, and without the benefit of hindsight.[74] In the absence of guiding metarules, a conscious and active process of reflection may thus be the only kind of safeguard an interpreter of CIL has.

4.3 *Reflexivity*

Thinking reflectively consists in 'turning a subject over in the mind and giving it serious and consecutive consideration', says John Dewey.[75] According to Dewey, reflective thinking can be a useful method to

[72] D Akande, 'International Law Immunities and the International Criminal Court' (2004) 98 AJIL 407, 417; also Chasapis Tassinis (n 1), 265–66.

[73] Kolb (n 56), 131–33; similarly, Hakimi (n 57) 1506–10 (arguing that CIL has no secondary rules – that is to say, rules that determine when the two-element test of state practice and *opinio juris* has been satisfied); and for a critical assessment of the ICJ's CIL methodology in essence along similar lines, S Talmon, 'Determining Customary International Law: The ICJ's Methodology between Induction, Deduction and Assertion' (2015) 26 EJIL 417.

[74] Schön (n 30) 49ff.

[75] J Dewey, *How We Think: A Restatement of the Relation of Reflective Thinking to the Educative Process* (2nd edn, DC Heath 1933) 3.

safeguard one's inferences from falling into obvious errors.[76] Perhaps the best-known contemporary exposition of reflective thinking comes from John Rawls and his concept of reflective equilibrium as a technique of justification.

Roughly put, the idea behind reflective equilibrium is that we must work back and forth in our reasoning between various levels of abstraction, including between our judgements about particular instances or cases, the principles that we believe underpin those judgements, and the theoretical considerations that we believe bear on accepting our judgements and principles, while revising any of these elements whenever necessary in order to achieve an acceptable level of convergence among them.[77] An acceptable level of convergence, according to Rawls, is 'wide' rather than 'narrow'. That is to say, we should not seek only mere consistency among our judgements, but we should also strive to ensure that some of these judgements provide the best justification for the others. Therefore, it is acceptable for prior judgements to be modified or new judgements to be added during this iterative process.[78] The goal is to achieve an 'optimal' equilibrium before stopping the enquiry. We arrive at an optimal equilibrium when the component judgements, principles, and theories of our reasoning are such that we are not inclined to revise any further, because, taken together, they have the highest degree of acceptability or credibility.[79]

The reflective equilibrium technique has strong similarities with the understanding of coherence put forward in this chapter as interdependence, mutual supportiveness, and a web of propositions exhibiting axiological compatibility. Not only is interdependence of judgements a core feature of reflective equilibrium, but also the latter's iterative process precisely seeks to ensure that one's judgements converge by being mutually supportive and able to stand together as a unit, as the concept of coherence indicates. In short, reflexivity and coherence are conceptually linked. Exhibiting reflexivity in one's practice is conducive to coherent reasoning, which, in turn, is conducive to a well-justified outcome, substantively as well as methodologically.

[76] Commenting on the importance of method in particular, ibid 166.

[77] J Rawls, *A Theory of Justice* (revised edn, Harvard University Press 1999) 18.

[78] ibid 42–43; also J Rawls, *Justice as Fairness: A Restatement* (E Kelly ed, Harvard University Press 2001) 29–32.

[79] N Daniels, 'Reflective Equilibrium', *The Stanford Encyclopedia of Philosophy* (Summer edn, 2020) <https://plato.stanford.edu/archives/sum2020/entries/reflective-equilibrium/> accessed 12 June 2024.

A reflexive attitude must thus permeate the entire process of CIL interpretation, permitting and indeed instructing interpreters to critically evaluate and, if need be, amend their interpretative choices and moves before fixing the exact scope of a concrete CIL rule to be applied in the case at hand.[80] No aspect of the process is beyond the possibility of re-assessment and amendment, including, critically, the framing of the legal issue/goal, the chosen level of contextualisation, and the concomitant normative weight assigned to every observable piece of evidence of practice. This makes CIL judgements essentially axiological overall.[81] Every interpretative step taken in ascertaining the content of CIL is to be assessed for its conformity to the identified normative background, its consistency with the implications created by earlier argumentative steps, and its practical consequences (whether desirable or problematic) – all combining to yield an appropriate resting place for the interpretative enquiry.[82]

I must make a caveat here. It is not at this point possible to offer a practical example of reflective thinking in CIL interpretation. Much like argumentation in general, putting forward legal arguments or handing down judicial decisions on the content of CIL are performative acts to some extent. That is to say, when expressed publicly, legal argumentation and judicial decision-making are constructed so as to persuade an audience that the argument or decision in question contains well-chosen premises and that the outcome follows rationally from these premises.[83] There is an inherent difficulty in examining reflective thinking taking place live in practice from that point of view, since any prior act of active reflection during the argument-forming or decision-making process would presently be obscured to the audience.[84] The audience may then only make reasonable retrospective inferences about the reflective thinking *likely* at play behind the finalised version of the argument or decision presented to them.

[80] cf Schön (n 30) 163–64.

[81] Hakimi (n 57) 1507–08 (citing to the ICRC's study on rules of customary international humanitarian law); and, more generally, Kolb (n 56) 130–31 (noting the level of 'axiology and subjectivity' entering into the CIL process).

[82] cf Schön (n 30) 93–102.

[83] E Jouannet, 'La Motivation ou le mystère de la boite noire' in H Ruiz Fabri and JM Sorel (eds), *La Motivation des décisions des juridictions internationales* (Pedone 2008) 267; and from a broader epistemological perspective, Dewey (n 75) 128–29.

[84] The research methodology required to identify active reflection in the course of one's practice goes beyond the scope and aims of the present chapter.

Nevertheless, this does not take away from the importance of reflexivity as good practice of an interpreter's moral responsibility, particularly in light of international law's arguable character and legal reasoning's practical nature.

5 Conclusion

This chapter has argued that it is both necessary and possible to strive towards coherence in the interpretation of CIL, once coherence is properly understood as an independent concept having both a substantive and a methodological dimension. This dual dimension of coherence is critical to law and legal reasoning. It means that coherence in law is more than a mere goal or a vague, results-oriented ideal. It is also a method of constructing one's reasoning and of deliberating about one's interpretative choices. The dual dimension is especially important when reasoning in practical settings (and legal reasoning is one such example), where one commits to action and where interpretability of ends is a core aspect of the process. The chapter has concluded by arguing that striving for coherence in the interpretation of CIL means being cognisant of three kinds of processes – namely, framing, contextualising, and iteration/reflexivity. These can serve as indicators of the coherence or incoherence of proposed CIL interpretations. However, the three processes are themselves interpretative in nature and therefore may be the subject of debate and reasonable disagreement.

To be sure, thinking about coherence, legal reasoning, and interpretation in the manner argued here raises fundamental questions about the nature of international law and the prevailing doctrine of sources. These are important and heavily implicated issues in the present analysis, which, however, I have not begun to address in this chapter. What can be said for the moment is that, if persuasive, the present analysis gives us at least an impetus to re-examine key tenets of legal positivism in international law and to re-assess the degree to which they comport with how international actors seem to reason and argue about international law in practice.

BIBLIOGRAPHY

Books, Theses and Chapters in Edited Volumes

Aarnio A, *The Rational as Reasonable: A Treatise on Legal Justification* (D Reidel Publishing 1987)

Alexy R, *A Theory of Legal Argumentation* (R Adler and N MacCormick trs, Oxford University Press 2011)

Allard J and Van den Eynde L, 'Le dialogue des jurisprudences comme source du droit: Arguments entre idéalisation et scepticisme' in I Hachez (ed), *Les sources du droit revisitées*, vol 3: *Normativités concurrentes* (Anthemis 2013) 285

Alter KJ, 'The Multiplication of International Courts and Tribunals after the End of the Cold War' in CPR Romano, KJ Alter and Y Shany (eds), *The Oxford Handbook of International Adjudication* (Oxford University Press 2014) 63

Alter KJ, Helfer LR and Madsen MR (eds), *International Court Authority* (Oxford University Press 2018)

Amaya A, *The Tapestry of Reason: An Inquiry into the Nature of Coherence and Its Role in Legal Argument* (Hart 2015)

Ammann O, 'The Court of Justice of the European Union and the Interpretation of International Legal Norms: To Be or Not to Be a "Domestic" Court?' in S Besson and N Levrat (eds), *L'Union européenne et le droit international – The European Union and International Law* (Schulthess 2015) 153

Ammann O, *Domestic Courts and the Interpretation of International Law: Methods and Reasoning Based on the Swiss Example* (Brill 2020)

Andenas M, Fitzmaurice M, Tanzi A and Wouters J (eds), *General Principles and the Coherence of International Law* (Brill 2019)

Anzilotti D, *Corso di diritto internazionale* (3rd edn, Athenaeum 1928)

Arajärvi N, *The Changing Nature of Customary International Law: Methods of Interpreting the Concept of Custom in International Criminal Tribunals* (Routledge 2014)

Arend AC, 'Toward Understanding of International Legal Rules' in RJ Beck, AC Arend and RD Vander Lugt, *International Rules: Approaches from International Law and International Relations* (Oxford University Press 1996) 289

Ayoub L, *Judicial Activism and Restraint in the Creation of the International Judicial Function: How Have Activism and Restraint Shaped the International Courts?* (Ridderprint 2021)

Bailey K, *Social Entropy* (State University of New York Press 1990)

Barnes FMM, 'International Investment Law and State-Owned Entities: Recurrent Key Issues and Future Directions' in LE Sachs, L Johnson and J Coleman (eds), *Yearbook on International Investment Law & Policy 2018* (Oxford University Press 2019) 432

Bartels L and Paddeu F (eds), *Exceptions in International Law* (Cambridge University Press 2020)

Bentivoglio LM, *Interpretazione del diritto e diritto internazionale* (Pavia University Press 1953)

Benvenisti E, 'Customary International Law as a Judicial Tool for Promoting Efficiency' in E Benvenisti and M Hirsch (eds), *The Impact of International Law on International Cooperation: Theoretical Perspectives* (Cambridge University Press 2004) 85

Besson S, 'Legal Philosophical Issues of International Adjudication: Getting Over the *amour impossible* between International Law and Adjudication' in CPR Romano, KJ Alter and Y Shany (eds), *The Oxford Handbook of International Adjudication* (Oxford University Press 2013) 413

Besson S and Gächter-Alge ML, 'L'interprétation en droit européen: Quelques remarques introductives' in S Besson, N Levrat and E Clerc (eds), *Interprétation en droit européen – Interpretation in European Law* (Schulthess 2011) 153

Bianchi A, 'Textual Interpretation and (International) Law Reading: The Myth of (In)determinacy and the Genealogy of Meaning' in PHF Bekker, R Dolzer and M Waibel (eds), *Making Transnational Law Work in the Global Economy: Essays in Honour of Detlev Vagts* (Cambridge University Press 2010) 34

Bianchi A, Peat D and Windsor M (eds), *Interpretation in International Law* (Oxford University Press 2015)

Boas G, *Public International Law: Contemporary Principles and Perspectives* (Edward Elgar 2012)

Bodansky D, 'Prologue to a Theory of Non-Treaty Norms' in MH Arsanjani, J Cogan, R Sloane and S Wiessner (eds), *Looking to the Future: Essays on International Law in Honor of W. Michael Reisman* (Brill 2010) 119

Boon M and Knuuttila T, 'Models as Epistemic Tools in Engineering Sciences' in AWM Meijers (ed), *Philosophy of Technology and Engineering Sciences* (Elsevier 2009) 695

Borelli S, 'The (Mis-)Use of General Principles of Law: *Lex Specialis* and the Relationship between International Human Rights Law and the Laws of Armed Conflict' in L Pineschi (ed), *General Principles of Law: The Role of the Judiciary* (Springer 2015) 265

Bos M, *A Methodology of International Law* (Asser Institute 1984)

Bradley CA, 'Customary International Law Adjudication as Common Law Adjudication' in CA Bradley (ed), *Custom's Future: International Law in a Changing World* (Cambridge University Press 2016) 34

Brandom R, *Making It Explicit: Reasoning, Representing, and Discursive Commitment* (Harvard University Press 1994)

Brink DO, 'Originalism and Constructive Interpretation' in W Waluchow and S Sciaraffa (eds), *The Legacy of Ronald Dworkin* (Oxford University Press 2016) 273

Broude T and Shany Y (eds), *Multi-Sourced Equivalent Norms in International Law* (Hart 2011)

Brown C, 'Inherent Powers in International Adjudication' in CPR Romano, KJ Alter and Y Shany (eds), *The Oxford Handbook of International Adjudication* (Oxford University Press 2013) 828

Brunnée J and Toope SJ, *Legitimacy and Legality in International Law: An Interactional Account* (Cambridge University Press 2010)

Burchard C, 'Judicial Dialogue in Light of Comparative Criminal Law and Justice' in P Lobba and T Mariniello (eds), *Judicial Dialogue on Human Rights: The Practice of International Criminal Tribunals* (Brill 2015) 56

Cardozo BN, *The Nature of the Judicial Process* (Yale University Press 1939)

Carnap R, *Logical Foundations of Probability* (University of Chicago Press 1950)

Carnap R, *The Continuum of Inductive Methods* (University of Chicago Press 1952)

Cassese A, *International Law* (2nd edn, Oxford University Press 2004)

Cassese A and Weiler JHH (eds), *Change and Stability in International Law-Making* (De Gruyter 1988)

Chayes A and Chayes AH, *The New Sovereignty: Compliance with International Regulatory Agreements* (Harvard University Press 1995)

Cheng B, *General Principles of Law as Applied by International Courts and Tribunals* (Stevens & Sons 1953)

Cheng B, *General Principles of Law as Applied by International Courts and Tribunals* (Cambridge University Press 1994)

Cheng B, *General Principles of Law as Applied by International Courts and Tribunals* (Cambridge University Press 2006)

Choi S and Gulati M, 'Customary International Law: How Do Courts Do It?' in CA Bradley (ed), *Custom's Future: International Law in a Changing World* (Cambridge University Press 2016) 117

Cocan S, *Le dialogue entre juridictions et quasi-juridictions internationales de protection des droits de la personne: L'exemple de la prohibition de la torture et autres peines ou traitements cruels, inhumains ou dégradants* (LGDJ 2020)

Cohen HG, 'International Precedent and the Practice of International Law' in MA Helfand (ed), *Negotiating State and Non-State Law: The Challenge of Global and Local Legal Pluralism* (Cambridge University Press 2015) 185

Cohen HG, 'Theorizing Precedent in International Law' in A Bianchi, D Peat and M Windsor (eds), *Interpretation in International Law* (Oxford University Press 2015) 268

Cohen HG, 'Culture Clash: The Sociology of WTO Precedent' in A Frese and J Schumann (eds), *Precedent as Rules and Practice: New Approaches and Methodologies in Studies of Legal Precedents* (CH Beck/Hart/Nomos 2021) 112

Corten O, *The Law Against War: The Prohibition on the Use of Force in Contemporary International Law* (2nd edn, Hart 2021)

Corten O and others, *A Critical Introduction to International Law* (Éditions de l'Université de Bruxelles 2019)

D'Amato A, *The Concept of Custom in International Law* (Cornell University Press 1971)

D'Aspremont J, 'The Multidimensional Process of Interpretation: Content-determination and Law-ascertainment Distinguished' in A Bianchi, D Peat and M Windsor (eds), *Interpretation in International Law* (Oxford University Press 2015) 111

D'Aspremont J, 'Canonical Cross-Referencing in the Making of the Law of International Responsibility' in S Forlati, M Mbengue and BK McGarry (eds), *The Gabčíkovo-Nagymaros Judgment and Its Contribution to the Development of International Law* (Brill 2020) 22

D'Aspremont J, *The Discourse on Customary International Law* (Oxford University Press 2021)

Dailler P, Forteau M and Pellet A, *Droit international public* (8th edn, LGDJ 2009)

De Beaugrande RA and Dressler WU, *Introduction to Text Linguistics* (Longman 1981)

De Visscher C, *Problèmes d'interprétation judiciaire en droit international public* (Pedone 1963)

De Visscher C, *Théories et réalités en droit international public* (4th edn, Pedone 1970)

Dennett DC, *Consciousness Explained* (Little Brown 1991)

Derrida J, *Specters of Marx: The State of Debt, the Work of Mourning and the New International* (Routledge 1994)

Descombes V, *Le raisonnement de l'ours: Et autres essais de philosophie pratique* (Seuil 2007)

Devitt M, *Realism and Truth* (2nd edn, Princeton University Press 1997)

Dewey J, *How We Think: A Restatement of the Relation of Reflective Thinking to the Educative Process* (2nd edn, DC Heath 1933)

Di Marco R, 'Customary International Law: Identification versus Interpretation' in P Merkouris, J Kammerhofer and N Arajärvi (eds), *The Theory, Practice, and Interpretation of Customary International Law* (Cambridge University Press 2022) 416

Diehl P and Ku C, *The Dynamics of International Law* (Cambridge University Press 2010)

Dolzer R and Schreuer C, *Principles of International Investment Law* (Oxford University Press 2012)

Dordeska M, *General Principles of Law Recognized by Civilized Nations (1922-2018): The Evolution of the Third Source of International Law through the Jurisprudence of the Permanent Court of International Justice and the International Court of Justice* (Brill 2020) 54

Douglas Z, 'Other Specific Regimes of Responsibility: Investment Treaty Arbitration and ICSID' in J Crawford, A Pellet and S Olleson (eds), *The Law of International Responsibility* (Oxford University Press 2010) 297

Droubi S and d'Aspremont J (eds), *International Organisations, Non-State Actors, and the Formation of Customary International Law* (Manchester University Press 2020)

Dworkin R, *Law's Empire* (Harvard University Press 1986)

Dworkin R, *Taking Rights Seriously* (Harvard University Press 1977)

Eggett C, 'General Principles as Systemic Elements of International Law' (PhD thesis, Maastricht University 2021)

Ehrlich E, *Fundamental Principles of the Sociology of Law, with an Introduction by Roscoe Pound* (Walter L Moll tr, first published 1936, Routledge 2017)

Farias AM and Lazzarini SG, *Reinventing State Capitalism: Leviathan in Business, Brazil and Beyond* (Harvard University Press 2014)

Fiore P, *International Law Codified and Its Legal Sanction* (Edwin M Borchard tr, Baker Voorhis 1918)

Fitzmaurice M, 'The Practical Working of the Law of Treaties' in M Evans, *International Law* (5th edn, Oxford University Press 2018) 138

Fitzmaurice M and Merkouris P, *Treaties in Motion: The Evolution of Treaties from Formation to Termination* (Cambridge University Press 2020)

Forrester JW, *World Dynamics* (2nd edn, Wright-Allen Press 1973)

Fortuna M, 'Different Strings of the Same Harp: Interpretation of Rules of Customary International Law, Their Identification and Treaty Interpretation' in P Merkouris, J Kammerhofer and N Arajärvi (eds), *The Theory, Practice, and Interpretation of Customary International Law* (Cambridge University Press 2022) 393

Fortuna M, 'Interpretation of Customary International Law in International Courts' (PhD thesis, University of Groningen 2023)

Friedmann W, *The Changing Structure of International Law* (Stevens & Sons 1964)

Frydman B, 'Conclusion: Le dialogue des juges et la perspective idéale d'une justice universelle' in *Le dialogue des juges : Actes du colloque organisé le 28 avril 2006 à l'Université Libre de Bruxelles* (Bruylant 2007)

Gadamer HG, *Wahrheit und Methode* (4th edn, JCB Mohr 1975)

Gadamer HG, *Truth and Method* (2nd revised edn, Continuum 2004)

Gaeta P, 'Inherent Powers of International Courts and Tribunals' in LC Vohrah (ed), *Man's Inhumanity to Man: Essays on International Law in Honour of Antonio Cassese* (Kluwer Law International 2003) 353

Gardiner RK, *International Law* (Pearson Longman 2003)

Giannakopoulos C, *Manifestations of Coherence and Investor–State Arbitration* (Cambridge University Press 2022)

Giddens A and others, *Essentials of Sociology* (WW Norton 2010)

Glock HJ, *A Wittgenstein Dictionary* (Blackwell Reference 1996)

Goldsmith JL and Posner EA, *The Limits of International Law* (Oxford University Press 2005)

Gorobets K, 'Peaks and Valleys: Contemplating the Authority of International Law' in K Gorobets, A Hadjigeorgiou and P Westerman (eds), *Conceptual (Re) Constructions of International Law* (Edward Elgar 2022) 171

Gorobets K, 'Practical Reasoning and Interpretation of Customary International Law' in P Merkouris, J Kammerhofer and N Arajärvi (eds), *The Theory, Practice, and Interpretation of Customary International Law* (Cambridge University Press 2022)

Groppi T and Ponthoreau MC, *The Use of Foreign Precedents by Constitutional Judges* (Hart 2013)

Grossman N, 'Solomonic Judgments and the Legitimacy of the International Court of Justice' in HG Cohen and others (eds), *Legitimacy and International Courts* (Cambridge University Press 2018) 43

Grotius H, *The Rights of War and Peace* (Richard Tuck ed, Liberty Fund 2005)

Gruber M, *Alfred Tarski and the 'Concept of Truth in Formalized Languages'* (Springer 2016)

Guilfoyle D, *International Criminal Law* (Oxford University Press 2016)

Hage JC, *Reasoning with Rules: An Essay on Legal Reasoning and Its Underlying Logic* (Springer 1997)

Hage J, 'Construction or Reconstruction? On the Function of Argumentation in the Law' in C Dahlman and E Feteris (eds), *Legal Argumentation Theory: Cross-Disciplinary Perspectives* (Springer 2012) 125

Hage J, *Foundations and Building Blocks of Law* (Eleven International Publishing 2018)

Hage J, 'Are the Cognitive Sciences Relevant for Law?' in B Brożek, J Hage and N Vincent (eds), *Law and Mind: A Survey of Law and the Cognitive Sciences* (Cambridge University Press 2021) 17

Hage J and Waltermann A, 'Logical Techniques for International Law' in D Krimphove and G Lentner (eds), *Law and Logic: Contemporary Issues* (Duncker und Humblot 2017) 125

Hage J, Waltermann A and Arosemena Solorzano G, 'Exceptions in International Law' in L Bartels and F Paddeu (eds), *Exceptions and Defences in International Law* (Oxford University Press 2018) 11

Hanson, NR *Patterns of Discovery* (Cambridge University Press 1965)

Hanson NR, *Perception and Discovery: An Introduction to Scientific Inquiry* (MD Lund ed, Springer 2018)

Hansson SO, 'The Varieties of Permission' in DM Gabbay and others (eds), *Handbook of Deontic Logic and Normative Systems* (College Publications 2013) 204

Hart HLA, *The Concept of the Law* (1st edn, Clarendon Press 1961)

Hart HLA, 'Positivism and the Separation of Law and Morals', *Essays in Jurisprudence and Philosophy* (Oxford University Press 1983)

Hart HLA, *The Concept of Law* (2nd edn, Clarendon Press 1997)

Hart HLA, *The Concept of Law* (3rd edn, Oxford University Press 2012)

Heidegger M, *Sein und Zeit* (Max Niemeyer 1979)

Heilbronner M and Martini S, 'The German Federal Constitutional Court' in A Jakab, A Dyevre and G Itzcovich (eds), *Comparative Constitutional Reasoning* (Cambridge University Press 2017) 356

Henckaerts JM and Doswald-Beck L (eds), *Customary International Humanitarian Law* (Cambridge University Press 2005)

Hernández GI, 'Interpretative Authority and the International Judiciary' in A Bianchi, D Peat and M Windsor (eds), *Interpretation in International Law* (Oxford University Press 2015) 166

Hernández GI, 'Effectiveness' in J d'Aspremont and S Singh, *Concepts for International Law: Contributions to Disciplinary Thought* (Edward Elgar 2019) 237

Hesse K, *Grundzüge des Verfassungsrechts der Bundesrepublik Deutschland* (20th edn, CF Müller 1999)

Higgins R, *Problems and Processes: International law and How We Use It* (Clarendon Press 1995)

Hollis DB, 'Sources in Interpretation Theories: An Interdependent Relationship' in S Besson and J d'Aspremont, *The Oxford Handbook on the Sources of International Law* (Oxford University Press 2017) 429

Horwich P, *Probability and Evidence* (Cambridge University Press 1982)

Howson C, *Hume's Problem: Induction and the Justification of Belief* (Oxford University Press 2000)

Hume D, *A Treatise of Human Nature* (Floating Press 2009)

Jennings R, 'The Identification of International Law' in B Cheng (ed), *International Law: Teaching and Practice* (Stevens & Sons 1982)

Jeutner V, *Irresolvable Norm Conflicts in International Law: The Concept of a Legal Dilemma* (Oxford University Press 2017)

Jouannet E, 'La motivation ou le mystère de la boite noire' in H Ruiz Fabri and JM Sorel (eds), *La motivation des décisions des juridictions internationales* (Pedone 2008) 267

Jovanovic M, *The Nature of International Law* (Cambridge University Press 2019)

Kammerhofer J, *Uncertainty in International Law: A Kelsenian Perspective* (Taylor & Francis 2010)

Keller H and Sweet AS (eds), *A Europe of Rights: The Impact of the ECtHR on National Legal Systems* (Oxford University Press 2008)

Kelsen H, *General Theory of Law and State* (A Wedberg tr, Harvard University Press 1945)

King G, Keohane R and Verba S, *Designing Social Inquiry: Scientific Inference in Qualitative Research* (Princeton University Press 1994)

Kirby M, *Judicial Activism: Authority, Principle and Policy in Judicial Method* (Sweet & Maxwell 2004)

Klenlein T, 'Customary International Law and General Principles: Rethinking Their Relationship' in B Lepard (ed), *Reexamining Customary International Law* (Cambridge University Press 2016) 133

Klingler J, Parkhomenko Y and Salonidis C (eds), *Between the Lines of the Vienna Convention? Canons and Other Principles of Interpretation in Public International Law* (Kluwer Law International 2019)

Kochenov D and Amtenbrink F (eds), *The European Union's Shaping of the International Legal Order* (Cambridge University Press 2014)

Kolb R, *Interprétation et création du droit international: Esquisse d'une herméneutique juridique moderne pour le droit international public* (Bruylant 2006)

Kolb R, *Good Faith in International Law* (Hart 2017)

Kolb R, 'General Principles of Law, *Jus Cogens* and the Unity of the International Legal Order' in M Andenas and others (eds) *General Principles and the Coherence of International Law* (Brill 2019) 60

Koskenniemi M, *From Apology to Utopia* (Cambridge University Press 2006)

Kotuby C, Jr and Sobota L, *General Principles of Law and International Due Process: Principles and Norms Applicable in Transnational Disputes* (Oxford University Press 2017)

Koutrakos P, *EU International Relations Law* (2nd edn, Hart 2015)

Kramer MH, *Objectivity and the Rule of Law* (Cambridge University Press 2007)

Kratochwil FV, *Rules, Norms, and Decisions: On the Conditions of Practical and Legal Reasoning in International Relations and Domestic Affairs* (Cambridge University Press 1989)

Kress K, 'Coherence' in D Patterson (ed), *A Companion to Philosophy of Law and Legal Theory* (2nd edn, Wiley-Blackwell 2010) 521

Kuhn TS, *The Structure of Scientific Revolutions* (2nd edn, University of Chicago Press 1970)

Kuijper PJ, '"It Shall Contribute to . . . the Strict Observance and Development of International Law": The Role of the Court of Justice' in A Rosas, E Levits and Y Bot (eds), *The Court of Justice and the Construction of Europe: Analyses and*

Perspectives on Sixty Years of Case-Law – La Cour de Justice et la construction de l'Europe: Analyses et perspectives de soixante ans de jurisprudence (TMC Asser Press/Springer 2013) 589

Lauterpacht H, 'Some Observations on the Prohibition of "Non Liquet" and the Completeness of the Law' in *Symbolae Verzijl* (Martinus Nijhoff 1958) 196

Lauterpacht H, *The Development of International Law by the International Court* (Cambridge University Press 1982)

Lauterpacht H, *The Function of Law in the International Community* (Oxford University Press 2011)

Lepard BD, *Customary International Law: A New Theory with Practical Applications* (Cambridge University Press 2010)

Lepard BD (ed), *Reexamining Customary international Law* (Cambridge University Press 2017)

Lerche P, *Übermaß und Verfassungsrecht: Zur Bindung des Gesetzgebers an die Grundsätze der Verhältnismäßigkeit und der Erforderlichkeit* (Heymann 1961)

Levi I, *Hard Choices: Decision Making under Unresolved Conflict* (Cambridge University Press 1986)

Levine DH, 'The Chronological Paradox in Customary International Law (Or, the Virtue of Sloppy Timing in a Messy World)' (PhD thesis, Georgetown University 2005)

Lindquist S, 'Identifying Judicial Activism' in SA Lindquist and FB Cross, *Measuring Judicial Activism* (Oxford University Press 2009)

Llewellyn KN, *The Bramble Bush: The Classic Lectures on the Law and Law School, with a New Introduction and Notes by Steve Sheppard* (Oxford University Press 2008)

Lorenzen P, *Constructive Philosophy* (University of Massachusetts Press 1987)

Lucy W, 'Adjudication' in JL Coleman, KE Himma and SJ Shapiro (eds), *The Oxford Handbook of Jurisprudence and Philosophy of Law* (Oxford University Press 2004) 206

MacCormick N, *Legal Reasoning and Legal Theory* (Oxford University Press 1978)

MacCormick N, *Rhetoric and the Rule of Law* (Oxford University Press 2005)

MacCormick N and Weinberger O (eds), *Institutional Theory of Law: New Approaches to Legal Positivism* (Springer 1986)

Mackenzie R and others, *Selecting International Judges: Principle, Process, and Politics* (Oxford University Press 2010)

Mangabeira Unger R, *Law in Modern Society: Toward a Criticism of Social Theory* (Free Press 1976)

Marcos H, 'A Study on Defeasibility and Defeaters in International Law: Process or Procedure Distinction against the Non-Discrimination Rule' in W Menezes, A Nunes Filho and PH Reis de Oliveira (eds), *Tribunais Internacionais e a Garantia dos Direitos Sociais* (Academia Brasileira de Direito Internacional 2021) 199

Marmor A, *Interpretation and Legal Theory* (2nd edn, Hart 2005)

Merkouris P, *Article 31(3)(c) VCLT and the Principle of Systemic Integration: Normative Shadows in Plato's Cave* (Brill 2015)

Merkouris P, *Interpretation of Customary International Law: Of Methods and Limits* (Brill Research Perspectives in International Legal Theory and Practice, Martinus Nijhoff/Brill 2022)

Merkouris P, 'Interpreting Customary International Law: You'll Never Walk Alone' in P Merkouris, J Kammerhofer and N Arajärvi (eds), *The Theory, Practice, and Interpretation of Customary International Law* (Cambridge University Press 2022) 347

Merkouris P, Kammerhofer J and Arajärvi N (eds), *The Theory, Practice, and Interpretation of Customary International Law* (Cambridge University Press 2022)

Methymaki E and Tzanakopoulos A, 'Freedom with Their Exception: Jurisdiction and Immunity as Rule and Exception' in L Bartels and F Paddeu (eds), *Exceptions in International Law* (Cambridge University Press 2020) 240

Milano E, 'The 2013 Fisheries Protocol between the EU and Morocco: Fishing 'too South' Continues . . .' in M Balboni and G Laschi (eds), *The European Union Approach towards Western Sahara* (Peter Lang 2017) 151

Milano E, 'General Principles *Infra, Praeter, Contra Legem*? The Role of Equity in Determining Reparation' in M Andenas and other (eds), *General Principles and the Coherence of International Law* (Brill/Nijhoff 2019) 65

Müllerson R, 'The Interplay of Objective and Subjective Elements in Customary Law' in K Wellens (ed), *International Law, Theory and Practice* (Kluwer 1998) 161

Neframi E, 'Customary International Law and the European Union from the Perspective of Article 3(5) TEU' in P Eeckhout and M Lopez-Escuerdo (eds), *The European Union's External Action in Times of Crisis* (Hart 2016) 217

Odermatt J, 'The European Union as a Global Actor and Its Impact on the International Legal Order' (PhD thesis, University of Leuven Department of Law 2016)

Odermatt J, *International Law and the European Union* (Cambridge University Press 2021)

Odermatt J, 'The International Court of Justice and the Court of Justice of the European Union: Between Fragmentation and Universality of International Law' in A Skordas (ed), *Research Handbook on the International Court of Justice* (Edward Elgar 2022) 696

Orakhelashvili A, *The Interpretation of Acts and Rules in Public International Law* (Oxford University Press 2008)

Paparinskis M, 'Conclusions: General Principles and the Other Sources of International Law' in M Andenas and others (eds), *General Principles and the Coherence of International Law* (Brill/Nijhoff 2019) 117

Pascual-Vives F, 'The Identification of Customary International Law before the Court of Justice of the European Union: A Flexible Consensualism' in F Lusa Bordin, ATh Müller and F Pascual-Vives (eds), *The European Union and Customary International Law* (Cambridge University Press 2022) 123

Pauwelyn J, *Conflict of Norms in Public International Law: How WTO Law Relates to Other Rules of International Law* (Cambridge University Press 2003)

Pauwelyn J, Wessel RA and Wouters J, 'Informal International Lawmaking: An Assessment and Template to Keep It Both Effective and Accountable' in J Pauwelyn, RA Wessel and J Wouters (eds), *Informal International Lawmaking* (Oxford University Press 2012) 508

Peat D, *Comparative Reasoning in International Courts and Tribunals* (Cambridge University Press 2019)

Peczenik A, *Scientia Juris: Legal Doctrine as Knowledge of Law and as a Source of Law* (Springer 2005)

Pellet A, 'Article 38' in Zimmermann A and others (eds), *The Statute of the International Court of Justice: A Commentary* (2nd edn, Oxford University Press 2012)

Pérez Bermejo JM, 'Coherence: An Outline in Six Metaphors and Four Rules' in M Araszkiewicz and J Šavelka (eds), *Coherence: Insights from Philosophy, Jurisprudence and Artificial Intelligence* (Springer 2013)

Petersmann EU, '"Constitutional Justice" Requires Judicial Cooperation and "Comity" in the Protection of "Rule of Law"' in F Fontanelli, G Martinico and P Carrozza (eds), *Shaping Rule of Law Through Dialogue* (Europa Law 2010)

Phoa P, *EU Law as a Creative Process: A Hermeneutic Approach for the EU Internal Market and Fundamental Rights Protection* (Europa Law 2021)

Plumpton Ramsey F, 'Truth and Probability' in F Plumpton Ramsey and RB Braithwaite (eds), *The Foundations of Mathematics and Other Logical Essays* (Martino Fine Books 1950)

Popper K, *The Logic of Scientific Discovery* (Hutchinson 1972)

Popper K, 'Science: Conjectures and Refutations' in JA Curd and M Cover (eds) *Philosophy of Science: The Central Issues* (Norton 1998)

Porto Macedo Júnior R, *Do Xadrez à Cortesia: Dworkin e a Teoria do Direito Contemporânea* (Saraiva 2013)

Postema GJ, 'Custom in International Law: A Normative Practice Account' in A Perreau-Saussine and JB Murphy (eds), *The Nature of Customary Law: Legal, Historical and Philosophical Perspectives* (Cambridge University Press 2007)

Postema GJ, *Legal Philosophy in the Twentieth Century: The Common Law World* (Springer 2011)

Powderly J, *Judges and the Making of International Criminal Law* (Brill 2020)

Proctor RW and Capaldi EJ, *Psychology of Science: Implicit and Explicit Processes* (Oxford University Press 2012)

Radi Y, 'Coherence' in J d'Aspremont and S Singh (eds), *Concepts for International Law: Contributions to Disciplinary Thought* (Edward Elgar 2019) 105

Rasmussen H, *On Law and Policy in the European Court of Justice: A Comparative Study in Judicial Policymaking* (Martinus Nijhoff 1986)

Rawls J, *A Theory of Justice* (revised edn, Harvard University Press 1999)

Rawls J, *Justice as Fairness: A Restatement* (E Kelly ed, Harvard University Press 2001)

Redgwell C, 'General Principles of International Law' in S Vogenauer and S Weatherill, *General Principles of Law: European and Comparative Perspectives* (Hart 2017)

Ricoeur P, *Hermeneutics and the Human Sciences: Essays on Language, Action, and Interpretation* (JB Thompson ed, Cambridge University Press 2016)

Rioul O, 'This Is IT: A Primer on Shannon's Entropy and Information' in B Duplantier and V Rivasseau (eds), *Information Theory* (Progress in Mathematical Physics vol 78, Springer 2021)

Rosas A, 'The European Court of Justice and Public International Law' in J Wouters, A Nollkaemper and E de Wet (eds), *The Europeanisation of International Law: The Status of International Law in the EU and Its Member States* (TMC Asser Press 2008)

Rosenne S, *The Law and Practice of the International Court, 1920–2005* (Brill 2006)

Rossi P, *International Law Immunities and Employment Claims* (Hart 2021)

Russell B, *Our Knowledge of the External World: As a Field for Scientific Method in Philosophy* (Routledge 2009)

Salacuse JW, *The Law of Investment Treaties* (3rd edn, Oxford University Press 2021)

Sanders Peirce C, *Philosophical Writings of Peirce* (Justus Buchler ed, Dover 1955)

Saunders I *General Principles as a Source of International Law: Article 38(1)(c) of the Statute of the International Court of Justice* (Hart 2021)

Scelle G, *Manuel de droit international public* (Domat Montchréstien 1948)

Schabas WA, *The International Criminal Court: A Commentary on the Rome Statute* (2nd edn, Oxford University Press 2016)

Schabas WA, *The Customary International Law of Human Rights* (Oxford University Press 2021)

Schauer F, *Playing by the Rules: A Philosophical Examination of Rule-Based Decision-Making in Law and in Life* (Oxford University Press 1991)

Schauer F, 'Pitfalls in the Interpretation of Customary Law' in A Perreau-Saussine and JB Murphy (eds), *The Nature of Customary Law: Legal, Historical and Philosophical Perspectives* (Cambridge University Press 2007)

Schlütter B, *Developments in Customary International Law: Theory and the Practice of the International Court of Justice and the International ad hoc Criminal Tribunals for Rwanda and Yugoslavia* (Brill 2010)

Schmalenbach K, 'Article 26' in O Dörr and K Schmalenbach (eds), *Vienna Convention on the Law of Treaties: A Commentary* (2nd edn, Springer 2018)

Schmitt M (ed), *Tallinn Manual 2.0 on the International Law Applicable to Cyber Operations* (2nd edn, Cambridge University Press 2017)

Schön DA, *The Reflective Practitioner: How Professionals Think in Action* (Basic Books 1983)

Schreuer C, 'Diversity and Harmonization of Treaty Interpretation in Investment Arbitration' in M Fitzmaurice, O Elias and P Merkouris (eds), *Treaty Interpretation and the Vienna Convention on the Law of Treaties: 30 Years On* (Martinus Nijhoff 2010)

Schreuer C, 'Coherence and Consistency in International Investment Law' in R Echandi and P Sauvé (eds), *Prospects in International Investment Law and Policy* (Cambridge University Press 2013)

Schreuer C and others, *The ICSID Convention: A Commentary* (Cambridge University Press 2009)

Schreuer C and Weiniger M, 'A Doctrine of Precedent?' in PT Muchlinski, F Ortino and C Schreuer (eds), *The Oxford Handbook of International Investment Law* (Oxford University Press 2008)

Schrijver NJ, 'Fifty Years Permanent Sovereignty over Natural Resources: The 1962 UN Declaration as the *Opinio Iuris Communis*' in M Bungenberg and H Stephan (eds), *Permanent Sovereignty over Natural Resources* (Springer 2015)

Schultz T, 'Against Consistency in Investment Arbitration' in Z Douglas, J Pauwelyn and JE Viñuales (eds), *The Foundations of International Investment Law: Bringing Theory into Practice* (Oxford University Press 2014)

Schwarzenberger G, *The Inductive Approach to International Law* (Stevens & Sons 1965)

Searle J, *Expression and Meaning: Studies in the Theory of Speech Acts* (Cambridge University Press 1979)

Searle J, 'The Background of Meaning' in J Searle, F Kiefer and M Bierwisch (eds), *Speech Act Theory and Pragmatics* (D Reidel Publishing 1980)

Searle J, *The Construction of Social Reality* (Free Press 1995)

Searle J, *Mind, Language, and Society: Philosophy in the Real World* (Basic Books 1999)

Searle J, *Making the Social World: The Structure of Human Civilization* (Oxford University Press 2010).

Sethna J, 'What Is Statistical Mechanics' in *Statistical Mechanics: Entropy, Order Parameters and Complexity* (2nd edn, Oxford University Press 2021)

Shany Y, *Assessing the Effectiveness of International Courts* (Oxford University Press 2014)

Smith B, 'John Searle: From Speech Acts to Social Reality' in B Smith (ed), *John Searle* (Cambridge University Press 2003) 19

Stahn C, *A Critical Introduction to International Criminal Law* (Cambridge University Press 2019)

Staubach PG, *The Rule of Unwritten International Law. Customary Law, General Principles and World Order* (Routledge 2018)

Streck LL, *Hermenêutica Jurídica e(m) Crise: Uma Exploração Hermenêutica da Construção do Direito* (Livraria do Advogado 2018)

Sureda AR, 'Precedent in Investment Treaty Arbitration' in C Binder and others (eds), *International Investment Law for the 21st Century: Essays in Honour of Christoph Schreuer* (Oxford University Press 2009) 830

Tan Y, *The Rome Statute as Evidence of Customary International Law* (Brill Nijhoff 2021)

Tasioulas J, 'Customary International Law and the Quest for Global Justice' in A Perreau-Saussine and JB Murphy (eds), *The Nature of Customary Law* (Cambridge University Press 2007) 307

Terris D, Romano CPR and Swigart L, *The International Judge: An Introduction to the Men and Women Who Decide the World's Cases* (Brandeis University Press 2007)

Thirlway H, *International Customary Law and Codification: An Examination of the Continuing Role of Custom in the Present Period of Codification of International Law* (Brill 1972)

Thirlway H, 'Judicial Activism and the International Court of Justice' in E McWhinney, N Ando and R Wolfrum (eds), *Liber Amicorum Judge Shigeru Oda* (Kluwer Law International 2002) 75

Thirlway H, *The Law and Procedure of the International Court of Justice: Fifty Years of Jurisprudence* (Oxford University Press 2013)

Thirlway H, *The Sources of International Law* (Oxford University Press 2014)

Thomas EW, *The Judicial Process: Realism, Pragmatism, Practical Reasoning and Principles* (Cambridge University Press 2008)

Tomuschat C, 'General International Law: A New Source of International Law?' in R Pisillo Mazzeschi and De Sena P, *Global Justice, Human Rights and the Modernization of International Law* (Springer 2018) 185

Tunkin GI, *Theory of International Law* (Harvard University Press 1974)

Ulfstein G, 'Towards an International Human Rights Judiciary?' in J Ebbesson and others (eds), *International Law and Changing Perceptions of Security: Liber Amicorum Said Mahmoudi* (Brill 2014)

Van den Herik L, 'The Decline of Customary International Law as a Source of International Criminal Law' in C Bradley (ed), *Custom's Future: International Law in a Changing World* (Cambridge University Press 2016) 230

Van Vooren B, Blockmans S and Wouters J (eds), *The EU's Role in Global Governance: The Legal Dimension* (Oxford University Press 2013)

Vandevelde KJ, 'The Liberal Vision of the International Law on Foreign Investment' in CL Lim (ed), *Alternative Visions of the International Law on Foreign Investment: Essays in Honour of Muthucumaraswamy Sornarajah* (Cambridge University Press 2016) 43

Villiger M, *Customary International Law and Treaties: A Manual on the Theory and Practice of the Interrelation of Sources* (2nd edn, Brill 1997)

Villiger M, *Commentary on the 1969 Vienna Convention on the Law of Treaties* (Brill 2009)

Viñuales JE, *The UN Friendly Relations Declaration at 50: An Assessment of the Fundamental Principles of International Law* (Cambridge University Press 2020)

Waltermann A, 'Why Non-Human Agency?' in A Waltermann (eds), *Law, Science, Rationality* (Eleven International 2020) 51

Westerman P, 'Open or Autonomous? The Debate on Legal Methodology as a Reflection of the Debate on Law' in M van Hoecke (ed), *Methodologies of Legal Research: Which Kind of Method for What Kind of Discipline?* (Hart 2011) 87

Westerman P, '*Opinio Juris*: Test, Filter, Ideal or Map?' in K Gorobets, A Hadjigeorgiou and P Westerman (eds), *Conceptual (Re)Constructions of International Law* (Edward Elgar 2022) 127

Wheatley S, *The Idea of International Human Rights Law* (Oxford University Press 2019)

Wittgenstein L, *Philosophical Investigations* (GEM Anscombe tr, 3rd edn, Basil Blackwell 1986)

Wolfke K, *Custom in Present International Law* (2nd revised edn, Martinus Nijhoff 1993)

Wouters J, Ryngaert C, 'The Impact on the Process of the Formation of Customary International Law' in MT Kamminga and M Scheinin (eds), *The Impact of Human Rights Law on General International Law* (Oxford University Press 2009) 111

Yates DS, Moore DS, Starnes DS, *The Practice of Statistics* (3rd edn, WH Freeman 2008)

Articles

Abi-Saab G, 'Cours général de droit international public' (1987) 207 RdC 9

Adam E, 'A Logic of Conditionals' (1965) 8 Inquiry 166

Akande D, 'International Law Immunities and the International Criminal Court' (2004) 98 AJIL 407

Akande D, 'Introduction to the Symposium on Zachary Mollengarden & Noam Zamir "The *Monetary Gold* Principle: Back to Basics"' (2021) 115 AJIL Unbound 140

Akande D and Shah S, 'Immunities of State Officials, International Crimes, and Foreign Domestic Courts' (2010) 21 EJIL 815

Akehurst M, 'Custom as a Source of International Law' (1975) 47 BYBIL 1

Alexy R and Peczenik A, 'The Concept of Coherence and Its Significance for Discursive Rationality' (1990) 3 Ratio Juris 130

Alexy R, 'On the Structure of Legal Principles' (2000) 13 Ratio Juris 294
Alland D, 'L'interprétation du droit international public' (2013) 362 RdC 41
Anscombe GEM, 'On Brute Facts' (1958) 18 Analysis 69
Baker RB, 'Customary International Law: A Reconceptualization' (2016) 41 BJIL 458
Baude W and Sachs SE, 'The Law of Interpretation' (2017) 130 Harv L Rev 1079
Benson PE, 'François Gény's Doctrine on Customary Law' (1983) 20 Can YIL 267
Benvenisti E, 'The Future of International Law Scholarship in Germany: The Tension between Interpretation and Change' (2007) 67 Heidelberg J Intl L 585
Bertea S, 'The Arguments from Coherence: Analysis and Evaluation' (2005) 25 OJLS 369
Bilder RB and others, 'Disentangling Treaty and Customary International Law: Remarks' (1987) 81 ASIL Proc 157
Bleckmann A, 'Zur Feststellung und Auslegung von Völkergewohnheitsrecht' (1977) 37 ZaöRV 505
Blutman L, 'Conceptual Confusion and Methodological Deficiencies: Some Ways That Theories on Customary International Law Fail' (2014) 25 EJIL 529
Bodansky D, 'Customary (And Not So Customary) International Environmental Law' (1995) 3(1) IJGLS 105
Bodansky D, 'Does Custom Have a Source?' (2014) 108 AJIL Unbound 179
Bogdan M, 'General Principles of Law and the Problem of Lacunae in the Law of Nations' (1977) 46 NJIL 37
Bogdandy A von and Smrkolj M, 'European Union Law and International Law' (2011) MPEPIL <https://opil.ouplaw.com/display/10.1093/law:epil/9780199231690/law-9780199231690-e620>
Bos M, 'The Identification of Custom in International Law' (1982) 25 GYIL 9
Broches A, 'The Convention on the Settlement of Investment Disputes between States and Nationals of Other States' (1972) 136 RdC 331
Brown C, 'The Inherent Powers of International Courts and Tribunals' (2006) 76 BYIL 195
Brunnée J and Toope S, 'International Law and the Practice of Legality: Stability and Change' (2018) 49 VUWLR 433
Bufalini A, 'The Principle of Legality and the Role of CIL in the Interpretation of the ICC Statute' (2015) 14 LPICT 233
Burgorgue-Larsen L, '"Decompartmentalization": The Key Technique for Interpreting Regional Human Rights Treaties' (2018) 16 IJCL 187
Cappelletti M, 'The Law-Making Power of the Judge and Its Limits: A Comparative Analysis' (1981) 8 Monash UL Rev 15
Carty A, 'Language Games of International Law' (2012) 13 Melb JIL 1
Cassese A, 'Remarks on Scelle's Theory of "Role Splitting" (*dedoublément fonctionnel*) in International Law' (1990) 1 EJIL 210

Cassese A, 'The *Nicaragua* and *Tadić* Test Revisited in Light of the ICJ Judgment on Genocide in Bosnia' (2007) 4 EJIL 649

Castellano C, Fortunato S and Loretto V, 'Statistical Physics on Social Dynamics' (2009) 81 RMP 591

Cattani M and others, 'Deterministic Chaos Theory: Some Basic Concepts' (2017) 39 (1) Revista Brasileira de Ensino de Fisica e1309-1

Charney JI, 'Universal International Law' (1993) 87 AJIL 529

Chasapis Tassinis O, 'Customary International Law: Interpretation from Beginning to End' (2020) 31 EJIL 235

Christensen D, 'Measuring Confirmation' (1999) 96 J Philos 437

Clark B, 'The Vienna Convention Reservations Regime and the Convention on Discrimination against Women' (1991) 85 AJIL 281

Cohen HG, 'International Law's *Erie* Moment' (2013) 34 MJIL 249

Corsi JL, 'An Argument for Strict Legality in International Criminal Law' (2018) 49 GJIL 1321

Crease RP, 'Comment: The Quantum Moment' (2013) 26(3) Physics World 25

Croquet NAJ, 'The Import of International Customary International Law into the EU Legal Order: The Adequacy of a Direct Effect Analysis' (2013) 15 CYELS 47

Daniels N, 'Reflective Equilibrium', *The Stanford Encyclopedia of Philosophy* (Summer edn, 2020) https://plato.stanford.edu/archives/sum2020/entries/reflective-equilibrium/

D'Amato A, 'A Brief Rejoinder' (1988) 21 VJIL 489

D'Amato A, 'Custom and Treaty: A Response to Professor Weisburd' (1988) 21 VJIL 459

D'Argent P, 'The *Monetary Gold* Principle: A Matter of Submissions' (2021) 115 AJIL Unbound 149

Daugirdas K, 'Reputation and the Responsibility of International Organizations' (2014) 25 EJIL 991

De Brabandere E and Baldini Miranda Da Cruz P, 'The Role of Proportionality in International Investment Law and Arbitration: A System-Specific Perspective' (2020) 89 NJIL 471

De Brabandere E, '(Re)calibration, Standard-Setting and the Shaping of Investment Law and Arbitration' (2018) 59 BCLR 2607

De Wet E, and Vidmar J, 'Conflicts between International Paradigms: Hierarchy versus Systemic Integration' (2013) 2 GlobCon 196

Deeks AS, 'Unwilling or Unable: Toward a Normative Framework for Extraterritorial Self-Defense' (2012) 52 VJIL 483

Delile JF, 'Les effets de la coutume internationale dans l'ordre juridique de l'Union européenne' (2017) 53 CDE 177

Dinstein Y, 'The Interaction between Customary International Law and Treaties' (2006) 322 RdC 243

Dorota G, 'Hard Cases' (2013) 2 UMSLR 240

Drew C, 'The East Timor Story: International Law on Trial' (2001) 12 EJIL 663

Duarte d'Almeida L, 'What Is It to Apply the Law?' (2021) 40 Law Philos 361

Durkee MJ, 'Interpretive Entrepreneurs' (2021) VLR 431

Dworkin R, 'The Model of Rules' (1967) 35 UCLR 14

Dworkin R, 'Objectivity and Truth: You'd Better Believe It' (1996) 25 Philos Public Aff 87

Eells E and Fitelson B, 'Measuring Confirmation and Evidence' (2000) 97 J Philos 663

Eggett C, 'The Role of Principles and General Principles in the "Constitutional Processes" of International Law' (2019) 66 NILR 197

Ehrlich I and Posner RA, 'An Economic Analysis of Legal Rulemaking' (1974) 3 JLS 257

Elias O, 'The Nature of the Subjective Element in Customary International Law' (1995) 44 ICLQ 501

Ellis J, 'General Principles and Comparative Law' (2011) 22 EJIL 949

Etkin B, 'The Changing Rivers of Customary International Law: The Interpretative Process as Flux' (2022) ESIL Reflections 11(5) <https://plato.stanford.edu/archives/sum2020/entries/reflective-equilibrium/>

Fan M, 'Custom, General Principles and the Great Architect Cassese' (2012) 10 JICJ 1063

Feyerabend PK, 'Science without Experience' (1969) 66 J Philos 791

Fitzmaurice G, 'The Law and Procedure of the International Court of Justice, 1954–9: General Principles and Sources of International Law' (1959) 35 BYIL 183

Fitzmaurice G, '*Vae Victis* or Woe to the Negotiators: Your Treaty or Our 'Interpretation' of It?' (1971) 65 AJIL 373

Franck TM, 'Legitimacy in the International System' (1988) 82 AJIL 705

Fuller LL and Winston KI, 'The Forms and Limits of Adjudication' (1978) 92 Harv L Rev 353

Gaja G, 'Positivism and Dualism in Dionisio Anzilotti' (1992) 3 EJIL 123

Gaja G, 'General Principles of Law' (2020) MPEPIL <https://opil.ouplaw.com/display/10.1093/law:epil/9780199231690/law-9780199231690-e1410>

Gallant KS, 'International Criminal Courts and the Making of Public International Law: New Roles for International Organizations and Individuals' (2010) 43 J Marshall L Rev 607

Gardbaum S, 'Human Rights as International Constitutional Rights' (2008) 19 EJIL 749

Gourgourinis A, 'The Distinction between Interpretation and Application of Norms in International Adjudication' (2011) 2 JIDS 31

Guilfoyle D, 'Lacking Conviction: Is the International Criminal Court Broken? An Organisational Failure Analysis' (2019) 20 Melb JIL 401

Guillaume G, 'The Use of Precedent by International Judges and Arbitrators' (2011) 2 JIDS 5

Gümplová P, 'Restraining Permanent Sovereignty over Natural Resources' (2014) 53 EQdF 96

Haack S, 'Coherence, Consistency, Cogency, Congruity, Cohesiveness, &c.: Remain Calm! Don't Go Overboard!' (2004) 35 NLH 167

Hage J, 'Consistency of Rules and Norms' (2000) 9 ICTL 219

Hage J, 'Law and Coherence' (2004) 17 Ratio Juris 87

Hage J, 'Legal Reasoning and the Construction of Law' (2012) i-Lex 81

Hage J, 'Two Concepts of Constitutive Rules' (2018) 4 Argumenta 21

Hage J, 'Constructivist Facts as the Bridge Between Is and Ought' (2022) 1 IJSL 1

Hage J and Verheij B, 'Reason-Based Logic: A Logic for Reasoning with Rules and Reasons' (1994) 3 ICTL 171

Haggenmacher P, 'La doctrine des deux éléments du droit coutumier dans la pratique de la Cour internationale' (1986) 1 RGDIP 1

Hakimi M, 'Making Sense of Customary International Law' (2020) 118 Mich L Rev 1487

Hart HLA, 'Positivism and the Separation of Law and Morals' (1958) 71 Harv L Rev 607

Hathaway O, Johnson L and Ní Aoláin F, 'An Introduction: Effectiveness in International Law' (2014) 108 ASIL Proc 1

Helfer LR and Slaughter AM, 'Why States Create International Tribunals: A Response to Professors Posner and Yoo' (2005) 93 CLR 901

Helfer L and Voeten E, 'International Courts as Agents of Legal Change: Evidence from LGBT Rights in Europe' (2014) 68 IO 77

Heller KJ, 'The Law of Neutrality Does Not Apply to the Conflict with Al-Qaeda, and It's a Good Thing, Too: A Response to Chang' (2011) 47 TILJ 115

Heller KJ, 'Specially-Affected States and the Formation of Custom' (2018) 112 AJIL 191

Henderson C, 'The UK Government's Legal Opinion on Forcible Measures in Response to the Use of Chemical Weapons by the Syrian Government' (2015) 64 ICLQ 179

Higgins R, 'The ICJ, the ECJ and the Integrity of International Law' (2002) 52 ICLQ 9

Hoffmann PL, 'The "Blank Stare Phenomenon": Proving Customary International Law in U.S. Courts' (1996) 25 GJICL 181

Jain N, 'Comparative International Law at the ICTY: The General Principles Experiment' (2015) 109(3) AJIL 486

Jaynes ET, 'Information Theory and Statistical Mechanics' (1957) 14 Phys Rev 620

Jia BB, 'The Relations between Treaties and Custom' (2010) 9 Chinese JIL 81

Johnston KA, 'The Nature and Context of Rules and the Identification of Customary International Law' (2021) 32 EJIL 1167

Jones A, 'Judicial Cross-Referencing and the Identity of the International Criminal Court' (2018) 43 NCJIL 72

Joyner DH, 'Why I Stopped Believing in Customary International Law' (2019) 9 Asian JIL 31

Kammerhofer J, 'The Binding Nature of Provisional Measures of the International Court of Justice: The "Settlement" of the Issue in the LaGrand Case' (2003) 16 LJIL 67

Kammerhofer J, 'Uncertainty in the Formal Sources of International Law: Customary International Law and Some of Its Problems' (2004) 15 EJIL 523

Kassoti E, 'Between *Sollen* and *Sein*: The CJEU's Reliance on International Law in the Interpretation of Economic Agreements Covering Occupied Territories' (2020) 33 LJIL 381

Kirgis FL, Jr., 'Custom on a Sliding Scale' (1987) 81 AJIL 146

Klabbers J, 'How to Defeat a Treaty's Object and Purpose Pending Entry into Force: Toward Manifest Intent' (2001) 34 VJTL 318

Kolb R, 'Selected Problems in the Theory of Customary International Law' (2003) 50 NILR 119

Kooijmans P, 'The ICJ in the 21st Century: Judicial Restraint, Judicial Activism, or Proactive Judicial Policy' (2007) 56 ICLQ 741

Kornhauser LA and Sager LG, 'Unpacking the Court' (1986) 96 Yale LJ 82

Kornobis-Romanowska D, 'Effects of International Customary Law in the Legal Order of the European Union' (2018) 8 WRLAE 405

Koutsoyiannis D and Sargentis GF, 'Entropy and Wealth' (2021) 23 Entropy 1356

Kriebaum U, 'Evaluating Social Benefits and Costs of Investment Treaties: Depoliticization of Investment Disputes' (2018) 33 ICSID Review 14

Kwiecień R, 'General Principles of Law: The Gentle Guardians of Systemic Integration of International Law' (2017) 37 PYIL 235

Kyburg HE Jr, 'Belief, Evidence, and Conditioning' (2006) 73 Philos Sci 42

Lauterpacht H, 'Restrictive Interpretation and the Principle of Effectiveness in the Interpretation of Treaties' (1949) 26 BYBIL 48

Lee M, 'The Interrelation between the Law of the Sea Convention and Customary International Law' (2006) 7 SDILJ 405

Lefkowitz D, '(Dis)Solving the Chronological Paradox in Customary International Law: A Hartian Approach' (2008) 21 CJLJ 129

Levenbook BB, 'The Role of Coherence in Legal Reasoning' (1984) 3 Law Philos 355

Lindquist SA and Cross FB, 'Empirically Testing Dworkin's Chain Novel Theory: Studying the Path of Precedent' (2005) 80 NYUL Rev 1156

Lusa Bordin F, 'Reflections of Customary International Law: The Authority of Codification Conventions and ILC Draft Articles in International Law' (2014) 63 ICLQ 535

Macagno F, Walton D and Sartor G, 'Pragmatic Maxims and Presumptions in Legal Interpretation' (2017) 37 Law Philos 69

MacCormick N, 'Argumentation and Interpretation in Law' (1993) 6 Ratio Juris 16

Mac-Gregor EF, 'What Do We Mean When We Talk about Judicial Dialogue? Reflections of a Judge of the Inter-American Court of Human Rights' (2017) 30 HHRJ 89

Maculan E, 'Judicial Definition of Torture as a Paradigm of Cross-Fertilisation: Combining Harmonisation and Expansion' (2015) 84 NJIL 456

Madsen MR, 'Who Rules the World? The Educational Capital of the International Judiciary' (2018) 3 UC Irvine J Intl Transl Comp L 97

Maher P, 'A Conception of Inductive Logic' (2006) 73 Philos Sci 513

Mahoney P, 'Judicial Activism and Judicial Self-Restraint in the European Court of Human Rights: Two Sides of the Same Coin' (1990) 11 HRLJ 57

Malenovský J, 'Le juge et la coutume internationale: Perspectives de l'Union européenne et de la Cour de justice' (2013) 12 LPICT 225

McDougal MS, 'The Hydrogen Bomb Tests and the International Law of Sea' (1955) 49 AJIL 356

McIntyre J, 'Rules Are Rules: Reconceiving Monetary Gold as a Rule of Procedure' (2021) 115 AJIL Unbound 144

McLachlan C, 'The Principle of Systemic Integration and Article 31(3)(c) of the Vienna Convention' (2005) 54 ICLQ 279

Mendelson MH, 'The Formation of Customary International Law' (1998) 272 RdC 155

Merkouris P, 'Interpreting the Customary Rules on Interpretation' (2017) 19 ICLR 126

Merkouris P, 'Principle of Systemic Integration' (2020) MPEiPro, <https://opil.ouplaw.com/view/10.1093/law-mpeipro/e2866.013.2866/law-mpeipro-e2866>

Merkouris P and Mileva N, 'Introduction to the Series: Customary Law Interpretation as a Tool' (2022) ESIL Reflections 11(2) <https://esil-sedi.eu/esilreflection-introduction-to-the-series-customary-law-interpretation-as-a-tool/>

Mesjasz C, 'Complexity of Social Systems' (2010) 117(4) Acta Phys Pol A 706

Michaelides E, 'Entropy, Order and Disorder' (2008) 2 Open Thermodyn J 7

Milano E, '*Front Polisario* and the Exploitation of Natural Resources by the Administrative Power' (2017) 2 EP 953

Mohamad R, 'Some Reflections on the International Law Commission Topic "Identification of Customary International Law"' (2016) 15 Chinese JIL 41

Mollengarden Z and Zamir N, 'The *Monetary Gold* Principle: Back to Basics' (2021) 115 AJIL 41

Moral Soriano L, 'A Modest Notion of Coherence in Legal Reasoning: A Model for the European Court of Justice' (2003) 16 Ratio Juris 296

Moreno-Lax V, 'Systematising Systemic Integration' (2014) 12 JICJ 907

Mudukuti A, 'Prosecutor v. Omar Hassan Ahmad Al-Bashir, Judgment in the Jordan Referral re Al-Bashir Appeal' (2020) 114 AJIL 103
O'Connell ME, 'Remarks: The Resort to Drones under International Law' (2011) 39 Denv J Intl L & Pol'y 585
O'Shea JR, 'What Is the Myth of the Given?' (2021) 199 Synthese 10543
Odermatt J, 'The Court of Justice of the European Union: International or Domestic Court?' (2014) 3 CJICL 696
Odermatt J, 'Council of the European Union v Front Populaire pour la Libération de la Saguia-El-Hamra et Du Rio de Oro (Front Polisario)' (2017) 111 AJIL 736
Okasha S, 'What Did Hume Really Show about Induction?' (2001) 51 Philos Q 27
Orakhelashvili A, 'State Immunity and International Public Order' (2002) 45 GYIL 226
Pair L, 'Judicial Activism in the ICJ Charter Interpretation' (2001–02) 8 ILSA J Intl Comp L 181
Paparinskis M, 'Revisiting the Indispensable Third Party Principle' (2020) 1 RDI 49
Pasqualucci JM, 'Interim Measures in International Human Rights: Evolution and Harmonization' (2005) 38 VJTL 1
Pellet A, 'The Normative Dilemma: Will and Consent in International Law-Making' (1989) 12 Aus YIL 3
Pereira R, 'Permanent Sovereignty over Natural Resources in the 21st Century: Natural Resource Governance and the Right to Self-Determination of Indigenous Peoples under International Law' (2013) 14 Melb JIL 8
Perin Shecaira F, 'Sources of Law Are Not Legal Norms' (2015) 28 Ratio Juris 15
Perrez FX, 'The Relationship between "Permanent Sovereignty" and the Obligation Not to Cause Transboundary Environmental Damage' (1996) 26 Envtl L 1187
Peters A, 'The Refinement of International Law: From Fragmentation to Regime Interaction and Politicization' (2017) 15 IJCL 671
Pocar F, 'Symposium on the Rome Statute at Twenty: Transformation of Customary Law through ICC Practice' (2018) 112 AJIL Unbound 182
Pomson O, 'Does the *Monetary Gold* principle Apply to International Courts and Tribunals Generally?' (2019) 10 JIDS 88
Posner EA and Yoo JC, 'Judicial Independence in International Tribunals' (2005) 93 CLR 1
Postema GJ, 'Custom, Normative Practice, and the Law' (2012) 62 DLJ 707
Priest G, 'The Structure of the Paradoxes of Self-Reference' (1994) 103 Mind 25
Rasmussen H, 'Between Self-Restraint and Activism: A Judicial Policy for the European Court' (1988) 13 Eur L Rev 28
Raz J, 'The Relevance of Coherence' (1992) 72 BULR 273
Raz J, 'Why Interpret?' (1996) 9 Ratio Juris 349
Reid L, 'The Judge as a Lawmaker' (1972) 12 J Soc Public Teachers of Law 22
Reinhold S, 'Good Faith in International Law' (2013) 2 UCLJLJ 40

Rettler B and Bailey AM, 'Object', *The Stanford Encyclopedia of Philosophy* (Winter edn, 2017) https://plato.stanford.edu/entries/object/

Ridi N, 'United States: Anti-dumping Measures Applying Differential Pricing Methodology to Softwood Lumber from Canada' (2020) 114 AJIL 735

Roberts A, 'Power and Persuasion in Investment Treaty Interpretation: The Dual Role of States' (2010) 104 AJIL 179

Roberts AE, 'Traditional and Modern Approaches to Customary International Law: A Reconciliation' (2001) 95 AJIL 757

Romano C, 'Deciphering the Grammar of the International Jurisprudential Dialogue' (2009) 41 NYUJILP 755

Rosenkrantz RD, 'Does the Philosophy of Induction Rest on a Mistake?' (1982) 79 J Philos 78

Roversi C, 'In Defence of Constitutive Rules' (2021) 199 Synthese 14349

Rudner R, 'The Scientist *qua* Scientist Makes Value Judgments' (1953) 20 Philos Sci 1

Ruys T, 'The Meaning of "Force" and the Boundaries of the *Jus ad Bellum*: Are "Minimal" Uses of Force Excluded from UN Charter Article 2(4)?' (2014) 108 AJIL 159

Ryngaert C and Hora Siccama D, 'Ascertaining Customary International Law: An Inquiry into the Methods Used by Domestic Courts' (2018) 65 NILR 1

Saul M, 'The Normative Status of Self-Determination in International Law: A Formula for Uncertainty in the Scope and Content of the Right?' (2011) 11 HRLR 628

Scharf M, 'Hugo Grotius and the Concept of Grotian Moments in International Law' (2022) 54 CWR J Int Law 17

Schladebach M, 'Praktische Konkordanz als Verfassungsrechtliches Kollisionsprinzip: Eine Verteidigung' (2014) 53 Der Staat 263

Schmitt MN, 'Military Necessity and Humanity in International Humanitarian Law: Preserving the Delicate Balance' (2010) 50(4) VJIL 795

Schuck PH, 'Legal Complexity: Some Causes, Consequences and Cures' (1992) 42 DLJ 9

Schwarzenberger G, 'The Inductive Approach to International Law' (1947) 60 HLR 539

Schweitzer F, 'Sociophysics' (2018) 71 Physics Today 2

Schwitzgebel E, 'Belief', *The Stanford Encyclopedia of Philosophy* (Winter 2021 edition) https://plato.stanford.edu/entries/belief/

Searle J, 'How to Derive "Ought" From "Is"' (1964) 73 Philos Rev 43

Seidenfeld T, 'Direct Inference and Inverse Inference' (1978) 75 J Philos 709

Shannon C, 'The Mathematical Theory of Communication' (1948) 27 BSTJ 379

Shany Y, 'Assessing the Effectiveness of International Courts: A Goal-Based Approach' (2012) 106 AJIL 225

Shao X, 'What We Talk about When We Talk about General Principles of Law' (2021) 20 Chinese JIL 219
Slaughter AM, 'A Typology of Transjudicial Communication' (1994) 29 URLR 99
Slaughter AM, 'Building Global Democracy' (2000) 1 CJIL 223
Slaughter AM, 'Judicial Globalization' (2000) 40 VJIL 1103
Slaughter AM, 'A Global Community of Courts' (2003) 44 HILJ 191
Solares EJ, 'Las normas internacionales convencionales de derechos humanos y su contribución al orden público internacional' (2014) 14 RDUNED 325
Sparks T, 'Reassessing State Consent to Jurisdiction: The Indispensable Third Party Principle before the ICJ' (2022) 91 NJIL 216
Sparks T and Somos M, 'Grotian Moments: An Introduction' (2021) 42 Grotiana 179
Sur S, 'La créativité du droit international' (2012) 363 RdC 9.
Talmon S, 'Determining Customary International Law: The ICJ's Methodology between Induction, Deduction and Assertion' (2015) 26 EJIL 417
Teller P, 'Goodman's Theory of Projection' (1969) 20 BJPhS 219
Tomuschat C, 'Obligations Arising for States without or against Their Will' (1993) 241 RdC 83
Townley S, 'The Rise of Risk in International Law' (2018) 18 CJIL 593
Treves T, 'Customary International Law' (2006) MPEPIL <https://opil.ouplaw.com/display/10.1093/law:epil/9780199231690/law-9780199231690-e1393>
Tunkin G, 'Is General International Law Customary International Law Only?' (1993) 4 EJIL 534
Tuomela R, 'Collective Acceptance, Social Institutions, and Social Reality' (2003) 62 AJES 123
Tzekvelos V, 'The Use of Article 31(3)(c) of the VCLT in the Case Law of the ECtHR: An Effective Anti-Fragmentation Tool or a Selective Loophole for the Reinforcement of Human Rights Teleology? Between Evolution and Systemic Integration' (2010) 31 MJIL 621
Van Aaken A, 'Interests, Strategies and Veto Players: The Political Economy of Interpreting Customary International Law' (2022) 19 ESIL Reflections 11(2) <https://esil-sedi.eu/wp-content/uploads/2022/09/ESIL-Reflection-Anne-van-Aaken_final-version.pdf>
Vandevelde KJ, 'Sustainable Liberalism and the International Investment Regime' (1997) 19 MJIL 373
Vanhamme J, 'Formation and Enforcement of Customary International Law: The European Union's Contribution' (2008) 39 NYIL 127
Verdier PH and Versteeg M, 'International Law in National Legal Systems: An Empirical Investigation' (2015) 109 AJIL 528
Verdier PH and Voeten E, 'Precedent, Compliance, and Change in Customary International Law: An Explanatory Theory' (2014) 108 AJIL 389

Verdross A, 'Les principes généraux du droit dans la jurisprudence internationale, 1935' (1935) 52 RdC 193

Vessey J, 'The Principle of Prevention in International Law' (1998) 3 ARIEL 181

Vickers J, 'The Problem of Induction', *The Stanford Encyclopedia of Philosophy* (Winter edn 2022) http://plato.stanford.edu/entries/induction-problem/

Vidmar J, 'The Use of Force as a Plea of Necessity' (2017) 111 AJIL 302

Voyiakis E, 'International Law, Interpretative Fidelity and the Hermeneutics of Hans-Georg Gadamer' (2011) 54 GYIL 385

Wallace RJ, 'Practical Reason', *The Stanford Encyclopedia of Philosophy* (Spring edn, 2020) https://plato.stanford.edu/entries/practical-reason/

Weeramantry CG, 'The Function of the International Court of Justice in the Development of International Law' (1997) 10 LJIL 309

Weisburd AM, 'Customary International Law: The Problem of Treaties' (1988) 21 VJIL 1

Weisburd AM, 'The International Court of Justice and the Concept of State Practice' (2009) 31 UPJIL 330

White JB, 'Law as Language: Reading Law and Reading Literature' (1982) 60 Tex L Rev 415

Williamson J, 'Inductive Influence' (2007) 58 BJPhS 689

Wolfke K, 'Some Persistent Controversies Regarding Customary International Law' (1993) 24 NYIL 1

Wood M, 'Customary International Law and the General Principles of Law Recognized by Civilized Nations' (2019) 21 ICLR 307

Worster W, 'The Inductive and Deductive Methods in Customary International Law Analysis: Traditional and Modern Approaches' (2014) 45 GJIL 445

Yee S, 'Sketching the Debate on Military Activities in the EEZ: An Editorial Comment' (2010) 9 Chinese JIL 1

Yeini SA, 'The Specially-Affecting States Doctrine' (2018) 112 AJIL 244

Yildiz E and Yüksel U, 'Limits of Behavioral Approaches: Lessons from the Field of Maritime Boundary Making' (2022) 23 GLJ 413

Zamir N, 'The Applicability of the *Monetary Gold* Principle in International Arbitration' (2017) 33 Arb Int'l 523

Zarbiyev F, 'Judicial Activism in International Law: A Conceptual Framework for Analysis' (2012) 3 JIDS 247

Online Unpublished Academic Papers, Blog Posts, Position Papers and Encyclopedia Entries

——'equilibrium', *Encyclopedia Britannica* (21 July 2022) <www.britannica.com/science/equilibrium-physics>

Ammann O, 'On the Interpretability of Customary International Law: A Response to Nina Mileva and Marina Fortuna' (*Opinio Juris*, 7 October 2019) <http://

opiniojuris.org/2019/10/07/on-the-interpretability-of-customary-international-law-a-response-to-nina-mileva-and-marina-fortuna/>

Bourcier D and Mazzega P, 'Toward Measures of Complexity in Legal Systems', *ICAIL '07: Proceedings of the11th International Conference on Artificial Intelligence and Law* (June 2007) <https://dl.acm.org/doi/10.1145/1276318.1276359>

Cohen HG, 'Methodology and Misdirection: Custom and the ICJ' (*EJIL: Talk!*, 1 December 2015) <www.ejiltalk.org/methodology-and-misdirection-a-response-to-stefan-talmon-on-custom-and-the-icj/>

D'Aspremont J, 'Bypassing the Authority of international law: The virtue of modern self-referentiality' (21 September 2017; forthcoming in G Hernandez and G Jokubauskaite (eds), *Constructing Authority in International Law*) <https://papers.ssrn.com/sol3/papers.cfm?abstract_id=3040975>

D'Amato A, 'Legal Uncertainty' (2010) Faculty Working Papers 108, <http://scholarlycommons.law.northwestern.edu/facultyworkingpapers/108>

Di Marco R, 'Customary International Law: A Foreword to Identification v. Interpretation', TRICI-Law Research Paper 009/2019 <www.academia.edu/43325436/Customary_International_Law_a_Foreword_to_Identification_v._Interpretation>

Drake GWF, 'thermodynamics' (*Encyclopedia Britannica*, 15 May 2023) <www.britannica.com/science/thermodynamics>

Eur-Lex, 'Treaties Currently in Force' (*EU*, 2022) <http://ec.europa.eu/world/agreements/viewCollection.do>

Fortuna M, 'Different Strings of the Same Harp: Interpretation of Customary International Rules, Their Identification and Treaty Interpretation' (2020, revised 2021) University of Groningen Faculty of Law Research Paper 48/2020 <https://papers.ssrn.com/sol3/papers.cfm?abstract_id=3798476>

German Federal Foreign Office, German Federal Ministry of Defence, and German Federal Ministry of the Interior, Building and Community, 'On the Application of International Law in Cyberspace' (Position paper, March 2021) <www.auswaertiges-amt.de/blob/2446304/32e7b2498e10b74fb17204c54665bdf0/on-the-application-of-international-law-in-cyberspace-data.pdf>

Goodstein D, 'mechanics', *Encyclopedia Britannica* (21 August 2020) <www.britannica.com/science/mechanics>

Hosch WL, 'isomorphism', *Encyclopedia Britannica* (15 July 2009) <www.britannica.com/science/isomorphism-mathematics>

ILC, 'Analytical Guide to the Work of the International Law Commission: General Principles of Law' (*UN*, 2023) <https://legal.un.org/ilc/guide/1_15.shtml>

Jeutner V and Paddeu F, 'Three Paradoxes of Customary Law' (The Logic of International Law Conference Maastricht University 2022)

Kades E, 'The Laws of Complexity and the Complexity of Laws: The Implications of Computational Complexity Theory for the Law' (1997) Faculty Publications 646 <https://scholarship.law.wm.edu/facpubs/646>

Kamensky JM, 'Managing the Complicated vs. the Complex' (IBM Center for the Business of Government, Fall/Winter 2011) <www.businessofgovernment.org/sites/default/files/JohnKamensky.pdf>

Marcos H, Waltermann A and Hage J, 'From Sovereignty to International Cooperation: Lessons from Legal Logic and Social Ontology' (2021) Maastricht Faculty of Law Working Paper Series 2021/01 <https://cris.maastrichtuniversity.nl/ws/portalfiles/portal/76750436/law_working_paper_series_2021_01_bezerra_marcos_waltermann_hage.pdf>

Martinich AP and Stroll A, 'epistemology', *Encyclopedia Britannica* (26 August 2022) <www.britannica.com/topic/epistemology>

Mileva N and Fortuna M, 'Emerging Voices: The Case for CIL Interpretation – An Argument from Theory and an Argument from Practice' (*Opinio Juris*, 23 August 2019) <http://opiniojuris.org/2019/08/23/emerging-voices-the-case-for-cil-interpretation-an-argument-from-theory-and-an-argument-from-practice/>

Siegenfeld and Y Bar-Yam A, 'An Introduction to Complex Systems Science and Its Applications' [2020] Complexity <https://onlinelibrary.wiley.com/doi/epdf/10.1155/2020/6105872>

Turner C, 'Interconstituted Legal Agents' (2022) University of Georgia School of Law Research Paper 2022-07<https://papers.ssrn.com/sol3/papers.cfm?abstract_id=4049942>

UK Government, 'Chemical Weapon Use by Syrian Regime: UK Government Legal Position' (Policy paper, 29 August 2013) <www.gov.uk/government/publications/chemical-weapon-use-by-syrian-regime-uk-government-legal-position/chemical-weapon-use-by-syrian-regime-uk-government-legal-position-html-version>

INDEX

www.ingramcontent.com/pod-product-compliance
Lightning Source LLC
LaVergne TN
LVHW011701200926
848484LV00004B/1018
* 9 7 8 1 0 0 9 5 4 1 3 2 9 *